SHAKESPEARE'S 'LADY EDITORS'

The basic history of the Shakespearean editorial tradition is familiar and well-established. For nearly three centuries, men – most of them white and financially privileged – ensconced themselves in private and hard-to-access libraries, hammering out 'their' versions of Shakespeare's text. They produced enormous, learnèd tomes, monuments to their author's greatness and their own reputations.

What if this is not the whole story?

A bold, revisionist, and alternative version of Shakespearean editorial history, this book recovers the lives and labours of almost seventy women editors. It challenges the received wisdom that, when it came to Shakespeare, the editorial profession was entirely male-dominated until the late twentieth century. In doing so, it demonstrates that taking these women's work seriously can transform our understanding of the history of editing, of the nature of editing as an enterprise, and of how we read Shakespeare in history.

MOLLY G. YARN completed her PhD at the University of Cambridge in 2019. She is a co-editor of the Royal Shakespeare Company's revised edition of Shakespeare's *Complete Works*, as well as an active theatre practitioner.

T0381699

SHAKESPEARE'S
'LADY EDITORS'

A New History of the Shakespearean Text

MOLLY G. YARN

CAMBRIDGE
UNIVERSITY PRESS

Shaftesbury Road, Cambridge CB2 8EA, United Kingdom

One Liberty Plaza, 20th Floor, New York, NY 10006, USA

477 Williamstown Road, Port Melbourne, VIC 3207, Australia

314–321, 3rd Floor, Plot 3, Splendor Forum, Jasola District Centre, New Delhi – 110025, India

103 Penang Road, #05–06/07, Visioncrest Commercial, Singapore 238467

Cambridge University Press is part of Cambridge University Press & Assessment,
a department of the University of Cambridge.

We share the University's mission to contribute to society through the pursuit of
education, learning and research at the highest international levels of excellence.

www.cambridge.org
Information on this title: www.cambridge.org/9781009001120

DOI: 10.1017/9781009000307

First published 2022
First paperback edition 2024

A catalogue record for this publication is available from the British Library

Library of Congress Cataloging-in-Publication data
NAMES: Yarn, Molly G., author.
TITLE: Shakespeare's 'lady editors' : a new history of the Shakespearean text / Molly G. Yarn.
DESCRIPTION: Cambridge, United Kingdom ; New York, NY : Cambridge University Press, 2022. |
Includes bibliographical references and index.
IDENTIFIERS: LCCN 2021027020 (print) | LCCN 2021027021 (ebook) | ISBN 9781316518359
(hardback) | ISBN 9781009001120 (paperback) | ISBN 9781009000307 (epub)
SUBJECTS: LCSH: Shakespeare, William, 1567-1616–Criticism, Textual. | Drama–Editing–History. |
Women editors–History. | Women editors–Great Britain–Biography. | Women editors–United
States–Biography. | Shakespeare, William, 1564-1616–Bibliography. | BISAC: LITERARY
CRITICISM / European / English, Irish, Scottish, Welsh | LCGFT: Literary criticism.
CLASSIFICATION: LCC PR3071 .Y37 2022 (print) | LCC PR3071 (ebook) | DDC 822.3/3–dc23
LC record available at https://lccn.loc.gov/2021027020
LC ebook record available at https://lccn.loc.gov/2021027021

ISBN   978-1-316-51835-9   Hardback
ISBN   978-1-009-00112-0   Paperback

For Lisa and Douglas Yarn,
insightful critics and editors,
and even better parents.

No story is the same to us after a lapse of time – or, rather we who read it are no longer the same interpreters.

–George Eliot

Contents

Figures

Acknowledgements

Given that this is a book about the unacknowledged labour of making books, I feel both a great desire and an acute pressure to properly acknowledge everyone who made this particular book possible.

It seems only right to first thank *my* editor, Emily Hockley, as well as Rachel Blaifeder, George Paul Laver, Bethany Johnson, Dhivyabharathi Elavazhagan, Stephanie Sakson, and the whole team at Cambridge University Press for your trust and support.

My dissertation supervisor, Jason Scott-Warren, welcomed my project to Cambridge and helped me shape it into the book that it is, reading countless drafts and asking big questions. Jason, thank you for your patience and your faith in my work. Hester Lees-Jeffries served as my faculty advisor and my emotional rock. Hester, I promise I'll talk about performance in the next project. Andrew Zurcher and Sonia Massai examined my dissertation and were the first people (other than my mother) to insist that 'This is a book!'

Over the past five years, many people have offered feedback, encouragement, and the occasional helping hand or editorial eye, including Ruth Abbott, Brandi K. Adams, Virginia Anderson, Jonathan Bate, Claire M. L. Bourne, Erin Capistrano, Hilary Clare, Ian De Jong, Mark Dudgeon, Megan Heffernan, Adam G. Hooks, John Jowett, Sawyer Kemp, Laura Kolb, Raphael Lyne, Tara L. Lyons, Laurie Maguire, Gordon McMullan, Kirk Melnikoff, Dianne Mitchell, Andrew Murphy, Margaux Nair, Kate Ozment, Aaron T. Pratt, Eric Rasmussen, Elizabeth Riordan, Ann Thompson, Valerie Wayne, Nadine Weiss, Susannah Williams, and Henry Woudhuysen. Nicholas Flower kindly spoke to me about his mother, Margaret. My writing accountability groups kept me on track and cheered me on. I received crucial suggestions and feedback from my anonymous Press readers. The staff of the Arden Shakespeare and Methuen Drama at Bloomsbury Publishing, led by the redoubtable

Margaret Bartley, took me behind the curtain to see what it really takes to publish an edition of Shakespeare.

I've been lucky enough to have friends on several continents providing both emotional and material support throughout this process. Thanks particularly to Katie Weiller, Ben and Kate Samuels, Margaux and Rishi Nair (and Harini and Rohit), and Rina and Jason Fox for hosting me during US research trips. In Cambridge, Tom Littler, Anastasia Bruce-Jones, Nadine Weiss, Kim Alexander, and Zak Ghazi-Torbati had faith when I didn't. Thanks to them and to my many Cambridge theatre friends, particularly my fellow Marlowe Society committee members, who provided me with many distractions, for better or for worse.

I am immensely grateful to the staff at the following libraries, special collections, and archives, who have assisted me both in person and via email: the University of Reading, the University of Chicago, the British Library, Wellesley College, Hunter College, Columbia University, the New York Public Library, Harvard University's Houghton Library, King's College London, Trinity College Cambridge, King's College Cambridge, St John's College Cambridge, Newnham College Cambridge, Somerville College Oxford, Smith College, the Senate House, the University of North Carolina Chapel Hill, Queen Mary University of London, the British Academy, the Kislak Center at the University of Pennsylvania, Yale University's Beinecke Library, the University of Virginia, the Boston Public Library, the University of Liverpool, the National Archives of the UK, the Kingston *Gleaner*, the University of Iowa, and the Harry Ransom Center at the University of Texas in Austin. Particular thanks to the staff at my 'home' libraries: the Cambridge University Library, the English Faculty Library, and the Lucy Cavendish College Library. At Cambridge, Lucy Cavendish College and the Faculty of English have both provided much-appreciated funding for travel and conferences and been sources of collegiality and support. I am also grateful to the University of Chicago's Special Collections Research Center for their award of the Robert L. Platzman Memorial Fellowship, which funded my work in their archives, and to the staff for their assistance and welcome during my visits. On a far broader scale, this book would not exist without large-scale digitisation of archives and library catalogues, so to all the unnamed people involved in those immense tasks: thank you.

Several chapters in this book contain material that has been previously published in other forms. Many thanks to the Arden Shakespeare, an imprint of Bloomsbury Publishing Plc, for allowing me to use sections of 'Katharine Lee Bates and Women's Editions of Shakespeare for

Students', in Valerie Wayne (ed.), *Women's Labour and the History of the Book in Early Modern England* (London, 2020), pp. 187–203. William Caldwell was kind enough to allow me to use material from "'All the Youth of England Are on Fire (for Shakespeare)": A Review of Evelyn Smith's *Henry V*, published in issue 5.3 of *The Hare: A Journal of Untimely Reviews in Early Modern Theatre* (2021).

Most of all, thank you to my family, especially my parents. You know what you did.

A Note on Citations

In order to emphasise the editor's role as author of the paratextual materials and mediator of the text, all editions are cited in a format that names both William Shakespeare and the editor as authors.

Abbreviations

Arden1	Arden Shakespeare, First Series (1899–1924)
Arden2	Arden Shakespeare, Second Series (1951–1982)
Arden3	Arden Shakespeare, Third Series (1995–2020)
BL	British Library
CUL	Cambridge University Library
DNB	*Dictionary of National Biography* (1885–1920)
EETS	Early English Text Society
NSS	New Shakespeare Society
ODNB	*The Oxford Dictionary of National Biography* (since 2004). A distinction is drawn between the old *DNB* and the modern *ODNB* because although the original process of producing the *Dictionary of National Biography* and its initial supplements is discussed within the text, all references come from the revised version and its updates, from 2004 onwards.
OED	*Oxford English Dictionary*

Prologue
The Mystery of Mrs Valentine

In 1868, publishers Frederick Warne & Co. released an edition of *The Works of William Shakespeare* in their Chandos Classics series. The Chandos Classics was an inexpensive home library series, initially priced from one shilling and sixpence to two shillings, depending on the cover. Affordable editions of classic literature, particularly Shakespeare's plays, were a lucrative market around the mid-century, and many publishers invested in creating impressive texts.[1] Charles Knight, Cassell & Co., and George Routledge all published strikingly elaborate, reasonably priced, illustrated editions of the complete works.[2] Unlike its competitors, the Chandos Shakespeare was not illustrated, making it fairly forgettable in comparison. Even so, Warne claimed that their Shakespeare edition eventually sold over 340,000 copies.[3] Stephen Greenblatt has recounted the story of explorer H. M. Stanley burning a copy of Shakespeare's plays in Africa in order to protect his notes – that copy was a Chandos edition.[4] James Joyce owned a copy of the Chandos Shakespeare, as did Arthur Conan Doyle.[5]

Also unlike its competitors, the Chandos Shakespeare did not identify its editor, even though its advertising particularly described it as 'a well edited Edition', superior to other inexpensive Shakespeares 'in size of Page, Quality of Paper, Easy Reading, and General Completeness'.[6] The Preface of the 1868 and 1875 editions explained that

> this Edition of Shakspeare has been carefully prepared from the earliest and more modern Editions. Where Commentators have differed as to the sense of obscure or doubtful passages, we have selected those readings which we believed to be most Shakspearian and best suited to a popular Edition.[7]

Neither edition named an editor. Warne reused the original text multiple times for variations such as the 'Albion Edition', the 'Universal Edition', and the 'Victorian Edition'. By the late 1880s, those editions were appearing with revised prefaces. The Preface of the 1889 'Universal Edition' expanded upon the editorial principles employed:

The First Folio and the Quartos have been used for the Edition; and fidelity
to the original text has been preserved as much as possible. In fact, the
emendations are few in number, and only made when absolutely required.
No new readings have been attempted, as it is believed by the editor that
the ever-increasing knowledge of Elizabethan literature – and of Shakspeare
especially – has removed former obscurities, and much that perplexed the
old commentators is clear and intelligible to the modern reader; new
readings generally rather injure than improve the text.[8]

The editions released in the 1880s also provide the first indication of the
editor's presence – the title pages and prefaces name 'the editor of the
Chandos Classics' (Figure 0.1).[9]

Finally, in December of 1894, after almost thirty years in print, advertisements began to appear describing someone as the editor of the Chandos
Classics, and thus, obliquely, the Chandos Shakespeare, for the first time
(Figure 0.2). William Jaggard deemed this identification certain enough to
include in his expansive 1911 *Shakespeare Bibliography* without the question mark with which he marked unconfirmed attributions.[10] The editor's
name was Mrs Valentine.

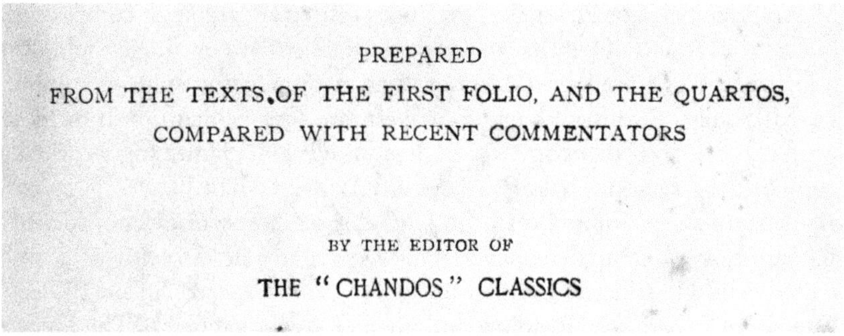

PREPARED

FROM THE TEXTS OF THE FIRST FOLIO, AND THE QUARTOS,

COMPARED WITH RECENT COMMENTATORS

BY THE EDITOR OF

THE " CHANDOS " CLASSICS

Figure 0.1   From the title page of Arthur Conan Doyle's copy of Warne's Shakespeare
text, printed in the 'Imperial Poets' series, c. 1896. Image used by permission of the
Harry Ransom Center, the University of Texas at Austin

**CAMEOS OF LITERATURE FROM STAN-
DARD AUTHORS.** Edited and prefaced with an Essay on
Literature by Mrs. VALENTINE, Editor of " The Chandos Classics."

Figure 0.2   Advertisement identifying Mrs Valentine as 'the editor of the Chandos
Classics' from an 1895 issue of *The Bookman* (vol. 7, no. 41, p. 163).

In 1915, Mr. Wm. H. Peet wrote to *Notes and Queries* with information gathered from W. Fruing Warne (the original Warne's son) about Mrs Valentine:

> Her full maiden name was Laura Belinda Jewry, her father being Admiral Jewry, and the place of her birth is supposed to have been the Victory. At an early age she became connected with the family of Lord Elphinstone, and spent some years of her maiden life in India. She married when young the Rev. R. Valentine, a clergyman of the Church of England, but he died within twelve months.[11]

Peet's claims seem to be a mixture of truths and slight exaggerations. Valentine was born in 1815 in Portsea, Hampshire. Her father was Lieutenant Henry Jewry, who commanded the HMS *Grecian* from 1815. Valentine's exact date of birth is unknown, but the *Grecian* was purchased by the Royal Navy on 3 November 1815, so if she was born earlier in the year, it is possible that her father was assigned to the *Victory* at that time.[12] The legendary HMS *Victory* was moored in Portsmouth Harbour beginning in 1812, after which she served as 'a residence, flagship and tender providing accommodation'.[13] In Valentine's novel *The Cup and the Lip* (1851), the heroine goes to live with her uncle, the captain of the *Victory*, and his family, who live aboard the ship itself. She describes family life aboard the ship, including an incident where the children hide in nooks and crannies to frighten visitors.[14] A review of her book *Sea Fights from Sluys to Navarino* describes her as 'a descendant of five generations of seamen, a lady who passed part of her childhood on board the "Victory"'.[15] So it seems likely that even if she was not born on the *Victory*, as Peet believed, Valentine lived on board the ship for a time during her childhood. The connection to Lord Elphinstone also appears to be a distortion of the facts. The 1841 census shows Valentine, then still Laura Jewry, working as a governess for the family of Eliza Arthur, who lived on the Royal Crescent in Bath.[16] Eliza Arthur's husband was George Arthur, formerly lieutenant governor of Van Diemen's Land and Upper Canada. The Arthurs had returned from Canada around 1840–41 and, apparently, hired Laura Valentine to teach their numerous children. In 1842, the East India Company appointed George Arthur governor of Bombay, a post later held by Lord Elphinstone.[17] Valentine may have moved with them to India, where the Arthurs remained until 1846.

Valentine's first book was *The Ransom*, a novel published in 1846, the same year that the Arthurs returned from India. The 1851 census lists her profession as 'Authoress'.[18] In 1853, she married the Reverend Richard

Valentine, only to be widowed a year later.[19] The case files of the Royal Literary Fund provide a deeper insight into this period of her life. Established in 1790 to assist writers experiencing financial difficulties, the Fund's files, lodged at the British Library, contain thousands of letters and documents about authors, well-known and forgotten, and their spouses and children. Valentine applied to the Fund for support after her husband's death. Several of the letters provided by friends in support of her request imply that he died of a fever contracted during his ministry. Valentine's letter reveals that at the time of his death, she was pregnant with their first child. Six weeks later, she delivered a stillborn baby. 'It may be very long – if I ever have strength again – before I can return to my pen for support,' she writes. 'My heart is well nigh broken and my head confused and troubled.'[20] One letter of support, written by Lady Cornwallis, president of the Ladies Committee that steered the Adult Orphan Institution, explains that Valentine had donated the proceeds of her novel *The Vassal* to the charity several years before, possibly worsening her situation after her husband's death.[21] The Fund provided her with several grants over the next eighteen months.

At some point during the next decade, Valentine did pick up her pen once more, and she completed and published several novels. After that initial period of bereavement and desperation, she moved to Battersea to live with her older sister, Mary, and their widowed mother. The 1861 Census described her occupation as 'Clergyman W[idow] and author of Tales, childrens books, Periodical articles'.[22] In *Notes and Queries*, Peet explains that following her husband's death

> Mrs. Valentine ... joined the staff of Messrs. Warne & Co., the well-known publishers, and rendered them very valuable service. She was practically the sole editor of 'The Chandos Classics,' and in the course of what may be called her 'business life' was on terms of friendship with many well-known literary people.[23]

As with the previous biographical details, Peet's claims must be taken with a grain of salt, but the in-house history of Warne, written for their centennial in 1965, confirms that she was 'Frederick Warne's editress in the early days and in fact the only female member of his staff at that time'.[24] Warne's own obituary in *The Athenaeum* described her as the firm's 'literary advisor'.[25] And when Valentine died in 1899, a note in *The Athenaeum* explained that she 'had acted as editor and confidential adviser on literary matters to Messrs. F. Warne & Co. since the foundation of the firm'.[26]

A letter from Mary Ann Evans, better known as George Eliot, to Valentine in 1867, responding to a request that Evans contribute something to a Warne publication, shows that Valentine already had a position at the firm two years after its founding.[27] Figure 0.3, which shows a contract between Warne and Valentine signed in 1874, confirms that Valentine's involvement dated back to the firm's inception in 1865. In exchange for a yearly increasing salary and due to 'her regard for the said Frederick Warne and for other good considerations', this contract gave Warne the rights to all published or unpublished 'books and portions of books and works and literary productions of whatever nature or kind ... written or edited' by Valentine between 15 April 1865 and 31 December 1873.[28] If she began working for Warne in 1865, Valentine could easily have been involved in the preparation of the Chandos Shakespeare, first published in 1868, and the contract indicates that she was editing something during that ten-year period.

Although this proves that Valentine *could* have edited the Chandos Shakespeare, definitive proof has not yet emerged that she *did*. The only Shakespeare-related work bearing Valentine's name was the illustrated *Shakespearian Tales in Verse* (1881), an attractive volume containing verse retellings of *The Tempest*, *The Winter's Tale*, *The Merchant of Venice*, and *The Taming of the Shrew*.[29] Gender may very well have been a factor in the decision not to identify Laura Valentine as the editor of the Chandos Shakespeare. Valentine wrote and edited prolifically for Warne, but her name was associated with domestic genres such as novels and children's books. Perhaps her authorial persona did not match the Chandos Classics brand that Warne wanted to develop. It was still unusual at the time for a woman to edit this kind of book; one reviewer simply assumed that the 'L. Valentine' who edited Milton's works for the Chandos Classics in the 1890s was a 'Mr' rather than a 'Mrs'.[30] Anonymous and pseudonymous publishing were common elements of Valentine's career – many of her books were published under the pseudonym 'Aunt Louisa', a name inspired by Warne's wife, Louisa.

Between this loss of name and the complete abdication of copyright that she agreed to in her contract, Valentine's authorial and editorial identity seems, in part, to have been annexed by the Warne firm and Warne himself. None of the early books of the Chandos Classics has a named editor; perhaps they were edited by multiple people at the publishing house, or perhaps Valentine was not involved with the Chandos Classics at all in the early years. Although incontrovertible proof has not survived, enough of Peet's claims have some basis in truth to justify our taking

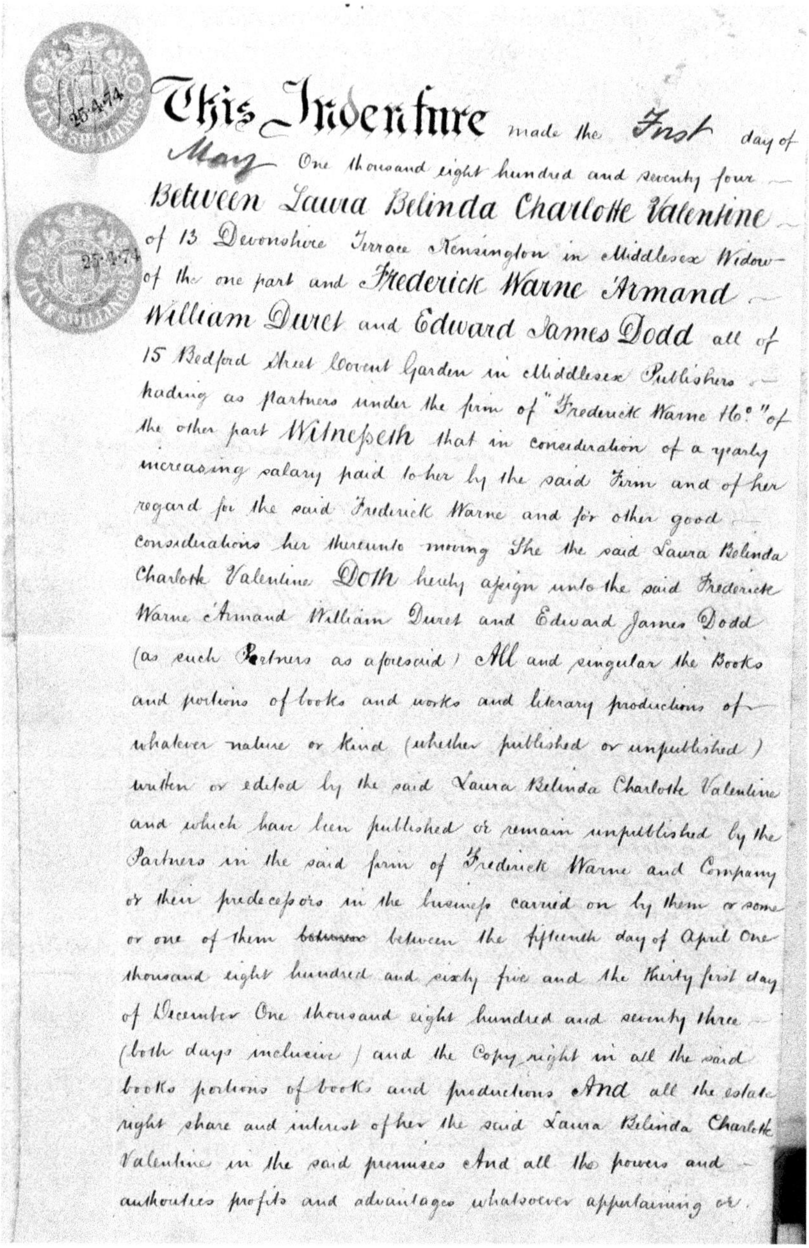

This Indenture made the First day of May One thousand eight hundred and seventy four Between Laura Belinda Charlotte Valentine of 13 Devonshire Terrace Kensington in Middlesex Widow of the one part and Frederick Warne Armand William Duret and Edward James Dodd all of 15 Bedford Street Covent Garden in Middlesex Publishers trading as partners under the firm of "Frederick Warne & Co." of the other part Witnesseth that in consideration of a yearly increasing salary paid to her by the said Firm and of her regard for the said Frederick Warne and for other good considerations her thereunto moving She the said Laura Belinda Charlotte Valentine Doth hereby assign unto the said Frederick Warne Armand William Duret and Edward James Dodd (as such Partners as aforesaid) All and singular the Books and portions of books and works and literary productions of whatever nature or kind (whether published or unpublished) written or edited by the said Laura Belinda Charlotte Valentine and which have been published or remain unpublished by the Partners in the said firm of Frederick Warne and Company or their predecessors in the business carried on by them or some or one of them ~~between~~ between the fifteenth day of April One thousand eight hundred and sixty five and the thirty first day of December One thousand eight hundred and seventy three (both days inclusive) and the Copyright in all the said books portions of books and productions And all the estate right share and interest of her the said Laura Belinda Charlotte Valentine in the said premises And all the powers and authorities profits and advantages whatsoever appertaining or

Figure 0.3 Contract of Indenture between Laura Valentine and Frederick Warne. Frederick Warne Archive. Image used by permission of the University of Reading, Special Collections seriously the claim that Laura Valentine was indeed 'practically the sole editor of the Chandos Classics', and that in the course of those duties, she edited *The Complete Works of William Shakespeare*, making her only the second woman to do so, in the wake of Mary Cowden Clarke's 1860 edition (Figure 0.4). Laura Valentine's story proves that the Shakespearean editorial tradition, as it is currently known, remains fundamentally incomplete. All of the information needed to connect Valentine with the Chandos Shakespeare was in place, but the connection has simply not been made before now. This book will explore possible reasons for that neglect, while also filling in some of the lacunae in editorial history.

Figure 0.4   Laura Jewry Valentine's occupation as shown in the 1891 UK Census. PRO RG 12/33/122/25. Image used by permission of The National Archives of the UK

Shakespeare's 'Lady Editors' examines women editors as a group and a cultural phenomenon, rather than as isolated and exceptional individuals. Women such as Mary Cowden Clarke, Teena Rochfort Smith, Charlotte Porter, and Helen Clarke have received attention in several excellent but closely delimited article-length studies.[31] However, no attempt has previously been made to comprehensively identify and study these women and the editions they produced as a driving force in the way the Shakespearean text has been shaped and transmitted. At the outset of this project, I knew of about twenty women editors who had at least been identified by name, although most were still unstudied; I hoped to find another ten or so. Instead, I found almost seventy, more than doubling my initial estimate.

This book draws on material from twenty-eight different university and library archives in the UK and the US, as well as the records of government agencies in both countries. It weaves together material from letters, diaries, ledgers, contracts, census documents, published reports, reviews, advertisements, wills, life records, and even novels to create as detailed an account as possible of the lives and work of female editors, placing them alongside over 160 editions of the plays, ranging from the eighteenth century to the present day, some edited by men, but most by women. The majority of this material has never been published or discussed in print, and it represents an enormous body of unique and original documentary evidence relating both to the Shakespeare text and to the lives and work of scholarly women during the nineteenth and early twentieth centuries.

The Lady Editors builds on the work of a number of scholars, but its largest methodological debts are owed primarily to two books: *Shakespeare in Print*, by Andrew Murphy, and *Women Reading Shakespeare, 1600–1900*, by Ann Thompson and Sasha Roberts.[32] Murphy's study, which surveys the history of Shakespeare publishing from the early modern period to the present day, in addition to being a major work in its own right, opened up vast areas of enquiry for future scholarship. His rejection of the teleological impulse underlying previous accounts of editorial history, and his insistence on including 'derivative', forgotten texts in the new narrative, are critical elements of the theory that underpins this book. In *Women Reading Shakespeare*, Thompson and Roberts persuasively demonstrated that women's work on Shakespeare could be taken seriously, both as part of the wider history of Shakespeare criticism and as a freestanding genre.

Ann Thompson, Sasha Roberts, Gail Marshall, Laurie Maguire, and Jeanne Addison Roberts have produced excellent work on individual women editors including Mary Cowden Clarke, Alice Walker, Teena Rochfort Smith, Charlotte Endymion Porter, and Helen Archibald Clarke.[33] By placing these individual editors within the larger context of a female editorial tradition, this book takes the next logical step in the field that they established, a step suggested by Henry Woudhuysen in a brief piece on women editors.[34] The concept of the social text, articulated by theorists such Jerome McGann, D. F. McKenzie, David Greetham, and Joseph Grigely, is crucial to this project, as are the studies of textual and book history carried out by scholars such as Sonia Massai, Helen Smith, Margreta de Grazia, Gabriel Egan, and Leah Marcus. Although not directly addressed here, given its more contemporary focus, work on feminist editing by Ann Thompson, Laurie Maguire, Valerie Wayne, and Suzanne Gossett has also contributed to my thinking.

Given the vast scope of this new material covered, *Shakespeare's 'Lady Editors'* is wide-ranging; however, rather than presenting a comprehensive fait accompli, it is intended to open up new avenues of enquiry that can build on this research. I am particularly aware, for example, that this account excludes performance texts – texts abridged for classroom or student performance, or texts reflecting real historical performances (either published or in prompt-book form) – and I hope that this book will inspire or contribute to future research on women's involvement in that textual genre. In an ideological sense, this appeal to future collaboration and

cooperation reflects a central concern of *Shakespeare's 'Lady Editors'* –
replacing the narrowly defined, male-coded image of the solitary
Shakespeare editor with an understanding of the editorial role that takes
into account a wider network of contributors and shaping forces.

Gender is a social construct too complex to be contained within the
simplistic male/female binary; however, over the centuries, that binary has
crept into editorial discourse, infecting it with misogyny and suppressing
diversity in the field, as discussed in the section entitled 'Gendered Labour,
Gendered Text' in Chapter 1. Following the lead of the *Women in Book
History Bibliography*, I 'define "woman" as a constructionist, not an essen-
tialist, identity'.[35] To the best of my knowledge, the editors discussed in
this book all identified as women, but I recognise the difficulty of making
that determination, particularly for historical figures unable to speak
for themselves.

Chapter 1 lays out the theoretical concerns at hand, particularly issues
of gendered labour and gendered texts, introducing the concept of the
domestic text and exploring how the established language, conventions,
and assumptions surrounding the editorial task conspire to exclude
women from Shakespearean editorial history. By profiling the women
editors who functioned within the network of the New Shakspere
Society, Chapter 2 digs deeper into issues of gendered labour, focusing
on how male-female collaborations can both empower and marginalise
women editors. Chapter 3 moves across the Atlantic to examine a very
different network – the community of women editors centred around the
American women's colleges. Chapter 4 considers both the advantages and
the dangers of studying editorial work through a biographical lens. In it,
I present three case studies, each focused on a single editor, laying out my
research process and the challenges I found along the way. Chapter 5
investigates how the rise of the New Bibliography disadvantaged women
editors, demonstrating how women's success remained dependent on male
mentorship and male-centred networks. The book also includes two brief
"sidebars" and appendices. The first sidenote, following Chapter 2, discusses women who edited authors other than Shakespeare, or who carried
out textual work other than editing. The second sidenote, which follows
Chapter 3, introduces the material forms and uses of student editions of
Shakespeare and proposes some approaches to developing a critical framework for the study of this neglected textual genre. Appendix A offers brief
biographies of the sixty-nine women editors who produced editions prior
to 1950; Appendix B is a list of all editions prepared by women up to the
present day.

But first, a note on the book's title: the naming of things is important, and I have thought extensively about the terms I use to refer to textual editors who happen to identify as women. This question arose during the earliest days of this project – one reader of the initial proposal expressed the concern that 'editrix' could be seen as flippant or insulting. 'Female editors' has always felt unwieldy to me, although I use it at times. Ultimately, I chose to rely primarily on the term 'women editors', although admittedly that also grates when used in the singular – 'woman editor'. Having made this compromise, however, I still wanted to find a way to use my personal favourite description – 'lady editor'. Appealing to the ear in both singular and plural forms, I enjoy this moniker for its irreverence, and I hope to reclaim it from its often-derogatory past use. In 1869, for example, a particularly critical anonymous reviewer of Charles and Mary Cowden Clarke's illustrated edition of the plays blamed 'the numberless alterations, mutilations, corruptions, or whatever we may choose to call them' on Mary Cowden Clarke and wished that 'the lady editor had refrained from thus tampering with our great poet's language'.[36]

Interestingly, gendered, nuanced uses of the title of 'editor' are not exclusive to the English literary tradition. In China, poet and courtesan Xue Tao (c. 768–831 CE) so impressed a governor of the Tang Dynasty that he requested that she be appointed his *jiaoshu*, or editor, an official position.[37] Although she never received the appointment, she was known thereafter as *nü jiaoshu* – 'female editor/collator/reviser of books'. *Nü jiaoshu* later became a euphemism for a courtesan.[38]

As Ann Thompson and Sasha Roberts have detailed, Charles Cowden Clarke actively defended his wife's intellectual achievements, disclaiming any credit in her solo work and praising the value of her contributions to their joint projects.[39] Mary Cowden Clarke was significantly more likely to recognise Charles's contributions to her work than he was; in her 1860 edition of the plays, while taking pride in the thought that she was (to her knowledge) 'the first of his female subjects who has been selected to edit his works', she proudly credited Charles with preparing the glossary, even though 'his own unwillingness to diminish the Editor's credit for the whole work would fain have made him forbid this acknowledgment'.[40] And while their language and intentions are far from modern, the Cowden Clarkes did anticipate modern feminist editors in pointing out the value of gender diversity in editing, noting in the preface to the same edition that so peeved the anonymous reviewer that for one who is so universal-minded as Shakespeare, we think it will be conceded that there may be peculiar advantage in having a man and woman as his joint editors. While the man-editor uses his masculine judgment as to what expressions are fittest to be expunged from a chastened edition of Shakespeare, the woman-editor is not without her use in bringing feminine discernment as an aid and exponent to some of his passages. It is, perhaps, good and befitting that Shakespeare, who is not so much a man as human – containing in himself the best parts of woman's as well as man's nature – should have a woman to assist in editing and analysing him.[41]

The framework of this claim is certainly antiquated, but the intention behind it is clearly recognisable – an assertion that every editor brings their own experiences to bear on the editorial task. This book takes up and advances that argument in ways which the Cowden Clarkes probably never imagined, but the subversive seeds of their point are present in the work of every woman editor, no matter how conservative or regressive her work seems to the modern eye. Therefore, in honour of Mary Cowden Clarke and all other 'lady editors', known and unknown, and in defiance of their misogynistic critics, I dub this book *Shakespeare's 'Lady Editors'*.

***

And, for the record, in its original Latin form, 'editor' is a masculine noun. The Latin word *editor*, however, comes from the verb *edo* (*edo, edare, edidi, editus*), which includes among its many meanings 'to bear, to beget, to give birth to'. Just something to consider.

Notes

1 Mary Hammond, *Reading, Publishing and the Formation of Literary Taste in England, 1880–1914* (Aldershot: Ashgate, 2006); Richard D. Altick, 'From Aldine to Everyman: Cheap Reprint Series of the English Classics 1830–1906', *Studies in Bibliography*, 11 (1958), 3–24; Terry I. Seymour, 'Great Books by the Millions: J. M. Dent's Everyman's Library', in *The Culture of the Publisher's Series, vol. II: Nationalisms and the National Canon*, ed. John Spiers (Basingstoke, Hampshire: Palgrave Macmillan, 2011), pp. 166–72.

2 Marvin Spevack, 'What Price Shakespeare?: James Orchard Halliwell-Phillipps and the Shilling Shakespeares of the 1860s', *The Papers of the Bibliographical Society of America*, 96.1 (2002), 23–47; Alan R. Young, 'John Dicks's Illustrated Edition of "Shakspere for the Millions"', *The Papers of the Bibliographical Society of America*, 106.3 (2012), 285–310; Alan

R. Young, *Steam-Driven Shakespeare, or Making Good Books Cheap: Five Victorian Illustrated Editions* (New Castle, DE: Oak Knoll Press, 2017); Stuart Sillars, 'Reading Illustrated Editions: Methodology and the Limits of Interpretation', *Shakespeare Survey*, 62 (2009), 162–81.

3 Arthur King and A. F. Stuart, *The House of Warne: One Hundred Years of Publishing* (London: Frederick Warne & Co., 1965), pp. 4–5.

4 Stephen Greenblatt, *Shakespearean Negotiations: The Circulation of Social Energy in Renaissance England* (Berkeley: University of California Press, 1988), pp. 161–62.

5 These copies are now held at the Ransom Centre. Joyce's copy was part of his library in Trieste; Conan Doyle's copy was a wedding gift from George Edalji, a man who had been convicted of a crime of which Conan Doyle believed him innocent. Conan Doyle had campaigned for Edalji to receive a pardon, which was granted a few months before Conan Doyle's wedding – thus the gift. I am grateful to Aaron T. Pratt for obtaining images of these books on my behalf.

6 'Advertisement', *The Athenaeum* (London, 20 June 1868), p. 849.

7 William Shakespeare and Laura Jewry Valentine, *The Works of William Shakspeare*, Chandos Classics (London: Frederick Warne & Co., 1868); William Shakespeare and Laura Jewry Valentine, *The Works of William Shakspeare. Life, Glossary, &c.* (London: Frederick Warne & Co., 1875).

8 William Shakespeare and Laura Jewry Valentine, *The Works of William Shakspeare*, 'Universal' Edition (London: Frederick Warne and Co., 1889).

9 Shakespeare and Valentine, *Works of Shakspeare (Universal)*; William Shakespeare and Laura Jewry Valentine, *The Works of William Shakspeare*, 'Victorian' Edition (London: Frederick Warne and Co., 1896). Other Warne publications explicitly attributed to 'the Editor of the Chandos Classics' include editions of Milton, Horace, and *Memoirs of the Life of Sir Walter Scott*.

10 William Jaggard, *Shakespeare Bibliography*, reprint (London: Dawsons of Pall Mall, 1971). This William Jaggard was obviously not the printer of the 1623 first folio, although he did claim to be a descendant.

11 Wm. H. Peet, 'Laura Jewry, Afterwards Mrs. R. Valentine', *Notes and Queries*, s11-XII.301 (1915), 266-a.

12 James Stanier Clarke and John McArthur, *The Naval Chronicle: Volume 34, July–December 1815: Containing a General and Biographical History of the Royal Navy of the United Kingdom with a Variety of Original Papers on Nautical Subjects* (Cambridge: Cambridge University Press, 2010), p. 262.

13 'History | HMS Victory', www.hms-victory.com/history.

14 Laura Jewry Valentine, *The Cup and the Lip: A Novel*, 3 vols (London: T. C. Newby, 1851), I, p. 168. *The Cup and the Lip* also employs Shakespearean epigraphs at the start of each chapter.

15 'History and Biography', ed. John Chapman, *Westminster Review*, 33., no. 1 (1868), 264–84.

16 '1841 England Census – Laura Jewry', National Archives of the UK, PRO HO 107/970/15/16/25; www.ancestry.com.

17 A. G. L. Shaw, 'Arthur, Sir George, First Baronet (1784–1854)', in *Oxford Dictionary of National Biography* (Oxford: Oxford University Press, 2004), doi.org/10.1093/ref:odnb/707.

18 '1851 England Census – Laura Jewry', National Archives of the UK, PRO HO 107/1659, Folio 832, Page 8; www.ancestry.com.

19 John Sutherland, *The Longman Companion to Victorian Fiction* (London: Routledge, 2014), p. 336.

20 Laura Belinda Charlotte Valentine, 'Letter to the Committee of the Literary Fund', 28 June 1854, British Library, Western Manuscripts, Royal Literary Fund, Case Files 1790s–1970s, Loan 96 RLF 1/1351/2.

21 Lady Cornwallis, 'Letter to Thomas Cautley Newby', 29 June 1854, British Library, Western Manuscripts, Royal Literary Fund, Case Files 1790s–1970s, Loan 96 RLF 1/1351/4. The Adult Orphans Institution, now the Princess Helena College, was founded in 1820 to educate the orphaned daughters of military or churchmen as governesses. 'History | The Princess Helena College', www.princesshelenacollege.co.uk/History.

22 '1861 England Census – Laura B. C. Valentine', National Archives of the UK, PRO RG 9/451, Folio 81, Page 30; www.ancestry.com.

23 Peet, 'Laura Jewry'.

24 King and Stuart, *The House of Warne*, p. 14.

25 'Mr. Frederick Warne', *The Athenaeum*, 16 November 1901, p. 663.

26 'Literary Gossip', *The Athenaeum*, 23 December 1899, p. 866.

27 Mary Ann Evans, 'Letter to Mrs. R. Valentine', 7 July 1867, Special Collections, the University of Iowa Libraries, Iowa City, MsL E927 va. Many thanks to Elizabeth Riordan for obtaining photos of this letter for me.

28 'Indenture between Laura Belinda Charlotte Valentine and Frederick Warne, Armand William Duret and Edward James Dodd', 1874, Frederick Warne Archive, University of Reading Special Collections, Ledger, p. 557.

29 Laura Jewry Valentine, *Shakespearian Tales in Verse, Illustrated* (London: F. Warne & Co., 1881).

30 'Poetry and Verse', *The Critic: A Weekly Review of Literature and the Arts*, 14 August 1897, 88.

31 Enumerated and cited below.

32 Andrew Murphy, *Shakespeare in Print: A History and Chronology of Shakespeare Publishing* (Cambridge: Cambridge University Press, 2003); Ann Thompson and Sasha Roberts, *Women Reading Shakespeare, 1600–1900: An Anthology* (Manchester: Manchester University Press, 1997).

33 Ann Thompson, 'Teena Rochfort Smith, Frederick Furnivall, and the New Shakspere Society's Four-Text Edition of Hamlet', *Shakespeare Quarterly*, 49 (1998), 125–39; Ann Thompson and Sasha Roberts, 'Mary Cowden Clarke: Marriage, Gender and the Victorian Woman Critic of Shakespeare', in *Victorian Shakespeare, vol. II: Literature and Culture*, ed. Gail Marshall and Adrian Poole (New York: Palgrave Macmillan, 2003), pp. 170–89; Gail Marshall and Ann Thompson, 'Mary Cowden Clarke', in *Jameson, Cowden*

Clarke, Kemble, Cushman, ed. Gail Marshall, Great Shakespeareans (London: Bloomsbury Arden Shakespeare, 2011), VII, pp. 58–91; Laurie E. Maguire, 'How Many Children Had Alice Walker?', in *Printing and Parenting in Early Modern England*, ed. Douglas A. Brooks (Aldershot: Ashgate, 2005), pp. 327–50; Jeanne Addison Roberts, 'Women Edit Shakespeare', *Shakespeare Survey*, 59 (2006), 136–46.

34 H. R. Woodhuysen, 'Some Women Editors of Shakespeare: A Preliminary Sketch', in *Women Making Shakespeare: Text, Performance and Reception*, ed. Gordon McMullan, Lena Cowen Orlin, and Virginia Mason Vaughan (London: Bloomsbury Arden Shakespeare, 2014), pp. 79–88 (p. 80).

35 With thanks to Cait Coker and Kate Ozment. 'Our Mission', in *Women in Book History Bibliography*, www.womensbookhistory.org/our-mission.

36 Quoted in Thompson and Roberts, 'Mary Cowden Clarke', pp. 178–79.

37 Victor Cunrui Xiong, *Historical Dictionary of Medieval China* (Lanham, MD: Rowman & Littlefield, 2009), p. 250.

38 Lily Xiao Hong Lee and Sue Wiles, *Biographical Dictionary of Chinese Women: Tang through Ming, 618–1644* (New York: Routledge, 2014), p. 522.

39 Thompson and Roberts, 'Mary Cowden Clarke', pp. 178–79.

40 William Shakespeare and Mary Cowden Clarke, *Shakespeare's Works. Edited, with a Scrupulous Revision of the Text, by M. Cowden Clarke* (New York: D. Appleton & Co., 1860), p. vii.

41 William Shakespeare, Mary Cowden Clarke, and Charles Cowden Clarke, *The Plays of Shakespeare*, Cassell's Illustrated Shakespeare, 3 vols (London: Cassell & Co., 1864), III, p. xiv.

CHAPTER I

'We Have Lost Our Labour'
Recovering Women Editors of Shakespeare

Gary Taylor once began an article with a cut-and-dried statement of the problem that he wished to highlight: 'Women may read Shakespeare, but men edit him. So it has been from the beginning, and so it remains.'[1] But this story is far more complex, and far more consequential, than it has seemed. Between 1800 and 1950, at least sixty-nine women in the United Kingdom and the United States edited Shakespeare. Their output of over 100 editions – some of single plays, some of complete works, with many others falling somewhere in between – does not square with the generally held understanding, as laid out by Taylor, that women have never edited Shakespeare in significant numbers. Taylor's misapprehensions are understandable; the gender imbalance in editing has always been significant, and it was particularly egregious by the last quarter of the twentieth century. So how did the number of women editors decrease so significantly during the twentieth century, and why were most women editors of the nineteenth and early twentieth centuries excluded from the editorial record?

The first element of the answer involves the assessment of nineteenth-century editors by modern critics. The current conception of the scholarly editor's role developed during the twentieth century as part of an immensely influential academic movement: the New Bibliography. Setting aside modern opinions on the validity of its principles, the New Bibliography fundamentally changed how scholars thought about textual studies and editing, formalising new methods of analytical bibliography and instituting a new focus on the search for 'ideal copy' that reflected the author's intentions, as interpreted by the editors. Because of the depth of that influence, there is a tendency when considering editors who worked prior to the New Bibliography to judge them against what are now considered the basic tenets of scholarly editing.[2] Those who displayed recognisably 'modern' practices in their work earn plaudits, while those who now seem outdated are chided, mocked, or ignored.[3] Discussing editorial intervention in the Shakespearean text prior to Rowe's edition of 1709, Sonia Massai notes that although the topic has not been entirely neglected, previous work has focused on 'exceptional examples which can best be understood as precursors of the editorial tradition associated with eighteenth-century editors', a trend which she attributes to 'a teleological desire which foregrounds familiar (and therefore *properly* editorial) strategies at the expense of ... much wider and more representative textual practices'.[4] Massai's work attempts to fill the gap between early modern printing house practices and the dawn of 'modern' editing in the eighteenth century; however, the paradigm shift between nineteenth-century and current editorial practice is also profound, and Massai's point transfers neatly across to this later context. Nineteenth-century editors were not presciently operating according to principles still decades away from articulation, and although they worked between two eras of intense and influential editorial work, the nineteenth century was by no means a fallow period in editorial history. Paul Salzman has recently called into question past judgements of nineteenth-century editorial work, and this book echoes his claims that this era of the Shakespearean editorial tradition deserves greater consideration.[5] Demanding proleptic modernity from nineteenth-century editors results in an unjustified elision of a large span of important editorial activity.

So, appropriating Massai's phrasing, what does it mean to be '*properly* editorial'? Does one particular element of the editorial process, taken on its own, make the person doing it an editor? Or is it a confluence of tasks that cumulatively earns one the title? Must one prepare the text *and* write the notes/commentary *and* compose the introduction to be called an editor? Taylor writes critically of the problematic paradigm he sees as the root of the gender imbalance in editing:

> Textual scholars generally believe that textual scholarship is the most important activity of academic humanism: it constructs the foundation upon which all other literary interpretation is built. Textual scholars – by recovering, editing, and publishing classical texts – made possible the Renaissance itself. Within this value system, editing is work, criticism is play; editing is primary, criticism is parasitic. This value system can easily overlay another: men work, men are primary; women are idle, parasitic, secondary. The paucity of female editors reflects and reinforces the sexist myth that men do the scientific problem-solving, while women indulge in various forms of 'appreciation': men make, women interpret.[6]

While Taylor's article undoubtedly arises from good intentions, it rests on shaky historical grounds, and his language and conclusions reinforce the gendered division of labour that he wants to critique. To fully parse the complex factors at play here, consider the word 'work' in two senses: work, as in the labour involved in producing something, and work, as in the thing produced. Work-as-process and work-as-product, both verb and noun. In both senses, work can be gendered – gendered labour and the gendered text. Although these concepts are inextricably linked, considering them separately enables a better understanding of their interplay.

Taylor's critique of the textual/critical binary relies on assumptions about gendered labour. He describes Elizabeth Inchbald and Anne Barton, who wrote introductions to plays but did not perform the work of collation/emendation, as playing the part of '"the good hostess," introducing readers to editors. The man does the work, and the woman takes care of the social arrangements.'[7] Taylor's assessment that it is unfair that women were allowed to do only part of the job, and not the most important part at that, is problematic on two fronts. First, it reinforces the paradigm according to which the traditional textual work of collation and emendation is the most serious and important element of editing – the editing is the 'work', and the introduction is the 'play'; therefore, the 'social arrangements' are the less important element. Second, it completely disregards historical context. Inchbald did not select or prepare the texts used for *British Theatre*, but like Johnson or Pope during the previous century, her name was a major selling point, and her critical introductions distinguished the series from its competitors. Anne Barton wrote the introductions to the comedies for the 1974 edition of *The Riverside Shakespeare*, the text of which was prepared by G. Blakemore Evans; however, Barton was only one of six scholars who wrote critical introductions or essays for the volume. The other five were men, but Taylor singles out only Barton as an underappreciated 'hostess'.[8]

A significant aspect of recent feminist thought involves reappraising the value of the emotional/social labour more often taken on by women, bringing it up to par in importance with more traditional (male-oriented) work. Viewed through this new lens, the traditionally 'social' elements of editorial work take on new significance. If the writer of the introduction is indeed the hostess for the rest of the edition, we should also remember that women have, throughout history, exerted significant political and cultural power through the role of hostess – establishing literary salons, setting the tone for political gatherings, bestowing financial or political patronage.[9] A well-placed, canny woman has often been able to influence events via her 'social' privileges. Take, for example, the case of a woman who seems to have been chosen very specifically to perform those 'hostess' tasks for a particular play. Between 1906 and 1909, New York publisher George

D. Sproul produced the Renaissance Shakespeare under Sidney Lee's general editorship. Lee wrote the general introduction and annotations, while authors and scholars such as Edmund Gosse, Algernon Charles Swinburne, and Henry James wrote introductions for individual plays. The list of editors was a who's who of the fin de siècle literary world, and all the names were male except for one – Alice Meynell.[10]

Essayist and poet Meynell, a well-known suffragist, wrote the introduction for *The Taming of the Shrew* for the Renaissance series. Meynell was the only woman to write an introduction in this series, and she wrote on arguably the most gender-problematic play in the Shakespeare canon.[11] Meynell derides critics who attempt to analyse *Shrew* seriously, singling out Mary Cowden Clarke's *Girlhood of Shakespeare's Heroines* for its unfortunate attempts to understand and explain Katharine's character.[12] Any attempt to delve too deep into *Shrew* reveals the appalling truth of the situation, she explains:

> Granting [Cowden Clarke], then, that the heroine of a tender story, a sentimental shrew honestly in need of love and a respectable master, is appropriately to be tamed by famine, cold, ignominy, insolence, and violence, to what end are these rigours practised in the play? To what end but to make of her a hypocrite – her husband the while happy to have her so? For a woman who feigns, under menace, to see a young maid where an old man stands, or a sun where the moon shines, is no other. Katharine does this for fear of the repetition of outrage – more famine, more cold, more contempt, at the hands of the strong man: the strong man of her girlish dreams, quotha![13]

Attacking the 'feminine' Shakespeare of the previous generation, characterised by the sentimental character criticism of writers like Cowden Clarke, Anna Jameson, and Helena Faucit, Meynell offers a particular approach to the play, priming the reader to approach it from a specific angle. Sidney Lee clearly selected well-known, established literary figures to write the introductions for this series, and both Lee and many readers would likely have been aware of Meynell's social, political, and intellectual leanings, which formed a major part of her public identity. An advertisement for Lee's later Caxton Edition, which used the same introductions, stresses that, thanks to their varied backgrounds, 'every school of thought and critical temper is represented among the contributors', and, of the forty-one contributors, Meynell was one of only twenty whose portraits were included in the advertisement, signalling her market appeal and name recognition.[14] As the writer of the introduction, does she qualify as an editor? In the old paradigm, which distinguishes social/frivolous/female labour from real/serious/male labour, she would not. But in cases like this, where the writer of the introduction seems to have been selected specifically for the play in question, the shaping influence of the introduction and its inextricability from the overall edition become obvious. Meynell's authorship of that editorial element is crucial to the edition as a whole. She should not be considered 'less than' general editor Sidney Lee.

Returning to the question of why women's contributions to editing have been neglected, a second part of the answer lies in the creation of a hierarchy of editions that occurs, in part, as a consequence of the procedures used for collation. Collation is the process by which textual variants are recorded and reported. Although collation protocols differ between series, the basic procedure involves comparing every iteration of a text and noting all the variations. Collation is recorded and explained through textual notes. Modern textual notes emphasise the originator of a textual emendation or conjecture, as is consistent with our overwhelming concern with intellectual property, a preoccupation dating back to the proprietary attitudes established by the Tonson publishing cartel in the eighteenth century.[15] Margreta de Grazia describes textual notes as 'a format for attribution, registering critical as opposed to literary property'.[16] In notes, the abbreviation 'subst.' means that another edition 'substantially' used the same conjecture for the basis of an emendation, with only minor differences not affecting the overall sense of the emendation. The all-important '*this edn*' marks an original emendation. If an edition is not considered to be textually 'significant' or original, it is not generally included in collation, and therefore does not appear in textual notes.

An editor of Shakespeare must be strategic in choosing which editions to collate because she is limited by the realities of time, space, publishing practice, and human endurance. As Leah Marcus has said, '*Ars longa, vita brevis*: there is only so much primary textual investigation that any given scholar can be expected to accomplish.'[17] According to one estimate, producing an edition of a play in the Arden series already requires the collation of between forty-five and ninety texts.[18] In the *Handbook* for the New Variorum Shakespeare, probably the most critically and textually expansive editions of Shakespeare ever produced, Richard Knowles writes that 'in general, editions should not be fully collated unless they are of real importance to our understanding of the text and its history'.[19] One could argue that 'real importance' is a subjective criterion – indeed, the *Handbook* goes on to say that each variorum editor must make these judgements for herself. The point is reinforced by Philip Gaskell in his classic work on editing: 'Neither can there be any rules governing the extent to which textual annotation should be carried out. Important variants, no doubt, should be annotated, but only the editor can decide which of the variants are important.'[20]

Recent studies have shown, however, that editing is a conservative practice, with each edition being substantially and often surreptitiously shaped by the editions that preceded it.[21] It is a rare editor who, embarking on the arduous process of textual collation, will not look to previous editions to see what their predecessors considered important. In doing so, however, they risk the creation of a self-perpetuating system of exclusions, shaped by generations of subjective judgements of the kind that Knowles and Gaskell describe. Comparably, when Taylor writes that '[between 1970 and 1990] women have been responsible for important editions of a few plays ... and less important editions of a few more', his criteria for measuring 'importance' are likely influenced by the judgements of past editors.[22] I currently know of twenty-two unique editions of *As You Like It* edited by women and published before 1950. This makes it the largest data set in my research. In the recent Arden3 edition of the play, Charles and Mary Cowden Clarke's Cassell edition is the only woman-edited, pre-1950 text collated. The same is true for the most recent New Cambridge and Oxford editions. Knowles's Variorum edition, which breaks texts down into three categories based on frequency of use, includes no women in the 'most used' category, has only the Cowden Clarkes' Cassell edition in the middle category (texts which are 'occasionally quoted in the textual notes and in the appendix or their notes quoted in the commentary'), and in the final category (never quoted in textual notes, but cited for critical material) lists editions by Katharine Lee Bates, Charlotte Endymion Porter and Helen Archibald Clarke, Martha Hale Shackford, Cecily Boas, and Isabel J. Bisson. This accounts for fewer than half of the women-edited editions I am aware of, even if we exclude dramatically expurgated editions from the final count. So which editions make the cut? And how do the criteria of selection relate to the exclusion of women from the editorial tradition?

Women and the Domestic Text

That question brings us to a discussion of gendered work-as-product. This book makes extensive use of the label 'domestic text' to describe a subset of Shakespeare editions intended for women, children, and working-class readers that is often left out of the editorial record. Although no word perfectly encompasses the elements of this somewhat disparate grouping, 'domestic' emerged as the most effective option during my research. 'Domestic' offers a slightly more neutral characterisation than options such as 'feminine' or 'low', and as Georgianna Ziegler has pointed out, 'home was the major location where most people first experienced Shakespeare's plays and poetry'.[23] This quote from an 1847 article in *Fraser's Magazine* demonstrates how the three audiences could be combined into one domestic image:

> Book-love is a home-feeling – a sweet bond of family union – and a never-failing source of domestic enjoyment. It sheds a charm on the quiet fireside, unlocks the hidden sympathies of human hearts, beguiles the weary hours of sickness or solitude, and unites kindred spirits in a sweet companionship of sentiment and idea. It sheds a gentle and humanising influence over its votaries, and woos even sorrow itself into a temporary forgetfulness. Book-love is the good angel that keeps watch by the poor man's hearth, and hallows it; saving him from the temptations that lurk beyond its charmed circle; giving him new thoughts and noble aspirations, and lifting him, as it were, from the mere mechanical drudgery of his every-day occupation. The wife blesses it, as she sits smiling and sewing, alternately listening to her husband's voice, or hushing the child upon her knee. She blesses it for keeping him near her, and making him cheerful, and manly, and kind-hearted, – albeit understanding little of what he reads, and reverencing it for that reason all the more in him.[24]

Here, the poor man, the wife, and the chattering child join together to reap the benefits of literature. Distinctions between target audiences were important factors in the development of Shakespeare editions in the nineteenth century, and modern critics have found various linkages among these three groups.[25] Erica Hateley has pointed out that the genre of children's literature, particularly children's Shakespeare, has a 'history of conflating "ladies" and "youths" as an implied audience', while Mary Hammond notes that when publishing inexpensive texts for working-class readers, 'publishers tended . . . to assume a patriarchal, teacherly role', and that 'the protection of these "innocent" readers [young students, women, and the self-educated] was very much a nineteenth century trope'.[26] Janet Bottoms has linked publications for women, children, and the working classes as three of the major strands in the development of methods of teaching the plays and of Shakespeare's place in the curriculum.[27]

The sizeable and lucrative market for commercially produced domestic Shakespeare is best known for its products aimed at children. Georgianna Ziegler has traced the market for children's Shakespeare back to the 1720s, revealing a rich history that encompassed excerpt books and expurgated editions as well as chapbooks, paper dolls, and toy theatres.[28] During the nineteenth century, influenced by changing educational philosophies and the growth of mass literacy, publishing companies began investing exten- sively in these products. In 1807, two books appeared that would deeply influence the world of Shakespeare publishing, both originating largely with female creators – Charles and Mary Lamb's *Tales from Shakespeare* and Henrietta Bowdler's *Family Shakespeare*. Although Mary wrote the majority of the *Tales*, the original imprints listed Charles Lamb as the sole author, thereby avoiding any negative publicity that might derive from Mary's well-known psychotic episode, during which she killed their mother.[29] The anonymous Bowdler edition, originally published in a small batch by a Bath publisher, did not achieve popularity until Henrietta's brother Thomas convinced a London publisher to re-release it in an expanded form under his name. Although Thomas has therefore received most of the credit (and the blame) for the *Family Shakespeare*, the idea originated with Henrietta, and many of her edits survive in the re-released edition and its subsequent revised printings.[30] These two books exemplify the tradition of nineteenth-century domestic Shakespeare.

Both books grew out of the impulse to make the works of Shakespeare available to those who could not previously access or understand them. The Lambs' *Tales* focused on the combined market of women and children, particularly female children; by the second edition, the 'Advertisement' section described them as 'not so precisely adapted for the amusement of mere children, as for an acceptable and improving present to young ladies advancing to the state of womanhood'.[31] Bottoms suggests that even during composition, 'the Lambs' dual aim caused them to substitute simple plotlines for children but to focus their stories on the women whenever possible'.[32] Both the *Tales* and *The Family Shakespeare* frame themselves in relation to a male authority controlling access to Shakespeare. The Lambs suggest that after a girl read the *Tales* to get a sense of the story, her brother, having access to the complete Shakespeare, could

> read to them (carefully selecting what is proper for a young sister's ear) some passage which has pleased them in one of these stories, in the very words of the scene from which it is taken; and it is hoped they will find that the beautiful extracts, the select passages they may choose to give their sisters, in this way will be much better relished and understood.[33]

The introduction to the Bowdler text explains that the edition is intended to replicate the mediated transmission methods of the Bowdlers' child- hood, in which a discriminating father exercised his good taste while reading Shakespeare aloud to the family, avoiding any immodest material that might provoke 'blushes'.[34] Both introductions therefore acknowledge the incompleteness of the text offered, and the necessity of a qualified mediator to dispense a sanctioned, sanitised version of Shakespeare.

As a result of that perceived necessity, the spectre of expurgation haunts domestic editions, making them easily dismissed, criticised, or mocked. Expurgated texts violate editorial norms by insisting on the visibility of the editor's intervention in the 'authorial' text. They refuse to allow the reader to indulge in the fantasy of direct, unmediated access to the author. This issue has been described by Sonia Massai and Jonathan Bate in relation to adaptation:

> The figure of the author is still very powerful, and the further a text departs from the author's holograph, the more marginal and negligible it becomes to the critic's attention. Editing is particularly affected by this prejudice, in that the editor's task is generally identified with the recovery of a partially lost original: a transcendental drive leads editors to try and fill the gap left by the disappearance of the natural author at the center of his work.[35]

The most famous expurgator of Shakespeare was a woman, and she (unintentionally) gave her name to the practice of expurgation on moral grounds. Henrietta Bowdler was the first woman to bowdlerise Shakespeare, and she was by no means the last. In her initial edition of the *Family Shakespeare*, published in 1807, Bowdler employed both aesthetic and moral judgement in her expurgations, cutting parts of the text that she found uninteresting in addition to those that were, one might say, too interesting.[36]

So as 'innocent' populations gained increased access to Shakespeare, cultural gatekeepers responded by making judgements regarding which parts of Shakespeare were safe and appropriate for the new readers, and even what elements they were most likely to enjoy. Access to printed Shakespeare was no longer contingent on parental approval – school boards and teachers now shared that responsibility. A working-class reader could acquire an inexpensive 'shilling Shakespeare' of their own. The images presented by the Lambs and Bowdlers of a male relative mediating contact for girls still existed, but a new social context also emerged: reading in a classroom with other children, overseen by a teacher. New approaches involved some trial and error, as demonstrated by a professor at Queen's College, London, in the 1890s, whose student later recalled that [we were] reading the sleep-walking scene in *Macbeth* when the Professor held up his hand: 'Ladies, before proceeding further we will turn to the next page. We will count one, two, three lines from the top. We will count one, two words in this line. We will erase or cross out the second word and substitute the word "thou". This line will then read "Out thou spot. Out I say."'[37]

The more efficient solution to this problem was to remove offending words prior to printing, and the popularity of expurgation as a defensive position meant that most domestic editions suffered from a lack of textual 'wholeness' that some found troubling. Some objected out of a desire to protect the sanctity of the Shakespeare text, accusing expurgators of 'mutilating' or even 'castrating' the text, removing from it the things that made it male.[38] One reviewer of the Cowden Clarkes' expurgated Cassell edition wondered, 'if we begin to rewrite Shakespeare, where is the operation to end?'[39]

Given that Bowdler's edition was far from the most extreme example of expurgated female-edited Shakespeare in the nineteenth century, certain aspects of this concern are understandable. Feeling that Bowdler had been overly conservative in her cutting, Rosa Baughan prepared her own version of the text.[40] The resulting *Shakespeare's Plays Abridged and Revised for the Use of Girls*, published in two volumes by T. J. Allman in 1863 and 1871, retains only the bare minimum of Shakespeare.[41] Volume 1, containing the 'Tragedies and Historical Plays', is a meagre, insubstantial book. *Hamlet* occupies only fifteen pages; Baughan dispenses with *Romeo and Juliet* in just nine.[42] She writes in her introduction that her initial intention was to publish a book of selections from Shakespeare in the style of the popular nineteenth-century excerpt books, the most famous of which was William Dodd's *Beauties of Shakespeare*.[43] Baughan recognised that, had she executed her plan, 'one of the greatest charms of Shakespeare – the fitness of the sentiment in the mouth of the speaker – would be entirely lost', so she chose instead to produce a severely expurgated edition.[44] She admitted that comedy was the primary victim of her expurgation, comedic scenes being where 'the greatest freedom of expression is to be found', but Baughan believed that the humour would be 'the quality least appreciable by the class of readers for whom I have laboured'.[45] In other words, the girls wouldn't get the jokes anyway.

As for prose adaptations, the Lambs themselves recognised the dangers of offering an incomplete Shakespeare to someone experiencing the plays for the first time, expressing the wish in their Preface that

if [the *Tales*] be fortunately so done as to prove delightful to any of the
young readers it is hoped that no worse effect will result than to make them
wish themselves a little older, that they may be allowed to read the Plays at
full length (such a wish will be neither peevish nor irrational).[46]

Others criticised editors and adaptors who admitted to the missing elements, and thus highlighted their existence. One review of the Lambs'
Tales complained about 'the language of the preface, where girls are told
that there are parts in Shakespeare *improper* for them to read at one age,
though they may be allowed to read them at another. This only serves as a
stimulus to juvenile curiosity, which requires a *bridle* rather than a *spur*.'[47]
In poet Emily Dickinson's Shakespeare reading group, the men suggested
that they go through all the copies of the plays and mark out anything
'questionable'. The women rejected this idea, informing the men that they
did not want those 'questionable' things emphasised, and that they would
read everything. Dickinson herself haughtily told them that 'there's nothing wicked in Shakespeare, and if there is I don't want to know it'.[48]

New strategies evolved to counter both concerns. One solution was to
use the Lambs' *Tales*, or similar prose versions, in concert with expurgated
texts or extracts in order to offer narrative contexts to students without
access to the full text.[49] Leah Price has described expurgations and
abridgements as 'photographic negatives', explaining that 'each retains
what the other discards'.[50] Seen in this light, a pairing of the two could
be seen as creating the complete picture. An example of this dual approach
is Mary Atkinson Maurice's *Readings from the Plays of Shakespeare, in
Illustration of His Characters* (1848), in which Maurice's own prose narratives were paired with expurgated texts. This volume has, until now, been
tentatively identified as being edited by the Winkworth sisters.[51] This
attribution is incorrect, and the mistake demonstrates how challenging
ascription can be when working on women authors with limited bodies of
known work. The title page says only that the book was 'Edited by the
Author of "Aids to Developement [*sic*];" "Memorials of Two Sisters;"
"Mothers and Governesses;" &c. &c.' Although there is a book entitled
Memorials of Two Sisters (1908) about the Winkworth sisters, the dates do
not allow for the same author to have edited *Readings* (1848) and written
Mothers and Governesses (1848). The elder Winkworth sister would have
been only twenty-one at that time. The author of the other two books, as
well as a different book called *Memorials of Two Sisters* (1837), was
education reformer Mary Atkinson Maurice.

Maurice represents an interesting link to the larger world of education,
for both girls and the working class. A lifelong teacher, Maurice ran her

own schools in Southampton and Reading before moving to London, where she became deeply involved with Queen's College, London (an institution pioneering education for girls), and the Governesses' Benevolent Institution. Both were early examples of the push for better education for girls in general, and more extensive preparation and support for women teachers specifically. Maurice's brother, Frederick Denison Maurice, served as the first principal of Queen's College and went on to found the Working Men's College as part of a group that also included Frederick Furnivall.[52] In the introduction to *Readings*, Maurice described previous efforts to avoid 'indelicacy' in Shakespeare as leading to publications that 'give no more notion of the magnificent whole, than a few pebbles picked from the sea-shore, or a bottle filled with salt water, would convey to one who had never seen it, an idea of the grand and boundless ocean'.[53] Bundling expurgated texts with prose stories offered a way to allow the reader a better idea of 'the magnificent whole' without sacrificing propriety.

Gendered Text, Gendered Labour

Despite some objections, expurgation proved to be a particularly persistent feature of student and domestic editions well into the twentieth century, and the association between expurgation and castration exemplifies the troubled intersection between the gendered text and gendered labour.[54] In a Western context, 'domestic' is almost inevitably a word with gendered connotations, and the inclination to gender texts, like the inclination to gender types of labour – that is, critical/feminine versus textual/masculine – is problematic. Editing as a discipline, and the theory surrounding it, is steeped in deeply gendered concepts.[55] The language used to describe texts themselves often betrays its inherent biases. The binary foundations of many New Bibliographical concepts – good/bad, fair/foul – lend themselves to gendered readings.[56] Leah Marcus points out that in Alfred Hart's formulation,

> [t]he 'bad' quartos are gendered as feminine – they are lax and chatty rather than rigorously formed and poetic, reminding 'us of the vulgar gossiping of the immortal Sairey Gamp or the chattering irrelevancy of the inane Mrs. Nickleby'. Worse yet, they are sexually suspect – a prostitution of the 'true' text.[57]

Criticising the eroticization and sexual violation inherent in Fredson Bowers's famous desire to 'strip the veil of print from the text',

Holderness, Loughrey, and Murphy characterise 'that virtually all-male club the New Bibliographers' as a group that 'evidently cherished beneath their respectable tweed jackets a perverse desire to ravish the printed text in order to release the perfect female body enclosed within it'.[58] In the 1987 *Textual Companion* to the Oxford Shakespeare, Gary Taylor called editors the 'pimps of discourse' and equated the text with a diseased female prostitute.[59] In 1970, Chaucer editor E. Talbot Donaldson embarked on a particularly fraught envisioning of the editorial task. It is worth quoting in full in order to demonstrate how far flights of rhetorical cleverness can lead critics into blatant sexism. Like a woman, no text is perfect in its natural state, says Donaldson:

> after careful analysis of the textual situation and long thought about the meaning, the editor, not unlike a bachelor choosing a bride, selects Line Form A for his text. For a time he lives in virtuous serenity, pleased with his decision. A year or more passes, and then one day it comes to him, like a bolt from the blue, that he should, of course, have chosen Line Form B; in short, he married the wrong girl. She is attractive, she is plausible, she has her points, but he just can't live with her; he lies awake at nights enumerating her faults, which seem considerable when she is compared with her rejected rival, who now appears infinitely preferable. So the editor (who is the least reliable of all possible husbands) obtains a divorce – an enormously expensive one, since it forces him to change his apparatus and also to worry endlessly whether other decisions he has made have not depended on this one (and, as in matrimony, he will find that they have), so that they will have to be changed, too. His marriage with Line Form B is now consecrated, and he settles down to live happily ever after. Then after a year or so, Wife B begins to prove incompatible in a different and even more annoying way than Wife A; and it occurs to him that if he could find someone who had the best characteristics of both A and B, without their objectionable traits, he could be truly happy. The editor is uniquely privileged to be able to bring this dream-girl into existence by amalgamating A and B, which he does, and then weds this AxB after another expensive divorce. But the chances are that by now he is less illusioned about the excellence of his judgment in choosing wives, and while he likes his third one basically, he is prepared to expect that as time passes he may want to make a few changes in her. And at what time in his life will he be ready to say that he is fully and permanently satisfied with his choice? Never, until he stops thinking entirely.[60]

So even after the editor engages in the Pygmalion fantasy of conflation to create his 'dream-girl', only death can bring an end to his search for the perfect woman/text. These examples support editor Ann Thompson's assertion that 'the typical rhetorical stance of the male editor is aloof, patronising and overtly or covertly misogynistic' and that 'editors are frequently more sexist than the text'.[61] In 2019, Laurie Maguire and Emma Smith reflected on the continued use of gendered metaphors in textual studies, concluding that the trope continues to have 'a dispiriting longevity'.[62]

Ultimately, all of these rhetorical conceits require the critic to ascribe humanity to the text. Laurie Maguire has discussed the persistent tendency to anthropomorphise texts, to 'present [them] as abused (orphaned, abandoned, mistreated) or nurtured (adopted, bandaged, patronized)'.[63] By anthropomorphising texts, Maguire suggests, we create a dynamic in which 'texts, like human beings, have parents, become orphans, seek guardians'.[64] The deeply rooted perceptions of sexual dimorphism in the traditional Western world view mean that when something is characterised as 'human', possessing parents and able to reproduce, it is often assigned a binary gender identity. In his Lacanian reading of editorial authority, Clayton Delery recognises that the gender binary inflects the author/ text/editor/reader relationship, but he is too quick to elide author with book, and to label them both as symbolically male.[65] As seen in Hart's, Bowers's, Donaldson's, and Taylor's formulations, and as explored by Wendy Wall, the text, particularly the imperfect or 'corrupted' text, is often portrayed as female.[66] Not only that, but female touch itself could be depicted as corrupting, as seen in the review of Charles and Mary Cowden Clarke's edition in which the reviewer blamed 'the lady editor' for the text's 'alterations, mutilations, [and] corruptions'.[67]

For a male-authored book to be purely male, it would have to be an inviolable object, entirely closed to outside influences; however, as Robert Darnton has pointed out, a book is part of a larger communications circuit, or communications web, in Helen Smith's more nuanced analogy.[68] The boundaries of a book are less brick walls than semi-permeable membranes, open to osmotic transfer between the book itself and its surroundings. In Smith's words, 'the gender of the text can only be the result of the numerous sexed encounters and acts which constitute its making and reception'.[69] The symbolic genders of all actors in the web affect the symbolic gender of the book. Delery suggests that student editions are 'most phallic and most dependent upon traditional notions of patriarchal authority' because they most entirely veil their textual castration (imperfection); however, when placed within Smith's web, the 'feminine' nature of the intended student audience exerts sway over the process of making the book and the gender of the eventual product.[70] Furthermore, Delery's analysis implies that the author and editor are always symbolically male. How does this change when the author or, more relevant to this case, the editor is literally female?

The involvement of female agents thoroughly disrupts the fantasy of parthenogenesis central to the traditional Western conception of authorship. Issues of fertility and potency arise constantly in discussions of authorship and editorship, and despite its Lacanian inflections in Delery's analysis, castration was an image that emerged in editorial discourse long before the advent of Freud. In response to a suggestion that he expurgate John Dryden's work in the edition he was preparing, Sir Walter Scott wrote that 'I will not castrate John Dryden. I would as soon castrate my own father.... What would you say to any man who would castrate Shakespeare, or Massinger, or Beaumont and Fletcher?'[71] Thomas Bowdler, the most famous example of an editor charged with 'castrating' Shakespeare, responded with outrage and offense to the accusation, but how much more complicated might those accusations have been if the critics had known that the original castrator was Henrietta?[72] Despite Thomas Bowdler's annexation and revision of the project, the *Family Shakespeare*'s female roots are important. When they are taken into account, the Bowdler text feels unintentionally subversive, despite the editor's stated aim of recreating the traditional paternal voice of Shakespearian authority. The cosy domesticity of the imagined scene, in which the father reads aloud to the family, prudently editing to preserve modesty, feels disrupted; there is a kind of editorial puppet act taking place when a female voice interjects itself into the male-authorised transmission of Shakespeare. To borrow Delery's Lacanian language, Henrietta has disrupted the inheritance of the phallus.

Inheritance and legacy are key concepts in the language of textual criticism. German philology deeply influenced the development of English textual studies, and with it came the Lachmannian formulations of textual genetics.[73] K. K. Ruthven writes that 'stemmatism, with its "filiation" of texts, ... seems to betray only too patently a displacement into the realm of scholarship of a characteristically patriarchal anxiety about legitimacy of descent, related in turn to nineteenth-century notions of property and inheritance'.[74] Just as a genealogist creates a family tree as a convenient graphic for organising the most basic facts of a person's origins, a textual scholar might employ stemmata to illustrate the relationships between texts. As David Greetham points out, this representation of taxonomy is inherently patriarchal in its assumption of a 'nonsexual, parthenogenic biology of descent' that requires the occlusion of the matrilineal line for the sake of two-dimensional representation.[75] In *The*

Calculus of Variants, W. W. Greg explicitly acknowledges that conceptualising textual reproduction as parthenogenic is necessary to his method of mapping a textual family tree.[76] In his *Prolegomena*, R. B. McKerrow is even more blatant, providing this explanation for the difference between 'monogenous' and 'polygenous' series of texts: 'The "monogenous" series may be considered as the equivalent of a family of father, son, grandson, great-grandson, &c., the father being still alive; the "polygenous" group to a family of brothers whose father is dead and each of whom may be the head of a family of his own.'[77] Joseph Grigely has taken Greetham's criticism a step farther, condemning many of the practices of editing as 'textual eugenics' and drawing connections between the focus on textual purity in the work of early and mid-twentieth-century bibliographers and the language and principles of Social Darwinism and other manifestations of eugenics.[78]

Women are similarly erased from the wider symbolic 'family' of Western authorship. Just as the editorial tradition places textual witnesses into family trees, so authors are often placed, to their detriment or benefit, in positions of kinship and inheritance with their predecessors and their successors – 'heir to Milton', 'Shakespeare's son', and so on. These relationships are primarily, although not exclusively, male-oriented, reflecting the standard Western system of patrilineal inheritance. In her book tracing the history of the kinship metaphor in literary biography, Jane Spencer explains that

> Women . . . are not expected to be artistic creators in the highest or spiritual sense. Nor do they have a clear place in literary genealogies. Kinship, in the Western world, is the organizing principle for inheritance, and the trope of inheritance is central to the idea of literary history. The patrilineal model of inheritance, based on ancient sources and still influencing cultural ideas today, has obviously made women's place within literature problematic, to say the least.[79]

Spencer relates this paradigm to the Aristotelian theory of conception, in which 'the male was the agent of generation, the female its passive receptacle'.[80] Sperm, the animating agent, activates the 'inert' maternal contribution. In other words, the man provides the generative, creative element, the woman the mechanical vessel of transmission. Both uses of stemmatism leave 'female' texts and women authors and editors in a critical catch-22. In the first, they are corrupt/corrupting, and 'corruption' must be stamped out, leaving neither the corrupt female bodies of problematic texts nor the 'corrupting' hand of the female editor with any place in an idealised family tree. In the second, they are passive and nongenerative and therefore irrelevant to the overall picture, easy to ignore in favour of emphasising the 'significant' or dominant genetic lines. Either paradigm leaves female editors and texts vulnerable to the same result: erasure.

The process of simplification is the enemy of women in textual history. As Bonnie Smith and Sonia Massai each point out, the urge to tell a complete, coherent story with a strong, forward trajectory leads to the elision of anything that does not fit that narrative.[81] Domestic texts, and the women who created them, do not fit this teleological trajectory. 'Castrated' and feminised, aimed at less elite readers, they lacked many of the markers that distinguished 'important' editions of Shakespeare in the eighteenth and nineteenth centuries. Some domestic editions are regularly included in textual notes – Charles Knight's illustrated edition, for example – but most are not. They have been treated as spinster texts, dead-end branches of the textual family tree, pruned off to serve short-sighted critical interpretations and editorial pragmatism. Previous accounts of the editorial tradition have overvalued the generative aspect of editions by considering them 'important' only if they demonstrate clear, textual innovation, the type of originality that can be claimed with '*this edn*' in the textual notes. Using outdated concepts of creative generativity, they have equated value with originality, innovation, or genius, excluding work, in the sense of both product and process, which does not fit into that ideal. By seeking anachronistic modernity in textual work, we doom ourselves to an almost exclusively male editorial tradition. Instead, it is vital to acknowledge that all editions are rooted in radically mixed motives, and that different processes of preparation, each tailored to the goals of a specific edition, can all fall under the definition of 'editing'.

It is hard to imagine editions like *The Boudoir Shakespeare* alongside Johnson, Clark and Wright, and Malone, and I do not contend that all domestic editions should be added to those ranks. They were created under different conditions and for different purposes and should not be judged or measured by the same criteria. In a student edition, for example, the preparation of the text may not be the most important part of the editorial task. But all editions share the same basic aim of presenting Shakespeare, in some form, to the reader, and it is vital to consider, in Leah Marcus's words, 'the subtle, pervasive rhetorical power exerted by the editions we use'.[82] This is particularly true of the editions in which readers encounter Shakespeare for the first time. In an article tracing the influence of Shakespeare in schools, Janet Bottoms pointed out that the classroom is 'one of the most powerful forces at work upon [the idea of Shakespeare]'.[83]

Many people first read the plays in domestic editions; therefore, those editions deserve attention, consideration, and analysis – as do their editors. Jerome McGann writes that 'every new edition, including every critical edition, is an act of re-imagining and redefining a text's audience(s) and its ways of interacting with those audience(s)'.[84] The principles of the social text suggest that every text is an iteration of the 'work' that deserves acknowledgement in its own right; in Grigely's words, every edition is a 'moment of inscription' that is 'unique, and in its uniqueness, telling'.[85] If this is true, then the editor of each text must be considered under the same democratising principles – each one telling in her uniqueness.

Notes

1 Gary Taylor, 'Textual and Sexual Criticism: A Crux in *The Comedy of Errors*', *Renaissance Drama*, 19 (1988), 195–225 (p. 195).
2 Marcus Walsh examined this in detail in the context of eighteenth-century editors. Marcus Walsh, *Shakespeare, Milton, and Eighteenth-Century Literary Editing: The Beginnings of Interpretative Scholarship* (Cambridge: Cambridge University Press, 1997).
3 See Margreta de Grazia, *Shakespeare Verbatim* (Oxford: Oxford University Press, 1991).
4 Sonia Massai, *Shakespeare and the Rise of the Editor* (Cambridge: Cambridge University Press, 2007), pp. 2–3.
5 Paul Salzman, *Editors Construct the Renaissance Canon, 1825–1915* (Basingstoke: Palgrave Macmillan, 2018), p. 136.
6 Taylor, 'Textual and Sexual Criticism', p. 197.
7 Taylor, 'Textual and Sexual Criticism', p. 198.
8 The others were Hallett Smith (introductions to romances and poems), Frank Kermode (introductions to tragedies), Harry Levin (general introduction), Herschel Baker (introductions to histories), and Charles H. Shattuck (essay on Elizabethan theatre). Another woman, Dr Marie Edel, was employed by Houghton Mifflin to assist with the edition; she was ultimately listed as an editor and co-wrote the notes to the comedies with G. Blakemore Evans.
9 See chapter 2 in Helen Smith, *'Grossly Material Things': Women and Book Production in Early Modern England* (Oxford: Oxford University Press, 2012); Elizabeth Muir Tyler, *England in Europe: English Royal Women and Literary Patronage, c. 1000–c. 1150* (Toronto: University of Toronto Press, 2017); David Roberts, *The Ladies: Female Patronage of Restoration Drama, 1660–1700* (Oxford: Clarendon Press, 1989); Anneliese Pollock Renck, *Female Authorship, Patronage, and Translation in Late Medieval France: From Christine de Pizan to Louise Labé* (Turnhout: Brepols, 2018).
10 Murphy, *Shakespeare in Print*, pp. 369–79.

11 For an overview of editorial treatments of *Shrew* and their contradictory attitudes towards gender roles and violence, see chapter 3 in Leah S. Marcus, *How Shakespeare Became Colonial: Editorial Tradition and the British Empire* (London: Routledge, 2017).

12 In *Girlhood*, Cowden Clarke writes backstories for Shakespeare's heroines that conclude with their first appearance in their plays. They tend to be simultaneously earnest and melodramatic, but after a long period during which they were out of fashion, critics have recently mined *Girlhood* to find deeper thought and meaning. In particular, see the work of Sarah Barber, Erica Hateley, Gail Marshall, Ann Thompson, and George C. Gross.

13 William Shakespeare, Alice Meynell, and Sidney Lee, *The Taming of the Shrew*, Renaissance Shakespeare (New York: George D. Sproul, 1907), VII, p. xii. Meynell's message may have been relatively progressive, but it certainly did not avoid classism – she claims that in her time, such a shrew may exist in 'the alleys of the town' but not in the country house (p. xiii).

14 'Advertisement for the Caxton Edition of the Complete Works of Shakespeare' (Caxton Publishing Company, undated), David Nichol Smith Papers, Osborn Collection, Beinecke Rare Book and Manuscript Library, Yale University, Box 2, Folder 11.

15 Eric Rasmussen, 'Editorial Memory: The Origin and Evolution of Collation Notes', in *Shakespeare and Textual Studies*, ed. Margaret Jane Kidnie and Sonia Massai (Cambridge: Cambridge University Press, 2015), pp. 391–97 (p. 392); Massai, *Shakespeare and the Rise of the Editor*, pp. 190–91; Evelyn B. Tribble, '"Like a Looking-Glas in the Frame": From the Marginal Note to the Footnote', in *The Margins of the Text*, ed. D. C. Greetham (Ann Arbor: University of Michigan Press, 1997), pp. 229–44.

16 De Grazia, *Shakespeare Verbatim*, p. 213.

17 Leah S. Marcus, *Unediting the Renaissance: Shakespeare, Marlowe, Milton* (London: Routledge, 1996), p. 4.

18 Valerie Wayne, 'The Gendered Text and Its Labour', in *The Oxford Handbook of Shakespeare and Embodiment: Gender, Sexuality, Race*, ed. Valerie Traub (Oxford: Oxford University Press, 2016), pp. 549–68 (p. 554).

19 Richard Knowles, *Shakespeare Variorum Handbook: A Manual of Editorial Practice*, 2nd ed. (New York: Modern Language Association of America, 2003), p. 58, www.mla.org/content/download/3330/81674/variorum_hndbk.pdf.

20 Philip Gaskell, *From Writer to Reader: Studies in Editorial Method* (Oxford: Clarendon Press, 1978), p. 7.

21 Random Cloud, 'FIAT FLUX', in *Crisis in Editing: Texts of the English Renaissance*, ed. Randall McLeod (New York: AMS Press, 1994), pp. 127, 148–49.

22 Taylor, 'Textual and Sexual Criticism', p. 197.

23 Georgianna Ziegler, 'Introducing Shakespeare: The Earliest Versions for Children', *Shakespeare*, 2.2 (2006), 132–51 (p. 133).

24 R. A. Willmott, 'Book-Love', *Fraser's Magazine* (1847). Quoted in Kate Flint, *The Woman Reader 1837–1914* (Oxford: Oxford University Press, 1995), pp. 11–12.

25 Leah Price, *The Anthology and the Rise of the Novel: From Richardson to George Eliot* (Cambridge: Cambridge University Press, 2000), p. 77.

26 Erica Hateley, *Shakespeare in Children's Literature: Gender and Cultural Capital* (New York: Routledge, 2009), p. 16; Hammond, *Reading, Publishing and the Formation of Literary Taste in England*, p. 106.

27 Janet Bottoms, '"Doing Shakespeare": How Shakespeare Became a School "Subject"', *Shakespeare Survey*, 66 (2013).

28 Ziegler, 'Introducing Shakespeare'.

29 In 1796, Mary Lamb stabbed her mother in the heart. The traditional explanation for the sudden violence was that 'the accumulated strain of nursing a senile father and a bedridden mother, while also maintaining the family through her needlework, had exacerbated a psychological disorder subsequently categorised by her brother's twentieth-century biographers as a manic-depressive illness'. Charles took custody of his sister, and they remained devoted partners throughout their lives, although Mary did periodically have to return to private madhouses due to relapses. Jane Aaron, 'Lamb, Mary Anne (1764–1847), Children's Writer', in *Oxford Dictionary of National Biography* (Oxford: Oxford University Press, 2004), doi.org/10.1093/ref:odnb/15918.

30 By 1850, eleven editions had been produced. For more on the history of the Bowdler text, see Adam H. Kitzes, 'The Hazards of Expurgation: Adapting *Measure for Measure* to the Bowdler *Family Shakespeare*', *The Journal for Early Modern Cultural Studies*, 13.2 (2013), 43–68; Noel Perrin, *Dr. Bowdler's Legacy: A History of Expurgated Books in England and America* (Boston: David R. Godine, 1992).

31 Quoted in Janet Bottoms, '"To Read Aright": Representations of Shakespeare for Children', *Children's Literature*, 32 (2004), 1–14; Kate Harvey, '"A Classic for the Elders": Marketing Charles and Mary Lamb in the Nineteenth Century', *Actes Des Congrès de La Société Française Shakespeare*, 34 (2016).

32 Bottoms, 'To Read Aright', p. 4; see also Jean I. Marsden, 'Shakespeare for Girls: Mary Lamb and *Tales from Shakespeare*', *Children's Literature*, 17.1 (2009), 47–63.

33 Mary Lamb and Charles Lamb, *Tales from Shakespeare: Illustrated with Paintings of Scenes from Shakespeare by Various Artists*, ed. Katherine Duncan-Jones (London: Folio Society, 2003), p. xviii. Price discusses the dynamic between brothers and sisters reading the *Tales*, but I believe she overstates the degree to which the Lambs intentionally tried to 'shame' boys into reading the full plays rather than the *Tales*. Leah Price, *The Anthology and the Rise of the Novel: From Richardson to George Eliot* (Cambridge: Cambridge University Press, 2000), pp. 87–88.

34 William Shakespeare and Henrietta Maria Bowdler, *The Family Shakespeare*, 4 vols (Bath: R. Cruttwell, 1807), p. vii.

35 Jonathan Bate and Sonia Massai, 'Adaptation as Edition', in *The Margins of the Text*, ed. D. C. Greetham (Ann Arbor: University of Michigan Press, 1997), pp. 129–53 (pp. 129–30).

36 Perrin, *Dr. Bowdler's Legacy*, p. xii; for more on the Bowdler text, see also Emily Burden, 'Pre-Victorian Prudery: *The Family Shakespeare* and the Birth of Bowdlerism' (master's thesis, University of Birmingham, 2007); Michael Dobson, 'Bowdler and Britannia: Shakespeare and the National Libido', *Shakespeare Survey*, 46 (1993), 137–44; Leah Price, 'The Poetics of Pedantry from Thomas Bowdler to Susan Ferrier', *Women's Writing*, 7.1 (2000), 75–88; David Skinner, 'A Critical and Historical Analysis of Charles and Mary Lamb's *Tales from Shakespeare* and Thomas Bowdler's *The Family Shakespeare*' (doctoral dissertation, University of Sheffield, 2011).

37 Quoted in Flint, *The Woman Reader*, p. 129; a similar logic can be found behind the concept of the *index expurgatorius*. Beginning in the sixteenth century, censors produced lists of heresies or other material in need of expurgation in printed books, with the intention that the reader would use the index to find the prohibited lines and cross them out. Paul Saenger, 'Benito Arias Montano and the Evolving Notion of Locus in Sixteenth-Century Printed Books', *Word & Image*, 17.1–2 (2001), 119–37.

38 Kitzes, 'The Hazards of Expurgation'; George Yeats, 'Shakespeare's Victorian Legacy: Text as Monument and Emendation as Desecration in the Mid-Nineteenth Century', *Victorian Literature and Culture*, 40.2 (2012), 469–86.

39 Christopher Decker, 'Shakespeare Editions', in *Shakespeare in the Nineteenth Century*, ed. Gail Marshall (Cambridge: Cambridge University Press, 2012), pp. 16–38 (p. 20).

40 Baughan was not alone in feeling that Bowdler had been too lax – Charles Dodgson, aka Lewis Carroll, agreed. See Georgianna Ziegler, 'Alice Reads Shakespeare: Charles Dodgson and the Girl's Shakespeare Project', in *Reimagining Shakespeare for Children and Young Adults*, ed. Naomi Miller (New York: Routledge, 2013).

41 Baughan became better known for her writing on palmistry, astrology, physiognomy, and graphology.

42 Baughan entirely excluded all three *Henry VI* plays, *Troilus and Cressida*, *Timon of Athens*, *Othello*, *Antony and Cleopatra*, *Measure for Measure*, *All's Well That Ends Well*, *Cymbeline*, *Merry Wives of Windsor*, and *The Winter's Tale*. The edition is unadorned with notes, introduction, or glossary.

43 For more on the development and legacy of extract books, see Georgianna Ziegler, 'Women and Shakespeare', in *Shakespeare in the Nineteenth Century*, ed. Gail Marshall (Cambridge: Cambridge University Press, 2012), pp. 205–28; Price, *The Anthology and the Rise of the Novel*, pp. 67–77.

44 William Shakespeare and Rosa Baughan, *Shakespeare's Plays Abridged and Revised for the Use of Girls*, 2 vols (London: T. J. Allman, 1863), I, p. v.

45 Shakespeare and Baughan, *Shakespeare's Plays Abridged and Revised for the Use of Girls*, I, p. v.

46 Lamb and Lamb, *Tales from Shakespeare*, p. xviii.

47 Quoted in Susan J. Wolfson, 'Explaining to Her Sisters: Mary Lamb's *Tales from Shakespear*', in *Women's Re-visions of Shakespeare: On the Responses of Dickinson, Woolf, Rich, H.D., George Eliot and Others*, ed. Marianne Novy (Urbana: University of Illinois Press, 1990), pp. 16–40 (p. 22).

48 Páraic Finnerty, *Emily Dickinson's Shakespeare* (Amherst: University of Massachusetts Press, 2006), p. 16.

49 Bottoms, 'Doing Shakespeare', p. 99; Harvey, '"A Classic for the Elders"', p. 4.

50 Price, *The Anthology and the Rise of the Novel*, p. 81.

51 Ziegler, 'Women and Shakespeare', p. 209.

52 Elaine Kaye, 'Maurice, Mary Atkinson (1797–1858)', in *Oxford Dictionary of National Biography* (Oxford: Oxford University Press, 2004), doi.org/10.1093/ref:odnb/51769.

53 William Shakespeare and Mary Atkinson Maurice, *Readings from the Plays of Shakespeare, in Illustration of His Characters* (London: John W. Parker, 1848), p. vi.

54 Perrin, *Dr. Bowdler's Legacy*, pp. 255, 265.

55 For an overview of this issue, including additional examples, see Laurie Maguire and Emma Smith, 'On Editing', *Shakespeare*, 15.3 (2019), 293–309.

56 For more on the use of binary elements, see Paul Werstine, 'Narratives about Printed Shakespeare Texts: "Foul Papers" and "Bad" Quartos', *Shakespeare Quarterly*, 41.1 (1990), 65; Laurie E. Maguire, *Shakespearean Suspect Texts: The 'Bad' Quartos and Their Contexts* (Cambridge: Cambridge University Press, 1996).

57 Marcus, *Unediting the Renaissance*, p. 102.

58 Graham Holderness, Bryan Loughrey, and Andrew Murphy, '"What's the Matter?" Shakespeare and Textual Theory', *Textual Practice*, 9.1 (1995), 93–119; Marcus, *How Shakespeare Became Colonial*, p. 101. Leah Marcus has recently discussed the racial and colonial inflections of this language in *How Shakespeare Became Colonial*.

59 Gary Taylor, 'General Introduction', in *The Oxford Shakespeare: A Textual Companion*, ed. Stanley Wells et al. (Oxford: Oxford University Press, 1987), pp. 7, 60.

60 E. Talbot Donaldson, *Speaking of Chaucer* (London: Athlone Press, 1977), pp. 103–4.

61 Ann Thompson, 'Feminist Theory and the Editing of Shakespeare: *The Taming of the Shrew* Revisited', in *Shakespeare, Feminism and Gender*, ed. Kate Chedgzoy, New Casebooks (Basingstoke: Palgrave, 2001), pp. 49–69 (p. 93).

62 Maguire and Smith, 'On Editing', p. 295.

63 Maguire, 'Alice Walker', p. 327.

64 Maguire, 'Alice Walker', p. 327.

65 Clayton J. Delery, 'The Subject Presumed to Know: Implied Authority and Editorial Apparatus', *Text: Transactions of the Society for Textual Scholarship*, 5 (1991), 63–80 (p. 64).

66 Wendy Wall, *The Imprint of Gender: Authorship and Publication in the English Renaissance* (Ithaca, NY: Cornell University Press, 1993).

67 Quoted in Thompson and Roberts, 'Mary Cowden Clarke', p. 179.

68 Smith, *'Grossly Material Things'*, pp. 6–10.

69 Smith, *'Grossly Material Things'*, p. 217.

70 Delery, 'The Subject Presumed to Know', p. 70.

71 Quoted in Jane Spencer, *Literary Relations: Kinship and the Canon 1660–1830* (Oxford: Oxford University Press, 2005), p. 2; for more on Scott's edition, see George Falle, 'Sir Walter Scott as Editor of Dryden and Swift', *University of Toronto Quarterly*, 36.2 (1967), 161–80.

72 Kitzes, 'The Hazards of Expurgation', p. 56.

73 See chapters 5 and 6 in James Turner, *Philology: The Forgotten Origins of the Modern Humanities* (Princeton, NJ: Princeton University Press, 2015).

74 K. K. Ruthven, 'Textuality and Textual Editing', *Meridian: The La Trobe University English Review*, 4.1 (1985), 85–87 (p. 87). For more on textual stemmatics and gender, see Emily Loney, 'Preposterous Revisions: Reordering Space and Time in the Sidney Circle' (doctoral dissertation, University of Wisconsin, Madison, 2020), and Yin-Jan Lin, *The Erotic Life of Manuscripts* (Oxford: Oxford University Press, 2016).

75 D. C. Greetham, *The Pleasures of Contamination: Evidence, Text, and Voice in Textual Studies* (Bloomington: Indiana University Press, 2010), pp. 153–54.

76 W. W. Greg, *The Calculus of Variants: An Essay on Textual Criticism* (Oxford: Clarendon Press, 1927), p. 2.

77 Ronald Brunlees McKerrow, *Prolegomena for the Oxford Shakespeare: A Study in Editorial Method* (Oxford: Clarendon Press, 1939), p. 36.

78 Joseph Grigely, *Textualterity* (Ann Arbor: University of Michigan Press, 1995), p. 23.

79 Spencer, *Literary Relations*, p. 11.

80 Spencer, *Literary Relations*, p. 11.

81 Massai, *Shakespeare and the Rise of the Editor*, p. 194; Bonnie G. Smith, *The Gender of History: Men, Women, and Historical Practice* (Cambridge, MA: Harvard University Press, 1998), p. 9.

82 Marcus, *Unediting the Renaissance*, p. 3.

83 Bottoms, 'Doing Shakespeare', p. 96.

84 Jerome J. McGann, *The Textual Condition*, Princeton Studies in Culture/Power/History (Princeton, NJ: Princeton University Press, 1991), pp. 65–66.

85 Grigely, *Textualterity*, p. 95.

CHAPTER 2

'It Is My Lady's Hand'
Female Collaborators and Ambiguous Literary Labour

'Could I not be preparing myself now to be more useful?' said
Dorothea to him, one morning, early in the time of courtship; 'could
I not learn to read Latin and Greek aloud to you, as Milton's
daughters did to their father, without understanding what they read?'

'I fear that would be wearisome to you,' said Mr. Casaubon, smiling;
'and, indeed, if I remember rightly, the young women you have
mentioned regarded that exercise in unknown tongues as a ground
for rebellion against the poet.'

'Yes; but in the first place they were very naughty girls, else they
would have been proud to minister to such a father; and in the
second place they might have studied privately and taught themselves
to understand what they read, and then it would have been interesting. I hope you don't expect me to be naughty and stupid?'
                                                —George Eliot, *Middlemarch*[1]

The time friendly to the Muses [Milton] fell to his Poetry; And hee
waking early (as is the use of temperate men) had commonly a good
Stock of Verses ready against his Amanuensis came; which if it
happened to bee later than ordinary, hee would complain, Saying,
hee wanted to be milked.
                                —Cyriack Skinner [?], *The Life of Mr. John Milton*[2]

Did Milton's daughters milk their father? Many have asked the question,
although perhaps not in such a grotesque, John Waters–esque fashion.
The image of Milton demanding to be 'milked', combined with the
reports of his daughters, Anne, Mary, and Deborah, resentfully reading
aloud to their blind father and, perhaps, taking dictation, provocatively
evokes issues surrounding paternity, authorship, textual labour, and gender.[3] Like many anecdotes about Milton, his call for milking is hearsay,
taken from an anonymous biography often attributed to Milton's student
and sometime amanuensis Cyriack Skinner. Similarly, the reports of his
daughters' involvement in his writing process remain – and will likely

always remain – contested and much discussed, but still very much a subsidiary element to the larger Milton legend. Kevin Pask has argued that eighteenth-century writers like Johnson employed the stories of Milton's daughters to demonstrate the hypocrisy of Milton's public republicanism in the face of his private tyranny, and that this usage was critical in the development of Milton's authorial legacy/persona. Although in some ways, Pask's analysis foregrounds the daughters, he still does so only within the context of making a point about Milton and the men who wrote about him.[4] Rather than proving something about Milton, however, the legend of Milton's daughters also supports a previously remarked-upon consequence of the hierarchical division of literary labour: the marginalisation of the ways in which women participated in the life cycle of a book.

Examples of women facilitating men's authorial and artistic efforts abound throughout history.[5] Milton's daughters, Wordsworth's sister, and nearly every woman ever married to an author participated somehow in the act of creation. Perhaps the most etymologically appropriate way to describe the traditional critical characterisation of these roles is 'ancillary', from the Latin *ancilla*, a handmaid. Helen Smith has challenged critics to 'reconceptualiz[e] women's work as co-creation', a process that 'may require us to recognize some of the ingrained heterosexist assumptions that situate certain textual interventions as secondary or derivative'.[6] The focus in this book is on one particular form of literary work – editing – but a rising tide lifts all boats. If, as Smith and others have shown, the printers, binders, scribes, translators, and copy editors who made books possible can be brought out of the shadows, so too can women previously considered mere 'hostesses' for their editions.

As mentioned in Chapter 1, female assistants and collaborators interfere with the myth of the (male) solitary genius. Although the process of dismantling this problematic archetype has been underway for several decades, much work remains to be done in order to disentangle, as much as possible, how agents other than the 'author' contributed to the creation of books. The Milton anecdote is interesting partly because it creates a conflict between Milton's biological and literary progeny – a sort of bibliographical sibling rivalry. The involvement of Milton's male protégés in the composition process, as both amanuenses and readers, tends to be portrayed as uncontroversial, and even his third wife, Katherine, is sometimes given credit for taking dictation.[7] Only his unruly female offspring throw a spanner in the works, both by their original reluctance to passively transmit words to and (possibly) from Milton and by the difficulty they present to scholars attempting to parse the nature of their involvement in the composition process. Work undertaken within a domestic environment is particularly challenging to analyse for component contributions, possibly because the larger family identity, generally represented by the paterfamilias, supersedes the individual identities of the women around him. The publishing process reinforces this by requiring the intermediary marginalia of corrections, suggestions, and additions by other agents to be evened out and subsumed within the monolithic 'authorial' identity associated with the completed book.

Sibling, filial, or spousal bonds often create a relationship conducive to literary partnership or assistance. If the goal of the amanuensis is to be, literally, an extension of the author's *manus*, hand, then what better hand exists than one related by blood or bound in marriage? The author–amanuensis relationship requires trust, as demonstrated by situations in which it went awry. Thomas Hardy, for example, concerned about how he would be portrayed in posthumous biographies, asked his second wife Florence to secretly co-author a biography that would be published under her name after his death. Florence Dugdale had assisted both Hardy and his first wife Emma with secretarial work and research for several years prior to Emma's death.[8] Florence, much younger than Hardy, often found their marriage restrictive and disappointing, particularly as Hardy began to create an idealised, romantic narrative surrounding his first wife. When he suggested the autobiography, Florence, a writer herself, agreed in the hope that it would offer her a literary outlet, but the process did not turn out that way:

> By 1918 the secret biography was under way, and Florence's 'collaborative' duties had come to be defined. First, she had to arrange Hardy's notebooks and letters in chronological order.... Using these documents Hardy wrote his narrative by hand and Florence typed it up. The typed copy went back to Hardy for revisions, which he did in a fake calligraphic hand. Florence then typed up a final script. All the documents and everything in Hardy's genuine handwriting were destroyed.[9]

Hardy's tortuous efforts to conceal his authorship of his own biography both foreground and de-legitimise his wife's position as author/creator. Hamilton notes that the writing style of the biography was distinctive enough that Hardy's friends 'politely' supported the fiction of Florence's authorship when it was finally published.[10] Still, her actions after Hardy's death reveal the potentially disruptive power of the amanuensis over the final work. Irritated by his posthumous deification of his first wife, Florence edited and

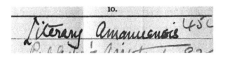

Figure 2.1   From Emma Gollancz's entry in the 1911 UK Census. PRO RG 14/634/19.
Image used by permission of The National Archives of the UK

minimised the presentation of several incidents related to Emma Hardy's role in her husband's life before the manuscript went to print.[11]

Metaphorical and physical hands (and handwriting) arise repeatedly in discussions of literary partnerships. Hardy falsified his handwriting during the revision process and insisted on destroying everything in his own writing – Florence was allowed only to type the manuscripts. Frances Burney disguised her handwriting when she submitted her first manuscript to publishers, afraid that it would be connected to her father's manuscripts, as she had served as his amanuensis.[12] Several of the women who figure in this chapter were described in their obituaries as the 'right hand' of their male partner; Emma Gollancz's obituary mentioned that her 'rare calligraphy' was 'selflessly placed at her brother Israel's service', and in the 1911 census (Figure 2.1), she specifically identified her occupation as 'Literary Amanuensis'.[13]

Many women with literary connections or aspirations made their living through their handwriting, copying manuscripts and undertaking research in the British Museum for scholars unable to travel to London, a task known as 'devilling'.[14] Frederick Furnivall's cousin Agnes supported herself and her two children partly by devilling.[15] Many jobs taken on by female collaborators tended to be the 'trans' jobs – translation, transcription – often classed as mechanical, rather than as creative or generative labour.[16] The female hand, in these cases, is seen to operate merely as a vessel of transmission for the male genius, detached from the whole person and her mind, like the hand of the medium channelling a deceased personality to produce automatic writing.[17] As Bette London points out in her discussion of literary secretaries and mediums, however, 'while mediums regularly represent themselves as amanuenses – as, in fact, recording machines or instruments – they are never *merely* that. Indeed, the qualities that make for an ideal private secretary are precisely the same as make for an ideal medium – a sensitive typewriter, a "machine" with intelligence and feeling.'[18] The hand cannot be detached from the (often female) body and mind to which it belongs.

In *Milton and the Victorians*, Erik Gray delves deeply into George Eliot's use of Milton in *Middlemarch* to reflect issues of transmission.[19] Dorothea is the archetypal frustrated female amanuensis, chafing against the limitations of her marriage and her assigned literary role. Her lack of agency in both is contrary to her own personality and needs; as Gilbert and Gubar have pointed out, 'textuality has been substituted for sexuality in her married life', and her husband's sterility and lack of vitality in both the domestic and the literary realms trap her in an unproductive position. Her own generative capabilities are subordinate.[20] From Dorothea's perspective, however, assisting her husband is the only way for her to make a lasting contribution to the cultural record. Although many achieved greater independence and fulfilment than Dorothea, the same basic situation was true for many early women editors of Shakespeare.

During the nineteenth and early twentieth centuries, male mentors, partners, or relatives both facilitated and concealed women's textual activities. Some women gained an entrée to literary circles through male sponsors, while others found editing opportunities through their male connections. This chapter considers this phenomenon in the case of the New Shakspere Society (NSS). Literary societies like the NSS, Stephanie Green writes, were 'crucial in supporting women of the period to pursue independent writing, editing and research'.[21] Founded by Frederick Furnivall in 1873, the NSS provided valuable connections for literary women, and the web of connections formed there encompassed no fewer than five women editors of Shakespeare directly, and even more to secondary degrees. The world of British Shakespeare scholarship was relatively small and interconnected, and the New Shakspere Society was an important element of that community.

Figure 2.2 offers an overview of some of the relationships orbiting the New Shakspere Society. The people directly connected to the central topic are those recorded either in the Society's *Transactions* or other sources as attending meetings of the NSS; secondary and sometimes tertiary relationships branch off from these.

In truth, these connections are too extensive to chart thoroughly in two dimensions. The chart also represents only one of the important societies of this period. Charlotte Stopes, for example, belonged to at least three of the major Shakespeare groups active during her life, as well as the Royal Society of Literature, Emmeline Pankhurst's militant Women's Social and Political Union, the Rational Dress Society, and many more on varying topics.[22] Additionally, to focus on the female subset of the society's membership may distract from the overall picture of its demographics. In 1875, the first annual report of the Society included a membership list in which, of the 498 members listed, thirty-six were women (about 6 per cent).[23] Even 498 is

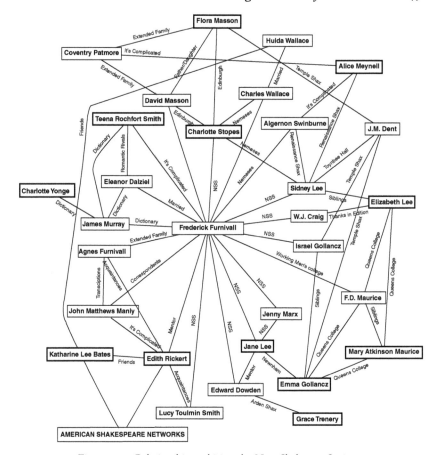

Figure 2.2 Relationships orbiting the New Shakspere Society.

a misleading number, as Shakespeare societies, libraries, colleges, and other institutions often paid for a single membership. That number also has no bearing on how many people actually attended meetings, since members resided all over the UK, Europe, America, and even India, and non-members likely attended meetings at times. Despite the shortcomings of these statistics, the number of women recorded as presenting papers or attending the meetings must be considered significant in light of the undeniable influence of the Society as a whole.

While male connections facilitated editing opportunities, the stories of the women in this chapter reveal how those same connections sometimes obscured women's involvement in textual work. Thompson and Roberts point out that 'while a man may gain prestige from a male-female literary partnership and be credited with playing a decisive role, a woman's literary reputation is compromised by working with a man – she becomes relegated to the position of needing "help" or becoming a "helpmate".'[24] So even when her name is known, or she is specifically credited as an author, the contribution of a female collaborator is liable to be ranked below that of the male partner. This could happen even when a known male collaborator was not involved in a specific work. Charles Cowden Clarke wrote in irritation to a reviewer at the *Daily News*, who had authored a generally positive review of Mary Cowden Clarke's solo edition of Shakespeare's *Complete Works* (1860), that

> I have but one objection to make against your 'review'; and that is, your having named me at all in reference to the 'Glossary'.... I know that the male world will give me credit for being the compiler of that Glossary; as I know of those who said of the 'Concordance' – 'Of course, her husband helped her.'[25]

This situation, in which the effacement of female labour became a cause of anguish for her male associate, is predictably rare in the documentary legacy, but Cowden Clarke was not the only man who went to great lengths to support women scholars. Frederick Furnivall, the founder of both the New Shakspere Society and the Early English Text Society (along with many other groups), seems to have been particularly friendly to women members, and encouraging to women interested in editing. He recommended his cousin Agnes Furnivall, who was attempting to support two daughters as a single parent, as a copyist to American scholars such as John Matthews Manly.[26] There are several letters to Furnivall suggesting that he assisted women scholars with finding posts and making connections with other scholarly women.[27] In the memorial volume assembled after his death, his friends J. C. Castell and C. F. W. Mead described him as 'a fearless and enthusiastic advocate of woman suffrage [whose] ardent democracy could tolerate nothing short of adult suffrage; and those who suggested the exclusion of a sex fared as ill at his hands as those who would shut out any class from the rights of citizenship'.[28] Alice B. Gomme wrote that '[h]e never suggested the learned man who condescends to impart knowledge.... [H]e never either suggested "man" the superior to me, a woman, and inferior; but was a friend and equal from first to last'.[29] Although those attitudes are admirable, Furnivall sometimes crossed the boundaries between the personal and the professional in troubling ways.

His first wife, Eleanor Dalziel, served as his amanuensis both before and after their marriage, and their relationship shocked some of his colleagues. Arthur Munby described a visit to Furnivall's home, where he met

> 'Lizzy' Dalziel, the pretty lady's maid whom he has educated into such strange relations with himself, and for whose sake he has behaved so madly to Litchfield & others of his best friends; & her brother, a student of our [Working Men's] College. After the meal . . . all four of them set to work, arranging and writing out words for the Philological Dictionary, of which Furnivall is now Editor in place of poor Herbert Coleridge. 'Missy,' as F. calls the girl, is his amanuensis and transcribes: takes long walks too with him and others, of ten and twenty miles a day; which is creditable to her; indeed she seems a quiet unassuming creature.[30]

According to Benzie, Eleanor ('Lizzy') was 'the daughter of a market gardener' rather than a lady's maid, and the scandal was less about the differences in class than the great disparity in their ages.[31]

This attraction to younger women is confirmed by Furnivall's later behaviour. At age fifty-eight, he left his wife to pursue a relationship with his young protégé Teena Rochfort Smith, then just twenty-one years old. This caused great consternation among his contemporaries and fellow scholars. Former NSS member Lucy Toulmin Smith wrote to a scandalised James Murray to explain her reasons for cancelling her subscription to the NSS:

> You asked me the other night why I did not continue to subscribe to the new Sh. Soc. I do not feel satisfied with its management this year, in one particular, which seems to me dishonest. But, there is a much worse thing which I must tell you, tho' odious to me.
>
> Furnivall is being separated from his wife, at his own desire, as he has become infatuated with a young girl [Teena Rochfort Smith]. He is selling his books & breaking up his house on 24 June.
>
> I tell you this for the sake of the poor innocent wronged wife, to whom he owes *much*. She needs all the manly & womanly sympathy of her friends.
>
> . . . Good heavens, what desecration! Pardon me I feel it deeply.[32]

Toulmin Smith later told a fellow scholar that Furnivall should not be considered 'a safe guide' in questions of propriety.[33] In contrast to Toulmin Smith, who emphasises how much Furnivall owed his wife, Benzie suggests that Eleanor's early charms had worn off:

> Teena Rochfort-Smith was an extremely attractive girl, deeply interested and involved in Furnivall's work. 'Lizzy,' on the other hand, had turned out to be rather indolent and dull, and was fond of sitting passively in a chair. In

1888, Furnivall told Mrs. Walter Slater, 'A wife's want of sympathy with her husband's work ruined Dickens's married life, mine too, & hundreds of others besides.' At sixty-three Furnivall was still 'youthful' and fond of pretty young women. It is most likely, however, that it was Teena's intellectual interest and involvement in his work rather than her looks that attracted Furnivall.[34]

Benzie's prejudicial description of Eleanor's behaviour, relying heavily on a hearsay comment by Furnivall, demonstrates how warped a woman's story can become within a male-written narrative. Furnivall was by no means an impartial source on the matter, and Benzie's sexist framing elides many possible realities about the Furnivalls' marriage. Perhaps Eleanor's willingness to act as amanuensis had faded as the years went by and she bore children (one of whom died young) and managed Furnivall's household. Thanks to Furnivall and his biographers, however, like Milton's daughters, Eleanor's lack of engagement with her male relative's work has come to define her role in literary history, with her previous contributions to projects like the *Philological Dictionary*, which went on to become the *Oxford English Dictionary*, forgotten.

Later in life, Furnivall actively embraced the role of patron to young women, founding the Hammersmith Sculling Club for working-class girls. His biography in the *Oxford Dictionary of National Biography* (*ODNB*) states that 'Furnivall entered into [the club's] activities with his usual boyish enthusiasm, for it brought together two of his favourite activities: vigorous outdoor exercise and enjoyment of the company of young women', noting also that Furnivall 'never remarried but managed to surround himself with attractive young women for the rest of his life'.[35] More recently, Jeffrey Kahan has edged closer to direct denunciation of Furnivall, whom he rather jocularly describes as 'the old letch', charging that he 'was an aggressive flirt. He liked women, working-class girls best, and often invited the pretty ones to spend afternoons with him punting on the River Cam. Furnivall would marry in 1862, but he continued to chase young, pretty, and needy women, including many that caught his eye in the various literary societies that he founded and controlled.'[36] A characteristic interaction was described by Edith Rickert, who visited the sculling club's boathouse: 'There we found a large party of young people – the boys rather sheepish in the corner with cigarettes – the girls dancing with one another & in their midst Dr. F. with red necktie & handkerchief (*is* he a socialist?) the gayest of the gay.'[37] There are no explicit records of Furnivall displaying actively predatory behaviour to the young women around him, but taken altogether, the evidence is unsettling. Although Kahan does not explore them, there are clear issues with the power dynamics inherent in his description of Furnivall's targets as 'young, pretty, and needy'. Becoming involved with one young female assistant might be called a romance; doing it twice is a pattern, and it was a pattern that Furnivall sought to replicate until his death by surrounding himself with young, attractive women who relied on him in various ways.

Whatever the truth about Furnivall's personal predilections, young female scholars clearly benefitted both from his patronage and from the generally egalitarian environment he established within the New Shakspere Society. After its first year of activity in 1874, the Society published its *Transactions*, containing lists of new members, minutes from meetings, and copies of the papers given. That first year, thirty women are named as members. Through the Society's *Transactions*, we are able to identify two particularly interesting women editors whose work was never published. At the twenty-seventh meeting of the Society, held on 13 October 1876, Miss Jane Lee presented a paper entitled 'On the 2nd and 3rd Parts of *Henry VI*, and Their Originals, *The Contention* and *The True Tragedy*'.[38] After the responses and counter-responses, Furnivall noted that 'Miss Lee has kindly undertaken to edit the *Contention* and *True Tragedy* for us in parallel columns with *2* and *3 Henry VI*', suggesting that the edition might need to be 'a 3- or 4-Text one, with the 4to of 1619, and perhaps a revis'd text'.[39] Furnivall admired 'the advance that [Miss Lee], so young, has made, after her start under her brilliant leader, Professor Dowden'.

Her three- or four-text *Henry VI* would indeed appear to have been a formidably ambitious undertaking, but sadly it never reached fruition. Furnivall adopted the conventions of the parallel-text edition for his Chaucer Society's editions and carried this over to the NSS, which published two parallel-text editions of the plays and commissioned several more that were never completed.[40] Jane Lee does not appear again in the Society's *Transactions*, and her identity has been lost to history until now. In an article on London theatre, Jenny Marx records her own attendance at that meeting and identifies Jane Lee as the 'daughter of the Archbishop of Dublin'.[41] Although no Lee served as Archbishop during the appropriate time frame, there was a William Lee, Archdeacon and professor at Trinity College Dublin. This identification lines up with Furnivall's mention of Jane Lee studying under Edward Dowden, also a professor at Trinity. William Lee's entry in the *ODNB* mentions his daughter Jane, saying that she 'studied Sanskrit and Lithuanian in Bonn, Germany, and was afterwards college administrator from 1889'.[42]

'College administrator' is a wholly unsatisfactory summary of Jane Lee's accomplishments, and the subordination of her biography to her father's aptly demonstrates the privileging of male stories over female. In fact, she was a lecturer in modern literature and languages at Newnham and an early Vice-Principal of the college. Although the Newnham archives contain no information suggesting that Lee did any work on Shakespeare, an 1881 column in *The Times* connects the Jane Lee of Dublin with the Jane Lee of the New Shakspere Society:

> Miss Jane Lee, the learned daughter of the Archdeacon of Dublin, was charged by her old teacher Professor Benfey, before his death, to English the whole of the great Sanskrit epic, the 'Mahabharata,' 80,000 lines, as only fragments of it had been translated before. Miss Lee has begun her task. She is also to help Professor Atkinson in his 'Old Irish Dictionary' for the Royal Irish Academy, and she will probably contribute papers to the New Shakespeare [*sic*] and the Browning Societies during the ensuing session.[43]

A letter held in the special collections of St John's College, Cambridge, further confirms that this is the correct Miss Lee, mentioning both her place at Newnham and the specific paper on *Henry VI* that she presented.[44]

The thorough and intimate records kept at Newnham fill in many details of Jane Lee's life story. Born on 13 June 1850, she had five siblings. Growing up in Dublin, she studied with Edward Dowden before travelling to Germany to attend Göttingen University.[45] She was a polyglot, skilled in Sanskrit, German, Lithuanian, and Italian, among others. She came to Newnham as a student in 1882 and was elected a lecturer in modern and medieval languages in the same year. In 1885, she took over running the Red House residence, where she remained until she became Vice-Principal of Old Hall in 1888. In a memorial article, which was printed along with a portrait (Figure 2.3), a former student named Miss Lyster explains that Lee's health was always 'feeble', but it worsened quickly, and she died young in 1895.[46] Having resigned her position at Newnham and moved in with a brother, her death seems not to have been unexpected, but probate records show that she died intestate. Perhaps she simply trusted her brother, a London barrister, to administer her estate, which totalled about £1,500 at the time of her death.[47] Her memorials depict a kind, quiet woman, much involved in the lives of her students and deeply disciplined and educated.

Although Lee's Shakespeare editions did not survive, her paper for the New Shakspere Society offers some insight into her scholarship. It explains her belief that the *Contention* and the *True Tragedy* are earlier plays, enlarged and revised by Shakespeare to create *2* and *3 Henry VI*.

Figure 2.3   Jane Lee. Image used by permission of the Principal and Fellows, Newnham College, Cambridge

Although the New Oxford Shakespeare made international news in 2016 for publishing new computer analysis–based evidence for Marlowe's involvement in all three parts of *Henry VI*, this basic premise was not new to Shakespeare scholarship. Edmond Malone influentially set forth a version of this hypothesis in 1778's *Book on the Three Parts of King Henry VI*, arguing that Shakespeare had rewritten earlier plays by Christopher Marlowe, Robert Greene, and George Peele.[48] In her paper, Lee laid out extensive evidence in support of Marlowe, Greene, and Peele's authorship of *Parts 2* and *3*, primarily in the form of parallel passages and other stylistic similarities.[49] Given the forensic detail she provides, it is not difficult to imagine her producing a three- or four-text edition, as Furnivall suggested. Contemporary evidence shows that Lee's iteration of this theory was influential. Fellow NSS member Israel Gollancz cited her paper in the introduction to the *Henry VI* plays in the Temple Shakespeare.[50]

The promised edition never materialised, however. Sometime between Lee's 1876 paper and 1883, the edition seems to have changed hands. In 1883, Furnivall mentioned that Teena Rochfort Smith 'had begun to prepare for press these Plays [the *Henry VI* plays], and those on which they were based – *The Contention*, and *True Tragedy* – for the "Old-Spelling Shakspere"'.[51] The society's edition of the *Henry VI* plays had been dogged by problems from its conception. In February 1874, Furnivall wrote to F. G. Fleay, who had originally agreed to edit the planned edition, explaining that '[w]e really are not in a position to print a parallel text of *Henry VI* yet. [Not with only] 300 pounds this year, & that is already taken up with *Transactions & text*.... I promise money should come in before June and we could do *Henry VI*.'[52] In the midst of a heated argument with Fleay several months later, Furnivall cancelled the edition and demanded the return of his personal copies of the *Contention* and *True Tragedy*.[53] About a month and a half after this letter, Furnivall announced that Lee had agreed to edit the parallel-text edition, although he did not mention Fleay's name. The Society's annual report in 1879 claimed that Lee's parallel-text edition could 'be sent to press at short notice', but this is set within a plea for more money and members in order to get the Society's new books to press in 1880, as they had more planned than usual. In a Society report, Furnivall berated his readers:

> What kind of tribute is a miserable £500 a year, to the memory of the man who has done for England and the world, what Shakspere has done, is doing, and will do? The sum is ludicrous in its pettiness. No Member can be satisfied with it. Every Member of the Society should make it his business to get the amount increast.[54]

Possibly the funds never appeared for the printing of Jane Lee's edition during that cash-strapped period of the Society's operations. No documentary evidence survives to indicate whether she had in fact completed the text, or if Furnivall was exaggerating in an effort to solicit funds. A few years later, in 1883, Jane Lee went to Newnham, where her focus may have shifted to new projects such as the ambitious translation of the Mahabharata mentioned in the *Times*.

Ensconced in the academic environment at Newnham, Lee probably relied less on public literary societies to provide her with stimulation and collegiality than did solitary scholars like Teena Rochfort Smith. Rochfort Smith's story was also that of a promising scholar struck down by tragedy at the very beginning of her career. Born in Calcutta (now Kolkata), she spent the first fifteen years of her life in India before moving to England, where she attended Dorothea Beale's Cheltenham Ladies' College. Supposedly unable to sit for the Cambridge and Oxford examinations due to ill health, she turned instead to the support and encouragement offered by Furnivall and his various London literary societies, including the

NSS and the Browning Society. In addition to transcribing early English manuscripts and contributing to Murray's *Dictionary*, she began to assist Furnivall with various projects, including the *Old-Spelling Shakspere* he was preparing with fellow NSS member W. G. Boswell-Stone. Apparently, she 'read every proof and revise of it, commenting on every point, little and great, and often suggesting the happiest way out of a difficulty that had puzzled all previous commentators'.[55] One tribute to Rochfort Smith (not written by Furnivall) described her as serving her male editorial superiors as an 'indefatigable auxiliary, who labored with the zeal of a woman and the power and intelligence that are claimed as the attributes of man'.[56] A woman could possess 'zeal' or 'enthusiasm' but brilliance, intelligence, and genius were seen as qualities appearing primarily in men, making Rochfort Smith's display of both unusual, in that writer's eyes. Eventually, she and Furnivall became romantically involved, and Rochfort Smith moved into his house even before his wife moved out.[57] Only a few months after Furnivall decided to obtain a divorce from Eleanor Furnivall, Rochfort Smith was visiting an uncle in the country in the wake of a serious illness. While burning letters in her room, she accidentally set herself on fire, resulting in horrific burns. She lingered for a week before finally dying.[58]

Her untimely death ended her plans for a remarkable four-text edition of *Hamlet*, but fortunately, in 1883 the NSS had printed and circulated a sample of her work, consisting of the first three scenes of the play, to their membership. Previously, only one copy of this item had been identified, residing at the Folger Shakespeare Library; however, I have located additional copies in the Furness Collection at the University of Pennsylvania and in the library of Trinity College, Cambridge.[59] Furnivall and Furness were correspondents, so the copy in the Furness collection was likely sent to him directly by Furnivall.[60] The Trinity copy came to the library from W. W. Greg's collection and contains his ownership marks, dated 1921. As Greg was only eight years old when the sample was originally circulated to NSS members in 1883, it is safe to say he was not the original owner. A pasted-in slip from a printed sale catalogue, describing the item and listing a five-shilling price, has 'F. Clarke. June 1921' handwritten on it. So presumably, Greg acquired it in 1921, probably from a bookseller called F. Clarke. There is one piece of handwritten marginalia in the Trinity copy. In the 'Revised text', Rochfort Smith proposed a substitution for a possible missing line at I.ii.126–27 in Q2. Rochfort Smith's line was 'While in the Heavens above were signs beheld.' The unknown annotator suggested, 'Whilst in the heavens were portents seen.' The handwriting does not appear to be Greg's, but the copy's original owner remains unknown at this time.

Rochfort Smith's original intention, according to the tribute written after her death by Frederick Furnivall, was to assemble a new concordance to Shakespeare's plays and poems, replacing Mary Cowden Clarke's opus of 1846. This idea being deemed too expensive and time-consuming, she moved on to Furnivall's suggestion of a four-text *Hamlet*.[61] The plans she developed for this edition, however, would have probably been just as expensive and time-consuming as a new concordance. Rochfort Smith proposed that the Q1, Q2, and F1 texts all be printed in separate, contiguous columns, in addition to a 'revized', conflated text. Six different typefaces and multiple typographical symbols were used to identify and classify variants.[62] Both Ann Thompson and Alan Galey have remarked on the incredibly elaborate system she developed, with Thompson claiming that it 'would have been the most complex presentation of the texts of *Hamlet* ever attempted' and Galey drawing attention to the ways in which it anticipated the twenty-first-century methods of digital tagging now a common part of the editorial process.[63]

In an anonymous memoir written by Furnivall after her death, Rochfort Smith is set up in direct competition with Lee, with Furnivall proclaiming that 'her knowledge of the Elizabethan dramatists was such, that she could from memory quote from Peele and Greene parallel passages to lines in *2* and *3 Henry VI*, which had evaded the search of even such an exhaustive commentator on these plays as Miss Jane Lee'.[64] The tributes to Lee and Rochfort Smith contain other similarities as well. Both are described as gentle, God-fearing women of 'delicate health' who dedicated themselves to scholarship despite physical challenges. Due to their premature deaths, neither Lee's nor Rochfort Smith's Shakespearean editorial projects ever reached fruition. Indeed, both women are often linked in contemporary and posthumous reports to the projects of the men around them rather than their individual work – the translation of the Mahabharata, the *Old Irish Dictionary*, the *Old-Spelling Shakspere*. Jane Lee's only published work was a school edition of Goethe's *Faust, Part I*, that received favourable reviews when published in 1886.[65] I have been unable to locate any remnants of her unpublished work. When Teena Rochfort Smith died, Furnivall wrote a loving tribute to her memory, but despite his assurances that her revolutionary four-text *Hamlet* would 'be finished by her friend Mr. Furnivall when he has time', it seems to have died with her.[66] Furnivall's memorial ends with the resolution of sympathy the NSS passed after hearing of her death: '[Furnivall] himself had, in Miss Rochfort

Smith, lost his right hand, his greatest helper and friend, the reader of his every proof and revise, the supplier of his many defects; he could not hope now to finish his share of the Comedies of the *Old-Spelling Shakspere* before next March.'[67] Rochfort Smith's untimely death delayed her partner's work, but he does not ultimately choose to complete her edition. Her death is an inconvenience and a source of grief, but it imposes no lasting obligation upon the men around her. Rochfort Smith's work, as laudable as it was, remained subordinate to that of her male collaborator.

Brothers and Sisters

Jane Lee and Teena Rochfort Smith illustrate a number of aspects of male-female literary relationships in the later nineteenth century, but their situations lack another major complicating factor: consanguinity. To explore that element, we need not venture from the circle of the NSS. Two of its most prominent members, Sir Israel Gollancz and Sir Sidney Lee, both relied on the collaboration and companionship of their older sisters, Emma Gollancz and Elizabeth Lee. The two stories contain many points of similarity, some of which are largely coincidental; other resemblances, however, reflect how common a certain experience was for women of their class. Emma (b. 1856) and Elizabeth (b. 1857/58) both came from relatively well-to-do Jewish families in London – Emma's father was a rabbi, Elizabeth's a merchant dealing in ostrich feathers. Both women were educated at Queen's College, Harley Street, London, the girls' school founded by F. D. Maurice, with the support of his sister Mary Atkinson Maurice.[68] Emma's brother attended Cambridge, Elizabeth's Oxford.[69] Here their stories diverge slightly: Elizabeth did not attend university. Emma followed her brother to Cambridge, beginning her study of English and modern languages at Newnham in 1888–89. At Newnham, she lived in Old Hall under its Vice-Principal, Jane Lee.[70] She left after 1890 without completing her degree in order to care for her parents.[71]

In his memoirs, publisher J. M. Dent describes the inception of the Temple Shakespeare, for which he wanted 'neither commentary nor personal impressions of a play, but only direct notes on data and dubious readings with some variorum work and a simple glossary of obsolete words, etc'.[72] After approaching several editors who declined to sign on, including Sidney Lee, he discussed the idea with Israel Gollancz, who 'offered to undertake the work with the help of his sister'.[73] Emma's name does not appear on the title page of the Temple Shakespeare, but a Gollancz family biographer claims that 'the assistance she gave to Israel in editing his many books was well-recognized in academic circles'.[74] Much documentation of the technical editorial process for the Temple Shakespeare and Temple Classics series survives due to a later court case between Dent and Israel Gollancz over royalties and rights to the Temple 'Shakespeare for Schools' series. Most of it, however, comes from the evidence compiled by Dent and his lawyers, giving it an implicit bias. In an archive of this material held at the University of North Carolina, Chapel Hill, there are several letters between the publishers and Emma Gollancz, attempting to ascertain her brother's location and the state of completion of various books. Israel seems to have been extremely peripatetic during this period, causing great frustration for the publishers attempting to track down overdue manuscripts.[75]

Emma edited four books for the Temple Classics while her brother served as series editor: these were Elizabeth Gaskell's *Cranford*, Mary Russell Mitford's *Our Village*, Charles Reade's *Peg Woffington*, and Robert Southey's *Life of Nelson*. Correspondence between Dent and Israel Gollancz indicates that there was a major problem with the draft of *Cranford* when it was sent to the printer. Whether the blame for this issue lay with the brother or the sister remains murky. Legal records list it as one of the major grievances Dent had with Israel Gollancz during their association. Dent's lawyers' notes explain that

> Our Village should have been issued in October but owing to the delay caused by G[ollancz] sending a bad text to the printers and it not being discovered until a great portion of the book had been set up [it was not issued on time].... G[ollancz] knew perfectly well that one of the leading features of this series was good uncorrupted text.[76]

Furthermore, they claim, 'nearly all of the books delayed in this period were those whose editors had been appointed by G[ollancz] or had been kept back for G[ollancz's] delay or neglect. *E.g. Cranford, Our Village, White's Selborne, Adam Bede.*'[77] The first two books on that list were edited by Emma herself, but the only reference to her in the legal papers was the complaint that the problematic editors had been chosen by Israel.

Whatever the trouble with the non-Shakespearean books in the Temple Classics series, Israel Gollancz did complete the Temple Shakespeare, and based on Dent's own recollections, Emma Gollancz likely served as a silent partner in this process. Both the 1891 and 1901 censuses list them as living together, and the Temple Shakespeare was published during the intervening ten years. The Temple Shakespeare became one of several important inexpensive Shakespeares released in the second half of the century – Dent's memoir cites the sales numbers as reaching 250,000 volumes a year.[78] As with Laura Valentine's Chandos Shakespeare, the Temple Shakespeare's impact was felt among popular rather than academic circles. Inexpensive editions of the plays like the Temple series provided an entrée into Shakespeare for those who could not previously afford copies, just as Dent had hoped when he conceived of the series.[79] In addition to its importance to individual (often working-class) readers, the Temple series also marked the beginning of Dent's experiments with attractive, inexpensive books which eventually led to Everyman's Library, one of the most far-ranging series of classic reprints published in the early twentieth century.[80]

Despite the significance of the Temple Shakespeare, Emma Gollancz has never before been credited with any work on the series. The books she edited on her own all appeared in a series edited by her brother, and even the legal trouble surrounding those particular books focuses on him, not her. Emma Gollancz thus never truly emerges from her brother's shadow. Her obituary in the *Times* focused on her 'selfless' role as 'his right-hand helper – trusty, able, and unsparing, making it possible for him to carry out the manifold duties of a many-sided academic life'. She asked that 'She tried to do her duty all her life' be her epitaph.[81] Her seemingly complete acceptance of the position of handmaiden to Israel's greatness effectively erased her work from the historical record.[82]

Elizabeth Lee's literary career is significantly better documented than Emma Gollancz's, and she established a stronger reputation as a scholar independent of her brother. Even so, Sidney Lee's relationships with the scholarly community provided his sister's initial admittance to the literary world.[83] Like so many others, Sidney Lee owed his literary success in part to Furnivall, who recommended him to Leslie Stephen as an assistant for the immense *Dictionary of National Biography* project.[84] Elizabeth Lee's contribution to the *DNB*, under her brother's editorship, is impressive in its own right, with 110 articles written under her own name, all but nine of which are about women. Gillian Fenwick suggests (in Lee's own well-earned *ODNB* entry, finally added in 2004) that Lee also wrote some of the articles published under her brother's name prior to her official employment, pointing out that

> Sidney had written twenty-two articles on women subjects in the twenty-seven volumes that appeared up to 1891 [the year he became the sole editor], but only six in the thirty-six volumes that followed. It is conceivable that, at a time when female contributors were rare, Lee's new editorial authority simply gave him the opportunity to introduce Elizabeth as a contributor in her own right.[85]

Elizabeth Lee eventually became an editor of the *DNB*, the only woman in an editorial staff of ten.[86] In her *Times* obituary, however, her contribution to the *DNB* receives very little attention next to her legacy as 'a stimulating lecturer on English literature, an editor of English texts for schools, a critic of foreign literature, a biographer, and an original thinker about educational problems'.[87]

After her time at Queen's College, Lee taught at girls' secondary schools. For many years, she wrote a regular column for *The Library* highlighting foreign literature; her focus on French literature in particular earned her the honour of Officier d'Académie from the French ministry of public affairs in 1909.[88] She became secretary of the English Association. She was a prolific translator, as well as an editor of school texts. In addition to authors such as Cowper, Carlyle, Walter Scott, and Elizabeth Barrett Browning, Lee edited *Twelfth Night* (1895) and *The Tempest* (1894) for Blackie's Junior School Shakespeare series. Aimed at younger students, the preface of these editions emphasised the teaching experience of the editors as an asset. Until the end of her life, Elizabeth Lee continued to assist her brother, but unlike Emma Gollancz's obituary, in which the last lines focused on her service to Israel, Elizabeth Lee's obituary ended with words about 'her sanguine spirit and independent judgment, her scholarly and orderly habit of mind and, above all, her intelligent sympathy with young people'.[89] The assistance she gave to her brother comprised only one element of the account. While the contributions she made to his projects were undoubtedly substantial, Elizabeth Lee's own literary work earned her a reputation semi-independent from that of her brother, whereas Emma Gollancz's life and work have been almost entirely forgotten, and her possible contributions to the Temple Shakespeare remain nebulous.

Charlotte Stopes

Finally, it is helpful to consider the experiences of a woman who operated in London literary circles at this time without extensive male support. Due to an improvident spouse who spent carelessly and died early, Charlotte Carmichael Stopes (1840–1929) became the sole breadwinner for herself and two daughters. Like Agnes Furnivall, she turned to the literary world for a living, but unlike Agnes, Stopes chose to carry out her own research, supporting her family by publishing books and articles primarily relating to Shakespeare. In the introduction to *Shakespeare Bibliography*, William Jaggard acknowledges his particular debt to 'that tireless enthusiast' Charlotte Stopes.[90] In many ways, this label, which rather damns with faint praise, sums up many aspects of Stopes's frustrations and the problems that haunt her legacy to this day. The same double-edged tone can be found here as was seen in the memorial of Teena Rochfort Smith discussed above, in which she was praised as a zealous 'indefagitable auxiliary'. Dogged in both her research and the promotion of her work, often to the point of provoking irritation in varying degrees among her friends and colleagues, Stopes fought constantly against the ignominy of being identified as an 'enthusiast' rather than a scholar. During this period, as the study of English took shape and the identity of the modern 'professional' scholar evolved, Stopes occupied a liminal space that would gradually narrow in the years to come.

Far from being a dilettante, Stopes was one of the first three women to qualify for a diploma at the University of Edinburgh. In 1873, although she could not be awarded a degree, she passed the examinations in English literature, logic and metaphysics, moral philosophy, geology, and chemistry. When Edinburgh began issuing degrees to women in 1892, they announced that women like Charlotte who had completed the earlier certificate programmes through the Edinburgh Association for University Education of Women would be retroactively awarded their degrees. To her great disappointment, because she had not taken examinations in Greek and mathematics, Charlotte was told she was not eligible for the full degree without additional classes.[91] A mother of two, with a husband recently jailed for non-payment of debts, Charlotte realised that she was unable to afford to take the required courses. Although she wrote to the University authorities explaining the situation and citing her scholarly achievements, both at Edinburgh and since, and even travelled to Edinburgh to make her case in person, they refused to make an exception. She later wrote, 'I had reluctantly to give up all hope of attaining the crown of my long labours. I left my children at school in Edinburgh, [and] returned baffled to my husband.'[92] This refusal to grant her institutional credentials, implicitly devaluing her scholarship, probably influenced much of her behaviour in the years to come. Charlotte took herself and her work seriously and wanted others to do the same.[93]

In the process of achieving this, Stopes did not scruple to step on toes and assert herself, as a result of which she ruffled a number of male feathers. This was not out of character for Stopes, an ardent suffragist whose best-known work was *British Freewomen: Their Historical Privilege* (1894), an overview of women's history in Britain used extensively by the suffrage campaign. Stopes herself frequently spoke in support of suffrage, including at one meeting at the University of Liverpool in 1906 at which '[a]ccording to the *Liverpool Daily Post*, a group of male students had "amused themselves by lighting cigarettes, throwing them half-smoked among the audience, howling, shouting and singing comic songs to the accompaniment of stamping feet". The meeting had broken up in disarray.'[94] Stopes met male aggression with her own confidence and lack of deference. This has earned her a somewhat complicated legacy. In *Shakespeare's Lives*, Schoenbaum openly struggles with the best way to characterise her as both a person and a scholar. He suggests that 'with all her feminist ardour, [Stopes] determined to excel in a field overwhelmingly dominated by men', and ultimately concludes that although 'lacking the discipline of the professional scholar, Stopes has her own eccentric strength'.[95] Her equivocal reputation stems, in part, from her own family. Her daughter Marie would far outpace her mother's fame as the author of *Married Love* and an advocate for birth control. Marie's complex relationship with her mother, as well as her vested interest in controlling her own public image, shaped Charlotte's depiction by biographers, many of whom were friends or admirers of Marie herself. Mother and daughter were, in fact, deeply similar: self-centred (in Marie's case, to the point of extreme narcissism later in life), competitive, and determined to succeed in traditionally male occupations.

Due to the combination of genuine rejection by scholarly institutions and an egocentric personality, Stopes nursed grudges against some of her colleagues, most particularly Elizabeth Lee's brother Sidney. According to Charlotte, Sidney Lee had used her work extensively in his *Life of William Shakespeare* without proper citation, leading her to gloat to Marie in 1908 that 'Sidney Lee has got into hot water, he has made some terrible bibliographical blunder and I rather fancy his wind-bag is pricked'.[96] She resented not having been asked to write the *Dictionary of National Biography* entry on the Elizabethan writer William Hunnis, about whom she considered herself an authority.[97] And she believed that Sidney Lee's *Times Literary Supplement* review of her book on the Burbages amounted to a 'deliberate attempt to crush it'.[98] It is indeed a crushing review. Sidney Lee writes that

> the truth is that Mrs. Stopes is a first-rate archivist and record searcher who lacks the gifts of the biographer or the literary historian.... Moreover, the author puts herself at some disadvantage by yielding too easily to the human failing of rating the importance of her own inquiries above those of her fellow-workers. The weakness leads her to ignore, or to appraise inadequately, pertinent explorations in which others than herself have engaged.[99]

Sidney Lee became a sort of metonymy for the resentment Stopes felt over her perceived lack of recognition, as when she wrote to Marie that 'I get glory on all sides, but little pay.... Dr. Furnivall said publicly that I was the "greatest living authority on Shakespeare" but they buy Sidney Lee's books.'[100]

Her own challenging personality met its match in scholar Charles Wallace, who, in partnership with his wife Hulda, made numerous significant archival discoveries about Shakespeare's life, including Shakespeare's signed deposition in the Belott–Mountjoy lawsuit.[101] Wallace claimed that Stopes shadowed him in the Record Office, attempting to figure out what papers he was working on in hopes of stealing a find from under his nose. He also claimed that when he did once tell her what he was doing, she published his findings under her own name.[102] Wallace himself displayed enormous paranoia and megalomania in relation to his work, as Schoenbaum emphasises, so this account cannot be entirely trusted. Stopes herself denied the accusations, claiming that Wallace had tried to pre-empt some of her work and insisting that everything she published had been found independently.[103] As with many such petty rivalries, the truth likely resides somewhere in the middle, but either way, the story demonstrates Stopes's willingness to adopt a combative scholarly persona rarely employed by women of her period.

Biographical and contextual research comprised the majority of Stopes's Shakespearean endeavours. Sidney Lee acknowledged her skills as an 'archivist' and 'record-searcher', even if he felt she lacked the talent for presenting her research in a coherent and persuasive fashion. She was a fixture in the reading room at the British Museum and the Public Records Office and travelled to archives around the country, where she carried out research for books such as *The Bacon-Shakespeare Question*, *Shakespeare's Warwickshire Contemporaries*, and *British Freewomen*. Stopes was also not without male allies. Her professor in Edinburgh, David Masson, provided an introduction to Furnivall when she moved to London, and Furnivall became a friend and supporter, even recommending her for a job editing the Sonnets.[104] Her edition was published in 1904 by the De la More Press.[105] In her 1978 biography of Marie Stopes, Ruth Hall writes that 'in spite of her ignorance [of sexual matters], Marie's reading suggests that her inclinations were more sensuous than her mother [Charlotte] would have approved. She read Browning and Swinburne and, ignoring Charlotte's advice, found "the real Shakespeare" not in the plays but in the Sonnets and *Venus and Adonis*.'[106] It seems unlikely that Charlotte Stopes would have told her daughter that she would find 'the real Shakespeare' in the

plays rather than the Sonnets or that she discouraged her from reading
them. In fact, after 1904, Marie could have read the Sonnets in an edition
prepared by Charlotte herself in which Charlotte expressed the view that
the Sonnets were precisely where Shakespeare had 'unlocked his heart'.

By editing the Sonnets in this period, Charlotte entered a major debate
over the question of the 'real Shakespeare', in which one of the loudest
voices was her nemesis Sidney Lee. Katherine Duncan-Jones suggests that
the reputation of the 1609 quarto edition of the sonnets as an
unauthorised or somehow illicit publication originated as a reaction to
the 1895 prosecution of Oscar Wilde, who cited them in his own defence
at his trial.[107] Duncan-Jones writes that

> Wilde's conviction and sentence to hard labour must have made it a matter
> of some urgency for ambitious Shakespeare scholars, whose own social
> standing depended to a large extent on the character of the material they
> studied, utterly to expunge the association that Wilde had set up between
> *Shakespeare's Sonnets* and his own friendships with numerous young
> men.... Shakespeare's works were increasingly taught in schools and uni-
> versities: how could he possibly have nourished – and have publicly
> articulated – passions of the sort that led to Wilde's being condemned to
> two years' imprisonment with hard labour?[108]

She singles out Sidney Lee's efforts in the years following the trial to
establish both that the Sonnets had been published illegally and without
Shakespeare's consent by Thomas Thorpe and that there was nothing
fundamentally incriminating in the sonnets themselves. On the contrary,
Lee claimed in his entry on Shakespeare for the 1897 American edition of
the *DNB* that 'hundreds of sonneteers had celebrated, in the language of
love, the charms of young men' without being homosexual.[109] This was a
major shift in position, and one undertaken quite suddenly, as Lee had
expressed the opposite viewpoint – that the Sonnets were biographically
based and offered significant insight into Shakespeare's mind and life – in
the London edition of the *DNB* earlier that same year.[110]

So, when Stopes agreed to edit the Sonnets in the early 1900s, she did so
within a hotly charged atmosphere. Stopes herself had a personal relationship with both Constance and Oscar Wilde in the decade leading up to the
trial, having corresponded and met with the Wildes while preparing her
articles for the *Rational Dress Society Gazette*, edited by Constance Wilde,
and *Woman's World*, edited by Oscar.[111] Whatever her feelings on the
potential homosexual content of the sonnets, Stopes also had an intensely
adversarial outlook regarding the main proponent for 'normalising' the
sonnets – Sidney Lee. Stopes had evidently been thinking about the

Sonnets for a long time prior to taking on the editing of the text. Schoenbaum relates an anecdote in which, after an 1884 meeting of the New Shakspere Society in which Thomas Tyler had expounded his theory that William Herbert was the addressee of the Sonnets and Mary Fitton the Dark Lady, Stopes approached Tyler with a challenge: "'I hope I may live long enough to be able to contradict you!" "No, you won't," he replied complacently, "for my theory is going down Time!" And she rejoined, "Not if I live long enough."'[112]

Stopes's edition immediately sets itself in opposition to Lee's school of thought, beginning with Wordsworth's sonnet counselling critics to 'scorn not the sonnet' for 'with this key / Shakespeare unlocked his heart'. Although she does not mention Lee by name, Stopes addresses his arguments immediately in her introduction, writing that

> many critics deny that 'Shakespeare unlocked his heart' in these poems, preferring to believe that they were mere literary exercises, improving on the efforts of other men; or that they were allegorical or hermetic writings, surcharged with hidden philosophical meaning; or that they also were written in dramatic form, voicing the feelings and giving expression to the thoughts of several of his friends. It is difficult to understand how those who have studied these literary epistles can see in them anything less than the poet's true expression of himself, not in deliberate, but unconscious autobiography.... They are, it is true, very unequal in poetical value; some of them seem self-contradictory in statement, some of them seem, at first sight, derogatory to the poet's character – but further study clears away many of the difficulties.[113]

Only that final, oblique mention of some aspects of the sonnets being 'derogatory to the poet's character' could refer to the controversy surrounding Wilde, but, as Stopes goes on to say, '"Clouds and eclipses stain both sun and moon" – but they pass, and leave the glory seeming brighter than before the temporary obscuring, which is visible only from the reader's standpoint.'[114] She then takes on Tyler's theories, which had already gone out of vogue by this time; instead, Stopes strongly advocates for the Earl of Southampton as the addressee of the sonnets, suggesting that a candidate for the 'Mr. W.H.' of the dedication could be William Harvey, who married Southampton's mother in 1598. In Stopes's imagined scenario, Harvey sent the manuscript of the sonnets to the publisher Thomas Thorpe after his wife's death in 1607. Rather than Mary Fitton, who several years earlier had been discovered to be blonde rather than 'dark', Stopes suggests Jacqueline Field, wife of printer Richard Field, as a candidate for the role of Dark Lady. She justifies this on the basis that the

Dark Lady was likely 'a woman who had been married just long enough to feel a sense of *ennui* creep into her leisured life, and a desire for new conquests steal into her veins', an observation that, given Stopes's own unhappy marriage, was probably based more on psychological projection than textual evidence. Furthermore, she says, Jacqueline Field 'was a Frenchwoman, and therefore likely to have dark eyes, a sallow complexion, and that indefinable "charm" which is so much referred to'.[115]

In keeping with her belief that the Sonnets were personal documents, Stopes retains the Q printing order in her edition but provides an appendix detailing her own proposed order, explaining that she does not attempt to '*better Shakespeare*, but to *find out what he means*, and to *get behind Thomas Thorpe*'.[116] Her major change involves the sonnets to the Dark Lady, which she believes to be contemporaneous with those to the youth, and therefore out of order in the sequence as it is represented in the 1609 quarto. Her theory for reordering involves linking 'catch-words' or 'catch-ideas' in order to 'pick up and piece together *some* of these separated pairs'. In a complex table, she divides the sonnets into three categories: 'To the youth', 'To or about the lady', and 'Impersonal'.[117] She then arranges them into twenty-seven different thematic groups. The 'Impersonal' category contains only four sonnets; of these, she positions 153 ('Cupid laid by his brand, and fell asleep') and 154 ('To the little love-god lying once asleep') at the very beginning, calling them 'Poetical Experiments'. Sonnets 1–23 come next but are followed by seven sonnets from the Dark Lady sequence, all out of order. From here, she alternates sonnets from each sequence, all reordered completely within their thematic grouping, in order to create a 'story' of the triangular relationship between the poet, the youth, and the Dark Lady. At the conclusion of that 'story' she inserts the other two 'Impersonal' sonnets (146, 'Poor soul, the centre of my sinful earth' and 129, 'Th'expense of spirit in a waste of shame'). From there, she classifies all the remaining sonnets under the category 'To the youth', with thematic groupings such as 'Gossip concerning Friend', 'The Poet forgets to sing', and 'Time's control of Nature'.

This edition of the Sonnets, rife as it is with rank speculation, is not the best example of the scholarship of Charlotte Stopes, but it is an excellent example of her fearless willingness to engage in debate. Although she eventually won the British Academy's Rose Mary Crawshay Prize and was elected a fellow of the Royal Society of Literature, Stopes's personal ambitions seem never to have slackened.[118] She continued working until her death in 1929.[119] Her legacy was damaged, however, by her daughter's biased recollections and by the ongoing prejudice against women who put themselves forward or refuse to conform to traditional gender roles. Like Rochfort Smith, she worked with 'the power and intelligence that are claimed as the attributes of man'; unlike Rochfort Smith, she did so without the sanctioning figure of a man, from whom those traits could be seen as borrowed or licensed, by her side.[120] This gave her a reputation as a virago, acting as a man; but however negative her reputation became, she *had* a reputation – her scholarly work survived better than any of the other four women in this chapter partly because it neither relied on nor was eclipsed by a proximal male. Only Elizabeth Lee came close to achieving a similar level of independence, and her primary legacy is still her connection to her brother's *DNB* project. Whatever the faults in the scholarship, no one could claim that a husband or brother or mentor 'helped' Stopes or deserved credit for her work. She advocated for herself and her scholarship, saw her work through to publication, and promoted it without false modesty or hesitation.

She also had a long life in which to pursue her goals; it is impossible to say what Jane Lee or Teena Rochfort Smith might have achieved if their lives had not been cut short. As it is, nothing of Jane Lee's Shakespearean work seems to have survived other than her NSS paper, and Rochfort Smith's prototypes for the four-text *Hamlet* were neglected until Ann Thompson connected them to her story. In the last decade, people have begun to re-evaluate Charlotte Stopes, scraping back the layers of prejudice that have obscured her legacy.[121] And hopefully, as we extend Helen Smith's challenge to reconceptualise different forms of textual work, women like Emma Gollancz will receive recognition as vital collaborators in the literary process, their 'manual' labour no longer relegated to second-class status, the distinctions between ancilla and virago erased. Milton's daughters may yet find a new place in literary history.

Notes

1 George Eliot, *Middlemarch: A Study of Provincial Life*, 8 vols (London: William Blackwood and Sons, 1871), I, pp. 105–6.
2 Quoted in Barbara K. Lewalski, *The Life of John Milton* (Oxford: Blackwell Publishing, 2003), p. 448.
3 Katharine Eisaman Maus, 'A Womb of His Own: Male Renaissance Poets in the Female Body', in *Printing and Parenting in Early Modern England*, ed. Douglas A. Brooks (Aldershot: Ashgate, 2005), pp. 89–108; Lynne Dickson Bruckner, 'Ben Jonson's Branded Thumb and the Imprint of Textual Paternity', in *Printing and Parenting in Early Modern England*, ed. Douglas A. Brooks (Aldershot: Ashgate, 2005), pp. 109–30.

4 Kevin Pask, *The Emergence of the English Author: Scripting the Life of the Poet in Early Modern England* (Cambridge: Cambridge University Press, 1997).

5 Possibly not pre-history, however. A recent study suggests that women may have been more involved than previously suspected in the creation of Paleolithic cave art. 'New Data on the Sexual Dimorphism of the Hand Stencils in El Castillo Cave (Cantabria, Spain)', *Journal of Archaeological Science: Reports*, 14 (2017), 374–81.

6 Smith, *'Grossly Material Things'*, p. 19.

7 Lewalski, *Life of John Milton*, p. 412.

8 Michael Millgate, *Thomas Hardy: A Biography Revisited* (Oxford: Oxford University Press, 2006), p. 412.

9 Ian Hamilton, *Keepers of the Flame: Literary Estates and the Rise of Biography* (London: Hutchinson, 1992), p. 247.

10 Hamilton, *Keepers of the Flame*, p. 247.

11 Hamilton, *Keepers of the Flame*, pp. 249–50.

12 Spencer, *Literary Relations*, pp. 49–50.

13 'Miss Emma Gollancz', *The Times* (London, 13 September 1929), p. 14; 'Miss Elizabeth Lee', *The Times* (London, 13 July 1920), p. 14; Frederick James Furnivall, *Teena Rochfort-Smith: A Memoir* (London, 1883); '1911 England Census – "Emma Gollancz"', National Archives of the UK (TNA), PRO RG 14/634 Sch 19; www.ancestry.com.

14 Susan David Bernstein, *Roomscape: Women Writers in the British Museum from George Eliot to Virginia Woolf* (Edinburgh: Edinburgh University Press, 2013), p. 37. The source of this terminology seems to be the printshop – Joseph Moxon uses 'devil' to describe a young assistant in the printshop. According to the OED, the term appeared in relation to 'a junior assistant of a barrister or other professional' by 1818, with a literary implication added by the end of the nineteenth century. The OED's quotation for that definition is from a newspaper article in 1888: 'Certain societies, the Early English Text, Chaucer, Shakspere, etc., though large employers of "devils", pay the highest wages.' 'Devil, n.', *OED Online* (Oxford University Press), www.oed.com/view/Entry/51468. By 1864, it was in use as a verb, 'to carry out research or other professional work in the name of someone else, esp. a lawyer or author, who receives the credit or remuneration'. 'Devil, v.', *OED Online* (Oxford University Press, 2018), www.oed.com/view/Entry/51469.

15 For more on Agnes Furnivall, see Molly G. Yarn, 'A Correction to the Identity of "Mrs Furnivall" in Harvard's Houghton Library Archives', *Notes and Queries*, 65.3 (2018), 401–2.

16 For more on translation and transcription, see chapter 2 in Bernstein, *Roomscape*, and chapter 1 in Smith, *'Grossly Material Things'*.

17 Victoria Olwell, 'The Body Types: Corporeal Documents and Body Politics circa 1900', in *Literary Secretaries/Secretarial Culture*, ed. Leah Price and Pamela Thurschwell (Aldershot: Ashgate, 2005), pp. 48–62; Jennifer L. Fleissner, 'Dictation Anxiety: The Stenographer's Stake in *Dracula*', in *Literary Secretaries/Secretarial Culture*, ed. Leah Price and Pamela Thurschwell

(Aldershot: Ashgate, 2005), pp. 63–90. Mediums appear surprisingly often in nineteenth-century Shakespeare studies. In 1866, poet and critic Gerald Massey released a book entitled *Shakespeare's Sonnets Never before Interpreted*, later reprinted as *The Secret Drama of Shakespeare's Sonnets*. In it, he argued that Shakespeare wrote the majority of the sonnets for the Earl of Southampton. Massey's wife, Rosina Jane Knowles, was a clairvoyant known as 'Somnambule Jane' who performed publicly both before and after her marriage. Massey explained in his introduction that Rosina used her clairvoyance to identify sources and references for Massey's work on the sonnets, carefully specifying that Rosina was not channeling Shakespeare himself. Andrew Murphy, *Shakespeare for the People: Working-Class Readers, 1800–1900* (Cambridge: Cambridge University Press, 2008), p. 119. Hester Dowden, daughter of renowned Shakespearean Edward Dowden, achieved fame as a particularly literary medium, conveying messages from no lesser personages than Oscar Wilde and Shakespeare himself. Bette London, 'Secretary to the Stars: Mediums and the Agency of Authorship', in *Literary Secretaries/Secretarial Culture*, ed. Leah Price and Pamela Thurschwell (Aldershot: Ashgate, 2005), pp. 91–110 (p. 102).

18 London, 'Secretary to the Stars', p. 101.

19 Erik Gray, *Milton and the Victorians* (Ithaca, NY: Cornell University Press, 2015).

20 Sandra M. Gilbert and Susan Gubar, *The Madwoman in the Attic: The Woman Writer and the Nineteenth-Century Literary Imagination* (New Haven, CT: Yale University Press, 1980), p. 505.

21 Stephanie Green, *The Public Lives of Charlotte and Marie Stopes*, Dramatic Lives (London: Pickering & Chatto, 2013), p. 53.

22 Green, *Public Lives*. The Rational Dress Society was dedicated to promoting practical, 'healthy' fashions for women, as opposed to the oppressive, impractical garments then in style. 'Rational Dress', *Saturday Review of Politics, Literature, Science and Art*, 61.1587 (1886), 433; Tracy J. R. Collins, 'Athletic Fashion, *Punch*, and the Creation of the New Woman', *Victorian Periodicals Review*, 43.3 (2010), 309–35; Patricia A. Cunningham, *Reforming Women's Fashion, 1850–1920: Politics, Health, and Art* (Kent, OH: Kent State University Press, 2003).

23 'Membership List', in *The New Shakspere Society's Transactions, 1874–75* (London: Trübner & Co., 1875).

24 Thompson and Roberts, 'Mary Cowden Clarke', p. 178.

25 Quoted in Thompson and Roberts, 'Mary Cowden Clarke', p. 178.

26 Frederick James Furnivall, 'Letter to J. M. Manly', 18 August 1894, John Matthews Manly Papers, Special Collections Research Center, University of Chicago Library, Box 1, Folder 2.

27 Margaret Lupton, 'Letter to Frederick Furnivall', 11 February 1900; Iris, 'Letter to Frederick Furnivall', n.d.; Anna Kellner, 'Postcard to Frederick Furnivall', n.d.; all in King's College London College Archives, Frederick Furnivall Collection, Group 1/2/7.

28 J. C. Castell and C. F. W. Mead, 'Memories of F. J. Furnivall, V', in *Frederick James Furnivall: A Volume of Personal Record* (London: Henry Frowde, Oxford University Press, 1911), pp. 16–25 (p. 21).

29 Alice B. Gomme, 'Memories of F. J. Furnivall, XIV', in *Frederick James Furnivall*, pp. 62–64 (p. 63).

30 Derek Hudson, *Munby: A Man of Two Worlds. The Life and Diaries of Arthur J. Munby, 1828–1910* (London: John Murray, 1972), pp. 123–24.

31 William Benzie, *Dr. F. J. Furnivall: Victorian Scholar Adventurer* (Norman, OK: Pilgrim Books, 1983), p. 23.

32 Letter in the James Murray Papers. Quoted in Benzie, *Dr. F. J. Furnivall*, pp. 29–30.

33 Lucy Toulmin Smith, 'Letter to J. M. Manly', 12 June 1896, Manly Papers, Box 1, Folder 4.

34 Benzie, *Dr. F. J. Furnivall*, p. 31.

35 William S. Peterson, 'Furnivall, Frederick James (1825–1910)', in *Oxford Dictionary of National Biography* (Oxford: Oxford University Press, 2004), doi.org/10.1093/ref:odnb/33298.

36 Jeffrey Kahan, *The Quest for Shakespeare: The Peculiar History and Surprising Legacy of the New Shakspere Society* (Basingstoke: Palgrave Macmillan, 2017), pp. 113, 3.

37 16 October entry in Edith Rickert, 'Diary, 1896' (London, 1896), Edith Rickert Papers, Special Collections Research Center, University of Chicago Library, Box 1, Folder 14.

38 Jane Lee, 'On the Authorship of the Second and Third Parts of *Henry VI*, and Their Originals, *The Contention* and *The True Tragedy*', in *Transactions of the New Shakspere Society, 1877–79*, ed. Frederick James Furnivall (London: Publisht for the Society by Trübner & Co., 1879), pp. 219–92.

39 Lee, 'On the Authorship of the Second and Third Parts', p. 284.

40 Turner, *Philology*, p. 264.

41 Jenny Marx, 'Shakespearian Studies in England: London, End of December 1876', in *Marx, Engels on Literature and Art*, by Friedrich Engels and Karl Marx (Moscow: Progress Publishers, 1976).

42 Gordon Goodwin and David Huddleston, 'William Lee', in *Oxford Dictionary of National Biography* (Oxford: Oxford University Press, 2004), doi.org/10.1093/ref:odnb/16317.

43 'The Linacre Professorship', *The Times* (London, 26 August 1881), p. 10. Theodor Benfey (1809–1881) taught Lee at Gottingen University. He studied comparative linguistics and was particularly well-known for his work on Sanskrit. 'Theodor Benfey | German Scholar', *Encyclopedia Britannica* (Encyclopedia Britannica, 2018), www.britannica.com/biography/Theodor-Benfey. Robert Atkinson taught Romance languages as well as Sanskrit, Telegu, and other Indian dialects at Trinity College, Dublin. David Greene, 'Robert Atkinson and Irish Studies', *Hermathena*, 102 (1966), 6–15.

44 R. P. Graves wrote: 'From what I have written you will infer that she must be possessed of a remarkable intellect: you will be not displeased to learn that she

is equally remarkable for simplicity of character, for unpretentiousness & lady-like feelings, & for moral qualities quite on a par with her intellectual.' R. P. Graves, 'Letter to Eliza Adams', 6 February 1883, St John's College Library, Papers of John Crouch Adams, 26/4/3.

45 The first professor of English literature at Trinity College, Dublin, Dowden was a towering figure in nineteenth-century Shakespeare studies, and author of the extremely influential *Shakespeare: A Critical Study of His Mind and Art*. Dowden was also the original editor of the Arden1 series but resigned in disappointment over his *Hamlet* edition's initial poor sales numbers. E. J. Gwynn and Arthur Sherbo, 'Dowden, Edward (1843–1913), Literary Scholar and Poet', in *Oxford Dictionary of National Biography* (Oxford: Oxford University Press, 2013), doi.org/10.1093/ref:odnb/32882.

46 E. H. Lyster, 'The Late Miss Jane Lee', in *Cambridge Letters, Etc, 1895* (London: Women's Printing Society, 1895), pp. 27–30, Newnham College Archives.

47 'Grant of Letters of Administration for Jane Lee', 1896, Principal Probate Registry, https://probatesearch.service.gov.uk.

48 William Shakespeare, John D. Cox, and Eric Rasmussen, *King Henry VI, Part 3*, Arden Shakespeare, Third Series (London: Bloomsbury Arden Shakespeare, 2001), pp. 45–46.

49 Lee, 'On the Authorship of the Second and Third Parts', p. 241.

50 William Shakespeare and Israel Gollancz, *Shakespeare's First Part of King Henry VI: With Preface, Glossary, &c*, The Temple Shakespeare (London: J. M. Dent and Co., 1898), p. ix.

51 Furnivall, *Teena Rochfort-Smith*, pp. 7, 10.

52 Kahan, *The Quest for Shakespeare*, p. 10.

53 Kahan, *The Quest for Shakespeare*, p. 51.

54 Frederick James Furnivall, 'Second Report', in *The New Shakspere Society's Transaction, 1877–79* (London: Publisht for the Society by Trübner & Co., 1879), p. 12.

55 Furnivall, *Teena Rochfort-Smith*, p. 7.

56 Joseph Crosby, 'Miss Teena Rochfort-Smith', *Shakespeariana; A Critical and Contemporary Review of Shakespearian Literature*, April 1884, 173.

57 Thompson, 'Teena Rochfort Smith', p. 136.

58 Crosby, 'Miss Teena Rochfort-Smith'; Thompson, 'Teena Rochfort Smith', pp. 135–36.

59 Alan Galey, *The Shakespearean Archive* (Cambridge: Cambridge University Press, 2014), p. 25; Thompson, 'Teena Rochfort Smith', p. 128.

60 I am grateful to John Pollack at the Kislak Center, University of Pennsylvania, for providing me with details about this copy.

61 Furnivall, *Teena Rochfort-Smith*, p. 5.

62 Thompson, 'Teena Rochfort Smith', p. 128.

63 Thompson, 'Teena Rochfort Smith', p. 131; Galey, *Shakespearean Archive*, p. 27.

64 Furnivall, *Teena Rochfort-Smith*, p. 10.

65 Johann Wolfgang von Goethe and Jane Lee, *Faust. Part I. With Introduction and Notes, and an Appendix on Part II*, Macmillan's Foreign School Classics (London: Macmillan, 1886); E. D. A. Morshead, 'Faust', *The Academy*, 752 (1886), 215–16.

66 Furnivall, *Teena Rochfort-Smith*, p. 5.

67 Furnivall, *Teena Rochfort-Smith*, p. 14.

68 See Chapter 1 for details of Maurice's edition.

69 Sidney Lee matriculated in 1878, Gollancz in 1883. Oxford and Cambridge had opened to Jewish students only in 1871 – the same year that Newnham opened its doors, and two years after Girton's founding in 1869.

70 *Cambridge Letter, &c., 1889* (London: Women's Printing Society, 1889), Newnham College Archives.

71 This was a common hazard for university women. The Shakespeare editor Fanny Johnson, whose sister served as the secretary to the principal of Newnham for many years, wrote a novel about a fictionalised version of Newnham called Hypatia. In it, one of the women explains to a male student that she was forced to intermit to care for a relative:

> 'Oh, I'm *very* sorry to hear about that,' said Gray, sympathetically; his beady eyes tried to express even more than he said. 'It's hard for you to have such interruptions.'
>
> 'It's the sort of thing we expect at Hypatia.'
>
> 'The sort of thing that very seldom happens to any of us. You know, Miss Blumberg, that is what makes one have such a tremendous respect for you.... Not for you only: you ladies, I mean. I'm serious; really I am, upon my word. To see you getting your first classes time after time, in spite of your having all that against you. You see, you *don't* give up being women in the true sense of the word, if you'll excuse my saying so.'

Fanny Johnson, *In Statu Pupillari*, ed. Anna Bogen, Women's University Narratives, 1890–1945, 4 vols (London: Pickering & Chatto, 2015), I, pp. 98–99.

72 J. M. Dent, *The House of Dent, 1888–1938; Being the Memoirs of J. M. Dent, with Additional Chapters Covering the Last 16 Years by Hugh R. Dent*, revised edition (London: J. M. Dent & Sons, 1938), p. 61. For more on the creation of the Temple Shakespeare, see the Primer.

73 Dent, *The House of Dent*, p. 62.

74 Ruth Dudley Edwards, *Victor Gollancz: A Biography* (London: Faber & Faber, 2012).

75 Emma Gollancz, 'Letter to J. M. Dent', 6 January 1898; Emma Gollancz, 'Letter to J. M. Dent', 19 August 1898; Emma Gollancz, 'Letter to J. M. Dent', 5 January 1899; J. M. Dent and Co., 'Letter to Emma Gollancz', 4 January 1898; all in J. M. Dent and Sons Records #11043, Rare Book Literary and Historical Papers, Wilson Library, University of North Carolina at Chapel Hill, Series 4.2, Folder 5139.

76 'Lawyer's Notes', n.d., J. M. Dent and Sons Records, Series 4.2, Folder 5141.

77 'Lawyer's Notes', p. 8.

78 Dent, *The House of Dent*, p. 63.

79 Young, *Steam-Driven Shakespeare*, pp. 15, 186–87; Murphy, *Shakespeare for the People*.

80 'Collecting Everyman's Library: 1906–1982', everymanslibrarycollecting.com.

81 'Miss Emma Gollancz'.

82 Although some collections of Israel's papers survive, including family corre-spondence, I have as yet been unable to find anything relating to Emma except for three letters from her property agent which seem to have been accidentally placed in the British Academy archives, probably while she assisted Israel in his role as secretary. (British Academy Archives, 'Miscellaneous Correspondence and Papers: 1908', BAA/SEC/1/34/6a-c.) More work should certainly be done to investigate Gollancz's archives at the British Academy and at Princeton for traces of Emma's life and voice.

83 Gillian Fenwick, 'Lee, Elizabeth (1857/8–1920), Biographer and Translator', in *Oxford Dictionary of National Biography* (Oxford: Oxford University Press, 2004), doi.org/10.1093/ref:odnb/41160.

84 Alan Bell and Katherine Duncan-Jones, 'Lee, Sir Sidney (1859–1926), Second Editor of the *Dictionary of National Biography* and Literary Scholar', in *Oxford Dictionary of National Biography* (Oxford: Oxford University Press, 2009), doi.org/10.1093/ref:odnb/34470.

85 Fenwick, 'Lee, Elizabeth'; for more on the increased number of women included in the 2004 release of the *ODNB*, see Alison Booth, 'Fighting for Lives in the *ODNB*, or Taking Prosopography Personally', *Journal of Victorian Culture*, 10.2 (2005), 267–79.

86 Fenwick, 'Lee, Elizabeth'.

87 'Miss Elizabeth Lee'.

88 'Miss Elizabeth Lee'.

89 'Miss Elizabeth Lee'.

90 Jaggard, *Shakespeare Bibliography*, p. xix. Jaggard, the proprietor of the Shakespeare Press in Stratford, was himself labelled an 'enthusiast', having spent over twenty years assembling his immense bibliography. 'Shakespeare Bibliography', *Saturday Review of Politics, Literature, Science and Art; London*, 111.2904 (1911), 782; 'Notes on Books', *Notes and Queries*, s11-IV.81 (1911), 59–60.

91 Green, *Public Lives*, p. 81.

92 Quoted in Green, *Public Lives*, pp. 81–82.

93 Stephanie Green, 'The Serious Mrs. Stopes: Gender, Writing and Scholarship in Late-Victorian Britain', *Nineteenth-Century Gender Studies*, 5.3 (2009), www.ncgsjournal.com/issue53/green.htm.

94 Carol Dyhouse, *No Distinction of Sex? Women in British Universities, 1870–1939*, Women's History (London: UCL Press, 1995), p. 217.

95 Schoenbaum is, however, using 'professional scholar' anachronistically, given that Stopes was working before and during the development of 'literary scholarship' as a profession. See Chapter 5 for more details. S. Schoenbaum, *Shakespeare's Lives*, new edition (Oxford: Clarendon Press, 1991), pp. 460, 463.

96 Green, *Public Lives*, p. 150.

97 Green, *Public Lives*, p. 150.

98 Kathleen E. McLuskie, 'Remembering Charlotte Stopes', in *Women Making Shakespeare: Text, Performance and Reception*, ed. Gordon McMullan, Lena Cowen Orlin, and Virginia Mason Vaughan (London: Bloomsbury Arden Shakespeare, 2014), pp. 195–205 (p. 200).

99 Sidney Lee, 'Shakespeare's Stage: England's Debt to the Burbages', *The Times Literary Supplement*, 610 (1913), 385.

100 Quoted in Green, *Public Lives*, p. 152.

101 Schoenbaum, *Shakespeare's Lives*, p. 467; see Charles Nicholl, *The Lodger: Shakespeare on Silver Street* (London: Penguin, 2008).

102 Schoenbaum, *Shakespeare's Lives*, pp. 469–70.

103 Schoenbaum, *Shakespeare's Lives*, p. 470.

104 Charlotte Carmichael Stopes, 'Memories of F. J. Furnivall, XLV', in *Frederick James Furnivall*, pp. 188–92. Masson, known as one of the founders of the study of English in universities, had a daughter named Flora, who edited *As You Like It* for Dent's Shakespeare for Schools, and was, along with Charlotte Stopes, in that first group of women to fulfil the degree requirements at Edinburgh. G. G. Smith and Sandra Miley Cooney, 'Masson, David Mather', in *Oxford Dictionary of National Biography* (Oxford: Oxford University Press, 2004), doi.org/10.1093/ref:odnb/34924; William Shakespeare and Flora Masson, *As You Like It*, Dent's Shakespeare for Schools (London: J. M. Dent & Co., 1903); Professor Basil Williams, 'Miss Flora Masson', *The Times* (London, 5 October 1937), p. 9.

105 William Shakespeare and C. C. Stopes, *Shakespeare's Sonnets*, King's Classics (London: De la More Press, 1904).

106 Ruth Hall, *Marie Stopes: A Biography* (London: Virago, 1978), p. 90.

107 William Shakespeare and Katherine Duncan-Jones, *Shakespeare's Sonnets*, The Arden Shakespeare, Third Series, revised edition (London: Arden Shakespeare, 2010), p. 78.

108 Shakespeare and Duncan-Jones, *Shakespeare's Sonnets*, p. 31.

109 Shakespeare and Duncan-Jones, *Shakespeare's Sonnets*, p. 32.

110 Schoenbaum, *Shakespeare's Lives*, p. 370.

111 Green, *Public Lives*, pp. 61, 63.

112 Schoenbaum, *Shakespeare's Lives*, p. 354.

113 Shakespeare and Stopes, *Shakespeare's Sonnets*, p. xi.

114 Shakespeare and Stopes, *Shakespeare's Sonnets*, p. xi.

115 Shakespeare and Stopes, *Shakespeare's Sonnets*, pp. xxxii–xxxiii.

116 Shakespeare and Stopes, *Shakespeare's Sonnets*, p. 157. For more information about the tradition of reordering the Sonnets, see Megan Heffernan, 'Turning Sonnets into Poems: Textual Affect and John Benson's Metaphysical Shakespeare', *Shakespeare Quarterly*, 64.1 (2013), 71–98; Kenneth Muir, 'The Order of Shakespeare's Sonnets', *College Literature*, 10.3 (1983), 244–50; Matthew Zarnowiecki, 'Responses to Responses to Shakespeare's Sonnets: More Sonnets', *Critical Survey*, 28.2 (2016), 10–26.

For more on the reception of the Sonnets, see Jane Kingsley-Smith, *The Afterlife of Shakespeare's Sonnets* (Cambridge: Cambridge University Press, 2019).

117 Shakespeare and Stopes, *Shakespeare's Sonnets*, p. 159.

118 The Rose Mary Crawshay Prize has also been awarded to editors Una Ellis-Fermor, Alice Walker, Evelyn Simpson, Anne Barton, and Molly Mahood, as well as numerous women who edited for the Malone Society and the Early English Text Society. See Chapter 5 and the sidenote 'On Women Editing Not-Shakespeare (or Not Editing)'.

119 Lesley A. Hall, 'Stopes, Charlotte Brown Carmichael (1840–1929), Feminist and Literary Scholar', in *Oxford Dictionary of National Biography* (Oxford: Oxford University Press, 2005), doi.org/10.1093/ref:odnb/53016.

120 Crosby, 'Miss Teena Rochfort-Smith', p. 173.

121 Green, 'The Serious Mrs. Stopes'; Green, *Public Lives*; McLuskie, 'Remembering Charlotte Stopes'.

Sidenote
On Women Editing Not-Shakespeare
(or Not Editing)

Although this book by its very nature plays into a Shakespeare-centric approach to editorial history, this brief mention of women editing early modern texts by other authors, or doing other types of bibliographical work, hopefully offers a slight counterbalance to that tendency. Some of this material warrants significantly more time and space than is available here. Many women editors and textual scholars are excluded from this book purely due to chronological technicalities. For example, Madeleine Doran's only edition of a Shakespeare play was *A Midsummer Night's Dream*, published in 1959 for the Pelican series, under the general editor-ship of Alfred Harbage.[1] This puts her beyond the time scope covered by this book; however, her influential bibliographical work during the 1920s and '30s deserves acknowledgement. Doran and Peter Alexander each developed, separately but simultaneously, arguments that the quartos of 2 and 3 *Henry VI* were memorial reconstructions.[2] Doran suggested that the quartos represent a shorter performance text intended for touring.[3] This theory proved very influential throughout the twentieth century.[4] Women's contributions to related fields such as attribution studies deserve greater attention. In addition to Jane Lee's and Madeleine Doran's studies, for example, Pauline Gertrude Wiggin, who edited two editions of Shakespeare, produced significant work on the authorship of Middleton and Rowley's collaborative plays.[5]

Although Madeleine Doran did not edit Shakespeare until 1959, she did produce an edition of Thomas Heywood's *If You Know Not Me You Know Nobody, Parts I and II* for the Malone Society in 1935.[6] In fact, almost all of the women discussed in this book who edited Shakespeare also edited other authors from many periods, including the early modern, and publications for scholarly societies such as the Malone Society and the Early English Text Society accounted for many woman-edited volumes. Under Greg's leadership as general editor, multiple women edited texts for the Malone Society, including Muriel St Clare Byrne, who edited

72

Anthony Munday's *John a Kent John a Cumber* (1932).[7] Several years prior to that, Byrne had assisted Greg by reading the proofs of *The Calculus of Variants*, which may have led to her being tapped to edit the Munday play.[8] Several years after the publication of the Munday play, Byrne edited *King Henry VIII* for the New Eversley Shakespeare (1937). Alice Walker also refers in one letter to an edition of Munday's complete works being edited by Byrne, but that project was never completed.[9]

In addition to the women Frederick Furnivall encouraged to edit Shakespeare, he also engaged female scholars to prepare non-dramatic texts for the Early English Text Society (EETS), beginning in 1870 with Lucy Toulmin Smith, who completed and edited her father's *English Gilds*, a collection of the ordinances of early English guilds. Toulmin Smith went on to publish many other texts, including the first edition of the York Mystery Plays in 1885, and to become the first librarian of Manchester College, Oxford. Around 1899, the number of women employed by the EETS increased significantly, and over the next fifty years, women edited thirty-six of the society's 109 publications.[10]

In America, Esther Cloudman Dunn, a long-time professor at Smith College and the first woman awarded a PhD by the University of London, edited *Eight Famous Elizabethan Plays* for the Modern Library series, containing *Doctor Faustus*, *The Shoemaker's Holiday*, *A Woman Killed with Kindness*, *Volpone*, *The Maid's Tragedy*, *The Duchess of Malfi*, *A New Way to Pay Old Debts*, and *'Tis Pity She's a Whore*.[11] Poet and essayist Louise Imogen Guiney played an important role in the rediscovery of poet Katharine Philips through the publication of the 'Orinda Booklets'.[12] Edith Rickert, who is discussed in Chapter 3, led the Chicago Chaucer Project, which produced the eight-volume *Text of the Canterbury Tales*.[13]

The growing appreciation of bibliographical work that does not fall within the traditional confines of 'editing' also allows for greater inclusion of women in textual history, as discussed in Chapters 1 and 2. Paul Salzman has recently highlighted the significance of Henrietta Halliwell's transcription in the recovery and publication of Mary Wroth's *Love's Victory*, suggesting that this is only one example of Henrietta working as an editorial team with her husband, James Orchard Halliwell-Phillips.[14] Agnes Furnivall's transcriptions were vital to editor John Matthews Manly's work.[15] Reference works such as concordances, indexes, lexicons, and dictionaries offered opportunities for many literary women, and demonstrate an interesting mix of feminine process and product. Cicely Palser Haveley has discussed the ways in which the reception of Mary Cowden Clarke's *Concordance* involved gendered values and a feminisation of her labour.[16] While Cowden Clarke's concordance of the plays is the best known of the genre, Helen Furness, wife of H. H. Furness, produced a concordance of Shakespeare's poems to supplement Cowden Clarke's work. Also responding to a perceived shortfall in the *Concordance* and other similar works, Evangeline M. O'Connor compiled *An Index to the Works of Shakspere*, published in 1887, offering 'references, by topics, to notable passages and significant expressions; brief histories of the plays; geographical name, and historical incidents; mention of all characters, and sketches of important ones; together with explanations of allusions and obscure and obsolete words and phrases'. In format, tone, and intent, O'Connor's *Index* strongly resembles the notes sections given in many single-text school editions, and it was bundled with a text by at least one publisher.[17]

The Boston Public Library's Barton Collection includes two letters from an H. Butler, proprietor of the *Isle of Wight Observer*, written in June 1860.[18] He mentions a ten-volume edition of Shakespeare that the paper printed in 1852–53 for 'Miss Lyndon'.[19] Sadly, this edition, which would have preceded Cowden Clarke's first edition of the complete works by about a decade, turns out not to be an edition at all, but a concordance. The publication history is somewhat obscure, as several of the volumes seem to have received slightly different titles, including *A Concordance to Select Quotations* ..., *A Collection of Select Quotations*, and *Apophthegms from the Plays of Shakespeare*; however, all seem to belong to a planned ten-volume set, sold for a shilling each, published by Simpkin, Marshall of London and G. Butler of Ryde, who also printed them.[20] Charlotte Sophia Lyndon was born in London in 1812; her parents, George Lyndon and Matilda Eliza Stearn, emigrated from Ireland to England in around 1803. Charlotte had a number of siblings, and the 1851 census shows Charlotte living with her sister Matilda's family on the Isle of Ryde, confirming the connection between Charlotte and the Ryde-printed *Concordance*.[21] By 1861, Charlotte and Matilda, now widowed, had moved to Wales, and Charlotte died in 1875.[22] Aside from her concordance, Charlotte published two novels, *The Voice of Ida* (1848) and *The Steadfast Ones; or, Safe at Last* (1849).

Teena Rochfort Smith originally intended to create a concordance to replace Cowden Clarke's, but Furnivall persuaded her that it would be too expensive to produce, and steered her towards the four-text *Hamlet* instead.[23] Rochfort Smith also contributed to James Murray's *Dictionary*, as did a number of other women, including Shakespeare editor Charlotte Yonge (the Dictionary's first female sub-editor, in charge of 'N').[24]

Murray's wife and children also toiled in his Scriptorium – his eldest daughter Hilda went on to become vice mistress of Girton College and to edit for the Early English Text Society.[25] Henrietta C. Bartlett catalogued *Mr. William Shakespeare: Original and Early Editions of His Quartos and Folios* (1922) and, in partnership with A. W. Pollard, *A Census of Shakespeare's Plays in Quarto, 1594–1709* (1916 and 1939). She was a member of the Hroswitha Club, a New York–based group of women book collectors, and taught courses on bibliography for women.[26]

Although there are many more examples, one stands out in particular. During Tudor Shakespeare editor Laura Wylie's undergraduate years at Vassar, she shared the campus with another student whose influence on the Shakespeare text would be profound, although her name does not appear on any edition's title page – Emily Folger, née Jordan. Soon after Wylie returned to Vassar as an instructor, Folger also returned, this time as a graduate student. She earned an MA in Shakespeare, writing her thesis on 'The True Text of Shakespeare'.[27] H. H. Furness served as her supervisor. By this time, Emily and her husband Henry were deep into their lifelong pursuit of collecting Shakespeare. According to her colleague James Waldo Fawcett, '[Emily] was [Henry's] librarian, clerk, and amanuensis. It was her responsibility to maintain a catalogue of books offered for purchase, of books actually bought, of books to be acquired. She read the bookseller's lists, marking interesting items for Mr. Folger's consideration. She regularly reviewed the periodical publications referring to Shakespeare.'[28] Emily and Henry built their collection collaboratively, with Emily performing much of the research while Henry continued in his day job at Standard Oil. That collection, which would become the Folger Shakespeare Library, is now a required stop for anyone preparing a critical edition of Shakespeare, a tribute to the couple's vision and to Emily's scholarship.

Notes

1 Two other women also edited for Pelican: Virginia Freund (*Henry V*, with Louis B. Wright, 1957) and Josephine Waters Bennett (*Much Ado About Nothing*, 1958). Murphy, *Shakespeare in Print*, p. 377.

2 Madeleine Doran, *Henry VI, Parts II and III: Their Relation to the Contention and the True Tragedy* (Iowa City: The University, 1928); Peter Alexander, *Shakespeare's Henry VI and Richard III*, Shakespeare Problems, 3 (Cambridge: Cambridge University Press, 1929).

3 For more on both Alexander's and Doran's theories, see Gabriel Egan, *The Struggle for Shakespeare's Text: Twentieth-Century Editorial Theory and Practice* (Cambridge: Cambridge University Press, 2010), p. 108; William

Shakespeare and Ronald Knowles, *King Henry VI Part 2*, Arden Shakespeare, Third Series (London: Bloomsbury Arden Shakespeare, 1999), p. 125. For more on Alexander's approach, see also Steven Urkowitz, "'If I Mistake in Those Foundations Which I Build Upon': Peter Alexander's Textual Analysis of "Henry VI Parts 2 and 3"', *English Literary Renaissance*, 18.2 (1988), 230–56.

4 Doran argued against the theories advanced by Jane Lee in her paper for the New Shakspere Society, in which Lee argued that the quartos were written by Marlowe and Greene. See Chapter 2 for more details on Lee. Lee, 'On the Authorship of the Second and Third Parts'.

5 Pauline G. Wiggin, *An Inquiry into the Authorship of the Middleton-Rowley Plays* (Boston: Ginn & Co., 1897).

6 Thomas Heywood and Madeleine Doran, *If You Know Not Me You Know Nobody*, Malone Society Reprints (London: Printed for the Malone Society by J. Johnson at the Oxford University Press, 1935).

7 Other Malone Society volumes edited by women prior to 1950: *Edmund Ironside*, ed. Eleanore Boswell (1927); Massinger's *The Parliament of Love*, ed. Kathleen Marguerite Lea (1928); *Thomas of Woodstock*, ed. Wilhelmina Paulina Frijlinck (Frijlinck also edited *The Tragedy of Sir John Van Olden Barnavelt* for a Dutch publisher); *The Two Noble Ladies*, ed. Rebecca G. Rhoads (1930); *Jack Juggler*, ed. Eunice Lilian Smart (1933); *Mother Bombie*, ed. Kathleen Marguerite Lea and W. W. Greg (1939). 'Malone Society Publication List', *The Malone Society*, 2017, http://malonesociety.com/wp-content/uploads/2012/02/Publication-List-July-2017.pdf. Lea, the Vice-Principal of Lady Margaret Hall, Oxford, also edited Milton's *Areopagitica* and *Of Education* for Oxford University Press.

8 Greg, *The Calculus of Variants*, p. vi.

9 Alice Walker, 'Letter to R. B. McKerrow', 2 March 1936, Trinity College Library, Cambridge: MCKW, A4/2.

10 The volumes edited by women for the EETS prior to 1950 were *English Gilds* (1870), ed. Lucy Toulmin Smith (with Lujo Brentano); *Queen Elizabeth's Englishings of Boethius, Plutarch and Horace* (1899), ed. Caroline Pemberton; *An Alphabet of Tales I & II* (1904 and 1905), ed. Mary Macleod Banks; *Emaré* (1906), ed. Edith Rickert; *Coventry Leet Book vols I and II* (1907, 1908, 1909), ed. Mary Dormer Harris; *The Middle English Poem Erthe upon Erthe* (1911), ed. Hilda M. R. Murray; *Lanterne of Lizt* (1917), ed. Lilian Mary Swinburn; *Early English Homilies from the Twelfth-Century MS. Vespasian D. xiv* (1917), ed. Rubie D. N. Warner; *The Wheatley Manuscript: Middle English Verse and Prose in BM MS Add 39574* (1921), ed. Mabel Day; *The Donet by Reginald Peacock* (1921), ed. Elsie Vaughan Hitchcock; *Meditations on the Life and Passion of Christ* (1921), ed. Charlotte D'Evelyn; *Folower to the Donet by Reginald Peacock* (1924), ed. Elsie Vaughan Hitchcock; *The Southern Passion* (1927), ed. Beatrice Daw Brown; *Seege or Batayle of Troye* (1926), ed. Mary Elizabeth Barnicle; *Alexander Barclay: The Eclogues* (1928), ed. Beatrice White; *William Nevill: The Castell of Pleasure* (1930), ed. Roberta Douglas Cornelius; *The Dance of*

Death (1931), ed. Florence Warren and Beatrice White; *John Audelay* (1931), ed. Ella Keats Whiting; *Nicholas Harpsfield: The Life and Death of Sr. Thomas More* (1932), ed. Elsie Vaughan Hitchcock; *John Stanbridge: The Vulgaria and Robert Whittinton: The Vulgaria* (1932), ed. Beatrice White; *Siege of Jerusalem* (1932), ed. Mabel Day (with E. Kölbing); *English Mediaeval Lapidaries* (1933), ed. Joan Evans and Mary Sidney Sergeantson; *Seinte Marherete* (1934), ed. Frances May Mack; *Quatrefoil of Love* (1935), ed. Magdalene Marie Weale (with Israel Gollancz); *William Roper: The Lyfe of Sir Thomas Moore, Knighte* (1935), ed. Elsie Vaughan Hitchcock; *Firumbras and Otuel and Roland* (1935), ed. Mary Isabelle O'Sullivan; *Mum and the Sothsegger* (1936), ed. Mabel Day; *Osborn Bokenham: Legendys of Hooly Wummen* (1938), ed. Mary Sidney Sergeantson; *The Liber de Diversis Medicinis in the Thornton Manuscript* (1938), ed. Margaret Sinclair Ogden; *The Book of Margery Kempe* (1940), ed. Hope Emily Allen (with S. B. Meech); *Charles of Orleans: The English Poems* (1941), ed. Mabel Day (with R. Steele); *The Latin Text of the Ancrene Riwle* (1944), ed. Charlotte D'Evelyn; *The Cloud of Unknowing and The Book of Privy Counselling* (1944), ed. Phyllis Hodgson; *The Lyfe of Syr Thomas More by Ro. Ba.* (1950), ed. Mabel Day (with P. E. Hallett). 'Publications', *The Early English Text Society*, http://users.ox.ac.uk/~eets/publications.html.
11 'Esther Cloudman Dunn Papers, 1864–1977 Finding Aid', Five College Archives & Manuscript Collections, https://asteria.fivecolleges.edu/findaids/smitharchives/manosca325_bioghist.html; *Eight Famous Elizabethan Plays*, ed. Esther Cloudman Dunn (New York: Modern Library, 1932).
12 Andrea Sununu, '"I Long to Know Your Opinion of It": The Serendipity of a Malfunctioning Timing Belt or the Guiney–Tutin Collaboration in the Recovery of Katherine Philips', *Women's Writing*, 24.3 (2017), 258–79.
13 Geoffrey Chaucer, John Matthews Manly, and Edith Rickert, *The Text of the Canterbury Tales* (Chicago, IL: University of Chicago Press, 1940).
14 Salzman, *Editors Construct the Renaissance Canon*, p. 52.
15 Yarn, 'Mrs. Furnivall'.
16 Cicely Palser Haveley, 'Mary Cowden Clarke's Labours of Love', in *Women, Scholarship and Criticism: Gender and Knowledge c. 1790–1900*, ed. Joan Bellamy, Anne Laurence, and Gill Perry (Manchester: Manchester University Press, 2000), pp. 110–24 (pp. 114–15).
17 Depending on the series and publisher, these notes sections could be titled 'Index', 'Glossary', 'Notes', or similar variations. O'Connor's glossary can be found in William Shakespeare, William Aldis Wright, et al., *The Works of William Shakespeare: With Prefaces, Notes, Glossaries, a Life of Shakespeare, and a History of Early English Drama*, Elsinore Edition (New York: University Society, 1901).
18 H. Butler, 'Letters Regarding Miss Lyndon', 9 June 1860, Boston Public Library, Thomas Pennant Barton Shakespeare Collection, No. 15 in G39.30.15.

19 James Mascarene Hubbard, *Catalogue of the Barton Collection, Boston Public Library. In Two Parts: Part I, Shakespeare's Works and Shakespeariana; Part II, Miscellaneous*, 2 vols (Bostons: Published by the Trustees, 1880), I, p. 151.

20 Charlotte Lyndon, *A Concordance to Select Quotations from the Plays of Shakespeare: Alphabetically Arranged with Full References* (London: Simpkin, Marshall, 1850).

21 '1851 England Census – Charlotte Lyndon', National Archives of the UK, PRO HO 107/1664, Folio 27, Page 21; www.ancestry.com. Their widowed brother Robert also lived on Ryde. Ten years later, Robert resided at the Charterhouse in London as one of their 'Poor Brothers', an official designation (established in 1613) for older gentlemen fallen on hard times, who, once admitted to the Charterhouse, received free board and a small annuity; however, by 1845, the institution had devolved so much that literary men Henry Morley and William Moncrief wrote essays decrying its corruption for Charles Dickens's *Household Words*. Robert was admitted to an asylum in 1862, then died in 1865.

22 '1861 Wales Census – Charlotte Lyndon', National Archives of the UK, PRO RG 9/4348/34/14; www.ancestry.com.

23 Furnivall, *Teena Rochfort-Smith*, p. 5.

24 Peter Gilliver, *The Making of the Oxford English Dictionary* (Oxford: Oxford University Press, 2016); Peter Gilliver, 'Women and the Oxford English Dictionary', *OxfordWords Blog*, 2016; https://blog.oxforddictionaries.com/2016/03/08/women-and-the-oed.

25 Editor Katharine Lee Bates also encountered the famously insalubrious Scriptorium. On a visit in 1890, she swooned from the heat and lack of air, much to the morbid pleasure of the staff, who appreciated any opportunity to demonstrate to Murray how unhealthy their working conditions were. Melinda M. Ponder, *From Sea to Shining Sea: The Story of the Poet of 'America the Beautiful'* (Chicago, IL: Windy City Publishers, 2017), pp. 95–96.

26 Thank you to Adam Hooks, who brought Bartlett to my attention. Adam G. Hooks, 'Precedent Bartlett', in the Women and Book History seminar (Shakespeare Association of America, Los Angeles, 2018).

27 Stephen H. Grant, *Collecting Shakespeare: The Story of Henry and Emily Folger* (Baltimore, MD: Johns Hopkins University Press, 2014), p. 36.

28 Quoted in Grant, *Collecting Shakespeare*, p. 35.

CHAPTER 3

'Give Ear, Sir, to My Sister'
Women Editors and Scholarly Networks in America

Whereas the previous chapter focused on women operating within primarily male networks, this chapter discusses the networks of female editors and academics that developed in nineteenth- and early twentieth-century America. As Andrew Murphy discusses in *Shakespeare in Print*, American Shakespeare publishing was slower out of the starting gate than its British counterpart. Large-scale printing and publication depended on the development of a practical infrastructure for such activities. To begin with, printing presses had to be built or shipped across the Atlantic. The first edition of the *Complete Works* printed outside Britain and Ireland was published in Philadelphia in 1795.[1] By the time of de Tocqueville's travels in 1831, when he commented on the omnipresence of Shakespeare in homes across America, multiple American editions existed, although many of them were reprints of British editions. An increasing number of texts edited by Americans appeared during the first half of the nineteenth century. The gradual acquisition of early exemplars of the folios and quartos by wealthy Americans facilitated more original editorial work, such as that done by Richard Grant White around 1860.[2] As a consequence of its slow growth, by the time home-grown Shakespeare publishing caught up with its British counterpart, American publishing houses already had a rich pool of educated editorial talent, male and female, on which to draw.

This was possible because while its Shakespearean publishing industry might have lagged behind, higher education for women began earlier in the United States than in England. Mount Holyoke Seminary, which would grow into one of the famed Seven Sisters schools, opened in 1837.[3] Its closest British equivalents, Queen's College and Bedford College in London, opened in 1847 and 1849, respectively. The early seminaries were not exact equivalents to all-male institutions, but they provided a testing ground for curricula and for the general precepts of women's higher education. Women's literacy in America has been estimated to have been

as high as 90 per cent by 1850, compared with 55 per cent in Britain. By
1872, women were writing almost three-quarters of the novels published in
the United States.[4] Experiments with coeducation began at Oberlin College
in Ohio in 1833. Founded on radical evangelical principles, Oberlin
admitted students of both genders, white and black; the first three women
graduated with bachelor's degrees in 1840. By 1870, when Girton College
was getting off the ground, 169 of the 582 institutions of higher education
in the United States were coeducational (29 per cent), and 70 schools
(12 per cent) were women's colleges.[5]

   It is rarely possible to trace a direct line of descent from woman editor to
woman editor, but the close connections among American academic
women during the period, particularly in the Seven Sisters schools, allow
us to do just that. None of this is to say that the women's colleges in
England, Scotland, Wales, and Ireland did not create networks of female
scholars. In terms of female editors, however, the materials needed to
demonstrate links have not been as well preserved. In general, the papers
of American women editors are more likely to have been preserved in large
collections than their transatlantic counterparts. The first generations of
American college women acknowledged and understood the historic
nature of their undertakings, so colleges such as Wellesley and Smith
maintain extremely rich archives relating to their faculty and alumnae.
Institutional affiliation significantly increases the odds that a woman
scholar's papers have been preserved. Obviously, any woman who achieved
fame in her own lifetime would be even more likely to preserve her papers
and to donate them to her own college. Several women editors fit this
description, but none more so than poet Katharine Lee Bates, who
attended Wellesley and became a professor of English there, serving as
head of department for many years. Best known for her poem 'America the
Beautiful', which became an iconic patriotic song and a top contender for
the national anthem, Bates edited numerous student editions, including
Merchant of Venice, *A Midsummer Night's Dream*, and *As You Like It*, all for
Boston-based Leach, Shewell, & Sanborn.[6] Bates's papers demonstrate the
depth of her scholarship, the significance of her influence, and her place at
the centre of a network of educated women editors.

Katharine Lee Bates

The Bates archive at Wellesley totals twenty-two catalogued boxes, as well
as an unknown amount of still unsorted material. It includes diaries,
letters, manuscripts, books, and lectures that span her life from childhood

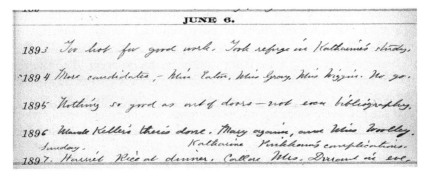

Figure 3.1 June 6 entry of Katharine Lee Bates's five-year diary. Image used by permission of the Wellesley College Archives, Library & Technology Services

until death.[7] Bates kept a five-year diary from 1893 until 1897, covering the years in which she produced her Shakespeare editions.[8] They are a remarkable resource, and provide enormous insight into Bates's life and work. The format of the journal allowed the diarist to record a few lines each day for five years, as shown in Figure 3.1.

Although the space was limited, Bates possessed a poet's ability to convey a great deal in very few words. Many entries consist of prosaic accountings of the weather or dinner guests, but in others her humour and intelligence shine through, as when on 24 April 1896 she writes, 'Almost made a friend today, but the stars are adverse.'[9] There are comments on the trials and tribulations of scholarship that will ring true for academics of any period: 'I don't know why anybody should write or read'; or, two days later, 'Life isn't worth living when it's making an index.'[10] More significantly, the diary makes it possible to chart exactly how much time she spent on *The Merchant of Venice*, her first edition, and gives a more general idea of the timeline of the other two projects. In addition, her archive contains letters that she wrote to her mother Cornelia and her sister Jane which expand on her progress and her opinions of her work.

Bates recorded in the diary that she '[broke] ground' on *Merchant* on 3 May 1894. Several frustrated entries followed that week, and then an entire month passed without mention of the play. During this month, Bates and her partner Katherine Coman travelled across the Atlantic to the United Kingdom, settling in Oxford for the summer. Coman was an economics professor at Wellesley. She and Bates spent their whole adult lives together, an arrangement common among educated middle-class women, particularly at women's colleges. These partnerships were sometimes called Boston (or Wellesley) marriages. When Coman died of cancer, Bates wrote a book of poetry entitled *Yellow Clover* in her memory.[11]

Beginning around 5 July, Bates worked in the Bodleian to collate the quarto and folio texts of *Merchant*.[12] A flurry of busy entries followed as she made her way through the text. On 8 July, she wrote to her mother that she had been 'enjoying my job so much that there's no telling when I shall finish it'.[13] To her sister, she explained that she had 'most unexpectedly become interested' in *Merchant*, but 'shall get it off presently'.[14] That same day, 12 July, she noted in her diary that she had finished the textual work. By 23 July, however, like every editor throughout history, she had discovered that the edition 'is more work than I had realized it would be' and averred that she must ignore her terrible toothache and stop writing letters or it 'will *never* be done'.[15] She gloomily predicted that even if she finished, the manuscript would probably be lost at sea before it reached the publishers in Boston. Luckily, it survived its sea voyage after being posted on 18 August. By the end of September, having returned to Wellesley, Bates noted that she was working on the proofs, which took her a month to complete back in the bustle of classes and coursework. On 26 October, she wrote that she was 'still busy' with the proofs, but 'almost done', and indeed, the preface of the published edition was dated November 1894. Overall, the process took her about seven months. At the end of the summer, just before sending off the manuscript, she told her mother that 'I have made a much more thorough piece of work than I expected, and I think it is, perhaps, a fairly good edition, but it has eaten up all the time.'[16]

Bates failed to give her work adequate credit. In fact, she produced a remarkable edition that demonstrates how insightful and useful a student edition could be when its execution was placed in the proper hands. Her editions appear to have been the first Shakespeare plays published in this series, the Student's Series of English Classics, so her approach to the format and contents may have been less constrained by precedent than that of the many editors who produced volumes for pre-existing series.[17] Bates's preface to *Merchant* explained the principles that guided her edition:

> Explanation is sometimes necessary, suggestion is often helpful; but the happiest and, in the end, the wisest student is he who makes the most discoveries. Taste and appreciation, critical judgment and discrimination, are developed through free exercise of the reader's own faculties, not by submission to authority.[18]

As detailed in her diary, Bates took the textual element of her edition extremely seriously, collating folio and quarto texts during her time at the Bodleian. The resulting text, she explained, followed the first folio 'somewhat closely', with quarto variations given in the notes. Although quarto readings or, very rarely, emendations were used in cases of 'manifestly' incorrect or 'inferior' folio options,

> in general the folio readings, even where the editor would personally reject them, are retained, with the design that each member of the class may have opportunity, by aid of the textual notes, of constructing a text for himself. It is suggested that the student, in hope of so sharpening his Shakespearian sense, con these notes carefully, and write into the play the readings which seem to him most worthy of the poet. Whatever perils wait upon the result, it is believed that the process will be beneficial.[19]

Each textual note included both the options available and a question prompting further thought and analysis, as seen in Figure 3.2. Bates thus created a democratic, open text in which her own opinions were subordinated to the goal of enhancing the student's experience. She invited engagement with the text's material history by deflecting the assumption of a single, authoritative reading, which had predominated in eighteenth-century editions, and by capitalising on students' pre-existing propensity to mark up their schoolbooks, encouraging them to take on an editorial role by writing in their preferred readings and emendations.

This approach is diametrically opposed to that of eighteenth-century editors, who adopted bombastic and argumentative tones in their notes, but it is in keeping with a shift towards more measured commentary that developed during the nineteenth century and had a particularly distinguished female proponent. Mary Cowden Clarke, the best-known woman editor of Shakespeare, eschewed the use of footnotes in her 1860 edition of the *Complete Works*, condemning notes as 'mere vehicles for abuse, spite, and arrogance ... written for the sole purpose ... of proving that other editors are wrong'.[20] Although Bates does not go so far as to exclude footnotes, her editorial approach, like Cowden Clarke's, feels both humble and entirely self-assured. Her references to other texts and critics are erudite, eclectic, and generally impartial, an attitude in keeping with her goal of encouraging reader engagement without demanding 'submission to authority'.

The year 1895 brought work on *A Midsummer Night's Dream* for the same series. Although the start date is less clear, Bates once again completed the bulk of the work over the summer vacation. A few of her notes from this period are particularly evocative: 'Have gotten to a state of calm

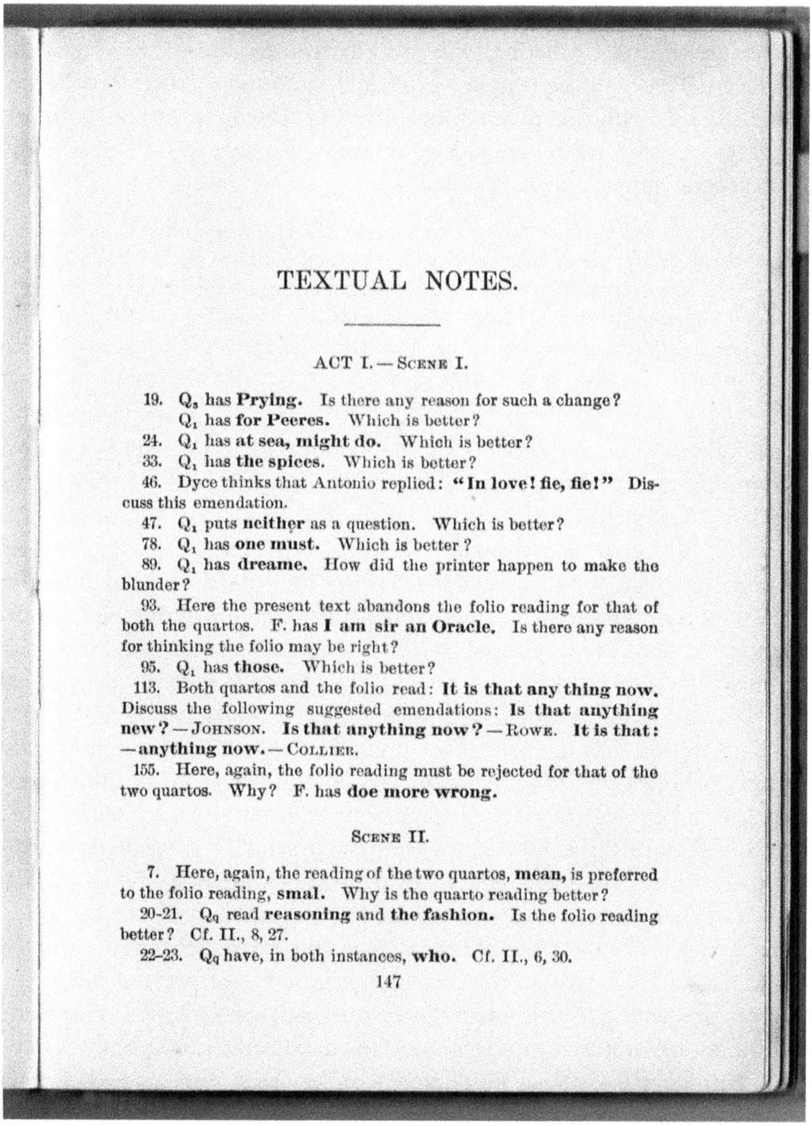

TEXTUAL NOTES.

ACT I. — SCENE I.

19. Q₂ has **Prying.** Is there any reason for such a change?
Q₁ has **for Peeres.** Which is better?

24. Q₁ has **at sea, might do.** Which is better?

33. Q₁ has **the spices.** Which is better?

46. Dyce thinks that Antonio replied: **"In love! fie, fie!"** Discuss this emendation.

47. Q₁ puts **neither** as a question. Which is better?

78. Q₁ has **one must.** Which is better ?

89. Q₁ has **dreame.** How did the printer happen to make the blunder?

93. Here the present text abandons the folio reading for that of both the quartos. F. has **I am sir an Oracle.** Is there any reason for thinking the folio may be right?

95. Q₁ has **those.** Which is better?

113. Both quartos and the folio read: **It is that any thing now.** Discuss the following suggested emendations: **Is that anything new ?** — JOHNSON. **Is that anything now ?** — ROWE. **It is that : — anything now.** — COLLIER.

155. Here, again, the folio reading must be rejected for that of the two quartos. Why? F. has **doe more wrong.**

SCENE II.

7. Here, again, the reading of the two quartos, **mean,** is preferred to the folio reading, **smal.** Why is the quarto reading better?

20-21. Q_q read **reasoning** and **the fashion.** Is the folio reading better? Cf. II., 8, 27.

22-23. Q_q have, in both instances, **who.** Cf. II., 6, 30.

147

Figure 3.2   First page of the 'Textual Notes' section of Bates's edition of *The Merchant of Venice* (p. 147). Photograph by the author.

despair over that *Introduction*' (7 August); 'Sunday, wrote hard in my wrapper all day on *Introd. to Mid. Night's Dream*' (18 August). The introduction that so vexed her ultimately began, 'When was *A Midsummer-Night's Dream* written? Three hundred years ago nobody cared, so to-day nobody knows.'[21] Like many editors before the advent of twentieth-century bibliography and its increased focus on an idealised editorial objectivity, Bates employed passionate, idiosyncratic, and occasionally overwrought prose to explore the play's history and contents. The play's structure garnered her particular attention, earning a description in her rather distinctive authorly voice: 'It ought to be all a jumble, and it is an artistic harmony. But how? What, in this that looks so helter-skelter, is the unifying truth? Here the scholars are at variance. The play is a twist of gold cord and rainbow silks, homespun yarn and shimmering moonbeams.'[22] Bates's analysis of the play cannot be called objective, but it is certainly engaging, as is appropriate for a volume intended to spark interest in students. The diagram of the plot included in the *Midsummer* introduction demonstrates Bates attempting to incorporate creative pedagogy into her editions. In *Midsummer*, she abandoned the separate section of questions that she had employed for *Merchant*. Instead, she incorporated questions into the literary notes, while decreasing their number significantly.

Bates's diary documented a similar four-month span of work on the 1896 edition of *As You Like It*. Again, the introduction showed her experimenting with the most useful content and format for the school edition. Bates returned to her original format in which the questions are separate from the notes, but she altered the design and page layout of the questions. In 1897, she wrote a letter to another publisher, who was interested in having her prepare student editions, explaining her philosophy on setting out questions, which had evolved in tandem with larger trends in school publishing: 'Groups of questions, following the chapters, break the narrative effect and are not, in themselves, invariably welcome to teachers.... Most of the present day school-histories of literature ... leave the questioning to the teacher.'[23] The introduction as a whole reflected Bates's long-standing interest in non-Shakespearian literature from the medieval and Renaissance periods. After referring the student to the earlier editions of *Merchant* and *Midsummer* for basic information on Shakespeare and Elizabethan theatre, suggesting the assumption that they would have access to those editions, Bates focused on a comparison between *As You Like It* and Lodge's *Rosalynde*. This included a twenty-four-page abridged version of *Rosalynde* in 'old-fashioned speech and spelling', edited by Bates specifically for this edition.[24] Since *As You Like It* is only extant in the Folio text, the preparation of the edition required less textual labour than *Merchant* or *Midsummer*; however, the abridged *Rosalynde* provided an opportunity for Bates to display additional editorial acumen.

Katharine Lee Bates's position at Wellesley and the longevity and success of her career allowed her to forge connections with many other editors of Shakespeare, including women. Bates's papers illuminate the extensive networks between women academics in the period, particularly those associated with women's colleges. Her diary reveals that during her time in Oxford in 1894, she wrote an article for *Poet Lore*, the magazine founded and edited by Shakespeare editors Charlotte Endymion Porter and Helen Archibald Clarke.[25] She also mentions meeting with them in person on a trip into Boston in 1895.[26] In 1896, she references a trip to Vassar during which she saw Laura Wylie, who went on to edit *A Winter's Tale* for the Tudor Shakespeare.[27] She maintained a long correspondence with the editor Edith Rickert, who was, along with Bates, hired to revise an edition of D. C. Heath's Arden Shakespeare series for reissue.[28] Bates's letters also include professional correspondence with British Shakespeareans such as F. G. Fleay and Sidney Lee, as well as a suggestion that she visit editor A. H. Bullen during an upcoming visit to Stratford.[29] In her preface to *Merchant*, Bates thanks William J. Rolfe, who, along with Henry Hudson, was one of the two biggest names in the field of American student editions of Shakespeare throughout the nineteenth century and well into the twentieth.[30] She also mentions Rolfe numerous times in her diaries. Horace Howard Furness wrote her a letter in 1895 after reading her edition of *Merchant*, expressing

> genuine admiration and delight, admiration for the thorough conscientious scholarship and wide reading of the Introduction, and delight of the sane and sympathetic dealing with the whole subject of notes, wherein it is most difficult to strike the happy mean between too little and too much. Happy as your selection of notes is, the best part of your book is the Introduction – a genuine contribution to the literature of the play.[31]

Bates's influence, like that of many editors of school editions, is difficult to quantify because her work was directed to students rather than the larger world of Shakespeare scholarship. Her editions were certainly used and read throughout the country. Charlotte Whipple Underwood, a Chicago teacher, acknowledged her debt to Bates's *Merchant* in her own 1899 edition of the play for Macmillan.[32] A used copy of Bates's *Merchant* includes marks identifying its owner as a resident of Salinas, California. Twenty years after their initial publication, *As You Like It* and *Midsummer* were reissued. Additional evidence of Bates's popular influence lies in the letters she received, most in response to 'America the Beautiful', but others regarding Shakespeare, such as the undated note from a teacher in Colorado named Ellen Louise Hill:

I'm in trouble here in my efforts to teach Shakespeare. I have a very large class, all bright and enthusiastic, and my wits are at a loss to know *how* to teach climaxes, incentive moments, catastrophe, and tragic moments! Can you help me? Will you? Will you place the above mentioned points in the following plays: Richard III, Hamlet, Othello, King Lear, Midsummer Night's Dream, and then tell me *what* to say to my class when they *insist* that it should be somewhere else?!

I know I am taking a great liberty in writing you in this strain, but in my despair I turn to you as an authority on everything Shakespearian. Please do pardon the liberty and give me a little light in my darkness.[33]

These two responses demonstrate the complex interplay between elevated and everyday scholarship present in the best examples of early student editions. Bates produced editions that spoke to students and distinguished Shakespeareans alike.

Perhaps most unusually, her relationship with another faculty member at Wellesley provides a direct link between two editions of the same play, both edited by women. Bates completed her edition of *As You Like It* in 1896. Martha Hale Shackford's edition of the same play was published by Macmillan as part of the Tudor Shakespeare series in 1911. Shackford attended Wellesley and subsequently became a member of the English department under Katharine Lee Bates. Bates was at once her teacher, her colleague, and her boss. They worked together for many years, and Bates was still head of the department when Shackford was preparing her edition. It is likely that Bates taught at least some of Shackford's classes on medieval and Renaissance literature during her time as a student. Shackford later wrote of Bates that

we who were undergraduates during the years when she established the major in English literature were constantly impressed by the range of her reading, the remarkable tenacity of her memory, the scope and aptness of her allusions, and, most of all, by her sensitiveness to aspects of imaginative beauty. Yet her awareness of ideal values did not prevent her from being a teacher who gently but firmly demanded from students sound knowledge, scrupulous accuracy of detail, and fastidiousness of form. Though often seeming shy in the classroom she was, when roused by argument, unmatched in repartee. Always there was a certain piquancy, in her conduct of a class, due to unexpected, stimulating modes of approaching a subject, and she was capable of gay and teasing innuendoes regarding the stolidity of some of our appreciation of great literature.[34]

This description of Bates is entirely consistent with the editorial voice present in her student editions and demonstrates how effectively Bates translated her own pedagogical personality into written guidance for students far outside the borders of the Wellesley campus.

The Tudor Shakespeare

Macmillan's Tudor Shakespeare series stands apart from its contemporaries in the number of women employed to edit individual volumes: five of the thirty-nine editors were women. The five women were Laura J. Wylie (*The Winter's Tale*, 1912), Virginia Gildersleeve (*King Lear*, 1912), Martha Hale Shackford (*As You Like It*, 1911), Elizabeth Deering Hanscom (*2 Henry IV*, 1912), and Louise Pound (*1 Henry VI*, 1911). Why did this series draw on the talents of so many women? The answer probably lies with one of the series editors, William Allan Neilson. Both Neilson and the other series editor, Ashley Horace Thorndike, clearly farmed out volumes to academics with whom they had pre-existing connections. At least eight of the editors came from universities at which Thorndike or Neilson had either studied or worked.[35] Neilson in particular had a strong connection to women's higher education. His first teaching job after moving to America from Scotland was at Bryn Mawr. He went on to Harvard, where one of his Radcliffe students was Helen Keller. He is remembered as the only professor who learned her version of sign language.[36] He later became the president of Smith College. It seems likely that his sympathy for women in academia extended to his practices as a series editor.

Neilson's career affiliations highlight an early argument amongst proponents of women's education in both America and England: whether single-sex colleges should hire only female faculty members. A major irony involved in discussing the female networks of American college women is that one must acknowledge how many men are involved in those networks. Of the Seven Sisters colleges, only Wellesley committed itself to hiring women academics.[37] At its most fundamental level, all-female Radcliffe was a Harvard annex, as all classes at Radcliffe were taught by Harvard professors. At Vassar, a quarter of the faculty and most department heads were male, and as president of Smith, Neilson recruited and promoted more men than women.[38] According to their advocates, these policies gave the colleges an advantage over women's colleges like Wellesley, where the primarily female faculty members would have had less formal education and fewer official degrees. Even a professor as distinguished as Katharine Lee Bates worried about whether she could be considered qualified to teach at the university level when hired by Wellesley in 1893. At the time, she held only her Wellesley bachelor's degree; she was later awarded a master's degree based on the strength of her academic publications since graduation.

By 1911, however, when the first volumes of the Tudor Shakespeare were published, opportunities for graduate studies had grown, and women were taking full advantage of them. All five of the women who edited for the Tudor Shakespeare held PhDs, while five of the male editors held only bachelor's or master's degrees. In fact, women were first admitted to some older universities through graduate courses, even while the undergraduate programs at the same universities refused to become co-educational. Laura J. Wylie and Elizabeth Deering Hanscom were two of the first seven women to graduate with PhDs from Yale in 1894, although Yale's undergraduate programs did not become co-educational until 1969.[39] After earning their PhDs, Wylie taught at Vassar, where she had received her undergraduate degree, and Hanscom at Smith.

The Tudor series represents a relatively rigid, standardised version of the student edition, very unlike Bates's experimental forms. It also demonstrates, however, an awareness of the sophistication of the consumer. All of the individual volumes used the 1906 Neilson text, published by Houghton Mifflin, so the volume editors did not make textual decisions, although they could comment on them in their notes. The use of Neilson's text led to a particularly interesting exchange between Neilson and a Macmillan staff member. Seeking publicity information about the text, Doris H. Taylor wrote to Neilson:

> It is our understanding that you went back to original sources and that so far as possible, existing editions were compared with old manuscripts line for line. Any information which you can give us which will help us to impress Shakespearean scholars with the merits and authenticity of the text will be greatly appreciated.[40]

Neilson replied rather firmly:

> Be sure not to say anything about manuscripts as there are no Shakespearian manuscripts. The earliest quartos and folios were collated word for word. I would be very glad if you could let me see your statement before it goes out since inaccuracies of a technical sort are apt to harm the publicity with teachers and others who may happen to have special knowledge.[41]

Neilson's concern about the details of the publicity suggests how competitive the school edition market had become by the 1920s, and how textually aware the potential consumer could be imagined to be.

Nationalism was also part of the Tudor Shakespeare's marketing, with the advertisements noting that all of the volume editors were American

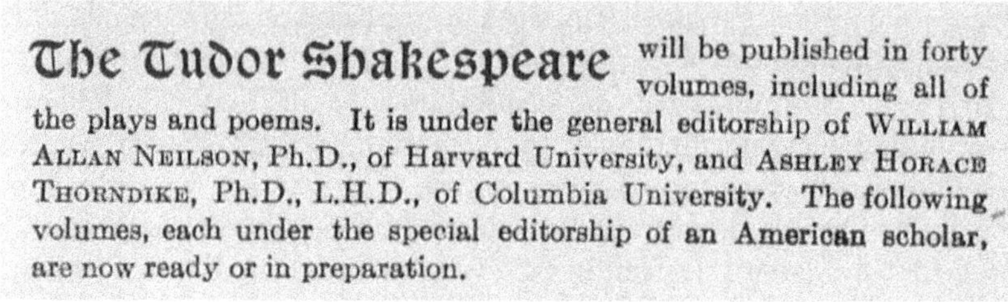

The Tudor Shakespeare will be published in forty volumes, including all of the plays and poems. It is under the general editorship of WILLIAM ALLAN NEILSON, Ph.D., of Harvard University, and ASHLEY HORACE THORNDIKE, Ph.D., L.H.D., of Columbia University. The following volumes, each under the special editorship of an American scholar, are now ready or in preparation.

Figure 3.3   Advertisement for the Tudor Shakespeare in Wylie's *The Winter's Tale* (1912). Photograph by the author.

scholars. Emphasising the 'Made in America' aspect of editions prepared by American scholars became a common selling point for school editions during the nineteenth century, as seen in Figure 3.3. William J. Rolfe, editor of one of the most important school series in America, encouraged American teachers and readers to use American editions (particularly his own, obviously), claiming that they were better suited to their educational needs than British editions could ever be.[42]

Royalty records kept by Neilson show each volume's sales in the two decades after its launch. Letters between Neilson and Macmillan reflect disappointment in sales numbers after the first few years of publication. They therefore initiated a marketing campaign and relaunch in 1922, which seem to have been successful.[43] Unfortunately, Neilson's papers include sales numbers only from 1917–21 and 1929–33, but Figure 3.4 gives a sense of the sales numbers for the five volumes edited by women, as well as four other popular titles in the series, during these periods and shows that the jump in sales after the relaunch decreased within five years.[44]

King Lear was by some margin the most popular of the five volumes edited by women, selling over 5,000 copies during the years documented in Neilson's accounts. In many ways, *Lear* editor Virginia Gildersleeve exemplified the deepening connections between women in academia. In 1919, she founded the International Federation of University Women with Caroline Spurgeon and Rose Sidgwick, with the goal of creating links between educated women to help prevent another war.[45] As the dean of all-women Barnard College, she built up the school's influence and increased opportunities for its students. Her legacy is not entirely unmixed, however; like Neilson, she primarily hired men for senior faculty positions, relegating women to more junior roles in an attempt to attract better-known male scholars. She later wrote that 'perhaps this was discrimination against women, but it was, I am sure, for the good of the college'.[46] In 1945,

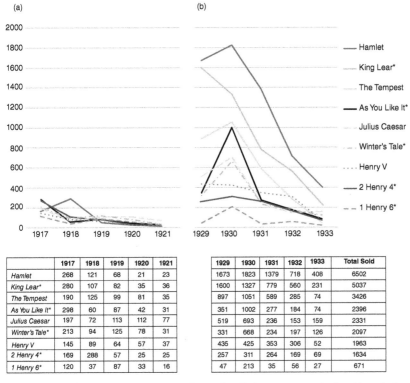

	1917	1918	1919	1920	1921
Hamlet	268	121	68	21	23
*King Lear**	280	107	82	35	36
The Tempest	190	125	99	81	35
*As You Like It**	298	60	87	42	31
Julius Caesar	197	72	113	112	77
*Winter's Tale**	213	94	125	78	31
Henry V	145	89	64	57	37
*2 Henry 4**	169	288	57	25	25
*1 Henry 6**	120	37	87	33	16

	1929	1930	1931	1932	1933	Total Sold
	1673	1823	1379	718	408	6502
	1600	1327	779	560	231	5037
	897	1051	589	285	74	3426
	351	1002	277	184	74	2396
	519	693	236	153	159	2331
	331	668	234	197	126	2097
	435	425	353	306	52	1963
	257	311	264	169	69	1634
	47	213	35	56	27	671

Figure 3.4 Sales figures of volumes in the Tudor Shakespeare series before (a) and after (b) the relaunch. Data compiled from documents in the William Allan Neilson Personal Papers, Box 47, Folder 1081, Smith College

President Franklin Delano Roosevelt chose Gildersleeve as the only female member of the United States delegation sent to help draft the United Nations' Charter. Neilson, her series editor and colleague, said that it was unfortunate that she was the only woman included, 'but that will not matter if only the men will listen'.[47] Her influence helped convince the delegates to include language on human rights in the Charter, and to require the appointment of the Commission on Human Rights.

The career of the editor of *1 Henry VI*, Louise Pound, also demonstrates the growing influence of women in public and professional academic circles. After receiving her BA and MA from the University of Nebraska, where she was an athletic star and co-editor of the literary magazine with her lifelong friend Willa Cather, she attended the

University of Heidelberg for her PhD before returning to Nebraska to teach at her alma mater. Throughout her life, she fought for increased opportunities for women in graduate studies and research posts. She served as the vice president of the American Association of University Women, and in 1955, she became the first woman president of the Modern Language Association.[48] Although it took several more decades for the MLA to begin seriously to address the needs of its women members – one critic pointed out in 1972 that although the MLA had had two female presidents in its history, it had yet to have a feminist president – Pound's election signalled the slow movement of women from the outskirts of academia into the mainstream.[49] Pound, Gildersleeve, and the other women leaders of their generation may not have accomplished as much as their descendants would have liked, but they made major strides in deepening the networks linking female academics in America and around the world.

Women as Revision Editors

Another avenue through which women became involved in the editorial process was the phenomenon of revising and re-releasing older editions. Many scholars consider Richard Grant White's first edition of the *Complete Works*, published in the 1860s, to be the first original, innovative edition of Shakespeare published in America.[50] White went on to edit the first edition of the *Riverside Shakespeare*, which remains an institution in America. Following the success of the *Riverside*'s initial release in 1883, publisher Houghton Mifflin decided to release the plays as individual school editions, supplemented and revised for students' use. Of the eleven individual editions that seem to have been completed for the first series, released from around 1892 till 1912, three – *Hamlet*, *Macbeth*, and *Twelfth Night* – were edited by Helen Gray Cone, while Laura Emma Lockwood of Wellesley edited *A Midsummer Night's Dream*. The hiring of Cone and Lockwood to revise and expand White's Riverside texts becomes particularly interesting in light of White's own statements denigrating women readers of Shakespeare.[51] In the preface to the *Riverside Shakespeare*, White wrote that 'in determining what passages were sufficiently obscure to justify explanation, the editor ... took the advice of his washerwoman', said woman being, presumably, on the lowest possible rung on the ladder of literacy, and therefore an appropriate marker to determine what was and was not comprehensible in Shakespeare.[52] Gender is an issue at several points in White's essay 'On Reading Shakespeare':

It is hard for these men [true lovers of Shakespeare] to apprehend that there are others not without intelligence and education, and who read, who have not read Shakespeare, or who having read a little of him do not read more. But there are such men; and there are still many more such women. On the whole I am inclined to think that Shakespeare is not a woman's poet. He deals too largely with life; he handles the very elements of human nature; he has a great fancy, but is not fanciful; his imagination moulds the essential and the central rather than the external; he is rarely sentimental, never except in his youngest work. Women, with the exception of a few who are not always the most lovable or the happiest of the sex, like something upon a lower plane, something that appeals more directly to them, because it was written to appeal directly to someone else (for in literature that which is directed to one point always keeps its aim); they like the personal, the external; that which seems to be showing them either themselves or some other real person. Shakespeare's humor ... is appreciated by still fewer women than the number who find pleasure in his poetry. They receive it in rather a dazed fashion, and don't know exactly what it means, all this, just as they would rather look at a woman of the first fashion in a dress of their time than at the grand simplicity of ideal woman in the Venus (so-called) of Melos.[53]

In his view, the shallowness of female thought prevents appreciation of Shakespeare, and even those who seek to improve have no recourse in White's eyes.

Like Katharine Lee Bates, White's fame as a Shakespeare scholar led people to write to him for advice on how best to approach Shakespeare. White had no patience for such inquiries:

Most of those who have asked [how to read Shakespeare] are, I am inclined to think, very young, as indeed some of them say they are; and a large proportion are plainly girls just beginning to feel their way in literature, and they ask, in the words of one of them, 'How shall I begin? and which plays shall I read first, so as to be sure to like them and their author?' Such uncertainty, I must confess, does not promise any genuine, strong taste for Shakespeare. Boys are of slower mental growth than girls, especially upon the poetical and sentimental side; but no boy who is a born Shakespeare-lover needs to ask such a question as that at sixteen. He has then already stepped in too far to pick his way or to turn back.[54]

Although based in similar precepts, his tone and attitude are a far cry from Katharine Lee Bates's urging that students develop their critical faculties through 'free exercise' of their own faculties rather than 'submission to authority'.[55] White speaks with authority even while scorning those who turn to authority for guidance, demanding submission as he criticises those who submit. His own advice to new readers was to eschew criticism and annotated editions altogether for one's first reading, relying only on one's own engagement with the words to establish the most full and true appreciation of Shakespeare. As such, the essential purpose of a student edition was antithetical to White's opinions. Unsurprisingly, the conversion of his edition into student texts did not take place until after White's death, when his widow held the copyright. Given his doubts about women's natural abilities in regard to Shakespeare, the fact that his work was co-opted and supplemented by female Shakespeareans feels particularly ironic.[56]

Helen Gray Cone (1859–1934) spent her entire career at her alma mater, the Normal College of the City of New York, now known as Hunter College. She achieved particular fame as a poet, but she was well-known within the college for her courses on Shakespeare and Romantic authors.[57] Like many early women academics, she demonstrated a remarkable loyalty to her school. In 1945, Vida Dutton Scudder wrote a letter to the new president of Hunter admitting that the Wellesley English faculty had unsuccessfully tried to poach Cone for their own program many years before.[58] Women like Laura Wylie, Martha Hale Shackford, and Louise Pound returned to their undergraduate colleges to take up teaching posts even after leaving to earn postgraduate degrees elsewhere.[59] In this way, the colleges began cultivating their own home-grown talent and using that talent to increase the prestige of their faculties. Cone became the first woman to hold a professorship at all-female Hunter College, that position having been previously held only by male faculty.

These changing standards and expectations sometimes created tension within departments. Laura Emma Lockwood (1863–1956) emerged from the same University of Nebraska programme that produced Louise Pound (1 Henry VI, Tudor Shakespeare) and Willa Cather. After earning her PhD at Yale, she took a teaching position in the English department at Wellesley in 1899 under the leadership of Katharine Lee Bates. There, she developed a rivalry with fellow professor Sophie Hart, who enjoyed seniority over Lockwood despite her lack of a doctoral degree. Coming from outside the Wellesley breeding ground, Lockwood may have felt less respectful of the generational mentor–protégé relationships common within the faculty. Patricia Palmieri cites another similar feud in which an outsider who came from a large co-educational university felt superior to her Wellesley-educated colleagues.[60] The period of overlap between the first generation of women professors and their more officially accredited successors was often characterised by strain among faculty members, particularly as the older 'war horses' refused to hand over responsibilities to the newer generation.[61]

In Cone's editions, in order to distinguish White's work from that of the new editor, all additional annotations appear within square brackets. Those square-bracketed notes far outnumber White's original, minimal glossing. The editions retain White's short introductions to each play but supplement them after the play text with a long section of questions and analysis, including extensive characterological commentary, by Cone. White did not engage in character analysis in the *Riverside*, so the limited critical material restricts the conclusions that can be drawn from the edition itself. Luckily, however, White wrote long critical pieces on both *Hamlet* and *Macbeth* for a different book, allowing for a fuller consideration of how Cone's influence shaped the student editions in opposition to White's stated views. The character of Lady Macbeth in particular offers a visible point of comparison and demonstrates the power that an editor wields when presenting texts to students.

Originally published in the *Massachusetts Ploughman and New England Journal of Agriculture*'s 'Ladies' Department' section in 1870, White's essay entitled 'The Lady Gruach's Husband' also appears in a posthumous collection of his writing called *Studies in Shakespeare*, published in 1885, a decade before Cone's revised edition of *Macbeth*.[62] In this aggressively misogynistic piece, White conspicuously uses the adjective 'imaginative' when describing Lady Macbeth, contrasting the 'less imaginative' woman to her husband. Here, 'imaginative' seems more related to idealism and abstract thought than creativity. White applies the descriptor to women in general, explaining that unlike men, who 'love power for its own sake … women, less imaginative, and, outside of love, more practical and material than men', desire power in part for the 'visible elevation' it provides them, but 'more for that which it enables them to give to those they love'.[63] In Lady Macbeth's case,

> unimaginative, without tenderness, with a cruel, remorseless nature and a bright, clear intellect that saw at once the end that she desired and the means of its attainment, she was a type of those female politicians who in the past ages of the world's moral rudeness have sought, and, by intrigue, by suggestion, and by the stimulus of sexual temptation and feminine craft which made the strength of men their instrument, have attained, that great end of woman's ambition, social preëminence.

'A tigress', White claims, 'has not less compunction when she bears a white gasping infant off into the jungle.'[64] Of course, many critics and readers have embraced the interpretation of Lady Macbeth as the primary instigator of the couple's crimes. White's larger misogyny lies in how he applies Lady Macbeth's actions and motives to the majority of woman-kind. Women, according to White, will sacrifice everything for the benefit of their men, 'and sometimes their sisters; and have been known to rejoice even in the triumphs of their dearest female friends', but a clever woman who lacks 'tenderness' is, perforce, 'the most unscrupulous and remorseless creature under the canopy of heaven'.[65]

Cone's analysis reuses some aspects of White's reading while also reformulating it, restricting it to Lady Macbeth as an individual rather than as an exemplar of her gender. In the process she reconfigures the adjective 'imaginative', which White deployed frequently. Regarding Act 2, Scene 1, Cone writes that

> Throughout this superb scene there is a contrast between the emotional and imaginative Macbeth, and his wife, who is not only far less emotional and imaginative, but who has all her powers under the control of an inflexible will. It must be strongly emphasized that this is a contrast of organization, and not of moral condition. At the end of the scene we cannot justly pronounce that Macbeth is remorseful, his wife incapable of remorse; judgment must be reserved until the end of the play.[66]

Here, 'imaginative' becomes a more neutral descriptor. Lady Macbeth possesses a 'singleness of purpose. Her nature ... is simple and balanced; all her powers work together. She is rapid, clear, and direct of thought, and her will is as strong as steel.'[67] While similar to White's interpretation in points such as her ambition on her husband's behalf, a reader can find more to admire in Cone's Lady Macbeth than in White's. A student first encountering Macbeth through White's critical materials would have a different experience than one primed with Cone's introduction. Cone appears to have constructed her arguments so as to build on and respond to White's original position, subverting his points while giving them a place in the editions that still bear his name and authority.

Other publishers did not grant their revising editors so much power. In the early part of the twentieth century, D. C. Heath's Arden Shakespeare series seemingly relaunched itself partly in an effort to appeal to the American market. As Andrew Murphy notes, the series has a convoluted print history, and was completely unrelated to the Arden Shakespeare published by Methuen.[68] Never completed, the earliest volumes appeared around 1895, and new editions continued to be released until around 1932. This included an edition of 2 Henry IV edited by Welsh academic Lilian Winstanley. At some point around 1910–15, Heath began reissuing earlier volumes revised by new editors. Unlike the originals, these were

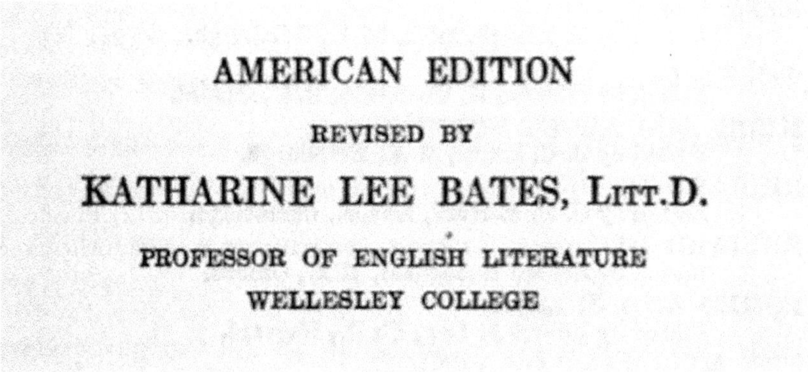

AMERICAN EDITION

REVISED BY

KATHARINE LEE BATES, Litt.D.

PROFESSOR OF ENGLISH LITERATURE

WELLESLEY COLLEGE

Figure 3.5   Title page of *The Tempest*, edited by Frederick Boas, revised by
Katharine Lee Bates (D.C. Heath, 1916). Courtesy of Hathitrust.
https://catalog.hathitrust.org/Record/004413347

'American editions', prepared by American editors. The publisher had
always been the Boston-based D. C. Heath, but the initial volumes were
mostly edited by British scholars. Like the Tudor Shakespeare, the publishers hoped to appeal to the American market with an emphasis on
'home-grown' scholarship, as illustrated in Figure 3.5.

Before the interruption in publication, an advertisement shows that
Professor Martha Foote Crow had been hired to edit *King Lear*, but the
Lear ultimately released in 1902 was edited by D. N. Smith.[69] Most of the
revision editors were men, but Heath hired Katharine Lee Bates to revise
Frederick Boas's edition of *The Tempest* (1916) and Edith Rickert to revise
E. K. Chambers's *A Midsummer Night's Dream* (1919).[70]

The changes made in the revised editions seem minimal, mostly
intended to bring the original introductions up to date with changes in
scholarship. Some of the possible restrictions placed on the revision editors
are visible in Edith Rickert's edition. In 1923, she published two articles in
Modern Philology, explaining her reasons for believing that *Midsummer* was
written in honour of the entertainment given for Queen Elizabeth by the
Earl of Hertford at Elvetham, rather than for the weddings to which it is
more commonly connected.[71] Although she begins the paper by explaining that she developed the theory while preparing the edition, no indication of her endorsement appears in the published edition, which sticks to
Chambers's original explanation regarding the possible wedding connections, mentioning Elvetham only briefly in an appendix.[72]

Ohio-born Edith Rickert attended Vassar as an undergraduate, completing her bachelor's degree in 1891. She then moved to London, where she wrote freelance and 'devilled' in the British Museum for others.[73] Martha Foote Crow, the University of Chicago professor originally hired by Heath to edit *King Lear*, was one of several academics who hired Rickert to carry out research in the Museum.[74] Rickert stayed in London until around 1897, during which time she registered as a doctoral candidate at the University of Chicago. In 1897, Rickert returned to Vassar, where she worked as an instructor while completing her thesis. She was supervised at Vassar by the Tudor Shakespeare editor Laura Wylie, who served as head of the English department for over two decades. After an initial positive impression, Rickert found Wylie to be extremely difficult. On 9 January 1898, Rickert wrote in her diary that

> an interview with Miss W. just used me up. I don't know what to think of her or myself any more. She appears to think me on the whole second-rate, but yet in her summing up, she is so inconsistent that I cannot feel that her judgment is right. It's all a perfect jumble. If I am losing my grasp of things, it's time to take hold of the matter & stop it. Is it true? Sally says not, but then she is prejudiced by our friendship. Perfectly helpless, hopeless, yet I've got to prove to her that she's wrong – got to – or I shall regret it all my life. It's hard because she admits that she is prejudiced agst [*sic*] me, but it's got to be done – somehow.[75]

Several weeks' worth of depressed entries follow before another meeting with Wylie on January 24:

> Another talk with my respected chief. Not much satisfaction. She grants that I may have a little brain – a little power to attack 'intellectual problems' but makes an entirely new charge – lack of 'literary sense'. Drop the subject. I am curious to know how it will come out; but I shall & cannot stay here more than one year longer. For Ethel's sake I'll do that, if possible. More dead than alive tonight.[76]

True to her word, Rickert left Vassar as soon as possible, returning to London to once again write freelance and research for herself and others.

While the Rickert–Wylie relationship demonstrates again that dealings amongst women academics were not always filled with sororal good will and fellowship, Rickert also maintained a long correspondence with a significantly more supportive mentor, her fellow Arden reviser Katharine Lee Bates. Bates admired Rickert for leaving teaching to write full-time, a consummation Bates devoutly wished for but never achieved. Bates remarked in one letter that 'we are all colleagues, are we not, in the patient years of teaching and the secret "urge" ... toward the free pen?'[77] In around 1909, Rickert moved from London to Boston, where she joined the editorial department at D. C. Heath and the *Ladies' Home Journal*, a situation that Bates judged 'better, but still not just right' for her friend.[78] Rickert therefore worked for Heath during the re-release of the Arden volumes, which explains her own involvement as volume editor, and potentially Bates's as well.

After a few years, Rickert moved to Washington, DC, to assist with the war effort. Both Edith and her sister Margaret worked as codebreakers during the world wars, Edith during the first, and Margaret during the second. In this they followed the urging of fellow editor Virginia Gildersleeve, who encouraged educated girls to join the war effort, insisting that their talents would be valued. She pointed out that 'even the training in research given to candidates for the Ph.D. degree, long held up to ridicule as the very epitome of uselessness, is in many cases proving its worth'.[79] In a speech after the First World War, Gildersleeve encouraged her listeners to 'never stop any research of your own that you are engaged in because you think it is of no use', justifying it with a Shakespeare-related anecdote:

> I have tried, at times, to teach Shakespeare, and like many who would be good Shakespeare scholars, I have had great contempt for the Baconians. There was a distinguished, rather prominent, enthusiastic Baconian in this country who had collected, in connection with his researches, the most complete set of books in codes and ciphers that I believe existed in the country. They found extraordinary codes and ciphers of use in explaining how Bacon began to write the books of Shakespeare, and books of codes are all interesting. This Baconian had collected a really remarkable library on codes and ciphers and when the United States entered the War, the decoding of ciphers was quite an important task that fell to the Intelligence department of the Army, and the Baconian's library proved very useful. So even such an eccentric field as this was practical.[80]

After the war, Rickert moved to Chicago to collaborate with John Matthews Manly, and in the 1920s, she joined the faculty at the University of Chicago.[81] She went on to co-edit one of the most important Chaucer projects of the twentieth century, the Chicago Chaucer Research Project. Unsurprisingly, the Chaucer project employed a number of women, including two of the three primary researchers who finished the project after Manly's and Rickert's deaths.[82] In this, Rickert carried on the legacy of supporting and offering opportunities to younger female colleagues.[83]

Charlotte Endymion Porter and Helen Archibald Clarke

Of all the women editing Shakespeare in America, the most well-known held no university posts. Their careers do not fit neatly into the preceding moulds and statistics. Rather, Charlotte Endymion Porter and Helen Archibald Clarke blazed their own trail into the increasingly rarefied world of Shakespeare studies. Nancy Glazener writes that the pair '[epitomised] some of the best tendencies of nineteenth-century public literary culture' because they 'combined scholarly seriousness, a taste for innovation, and fandom'.[84] Their uniqueness has also ensured that when scholars began investigating the history of women editing Shakespeare, they were among the first to be rediscovered and lauded. In the conclusion to her article on their literary accomplishments, Jeanne Addison Roberts suggests that 'their work should be belatedly recognized as a landmark in the history of editing, and that they should be recognized as a welcome addition to the long-standing brotherhood of "the Shakespearian editorial club"'.[85] Although modern recognition is well-deserved, there is no need to retroactively add Porter and Clarke to a club in which they were, in their own time, card-carrying members. Porter and Clarke represent the most visible point of osmosis between the supposed 'brotherhood' and 'sisterhood' of Shakespeare editors in America.

Clarke and Porter met when Clarke submitted an article to *Shakespeariana*, a literary publication edited by Porter. Neither came from the better-known women's colleges or coeducational schools – Porter attended Wells College in upstate New York, and Clarke received a certificate from the University of Pennsylvania (not yet co-educational at the time) and studied at the Sorbonne. After Porter resigned from *Shakespeariana*, the pair founded the literary magazine *Poet Lore*, now the oldest continuously running poetry journal in the United States, in 1889.[86] As editors of both publications, Porter and Clarke occupied a significant place in the American literary world around the turn of the century. They served as gatekeepers and tastemakers. Although they founded *Poet Lore* to promote the study of Shakespeare and Robert Browning, Porter and Clarke also championed Ibsen, Strindberg, Chekhov, and the emerging Irish literary drama in its pages.[87] They also supported other women. Not including its editors, in its first decade, *Poet Lore* included work by ninety-five female contributors, many of whom wrote multiple pieces for the journal during that period.[88] When Porter and Clarke's substantial contributions are taken into account, more than half the material published in that decade came from women, including women editors Katharine Lee Bates, Pauline Wiggin, and Charlotte Carmichael Stopes. In the following years, they also published work by editors Helen Gray Cone and Maud Elma Kingsley.[89]

Over a decade after founding *Poet Lore*, the first volumes of Porter and Clarke's First Folio and Pembroke editions appeared, printed by Thomas Y. Crowell of New York.[90] The Pembroke was a simplified, 'general reader' version of the forty-volume First Folio edition. The first four volumes of the First Folio edition were prepared by both women, after which Clarke moved on to other interests, leaving Porter to complete the other thirty-six on her own.[91] In terms of sheer volume of work, this was an incredible achievement. As John Dover Wilson wrote in a 1937 letter to bibliographer Henrietta Bartlett, 'I had no idea ... that Charlotte Porter could possibly have been responsible for two complete editions of the Works of Shakespeare, both beginning in 1903, but such is the incredible fact.'[92] Emma Smith identifies Porter and Clarke's edition as the first 'First Folio' edition prepared for modern readers following a century of calls for it and an increasing reliance on the First Folio's authority by editors.[93] When the first volumes appeared, Oxford professor Walter Raleigh, who had been attempting to convince Oxford University Press to do a First Folio edition, wrote to Charles Cannan at the Press that '[t]his is a hard business. It's exactly the book. I could do without the introductions, and the side-notes are often unnecessary and sometimes wrong. But the rest is all right, and I think, is exactly what is needed.... I don't see a way past ... these two advanced ladies.'[94] Some references to the editions among Press employees and editors were decidedly gendered. One letter to editor David Nichol Smith referred to their edition of *King Lear* as 'the Ladies' Lear'.[95] In another letter, Clarendon Press secretary R. W. Chapman noted that 'I daresay you know the "Folio" Shakespeare which is being dribbled out of two American ladies.... It is said to be good.'[96] Perhaps 'dribbling' is exactly the verbiage one should expect from a man who would later crib and fail to credit his wife Katherine Metcalfe Chapman's editorial work on Jane Austen.[97]

In the introduction to the London printing of the First Folio edition, John Churton Collins writes that Porter and Clarke's goal has been to empower everyday readers, to free them from dependence on 'what the poet's editors have chosen to give' them, those editors mostly being 'cranks and fribbles'.[98] That inherited text, Collins asserts, is 'a concoction the quality and characteristics of which have been determined partly by the idiosyncrasies of particular editors, and partly by the literary tastes and fashions of particular epochs'.[99] This is a fairly accurate summary of

Porter's feelings on the matter. Discussing a crux in Keats in a letter to Richard Gilder, poet and editor of *The Century Magazine*, Porter colourfully expresses her opinion of many Shakespeare editors:

> I am sure it is one of those punctilious external corrections of prosaic editors, such as they have administered to that 'careless' consummate artist, Will Shakespeare, till they have made that curious amalgam of three centuries they call the 'standard text' more multifariously and anachronistically *corrupt* with their 'corrections' than that of any other English poet.
>
> I came across an interesting instance recently wherein the *real* word has since the First Folio never seen the light. And it is most up to date. It puts Willy in the category of those who see that disadvantage to the younger brother where the laud is taken from him, and he is legally made poor.[100]

Although Raleigh and the Oxford University Press delegates criticised Porter and Clarke's paratextual materials, other critics have found useful details in their introductions; J. Dover Wilson, for example, was impressed by Porter's foresight in demonstrating that Richard Grant White's then-popular theory regarding the date of *Richard II*'s composition arose from a bibliographical error.[101] In addition to the critical material in their editions, the two women also produced an extremely well-regarded set of study guides for the plays, originally published in *Poet Lore*, then collected and released separately.[102] The guides were aimed at study circles or clubs. Self-education and social learning were immensely popular in nineteenth-century America, particularly among women, and *Poet Lore* published the reports of Browning, Shakespeare, and general literary clubs across the country.[103] Their editions of Shakespeare cannot be regarded as 'school texts' on their own, but taken in conjunction with their study guides, Porter and Clarke's body of work contain a strong emphasis on education and teaching. Via *Shakespeariana*, *Poet Lore*, and their editions, they reached many readers of varying education levels, bridging, like Katharine Lee Bates, the divide between 'high' and 'low' scholarship. While doing so, they also helped to create space for women in the national literary dialogue. And in fact, their Shakespeare text immediately became a multigenerational part of women's editorial history – only a year after its 1903 publication, the publishers licensed the Pembroke text to Doubleday, Page, who reprinted it as a new illustrated series, complete with new introductions by Esther Wood.[104]

Porter and Clarke were exceptional in their degree of scholarly independence; however, for those less fortunate, the spaces and networks established around the framework of the American women's colleges provided crucial support for scholarly activities. As a result, many of the American women who edited Shakespeare were directly connected via the extensive network of women's and coeducational colleges. They attended the same schools, taught in the same departments, and wrote for the same publications. These relationships involved but did not revolve around male scholars. As is still the case, carrying out editorial work required a high level of financial, institutional, and social privilege. Women editors relied not only on the financial support of their universities but often on the domestic support of family and partners. Although most remained unmarried, or stopped working after marriage, many early women professors, including Katherine Lee Bates, lived with widowed mothers and unmarried sisters, who often handled domestic duties and assisted with their research, even serving as their amanuenses. They formed lifelong domestic partnerships, or 'Boston marriages', with fellow professors. These stories further underscore the point that no editor is an island – all editorial work involves the support and input of myriad people and institutions.

Notes

1 Murphy, *Shakespeare in Print*, p. 145.
2 Murphy, *Shakespeare in Print*, p. 154; for details about the transatlantic migration of the First Folios, see Anthony James West, *The Shakespeare First Folio: The History of the Book, vol. II: A New Worldwide Census of First Folios* (Oxford: Oxford University Press, 2003); Emma Smith, *Shakespeare's First Folio: Four Centuries of an Iconic Book* (Oxford: Oxford University Press, 2016). For a 1916 census of the quartos, prepared in part by a woman, see Henrietta C. Bartlett and Alfred W. Pollard, *A Census of Shakespeare's Plays in Quarto, 1594–1709* (New Haven, CT: Yale University Press, 1916). Bartlett is discussed further in this book in the sidenote 'On Women Editing Not-Shakespeare (or Not Editing)'.
3 'History', Mount Holyoke College, 2012, www.mtholyoke.edu/about/history.
4 Barbara Sicherman, *Well-Read Lives: How Books Inspired a Generation of American Women* (Chapel Hill: University of North Carolina Press, 2010), pp. 38–39.
5 Barbara Miller Solomon, *In the Company of Educated Women: A History of Women and Higher Education in America* (New Haven, CT: Yale University Press, 1985), p. 44.
6 For more on 'America the Beautiful', see chapters 6 and 8 in Ponder, *From Sea to Shining Sea*.
7 For a recent biography that makes extensive use of these archival materials, see Ponder, *From Sea to Shining Sea*; for an older, but more personally inflected biography written by Bates's niece, see Dorothy Burgess, *Dream and Deed: The Story of Katharine Lee Bates* (Norman: University of Oklahoma Press, 1952).

8 Katharine Lee Bates, 'Diary, 1893–1897', Wellesley College Archives, Katharine Lee Bates Papers, Box 2, Folder: Diaries (1893–97, 1894). The Bates papers at Wellesley are hereafter referred to as 'KLB Papers'.

9 Bates was either hypochondriacal or possessed of unusually poor health, as the majority of entries make some mention of a physical complaint. Of course, given the limited health care options of the period, any malady could affect day-to-day life significantly.

10 8 and 10 September 1897 entries.

11 Judith Schwarz, '"Yellow Clover": Katharine Lee Bates and Katharine Coman', *Frontiers: A Journal of Women Studies*, 4.1 (1979), 59; for more on homosocial relationships at Wellesley and other women's colleges, see chapters 4 and 8 in Patricia Ann Palmieri, *In Adamless Eden: The Community of Women Faculty at Wellesley* (New Haven, CT: Yale University Press, 1995); chapter 7 in Solomon, *In the Company of Educated Women*.

12 Katharine Lee Bates, 'Letter to Jane Bates', 6 July 1894, p. 2, KLB Papers, Box 4.

13 Katharine Lee Bates, 'Letter to Cornelia Bates', 8 July 1894, p. 3, KLB Papers, Box 4.

14 Katharine Lee Bates, 'Letter to Jane Bates', 12 July 1894, pp. 2–3, KLB Papers, Box 4.

15 Katharine Lee Bates, 'Letter to Cornelia Bates', 23 July 1894, p. 3, KLB Papers, Box 4.

16 Katharine Lee Bates, 'Letter to Cornelia Bates', 12 August 1894, pp. 2–3, KLB Papers, Box 4.

17 Leach, Shewell, & Sanborn employed at least six women as editors for this series, including Bates's Wellesley colleagues Louise Manning Hodgkins and Vida Dutton Scudder.

18 William Shakespeare and Katharine Lee Bates, *Shakespeare's Comedy of the Merchant of Venice*, The Students' Series of English Classics (Boston: Sibley & Ducker, 1894), p. iii.

19 Shakespeare and Bates, *Merchant of Venice*, p. iv.

20 Shakespeare and Clarke, *Shakespeare's Works*, p. vii.

21 William Shakespeare and Katharine Lee Bates, *Shakespeare's Comedy of A Midsummer-Night's Dream*, The Students' Series of English Classics (Boston: Sibley & Ducker, 1895), p. 1.

22 Shakespeare and Bates, *Midsummer Night's Dream*, p. 11.

23 Katharine Lee Bates, 'Letter to George P. Brett', 12 November 1897, Macmillan Company Records, Manuscripts and Archives Division, New York Public Library, Box 34.

24 William Shakespeare and Katharine Lee Bates, *Shakespeare's Comedy of As You Like It*, The Students' Series of English Classics (Boston: Sibley & Ducker, 1896), pp. 14–48.

25 28 and 29 June 1894 entries.

26 9 November 1895.

27 19 January 1896 entry.

28 These letters are preserved in the Edith Rickert Papers, Special Collections Research Center, University of Chicago Library, and are discussed later in this chapter.

29 F. G. Fleay, 'Letter to Katharine Lee Bates', 14 July 1902, KLB Papers, Box 24; Sidney Lee, 'Letter to Katharine Lee Bates', 5 April 1913, KLB Papers, Box 23; Charles William Wallace, 'Letter to Katharine Lee Bates', 25 July 1910, KLB Papers, Box 23.

30 Nancy Glazener, *Literature in the Making: A History of U.S. Literary Culture in the Long Nineteenth Century* (Oxford: Oxford University Press, 2015).

31 Despite his admiration, Furness could not resist correcting the only mistake he noticed in the book: the failure of the bibliography to distinguish between two different German critics both named Elze. Horace Howard Furness, 'Letter to Katharine Lee Bates', 27 March 1895, KLB Papers, Box 24.

32 William Shakespeare and Charlotte Whipple Underwood, *Shakespeare's The Merchant of Venice*, Macmillan's Pocket Classics (New York: The Macmillan Company, 1899), p. x

33 Ellen Louise Hill, 'Letter to Katharine Lee Bates', KLB Papers, Box 24.

34 Burgess, *Dream and Deed*, p. 121.

35 Arthur C. L. Brown, Northwestern University (*Macbeth*); Harry M. Ayres, Columbia University (*The Merchant of Venice*); William W. Lawrence, Columbia (*Much Ado About Nothing*); John William Cunliffe, Columbia University (*A Midsummer Night's Dream*); Elmer E. Stoll, Western Reserve University (*Titus Andronicus*); George Pierce Baker, Harvard University (*Hamlet*); Carleton Brown, Bryn Mawr College (*Venus and Adonis*); Virginia Gildersleeve, Barnard College (*King Lear*); Elizabeth Deering Hansom, Smith College (*2 Henry IV*).

36 William Allan Neilson, 'Office of President William Allan Neilson Files, 1917–1939, Finding Aid', *Five College Archives & Manuscript Collections*, http://asteria.fivecolleges.edu/findaids/smitharchives/manosca13.html.

37 This policy continued until the 1930s, when changing social attitudes, and a refutation of the 'separatism' inherent in Wellesley's founding principles, led Wellesley's president to advocate for hiring married men. New medical theories about lesbianism also led to increased stigma against homosocial environments like the women's colleges. Palmieri, *In Adamless Eden*, p. 260.

38 Palmieri, *In Adamless Eden*, pp. 261–62.

39 'Biographies of Yale's First Women Ph.D.'s | Women Faculty Forum', http://wff.yale.edu/biographies-yales-first-women-phds.

40 Doris H. Taylor, 'Letter to W. A. Neilson', 21 June 1922, Smith College Archives, William Allan Neilson Personal Papers, Box 47, Folder 1081.

41 W. A. Neilson, 'Letter to Doris H. Taylor', 24 June 1922, Smith College Archives, William Allan Neilson Personal Papers, Box 47, Folder 1081.

42 Stephen Petersen, '"I Do Know Your Tongue": The Shakespeare Editions of William Rolfe and H. H. Furness as American Cultural Signifiers', *The Kentucky Review*, 13.1 (1996), 3–44 (p. 19).

43 A. H. Nelson, 'Letter to William A. Neilson', 23 December 1921, William Allan Neilson Personal Papers, Box 47, Smith College Archives, Folder 1081.

44 Although the figures are simplified into a single total for each title here, the records do break each play down into sales of 'cheap', 'cloth', and 'leather' copies.

45 The IFUW is now known as Graduate Women International. 'GWI History – Graduate Women International (GWI)', *Graduate Women International (GWI)*, www.graduatewomen.org/who-we-are/our-story/gwi-history.

46 Moreover, as Rosenberg has discussed, Gildersleeve's positions and actions regarding race and student body diversity were decidedly equivocal. Enrolment of African American students did not increase under her administration, although she personally supplied a full scholarship for at least one black student in the early 1940s. Although she 'disdained religious exclusivity', the proportion of Jewish students steadily decreased during her tenure. That last statistic is further complicated in light of Gildersleeve's firm opposition to the creation of the state of Israel. Cynthia Farr Brown, 'Gildersleeve, Virginia Crocheron (1877–1965), College Administrator and International Affairs Expert', in *American National Biography* (Oxford: Oxford University Press, 2000), doi.org/10.1093/anb/9780198606697.article.0900297.

47 Rosalind Rosenberg, 'The Legacy of Dean Gildersleeve', Barnard College, 2010, https://web.archive.org/web/20100624022420/http://beatl.barnard.columbia.edu/learn/documents/gildersleeve.htm; for more on Gildersleeve, see Virginia Crocheron Gildersleeve, *Many a Good Crusade: Memoirs* (New York: Macmillan, 1954); Rosalind Rosenberg, 'Virginia Gildersleeve: Opening the Gates', Living Legacies: Great Moments and Leading Figures in the History of Columbia University, www.columbia.edu/cu/alumni/Magazine/Summer2001/Gildersleeve.html. Although her career ultimately focused more on public service and university administration than pure academics, Gildersleeve's early monograph on Elizabethan drama was very well regarded. See Virginia Crocheron Gildersleeve, *Government Regulation of Elizabethan Drama* (New York: Columbia University Press, 1908).

48 Robert Cochran, 'Pound, Louise (1872–1958), Folklorist', *American National Biography* (Oxford: Oxford University Press, 2000), doi.org/10.1093/anb/9780198606697.article.0900606; for more on Pound's life and work, see Robert Cochran, *Louise Pound: Scholar, Athlete, Feminist Pioneer* (Lincoln: University of Nebraska Press, 2009).

49 Virginia Barber, 'The Women's Revolt in the MLA', *Change: The Magazine of Higher Learning*, 4.3 (1972), 24–27.

50 Murphy, *Shakespeare in Print*, p. 154; Justin Winsor, 'A Choice of Shakespeares', *The Literary World; A Monthly Review of Current Literature*, 8.10 (1878), 179.

51 Glazener, *Literature in the Making*, p. 134. White might, like Furnivall, have engaged in some inappropriate behaviour in his personal life, adding to the problematic nature of his remarks on women. John W. Velz, 'Joseph Crosby

and the Shakespeare Scholarship of the Nineteenth Century', *Shakespeare Quarterly*, 27.3 (1976), 316–28 (p. 324).

52 William Shakespeare and Richard Grant White, *Mr. William Shakespeare's Comedies, Histories, Tragedies, and Poems*, Riverside Shakespeare, 4 vols (Boston: Houghton Mifflin and Company, 1883), I, p. xii. White may have had a particularly clever and educated washerwoman, given the paucity of glosses he deemed necessary in the Riverside.

53 Richard Grant White, *Studies in Shakespeare* (Boston: Houghton Mifflin, 1885), pp. 1–2.

54 White, *Studies in Shakespeare*, p. 3.

55 Shakespeare and Bates, *Merchant of Venice*, p. iii.

56 While Cone and Lockwood engaged with White's texts after his death, another woman editor had thrown down a textual gauntlet at White's feet many years before. White served as the vice president of London's New Shakspere Society, a largely ceremonial position given that he lived on the other side of the Atlantic. White wrote negatively about most Shakespeare clubs, calling them 'pure vanity', given that 'the true Shakespeare lover is a club unto himself'. He exempted the NSS from his denunciation, however, claiming that the NSS and groups like it derived legitimacy and authority from the seriousness of the scholars involved, the work they produced, and the texts they published. (White, *Studies in Shakespeare*, pp. 56–57; for White's early distinctions between 'amateur' and 'professional' Shakespeare studies, see Glazener, *Literature in the Making*, p. 134.) So, when Jane Lee presented a direct challenge to White's theories about the authorship of *Henry VI* at an NSS meeting in 1876, White deigned to send a response to be read by Furnivall in his absence. Regrettably, it was not printed in the Society's *Transactions*.

57 Julio L. Hernandez-Delgado, 'The Helen Gray Cone Collection, 1859–1934, Finding Aid', https://library.hunter.cuny.edu/sites/default/files/documents/archives/finding_aids/Helen_Gray_Cone_1859_1934.pdf.

58 Vida Dutton Scudder, 'Letter to Dr. George N. Shuster', 31 January 1945, Hunter College Archives, Helen Gray Cone Papers, Box 1, Folder 5.

59 Vassar, Wellesley, and the University of Nebraska, respectively.

60 Palmieri, *In Adamless Eden*, p. 128. From the founding of the first women's college to the modern day, preferences have been split over the benefits of co-education versus single-sex education for women, in both the United States and England. Statistically, co-education was more common, but proponents were vociferous in their belief in the superiority of single-sex colleges. Solomon, *In the Company of Educated Women*, p. 61.

61 Palmieri, *In Adamless Eden*, pp. 245–51.

62 Richard Grant White, 'The Lady Gruach's Husband', *Massachusetts Ploughman and New England Journal of Agriculture*, 23 April 1870, 3 (p. 58).

63 White, *Studies in Shakespeare*, p. 60.

64 White, *Studies in Shakespeare*, p. 61.

65 White, 'The Lady Gruach's Husband'.

66 William Shakespeare, Helen Gray Cone, and Richard Grant White, *Macbeth*, The Riverside Literature Series, 106 (Boston: Houghton Mifflin and Company, 1897), p. 105.

67 Shakespeare, Cone, and White, *Macbeth*, p. 103.

68 Murphy, *Shakespeare in Print*, p. 366.

69 See advertisement in William Shakespeare and J. C. Smith, *As You Like It*, Heath's English Classics (Boston: D. C. Heath & Co., 1902); Murphy, *Shakespeare in Print*, p. 366.

70 D. C. Heath also employed Sarah Willard Hiestand to edit abridged editions for a series entitled The Beginner's Shakespeare and Pauline Gertrude Wiggin to edit for the Golden Key series. See Appendix A for biographical information and publication details.

71 Edith Rickert, 'Political Propaganda and Satire in "A Midsummer Night's Dream". (To Be Continued)', *Modern Philology*, 21.1 (1923), 53–87; Edith Rickert, 'Political Propaganda and Satire in "A Midsummer Night's Dream." II', *Modern Philology*, 21.2 (1923), 133–54. For images of a 1591 pamphlet describing the Elvatham entertainment, see 'An Entertainment for Elizabeth I at Elvetham, 1591', *The British Library*, www.bl.uk/collection-items/an-entertainment-for-elizabeth-i-at-elvetham-1591.

72 William Shakespeare, Edith Rickert, and E. K. Chambers, *A Midsummer Night's Dream*, The Arden Shakespeare, revised edition (Boston: D.C. Heath & Co., 1916), pp. 135–36.

73 See Chapter 2 for details of 'devilling'.

74 Edith Rickert, 'Diary, 1896–97' (London, 1896), Edith Rickert Papers, Special Collections Research Center, University of Chicago Library, Box 2, Folder 1.

75 Edith Rickert, 'Diary, 1898–1899' (Poughkeepsie, NY, 1898), Edith Rickert Papers, Box 2, Folder 5.

76 Rickert, 'Diary, 1898–1899'. Ethel was one of Rickert's dependent younger sisters. Her other sister, Margaret Rickert, eventually earned her own PhD in art history from the University of Chicago, where she also served on the faculty.

77 Katharine Lee Bates, 'Letter to Edith Rickert', 8 March 1900, Edith Rickert Papers, Box 1, Folder 6.

78 'Guide to the Edith Rickert Papers 1858–1960', University of Chicago, Special Collections Research Center, www.lib.uchicago.edu/e/scrc/findin gaids/view.php?eadid=ICU.SPCL.RICKERTE; Katharine Lee Bates, 'Letter to Edith Rickert', 19 July 1910, Edith Rickert Papers, Box 1, Folder 7.

79 Virginia Gildersleeve, 'War Time Education for Girls', 1918, Virginia Crocheron Gildersleeve papers, Rare Book and Manuscript Library, Columbia University Library, Series IV, Box 58.

80 Virginia Gildersleeve, 'Convocation Hour', 1919, Virginia Crocheron Gildersleeve papers, Rare Book and Manuscript Library, Columbia University Library, Series IV, Box 58.

81 'Guide to the Edith Rickert Papers 1858–1960'.

82 'Guide to the Chaucer Research Project Records 1886–1965', www.lib.uchicago .edu/e/scrc/findingaids/view.php?eadid=ICU.SPCL.CHAUCER&q=chaucer.

83 For more information on Manly and Rickert's female research network, see Molly G. Yarn, 'Rickert's Network of Women Editors', in *Collaborative Humanities Research and Pedagogy: The Networks of John Matthews Manly and Edith Rickert*, ed. Katherine Ellison and Susan Kim (Basingstoke: Palgrave Macmillan) (forthcoming).

84 Glazener, *Literature in the Making*, p. 145.

85 Jeanne Addison Roberts, 'Women Edit Shakespeare', p. 146.

86 'Our Story – Poet Lore', https://poetlore.com/about/ourstory.

87 Frank R. Holmes, *A Complete Index: Volumes 1–25 of Poet-Lore* (Boston: Richard G. Badger, Gorham Press, 1916), pp. i–iii.

88 This number includes articles, shorter notes, questions, answers to questions, reviews, poetry, translation, and short fiction. It does not include the women from around the country who submitted reports of their Browning and Shakespeare club activities, on the basis that these entries were less curated than the rest of the journal's content.

89 Holmes, *A Complete Index*, pp. 6, 23, 57, 103, 115.

90 William Shakespeare, Helen Archibald Clarke, and Charlotte Endymion Porter, *Shakespeare: First Folio Edition*, 40 vols (New York: T. Y. Crowell & Co., 1903); William Shakespeare, Helen Archibald Clarke, and Charlotte Endymion Porter, *Shakespeare's Complete Works*, Pembroke Edition, 12 vols (New York: Thomas Y. Crowell & Co, 1903).

91 Roberts, 'Women Edit Shakespeare', p. 140.

92 J. Dover Wilson, 'Letter to Henrietta C. Bartlett', 17 December 1937, Henrietta C. Bartlett Papers. General Collection, Beinecke Rare Book and Manuscript Library, Yale University, Series I, Box 5, Folder 264.

93 Emma Smith, *Shakespeare's First Folio*, p. 204; for more on editorial use of the First Folio, see Edmund G. C. King, 'Editors', in *The Cambridge Companion to Shakespeare's First Folio*, ed. Emma Smith (Cambridge: Cambridge University Press, 2016), pp. 120–36; Adam G. Hooks, 'Afterword: The Folio as Fetish', in *The Cambridge Companion to Shakespeare's First Folio*, ed. Emma Smith (Cambridge: Cambridge University Press, 2016), pp. 185–96; Brian Cummings, 'Shakespeare's First Folio and the Fetish of the Book', *Cahiers Élisabéthains*, 93.1 (2017), 50–69.

94 Quoted in Murphy, *Shakespeare in Print*, p. 165.

95 H. S. Milford, 'Letter to David Nichol Smith', 26 July 1905, David Nichol Smith Papers, Osborn Collection, Beinecke Rare Book and Manuscript Library, Yale University, Box 2, Folder 9.

96 R. W. Chapman, 'Letter to David Nichol Smith', 4 April 1907, David Nichol Smith Papers, Box 2, Folder 8.

97 Janine Barchas, 'Why K. M. Metcalfe (Mrs Chapman) Is "Really the Originator in the Editing of Jane Austen"', *The Review of English Studies*, 68.285 (2017), 583–611.

98 William Shakespeare, Charlotte Endymion Porter, and Helen Archibald Clarke, *The Complete Works of William Shakespeare, Reprinted from the*

First Folio Edition. (London: George G. Harrap, 1906), I, pp. ii, xiiii. Although advertised as the First Folio edition, the Harrap printing is comprised of thirteen volumes without extensive explanatory material, so it would more properly be considered a reprint of the Pembroke edition. For this London reprint Harrap replaced all of Porter and Clarke's introductory material with a forty-three-page introduction by Collins, an English critic and professor at Birmingham. This may have been a response to some of the America-centric language Porter and Clarke used in their original preface:

> In a word, the English editors of Shakespeare have continuously groped backward from the most modern toward the most ancient text. And it was reserved for the American editor Dr. Horace Howard Furness to be the first to adopt the rational and scientific method which alone makes it possible to catch all preceding slips and to forestall new causes of error by printing the First Folio as it stands, and noting variations from that in chronological order. (Shakespeare, Clarke, and Porter, *Shakespeare: First Folio Edition*, IV, pp. xi–xii)

> [Our thanks] to Dr. Furness, whose new and thoroughly American lead [the editors] have followed in adopting for this edition the First Folio text. (Shakespeare, Clarke, and Porter, *Shakespeare: First Folio Edition*, IV, p. xv)

For more on Porter and Clarke and American nationalism, see Tricia Lootens, 'Shakespeare, King of What? Gender, Nineteenth-Century Patriotism, and the Case of *Poet-Lore*', *Borrowers and Lenders: The Journal of Shakespeare and Appropriation*, 8.1 (2013), 8.

 99 William Shakespeare, Helen Archibald Clarke, and Charlotte Endymion Porter, *The Complete Works of William Shakespeare*, reprinted from the First Folio (London: George G. Harrap, 1906), I, p. ii.

100 Charlotte Endymion Porter, 'Letter to Richard Gilder', 12 March 1908, New York Public Library Archives and Manuscripts, Richard Watson Gilder Papers, Box 13, Folder 8.

101 J. Dover Wilson, 'Letter to Henrietta C. Bartlett', 13 November 1937, Henrietta C. Bartlett Papers, Series I, Box 5, Folder 264.

102 Murphy, *Shakespeare in Print*, p. 165; Glazener, *Literature in the Making*, p. 146.

103 For more on this, see Lootens, 'Shakespeare, King of What?'; Glazener, *Literature in the Making*. For Shakespeare clubs in particular, see Katherine West Scheil, *She Hath Been Reading: Women and Shakespeare Clubs in America* (Ithaca, NY: Cornell University Press, 2012); Christy Desmet, '*Shakespeariana* and Shakespeare Societies in North America, 1883–1893', *Borrowers and Lenders: The Journal of Shakespeare and Appropriation*, 2.2 (2006); Ann Thompson, 'A Club of Our Own: Women's Play Readings in the Nineteenth Century', *Borrowers and Lenders: The Journal of Shakespeare and Appropriation*, 2.2 (2006), 14.

104 William Shakespeare, Esther Wood, et al., *The Personal Shakespeare*, 15 vols (New York: Doubleday, Page & Co., 1904).

Sidenote
A Primer on Early Student Editions
of Shakespeare

Some sunshiny spring or summer Saturday, go out into ... the woods, ask your best ... friend to go with you, and take a volume of Shakespeare [along]. Do not take the school edition, but the daintiest and prettiest volume you can find ... and lay in it a sprig of scented geranium ... to mark the place and be a pleasure to the senses ... read the play through with your friend ... the next Shakespeare day in class, I think, some breath of the summer wood and the scent of geranium will blow on your Clarendon Press edition, and you and your friend will exchange a sly smile of superior intelligence! Do this, not once, but many times, and ... the temptation to take out 'an amusing book' [will] become less and less.
—Kathleen Knox[1]

In preparation for the next chapter, which focuses on student editions and their editors, this sidenote offers a brief introduction to student editions of Shakespeare. Publishers have produced hundreds of student editions since their rise to prominence in the mid- to late nineteenth century, and the majority of woman-edited editions were intended for school use. It is impossible to do them full justice in this context, particularly given the limited scholarly attention they have received thus far. Rather than attempt to be comprehensive, this section includes a brief introduction to the material form and format of standard student editions of Shakespeare, as well as some suggestions regarding how to establish a theoretical standard for evaluating student editions and positioning them within the larger context of Shakespearean texts. At the risk of engaging in the sort of hermeneutical shaping of editorial history discussed in Chapter 1, this sidenote suggests that student editions should be either considered in the overall development of the modern Shakespeare edition, rather than shunted to the side as a cadet branch of the editorial family tree, or evaluated within a separate framework.

The standard format for the student edition originated in the United Kingdom, where a century-long push to reform education reached its height during the last third of the nineteenth century. In both *Shakespeare in Print* and *Shakespeare for the People*, Andrew Murphy discusses the publishing industry's response to educational reform and enfranchisement, which resulted in a massive wave of both inexpensive Shakespeare for the home and Shakespearean school editions, an entirely 'new genre … specifically catering for the schools and examinations market'.[2] What Murphy and others do not discuss is the fact that this expansion provided the initial impetus for women to become involved in Shakespeare editing on a wide scale. Increasing literacy levels and growing demand for school texts propelled the publishing market to produce inexpensive printings of the 'classics', as determined by the new curricular requirements. Prior to this, as a teacher at Dorothea Beale's Cheltenham Ladies' College explained, 'it was impossible to place texts freely in the pupils' hands, because, for instance, to study *The Ancient Mariner*, one had to buy the complete works of Coleridge'.[3] In the same way, single-text editions of Shakespeare's plays were preferable to a hefty, expensive copy of the complete works. One alternative to the complete works was a reader such as William Enfield's *The Speaker* (1774) or Vicesimus Knox's *Elegant Extracts* (1781), which offered excerpts of Shakespeare alongside various other well-known authors.[4] These remained in use for less-affluent students throughout the nineteenth century.[5]

Another alternative was the severely expurgated and abridged edition of multiple plays.[6] Rex Gibson identifies Reverend J. R. Pitman's 1822 *The School Shakespeare; or, Plays and Scenes from Shakespeare* as the first 'school edition' of Shakespeare.[7] Pitman may have been the first, but he had many imitators, including women like Mary Atkinson Maurice and Rosa Baughan, as discussed in Chapter 1. Gradually, it became desirable to present more complete editions of single plays, leading to the familiar single-text student editions still used today. As the monolithic physical volumes of the complete works splintered into their component parts, editorial authority splintered too. Publishers began to employ a series editor to select and oversee volume editors, who were each assigned to individual plays. This significantly increased the number of editors working at any given time. Where once a single editor would be responsible for the complete works now thirty or more editors could be employed by a single series. University-educated women working as teachers or writers embraced the opportunities created by this new market, many of them capitalising on the advantages that their practical classroom experience offered them in understanding how best to teach the plays to students. The vast majority of editions by women were aimed at the student market;

therefore, it is impossible to assess women's editorial contributions without understanding student editions.

The physical form of school editions grew out of their conditions of use and the exigencies of production. Technological innovations in printing and paper-making made it possible to publish inexpensive books in greater quantities.[8] Paper could be made by machines instead of by hand, using less expensive materials, significantly reducing production time and costs.[9] Steam-powered printing presses and new methods in stereotyping and electrotyping increased output.[10] For student editions the primary factor, as with many mass-produced books, was cost, and the need to keep prices competitive led to some rather uninspiring, utilitarian printings, as the epigraph that begins this sidenote implies. This did not, however, preclude some attempts at both aesthetic and functional design, enabled by new techniques for reproducing illustrations.[11] Beginning around 1890, publishers such as J. M. Dent began embracing the goals of William Morris and the Arts and Crafts movement, attempting to make even inexpensive books into appealing objects. In his memoir, Dent exultantly described the planning of his Temple Shakespeare series:

> With the utmost pains I planned a special format. It should be printed on the best paper, shaped to require no turned lines, and finally it should be as far as I could make it a thing of beauty. All this was to be done and I must be able to sell at one shilling per volume. I discussed every detail with my friends Evans and Simmons [printers], worked out the cost to the uttermost farthing as I had thought, and we found it could be done. Every detail had its purpose: e.g. the red rubric of the act and scene printed at the head of each page, and the numbering of the lines was to aid in quick references when reading or discussing the play in a class. The paper was in the first instance a Dutch hand-made paper; later owing to the difficulty of getting a sufficient supply from Holland, we were compelled to make it in England. Mr. Gollancz [the editor] proposed that we should use the fly-leaf between the frontispiece and the title-page for a eulogy of Shakespeare by one of his contemporaries or by a modern author, and print on the back of the title-page itself some short critique of the particular play. I persuaded Walter Crane to draw the emblematic title-pages. For frontispieces we reproduced portraits, or had etchings made of scenes that were in some way connected with Shakespeare.... No piece of work has ever given me so much satisfaction, and the reader must therefore forgive my exuberance.[12]

Inspired partially by his work with Toynbee Hall, the first institution of the Settlement movement, which brought middle-class volunteers to poor urban areas, Dent explained that

as secretary of the Toynbee Shakespeare Society, I keenly felt the want of
such an edition, for members read aloud in class each scene and commented
thereon before turning to the next. It was amusing to see the texts brought
to our readings – second-hand editions, quartos, Bowdlerised school
editions – no two being the same and all without proper machinery
for elucidating difficulties. Neither types nor pages gave proper help to
reading aloud.[13]

Clearly, some publishers (and reviewers) thought carefully about the
physical experience of reading editions of Shakespeare. The librarian
Justin Winsor, recognising that all readers need 'a convenient little edition,
which will allow you physical comfort as well as intellectual elevation',
recommended a particular edition as being 'the best size and print for a
lounger on a couch', and for having 'a gentleman-like air'.[14] He, like Dent,
also recognised that clear type was an important factor for many readers.
One edition of *King Henry the Fifth*, published in London in 1888,
included this description amongst its promotional reviews:

> The book is prettily got up, being neatly bound in a dark blue cloth,
> pleasant to handle; and besides – a matter of serious importance to young
> as well as to elder eyes – is printed in a bold clear type on the buff tinted
> paper recommended by Mr. White Cooper, the eminent oculist. The
> corners, too, are rounded; an improvement which goes far to prevent the
> unsightly dog's ears so often characteristic of the well-thumbed volumes of
> younger folk.[15]

That last feature reflects a widespread reality about school editions that
has affected their consideration in later study. Both the scarcity and the
unassuming appearance of student editions have contributed to their
neglect in scholarly work. Due to their inexpensive construction and
the hard use they were put to, school editions tended not to survive or
to be preserved in libraries.[16] Companies often produced new editions
of the same text that superseded the previous printing and won out in
the battle for institutional and commercial shelf space. Many of the
editions examined in this book survive only in legal repository libraries
such as the Cambridge University Library and the British Library.[17] As
repository copies, they went directly from the printer to the library
without passing through students' hands, and thus lack signs of usage
that could indicate how they were employed in classrooms; however,
the ever-increasing digitisation of books and catalogues now facilitates
the location and examination of previously forgotten editions in libraries around the world, some of which do include marginalia and
other markings.

Additionally, old student editions are still in wide circulation within the rare and used book trades, and privately owned copies provide much more information than unused library copies. From the names written on fly leaves and title pages of Figure S.1a–d, we can infer that some students owned their own copies, or at least had exclusive use of them, while some editions were passed from student to student within a school or a family. Some student editions, such as Figures S.2 and S.3, show signs of having been used for performance or reading, with the lines of specific characters marked for learning, annotations indicating that lines or speeches were cut, or the metre marked for scanning. Actual classroom use of these editions varied, but having the students read aloud was a common element of the school experience in both America and the UK, rooted in the tradition of rhetorical and elocution training.[18] The Millard and Swending copies offer evidence of homework and assignments (Figures S.4–S.6), including one that made use of the edition's pedagogical

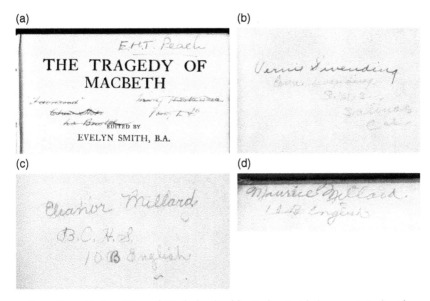

Figure S.1 (a) An edition of *Macbeth*, edited by Evelyn Smith (1937 printing) with multiple users. (b) *The Merchant of Venice* (1894), edited by Katharine Lee Bates, with signatures showing that it was owned by the Swending siblings of Salinas, California. (c and d) *The Merchant of Venice* (Bates, 1894), owned by Eleanor and Maurice Millard. Two other names have been erased, indicating that the book had at least two more users. All photographs taken by the author of items in her personal collection.

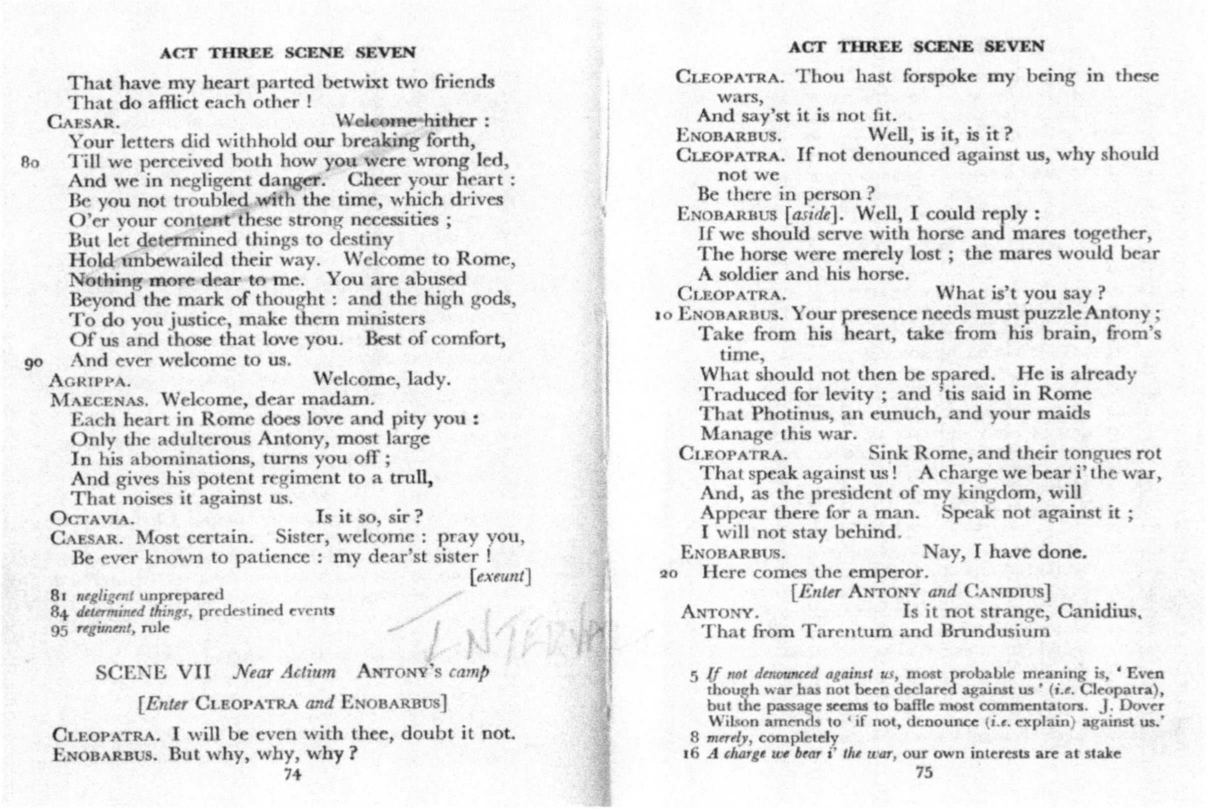

ACT THREE SCENE SEVEN

That have my heart parted betwixt two friends
That do afflict each other!
CAESAR.   Welcome hither!
Your letters did withhold our breaking forth,
Till we perceived both how you were wrong led,
And we in negligent danger. Cheer your heart:
Be you not troubled with the time, which drives
O'er your content these strong necessities;
But let determined things to destiny
Hold unbewailed their way. Welcome to Rome,
Nothing more dear to me. You are abused
Beyond the mark of thought: and the high gods,
To do you justice, make them ministers
Of us and those that love you. Best of comfort,
And ever welcome to us.
AGRIPPA.   Welcome, lady.
MAECENAS. Welcome, dear madam.
Each heart in Rome does love and pity you:
Only the adulterous Antony, most large
In his abominations, turns you off;
And gives his potent regiment to a trull,
That noises it against us.
OCTAVIA.   Is it so, sir?
CAESAR. Most certain. Sister, welcome: pray you,
Be ever known to patience: my dear'st sister!
                                        [exeunt]

81 *negligent* unprepared
84 *determined things*, predestined events
95 *regiment*, role

SCENE VII *Near Actium* ANTONY's *camp*
[*Enter* CLEOPATRA *and* ENOBARBUS]

CLEOPATRA. I will be even with thee, doubt it not.
ENOBARBUS. But why, why, why?

74

ACT THREE SCENE SEVEN

CLEOPATRA. Thou hast forspoke my being in these
    wars,
And say'st it is not fit.
ENOBARBUS.   Well, is it, is it?
CLEOPATRA. If not denounced against us, why should
    not we
Be there in person?
ENOBARBUS [*aside*]. Well, I could reply:
If we should serve with horse and mares together,
The horse were merely lost; the mares would bear
A soldier and his horse.
CLEOPATRA.   What is't you say?
ENOBARBUS. Your presence needs must puzzle Antony;
    Take from his heart, take from his brain, from's
    time,
What should not then be spared. He is already
Traduced for levity; and 'tis said in Rome
That Photinus, an eunuch, and your maids
Manage this war.
CLEOPATRA.   Sink Rome, and their tongues rot
That speak against us! A charge we bear i' the war,
And, as the president of my kingdom, will
Appear there for a man. Speak not against it;
I will not stay behind.
ENOBARBUS.   Nay, I have done.
    Here comes the emperor.
            [*Enter* ANTONY *and* CANIDIUS]
ANTONY.   Is it not strange, Canidius,
That from Tarentum and Brundusium

5 *If not denounced against us*, most probable meaning is, 'Even
though war has not been declared against us' (*i.e.* Cleopatra),
but the passage seems to baffle most commentators. J. Dover
Wilson amends to 'if not, denounce (*i.e.* explain) against us.'
8 *merely*, completely
16 *A charge we bear i' the war*, our own interests are at stake

75

Figure S.2 *Antony and Cleopatra* (edited by Nora Ratcliff, 1947), marked for performance. Photograph by the author of an item in her personal collection.

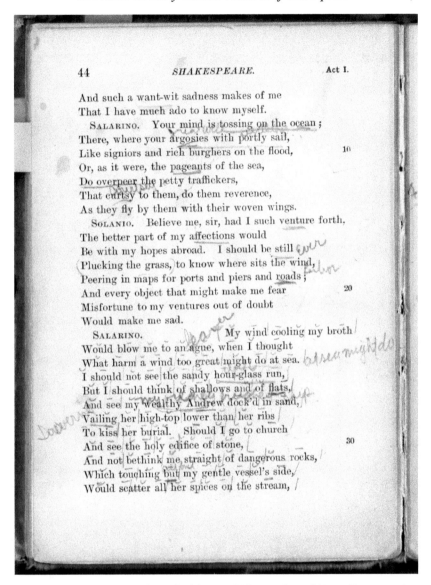

Figure S.3 Marginalia in the Millards' copy of *The Merchant of Venice* (Bates, 1894), suggesting that it was used for classroom performance or recitation. Photograph by the author of an item in her personal collection.

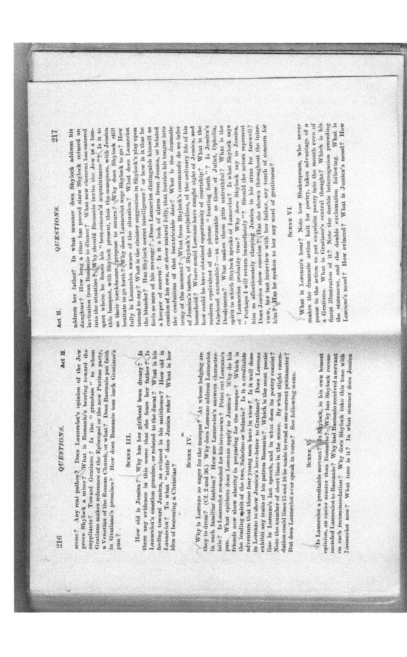

Figure S.4 A page from the questions section of the Swendings' copy of *The Merchant of Venice* (Bates, 1894). The marks seem to indicate either questions answered or questions to be answered. Photograph by the author of an item in her personal collection.

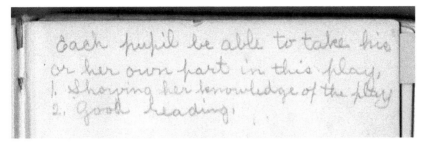

Figure S.5   One of the Millards recorded the overall goal that 'each pupil be able to take his or her own part in this play', demonstrating both knowledge and 'good reading' (Bates, 1894). Photograph by the author of an item in her personal collection.

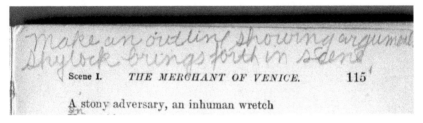

Figure S.6   The same Millard wrote down an assignment asking the students to outline Shylock's argument in Act IV, Scene 1, of *Merchant* (Bates, 1894). Photograph by the author of an item in her personal collection.

apparatus. Figures S.7 and S.8 show extensive marginal annotation relating to schoolwork, while Figure S.9 is a slightly less focused example, a poem recorded by one of the Millard siblings. Although tastes changed, certain plays remained popular for schools throughout the long nineteenth century, particularly *The Merchant of Venice, Julius Caesar*, and *As You Like It*.[19]

The standard format of Shakespeare school editions originated largely in the Latin and Greek school texts that developed earlier in the nineteenth century.[20] Despite Dent's initial inspiration by the adult-learning context of Toynbee Hall, many student editions were oriented towards the new Oxford and Cambridge Local Examinations.[21] The Clarendon Press Select Shakespeare and Pitt Press Shakespeare for Schools (published by Oxford and Cambridge University Presses, respectively) were two of the most popular and most long-lived school Shakespeare series in the UK. By 1907, almost forty years after its initial publication in 1869, the *Clarendon Macbeth* had sold 107,738 copies. In a similar time span

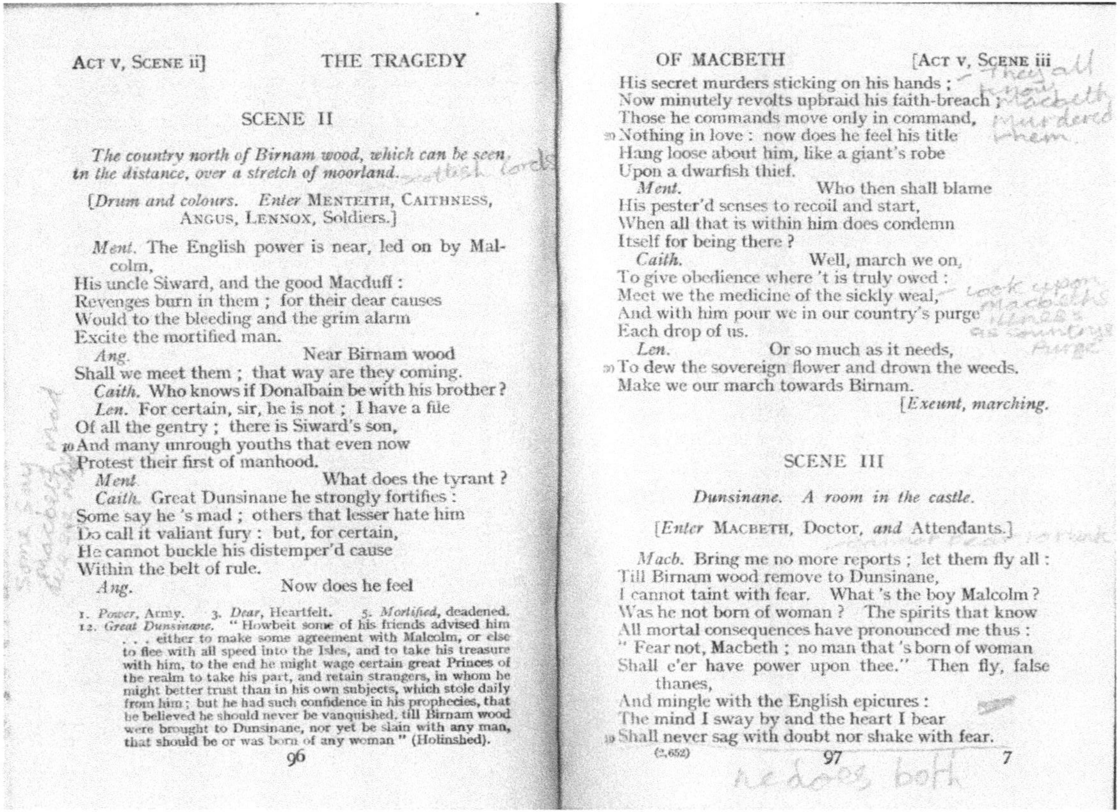

SCENE II

The country north of Birnam wood, which can be seen, in the distance, over a stretch of moorland.

[*Drum and colours. Enter* MENTEITH, CAITHNESS, ANGUS, LENNOX, *Soldiers.*]

Ment. The English power is near, led on by Malcolm.
His uncle Siward, and the good Macduff:
Revenges burn in them; for their dear causes
Would to the bleeding and the grim alarm
Excite the mortified man.
Ang.   Near Birnam wood
Shall we meet them; that way are they coming.
Caith. Who knows if Donalbain be with his brother?
Len. For certain, sir, he is not; I have a file
Of all the gentry; there is Siward's son,
And many unrough youths that even now
Protest their first of manhood.
Ment.   What does the tyrant?
Caith. Great Dunsinane he strongly fortifies:
Some say he 's mad; others that lesser hate him
Do call it valiant fury: but, for certain,
He cannot buckle his distemper'd cause
Within the belt of rule.
Ang.   Now does he feel

1. *Power*, Army.   3. *Dear*, Heartfelt.   5. *Mortified*, deadened.
12. *Great Dunsinane.* "Howbeit some of his friends advised him ... either to make some agreement with Malcolm, or else to flee with all speed into the Isles, and to take his treasure with him, to the end he might wage certain great Princes of the realm to take his part, and retain strangers, in whom he might better trust than in his own subjects, which stole daily from him; but he had such confidence in his prophecies, that he believed he should never be vanquished, till Birnam wood were brought to Dunsinane, nor yet to be slain with any man, that should be or was born of any woman" (Holinshed).

96

His secret murders sticking on his hands;
Now minutely revolts upbraid his faith-breach:
Those he commands move only in command,
Nothing in love: now does he feel his title
Hang loose about him, like a giant's robe
Upon a dwarfish thief.
Ment.   Who then shall blame
His pester'd senses to recoil and start,
When all that is within him does condemn
Itself for being there?
Caith.   Well, march we on,
To give obedience where 't is truly owed:
Meet we the medicine of the sickly weal;
And with him pour we in our country's purge
Each drop of us.
Len.   Or so much as it needs,
To dew the sovereign flower and drown the weeds.
Make we our march towards Birnam.
    [*Exeunt, marching.*

SCENE III

Dunsinane. A room in the castle.

[*Enter* MACBETH, Doctor, *and* Attendants.]

Mach. Bring me no more reports; let them fly all:
Till Birnam wood remove to Dunsinane,
I cannot taint with fear. What 's the boy Malcolm?
Was he not born of woman? The spirits that know
All mortal consequences have pronounced me thus:
"Fear not, Macbeth; no man that 's born of woman
Shall e'er have power upon thee." Then fly, false thanes,
And mingle with the English epicures:
The mind I sway by and the heart I bear
Shall never sag with doubt nor shake with fear.

97

Figure S.7   *Macbeth* (edited by Evelyn Smith) with extensive marginalia by an unknown annotator. Photograph by the author of an item in her personal collection.

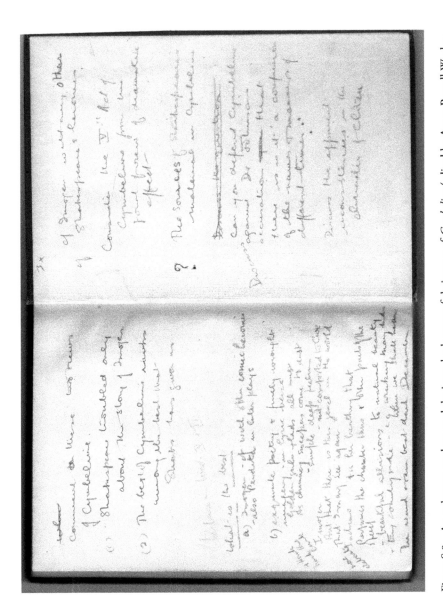

Figure S.8   An unknown student used the inner back cover of their copy of *Cymbeline* (edited by Agnes Russell Weekes, 1919) to take notes. Photograph by the author of an item in her personal collection.

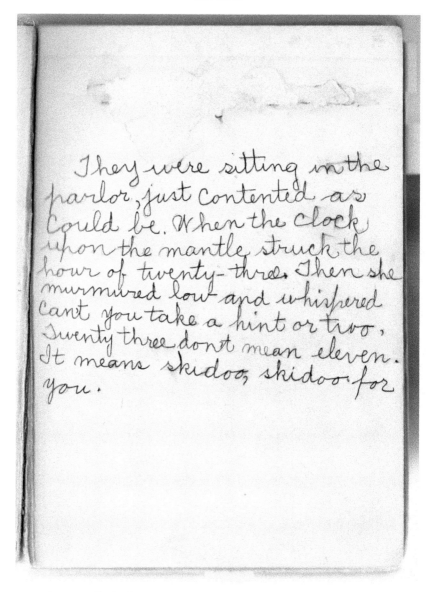

Figure S.9   A Millard sibling immortalised a bit of doggerel verse on her edition's flyleaf.
Photograph by the author of an item in her personal collection.

(1893–1936), the *Pitt Press Midsummer Night's Dream* sold 210,000 copies.[22] Both series published new editions of their *Henry V* in 1900, and these editions provide us with a template for the standard format of school editions around the turn of the century. The Pitt Press editions were the more elaborate of the two series. Edited by A. W. Verity, they included an introduction, the text, notes, a glossary, an appendix containing longer notes, extracts from a historical source like Holinshed or Lodge, 'Hints on Metre' and 'Hints on Shakespeare's English' (both identical in all editions), and indexes. Compared with the Pitt Press, the Clarendon, edited primarily by William James Craig, is spartan, containing only an introduction, the text, and notes.

The American equivalents of these editions were the Hudson series and the Rolfe series. In an 1889 column of an American publication, a list of the most important editors of Shakespeare included Henry Hudson and William Rolfe alongside luminaries like Johnson, Pope, and Malone.[23] Supposedly, the Rolfe editions sold more than half a million copies between 1870 and 1898; Bayer puts the number at closer to 100,000, which would make it very similar to the sales of the Clarendon.[24] The Hudson and Rolfe editions were extremely similar in format to their British counterparts; the Rolfe and Clarendon editions 'were virtual twins'.[25] Similarity in format did not necessarily equate to similarity in tone and educational approach, however. American critics and editors tended to emphasise a narrative in which the teaching of Shakespeare in America retained a more 'humanist' element compared with the philological methods adopted by British educators, resulting in differences between American and British school editions.[26] This distinction largely played out in forms of advertising, as discussed in Chapter 3; therefore, at its most basic, a school edition at this time in either America or the United Kingdom contained a critical introduction, a (usually expurgated) text, and glossarial notes.

In an 1887 article on 'Shakespeare as a Text-Book', teacher Charles Johnson suggests keeping a reprint of the First Folio in the room for the class to consult but dismisses the idea that the specific edition used by the students is important. He does 'utterly deny' that an expurgated edition is needed but admits that 'of course if there were young women in the class the case might be different'.[27] In the same article, however, the author recommends the Hudson and Rolfe editions, both of which were expurgated. Female students were sometimes assigned different editions than their male counterparts, although, as discussed in Chapter 1, this caused arguments between those who thought it best to remove 'inappropriate'

material and those who believed that expurgation drew unnecessary attention to topics unsuitable for children or girls. The editor S. P. B. Mais
prepared editions of thirteen of the plays for the Bell's Shakespeare for
Schools series. In his 1917 novel *Rebellion*, written during or just after the
years in which he was editing (1914–15), Mais expressed the second view,
describing his heroine's use of and reaction to school editions:

> [Sylvia] had never been able to understand, for instance, why the school
> text of the Shakespeare the girls used in form should be so different from
> the complete cheap Oxford edition which her father had given her. When
> she brought this difficulty to him to be solved he explained exactly why it
> was that school editors were expected to 'Bowdlerize' any work of art: she
> replied by showing him the sort of effect that such a conspiracy of silence
> had upon the other girls; she told him of the flushed faces of giggling
> 'innocents' dabbling in secret 'bawdy' talk. Sylvia was not innocent as
> these others were supposed to be, through ignorance. Her father had
> never beaten about the bush on any subject whatever: whatever she asked,
> to the best of his ability he answered. Consequently her mind was pure
> and she had no need to resort to these illicit indecencies in order to please
> her sensual side.[28]

Regardless of the theoretical debate over the issue, in practice, student
editions were almost always expurgated to some degree throughout the
nineteenth and twentieth centuries.[29]

Student editions have contributed to the development of the modern
critical edition in significant ways. For example, the practice of hiring
editors for each play originated with student editions. This practice was
later adopted by the first Arden Shakespeare series, and thereafter became a
common practice for series targeted at audiences other than younger
students.[30] Staking a claim for student editions and other domestic texts
within the mainstream history of critical editions, however, has been met
with resistance by those who view them as second-order, or even illegiti-
mate, texts. Fredson Bowers claimed in 1968 that most student editions,
which he called 'practical editions', were 'a disgrace', born of a process in
which 'having committed himself to a hack job, some scholar contents
himself with writing a general introduction and sends this off to the
publisher with a note about the text of some edition that can be reprinted
without charge'.[31] Many student editions did reuse the texts of well-
known editions, and, as discussed in Chapter 1, textual originality has
typically been the metric by which to judge an edition's value. Without
question, the text is important in a student edition, but it cannot reasonably be claimed that an editor needs to carry out extensive, original textual

work in order to produce a functional student edition. Student editions exist in a nebulous interstitial space between public- and academia-oriented scholarship, and as a result, they tend to be damned if they do, damned if they don't – although Bowers complained about school editors' lackadaisical approach, late twentieth-century school editor Rex Gibson claims that older school editions failed because they 'thoughtlessly imitated scholarly editions'.[32] While Bowers's 'practical text' nomenclature possesses patronising undertones, it also reflects an important reality. A student edition is intended to fulfil a specific function; therefore, its resulting form cannot be evaluated outside that context.

Additionally, assigning value to editions based on the originality of the textual work behind them privileges the single (usually white, male) editor as a surrogate author-figure. In order to take into account alternative models of textual labour, as well as editorial intentions other than scholarly use, I propose that collage/collaboration should be admitted as an equally viable metric for assessing value, drawing on Juliet Fleming's emphasis on the power of 'the compilation rather than the invention of thought', which she discusses in relation to the practice of 'collaging' books during the early modern period. This concept offers a foundation upon which to counter the prejudice against 'derivative' texts and to reassess the process of editing a student edition.[33] It imbues the aggregatory nature of the editorial task with increased power and importance, rejecting what Peter Stallybrass has called 'the regime of originality'.[34] It disengages student editions and other 'derivative' domestic texts from the inapplicable but pervasive value systems established by twentieth-century textual scholarship. When it becomes possible to consider student editions on their own merits, a picture begins to form of a centuries-long Anglophone women's editorial tradition centred less around a specific text than a specific purpose: pedagogy.

In addition to the hiring of single-text editors, another innovation popularised by school editions of Shakespeare became an important feature of modern critical editions: the lengthy critical introduction. Prior to the mid-nineteenth century, an edition's preliminaries tended towards disparate miscellany, often including a 'Life of Shakespeare', a selection of quotes about Shakespeare's greatness and legacy, reproductions of documents about Shakespeare's life, and, sometimes, a statement of editorial intent. The 'univocal' critical introduction, characterised by the voice of a single editor, originated with some single-editor texts in the 1850s, but the school editions of the 1860s onwards developed it and made the format familiar to generations of British and American schoolchildren.[35] Leah Marcus particularly focuses on editions of Shakespeare aimed at Indian students as crucial to the development of the critical introduction. Like Murphy in regard to single-text editors, Marcus identifies Arden1 as the link between the student edition and the developing format of the scholarly edition, pointing out that Kenneth Deighton produced three editions for Arden1, as well as multiple editions for the Macmillan 'English Classics for Indian University Students' series, launched in 1888.[36]

Marcus employs a univocal/multivocal binary to characterise the changing character of introductions. Since Marcus's binary applies to the makers/authors of the introductions, I propose outward/inward as a correlated framework that encompasses readers/users. Prior to the nineteenth century, editors directed paratexts largely towards an audience with a pre-existing knowledge of Shakespeare – essentially, insiders who did not need help understanding Shakespeare. These readers were primarily educated, male, native English speakers. Marcus draws attention to Mr. Crawford's claim in *Mansfield Park* that 'Shakespeare one gets acquainted with without knowing how. It is a part of an Englishman's constitution.'[37] Even Samuel Johnson's famous introduction is primarily an extended philosophical meditation on the editorial task rather than an attempt to convey information to an ignorant reader. Commentary notes often devolved into petty, personal exchanges with fellow editors, requiring an enormous amount of inside information to appreciate.

As Shakespeare became a subject to be *taught*, however, the editorial apparatus changed to reflect the more realistic needs of a first-time reader of Shakespeare. The turn to outwardly focused paratexts is inextricably bound up in education reform and increased literacy. While the concept of a univocal introduction seems inherently inconsistent with collage, pairing an outward-facing, explanatory introduction with a text represents a form of pedagogical piecework. The apparatus of a student edition consists of a series of elements designed to guide and enhance the experience of reading; in this sense, the apparatus can be considered a form of collage that derives value from compilation rather than invention.

I propose that Lamb-style narrative adaptations are the predecessors of outwardly focused paratexts, and that the practice of pairing Lamb-style narratives with expurgated editions to produce books like Mary Atkinson Maurice's *Readings from the Plays of Shakespeare* (1848), as discussed in Chapter 1, is a missing link in the development of the critical introduction – and, therefore, the modern critical edition. In books like Maurice's, the plot summary functions in the same way an introduction would: it offers readers extra assistance in understanding Shakespeare. As pedagogical use of the plays developed and became formalised, more comprehensive critical introductions replaced plot narratives. Charlotte Mary Yonge represents a direct link between prose narratives, expurgated texts, and student editions. Yonge was an immensely popular and prolific novelist during the nineteenth century, who published over 160 works while also founding and editing a long-running magazine. Yonge's moralistic, sentimental stories were beloved during her lifetime, and her name was a major selling point, so much so that in a reversal of the usual trend of a sister's work being presented under her brother's name, Yonge's brother Julian's work seems to have been published under her name.[38] As a child, like Henrietta Bowdler and many others, she first heard Shakespeare read aloud – and expurgated – by her father. When her parents were out of the house, she was allowed to read the Lambs' *Tales* aloud to her grandmother, and, when she turned twelve, Charlotte's mother 'turned [her daughter] loose on the plays, though only in Bowdler's version'.[39] In the 1880s, Yonge edited five editions of Shakespeare for the National Society's Depository: *1 Henry IV, 2 Henry IV, Henry V, Richard II*, and *Julius Caesar*.[40]

As a school editor nurtured on the Lambs and the Bowdlers, Charlotte Yonge exemplifies the connection between narrative tales, expurgated texts, and student editions. Yonge's introductions included discursive commentary, usually related to the historical contexts of the plays, as well as detailed, scene-by-scene plot summaries. The commentary is deeply moralising, and the texts are thoroughly expurgated. In *1* and *2 Henry IV*, she had to contend with the crudeness of John Falstaff, and there, in her scene breakdown, she marked full scenes as 'omitted' entirely.[41] Likewise, in *Henry V*, the slyly ribald scene between Katherine and her nurse disappeared completely, with Yonge explaining in the introduction that Shakespeare had introduced some comedic 'broken French, in scenes that could not be given here'.[42] Yonge's simple, explanatory tone in the introductions and summaries strongly resembles the Lambs' authorial voice; her approach to expurgating echoes the Bowdlers'.

Given the significance of women in both the prose narrative and expurgated text traditions, linking these two categories with student editions adds a substantial female component to the textual genetics of critical editions, as illustrated in Figure S.10. In other words, if Marcus is correct about the connection between student editions and critical editions, then Mary Lamb and Henrietta Bowdler also played roles in the evolution of the modern Shakespeare edition.

The value of the edition-as-collage framework carries over into student use as well. Chapter 3 discussed how Katharine Lee Bates encouraged students to embrace their own textual agency by writing their preferred

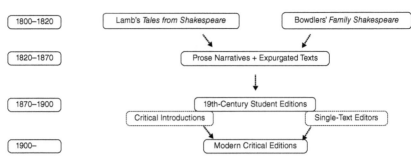

Figure S.10   An overview of the proposed relationship between narrative adaptations, expurgated editions, student editions, and modern critical editions.

textual variants into their books. Bates's suggestion that students mark their own editorial judgements in the text drew on the sense of investment that the act of customising a book creates for the reader, as noted by Fleming.[43] Even the multitudinous doodles and drawings that abound in schoolbooks contribute to this feeling of ownership. When viewed through Fleming's lens, writing notes or marking the text of an edition becomes not a rote or manual task but an act of customization that elevates the student from reader to co-editor. Moreover, while Bates's instruction to mark variants in the text is unusually specific, hers were not the only student editions to include basic lists of variants and prompts about editorial decision-making, and at least one other woman editor, Evelyn Smith, employed similar methods.[44] This starkly contradicts Clayton Delery's characterisation of student editions, which, he claims, '[give] the reader little reason to doubt the authority of either the text or of the editor' and, as a result, '[discourage] all that which students should be encouraged to do: to read critically, to investigate difficulties, and to evaluate claims of authority'.[45] While Delery's evaluation might apply to many student editions, it is not consistent with all student editions of the nineteenth and early twentieth centuries, and the work of these two women editors offers a strong rebuttal to Delery's premise.

A supportive but non-dictatorial style of collage pedagogy can be found in women's editorial work dating back to at least the seventeenth century. Whitney Trettien has pointed out that through the arrangement of their cut-and-paste Gospel for King Charles I, now known as the King's Harmony (c. 1635), the women of Little Gidding created 'navigational tools' that guided the reader through Scriptural interpretation but did not 'dictate or clamp down on individual exploration'.[46] In the preface to the

King's Harmony, the Little Gidding women echo the language in Bates's preface, as well as those of many other student editions, when explaining that 'these [reading strategies] are not to infringe [th]e Liberty of any others judgement; but to be Directions and Helps for them, who cannot intend the doing it themselves'.[47] Like the Little Gidding creators, Bates insisted that 'taste and appreciation, critical judgment and discrimination, are developed through free exercise of the reader's own faculties, not by submission to authority'.[48] In modern terminology, both Bates and the women of Little Gidding encouraged a form of experiential learning.

During the eighteenth century, women led the way in creating literary and pedagogical materials for English children – in 1749, Sarah Fielding wrote *The Governess, or The Little Female Academy*, the first full-length English novel written for children.[49] In her conduct book *Letters on the Improvement of the Mind* (1773), Hester Chapone laid out a guide for reading the Bible.[50] Mary Wollstonecraft edited an anthology entitled *The Female Speaker* (1789); two decades later, Anna Laetitia Barbauld produced her own anthology, also entitled *The Female Speaker* (1811).[51] Barbauld's popular and influential primers, *Lessons for Children* (1778–79), demonstrate a particularly well-developed pedagogical method. Barbauld thought carefully about children's needs in designing the books, insisting on wide margins and typography that grew gradually more sophisticated as the primers advanced. Thanks to their conversational tone and an emphasis on learning through engagement with the natural world, Barbauld's primers are considered by many to be the first example of Anglo-American experiential pedagogy. Moreover, their progression exemplifies the principle of student-focused rather than didactic learning – whereas the mother's voice initially dominates the dialogue, the child, Charles, gradually becomes the main speaker.[52]

As referenced in connection with Bates's editions in Chapter 3, while eighteenth-century Shakespeare editors adopted bombastic and argumentative tones in their notes, a shift towards more measured commentary and guided reading developed during the nineteenth century. In order to avoid the petty, insider arguments that dominated notes, Mary Cowden Clarke eliminated footnotes entirely in her 1860 edition of the *Complete Works*.[53] Like Yonge, Mary Cowden Clarke read the Lambs' *Tales* as a child; in fact, Mary Cowden Clarke was Mary Lamb's namesake, and Lamb herself tutored Cowden Clarke in Latin and poetry.[54] Explaining her editorial choices, Cowden Clarke mused that 'the time may come, when every reader of Shakespeare will be to a certain extent, his own editor; and the difficulties arising out of the early and original copies almost demand this'.[55] This

statement contains echoes of Johnson, who deemed collation notes 'necessary evils' since they allow the reader, if 'not satisfied with the editor's
determination', to 'have the means of choosing better for himself'.[56]
Cowden Clarke, however, directed interested readers to consult other
editions for this sort of information; she preferred to avoid 'the squabbles
of commentators' and 'the tedium of discussion' in favour of an edition
'intended for purely enjoyable reading – Shakespeare's book itself, and
nothing else'.[57]

Cowden Clarke's rejection of both commentary and textual notes had
deep implications for both the use and the reception of her text. As
discussed in Chapter 1, collation notes developed as a method of staking
out intellectual property in editorial work.[58] Notes also allow the editor to
show her work – that is, both to justify her decisions and to demonstrate
the amount of labour that has gone into the decision-making process. This
leads to the perception that 'a good rule of thumb is that the more
collation there is, the more work the editor has done', a criterion for
judgement that can affect an edition's commercial and scholarly reception.[59] Cowden Clarke felt confident that 'there being neither note nor
commentary to mark the editorial labour, will serve merely to save the
reader's toil, while that of the editor shall be none the less for being
unseen', assuring her readers that no decision had been made without
careful deliberation. This level of confidence and self-effacement in pursuit
of optimal reader experience, however, sets Cowden Clarke's edition apart.
Although she cared deeply about giving '*the pure text of Shakespeare* as far as
my judgment and long study of him enable me to discern', her priority is
to present the most enjoyable and functional reading text possible. As a
result, a casual reader who skips the preface might assume that Cowden
Clarke, like many editors both before and after her, simply affixed her
name to a reprint of another editor's text.

This brings us back to student editions and the question of priorities.
Like Cowden Clarke, editors of student editions prioritise utility and user
experience over proving their own scholarly acumen – an outward, rather
than inward, focus. This *practical* goal puts their editions outside the clear
parameters for 'scholarly editions'. Bowers acknowledged that in some
cases, practical editions 'can represent a certain small contribution to
scholarship', but hastened to urge readers not to 'confuse them with the
real thing ... An editor who thinks that he is really establishing a text when
working on a practical basis is deluding himself and his readers.'[60] Bowers's
bias is clear – the only 'real', valuable text is one that represents original
textual labour. The primary goal of editing, for Bowers, is establishing a

text. This is clearly an extremely narrow and limiting view of editorial work. 'Practical' editors may not produce original textual work, but surely the person who guides the reader and directs her attention is at least as important as the person who decides whether the word should be 'Indian' or 'Judean'.

Moreover, expanding the search for women's work focused on 'the compilation of thought' beyond the early modern period and outside the Anglophone literary tradition could further expand this picture of a women's editorial tradition. Even a brief survey reveals numerous possibilities. Beginning in the late Ming era (1368–1644), many Chinese women edited poetry anthologies.[61] The pedagogical emphasis also remains visible. During the Han Dynasty, Ban Zhao (c. 45–120 CE), a respected scholar and member of the imperial court, wrote *Lessons for Women*, a popular conduct book, and edited *Biographies of Eminent Women* by Liu Xiang. Fourth-century Roman poet Faltonia Betitia Proba may have composed *Cento Vergilianus de laudibus Christi*, which rearranged the work of Virgil to tell stories from the Christian Bible, for pedagogical purposes. A cento, by the way, is a piece of writing comprised entirely of quotes by other authors. In Latin, *cento* means 'patchwork quilt'.[62] During the twelfth century, Marie de France translated Aesop's fables into Anglo-Norman; her prologue emphasised the importance of moral instruction.[63] Herrad of Landsberg oversaw the creation of the *Hortus Deliciarum* (1159–1185), an illustrated encyclopaedia intended for the instruction of the women in her convent, Hohenburg Abbey. Herrad wrote original material, compiled quotations, and likely oversaw the illustration of the manuscript.[64]

In other words, if we reject modern value judgements about textual work – both process and product – and look beyond the Anglocentric literary tradition, how much deeper and more expansive might our understanding of editorial history become? These questions have become increasingly relevant to modern editorial practice, as the ongoing transition to digital editions offers an opportunity to make dramatic changes in how we understand both the editorial task and the editions themselves.[65] Hans Walter Gabler has already suggested that editors look to older traditions of scholarly editing as part of developing digital editions that operate as 'a functional whole'.[66] Building on that, Sarah Neville has urged that we refigure our use of citation, annotation, and commentary as 'a relational web of knowledge' in order to 'transform editorial authority from a traditional top-down hierarchy into a lateral and contingent arrangement that makes room for readers' participation in the production of knowledge'.[67] Like Fleming's collage, the imagery of Gabler's and Neville's web highlights the functional, the experiential – the *practical* – and throughout Shakespearean editorial history, few formats have embraced practicality as a guiding principle as fully and creatively as student editions. These little books could still have a great deal to teach us.

Notes

1 Kathleen Knox, 'On the Study of Shakespeare for Girls', *Journal of Education*, 1895, 222–23; quoted in Linda Rozmovits, *Shakespeare and the Politics of Culture in Late Victorian England* (Baltimore, MD: Johns Hopkins University Press, 1998), p. 40.

2 Murphy, *Shakespeare in Print*, p. 182; Murphy, *Shakespeare for the People*, p. 85.

3 Cecily Steadman, quoted in Flint, *The Woman Reader*, p. 128.

4 For more on extract books, see Price, *The Anthology and the Rise of the Novel*.

5 Leslie Howsam et al., 'What the Victorians Learned: Perspectives on Nineteenth-Century Schoolbooks', *Journal of Victorian Culture*, 12.2 (2007), 262–85 (p. 278).

6 Bottoms, 'Doing Shakespeare', p. 98.

7 Rex Gibson, 'Editing Shakespeare for School Students', in *Problems of Editing*, ed. Christa Jansohn (Berlin: Walter de Gruyter, 1999), pp. 180–99 (p. 180).

8 On the development of inexpensive Shakespearean editions, see the introduction to Young, *Steam-Driven Shakespeare*.

9 Alexis Weedon, *Victorian Publishing: The Economics of Book Production for a Mass Market, 1836–1916* (Aldershot: Ashgate, 2003), p. 64.

10 Weedon, *Victorian Publishing*, pp. 70, 73.

11 Weedon, *Victorian Publishing*, pp. 79–81.

12 Dent, *House of Dent*, pp. 62–63.

13 Dent, *House of Dent*, p. 61.

14 Winsor, 'A Choice of Shakespeares'.

15 William Shakespeare and Benjamin Dawson, *King Henry the Fifth*, The University Shakespeare (London: Simpkin, Marshall & Co.; Hamilton, Adams & Co., 1888), p. 147.

16 Megan A. Norcia, *X Marks the Spot: Women Writers Map the Empire for British Children, 1790–1895* (Athens: Ohio University Press, 2010), p. 3; for history primers, see the epilogue of Leslie Howsam, *Past into Print: The Publishing of History in Britain, 1850–1950* (London: British Library; Toronto: University of Toronto Press, 2009).

17 Many student editions were printed without dates, making them difficult to date accurately. When this is the case for editions discussed in this book, it has been noted. The estimated dates given are based on the library stamps in each book. Generally, in the Cambridge University Library (CUL), student editions that are both dated and stamped have stamp dates within a few years of

the initial publication date. This would make sense if the books were being deposited in the legal depository library for copyright reasons. Therefore, date ranges of up to three years before the stamp date have been assumed for undated editions. Where possible, this has been compared with the dates in Jaggard's *Shakespeare Bibliography* and other major library catalogues.

18 Nan Johnson, 'Shakespeare in American Rhetorical Education, 1870–1920', in *Shakespearean Educations: Power, Citizenship, and Performance*, ed. Coppélia Kahn, Heather S. Nathans, and Mimi Godfrey (Newark: University of Delaware Press, 2011), pp. 112–30; Bottoms, 'Doing Shakespeare', p. 98; Gibson, 'Editing Shakespeare for School Students', p. 181; Sandra M. Gustafson, 'Eloquent Shakespeare', in *Shakespearean Educations*, pp. 71–93.

19 W. J. Rolfe, 'A School of Shakespeare: School Courses in Shakespeare', *Shakespeariana: A Critical and Contemporary Review of Shakespearian Literature*, 1 July 1887, p. 313; for a particularly interesting study that examines *The Merchant of Venice* in Victorian educational contexts, see Rozmovits.

20 Russell Jackson, 'Victorian Editors of *As You Like It* and the Purposes of Editing', in *The Theory and Practice of Text-Editing*, ed. Ian Small and Marcus Walsh (Cambridge: Cambridge University Press, 1991), pp. 142–56 (p. 147).

21 Bottoms, 'Doing Shakespeare', p. 101.

22 Murphy, *Shakespeare in Print*, pp. 185–86.

23 'Books and Authors: The Bankside Shakespeare. List of Editions of Shakespeare for Critical Students', *Christian Union (1870–1893)*, 3 October 1889, 396; Rolfe referred to one of his series as 'the Friendly Edition', a name suggested by Mary Cowden Clarke, whom he called the series' 'godmother'. Murphy, *Shakespeare in Print*, p. 159.

24 Petersen, 'I Do Know Your Tongue', p. 14; Mark Bayer, 'Henry Norman Hudson and the Origins of American Shakespeare Studies', *Shakespeare Quarterly*, 68.3 (2017), 271–95 (p. 290).

25 Petersen, 'I Do Know Your Tongue', p. 20.

26 Thomas Dabbs, 'Shakespeare and the Department of English', in *English as a Discipline, or Is There a Plot in This Play?*, ed. James C. Raymond (Tuscaloosa: University of Alabama Press, 1996), pp. 82–98 (pp. 92–94).

27 Charles F. Johnson, 'Shakespeare as a Text-Book', *Shakespeariana: A Critical and Contemporary Review of Shakespearian Literature*, 1 November 1887, p. 487 (p. 487).

28 S. P. B. Mais, *Rebellion* (London: Grant Richards, 1917), p. 13. For more on this debate, see chapters 2 and 5 in Flint, *The Woman Reader*.

29 Rex Gibson, '"O, What Learning Is!" Pedagogy and the Afterlife of *Romeo and Juliet*', *Shakespeare Survey*, 49 (1996), 141–52 (p. 142).

30 Murphy, *Shakespeare in Print*, p. 207; for more on Arden1, see Mary Ann Kernan, 'The Launch of the First Series of the Arden Shakespeare in 1899: An Exploration of Bourdieu's Concept of Consecration', *Logos*, 27.2 (2016), 32–47; Gabriel Egan, '"A Complicated and Unpleasant Investigation": The

Arden Shakespeare 1899–1924' (presented at Open the Book, Open the Mind: The 2007 meeting of the Society for History of Authorship, Reading, and Publishing (SHARP), University of Minnesota, Minneapolis, 2007).

31 Fredson Bowers, 'Practical Texts and Definitive Editions', in *Essays in Bibliography, Text, and Editing* (Charlottesville: Published for the Bibliographical Society of the University of Virginia by the University Press of Virginia, 1975), pp. 412–39 (p. 416).

32 Gibson, 'Editing Shakespeare for School Students', p. 183.

33 Juliet Fleming, 'The Renaissance Collage: Signcutting and Signsewing', *Journal of Medieval and Early Modern Studies*, 45.3 (2015), 443–56 (p. 448).

34 Peter Stallybrass, 'Against Thinking', *PMLA*, 122.5 (2007), 1580–87 (p. 1582).

35 Marcus identifies the following as the earliest examples: Halliwell-Phillipps 1853; Singer 1856; Collier 1858 (2nd ed.). Leah S. Marcus, 'A Man Who Needs No Introduction', in *Shakespeare and Textual Studies*, ed. Margaret Jane Kidnie and Sonia Massai (Cambridge: Cambridge University Press, 2015), pp. 285–99 (p. 289).

36 Marcus, 'A Man Who Needs No Introduction', p. 293; Marcus, *How Shakespeare Became Colonial*, p. 138. Deighton's three Arden1 editions were *Timon of Athens* (1905), *Troilus and Cressida* (1906), and *Pericles* (1907).

37 Quoted in Marcus, 'A Man Who Needs No Introduction', p. 285.

38 Charlotte Mitchell, 'Charlote M. Yonge's Bank Account: A Rich New Source of Information on Her Work and Her Life', *Women's Writing*, 17.2 (2010), 380–400 (pp. 385–86).

39 Georgina Battiscombe, *Charlotte Mary Yonge: The Story of an Uneventful Life; With an Introduction by E. M. Delafield* (London: Constable and Company, 1943), p. 33.

40 The Anglican National Society for the Education of the Poor in the Principles of the Established Church throughout England and Wales, founded in 1811, established and operated schools for the poor throughout England. Religious organisations dominated British education until the late nineteenth century.

41 William Shakespeare and Charlotte Mary Yonge, *The Second Part of Shakespeare's King Henry IV* (Westminster: National Society's Depository, 1884), pp. x, xiii.

42 William Shakespeare and Charlotte Mary Yonge, *Shakespeare's King Henry V* (Westminster: National Society's Depository, 1885), p. xi.

43 Fleming, 'The Renaissance Collage', p. 449.

44 Smith's editions are discussed in detail in Chapter 4.

45 Delery, 'The Subject Presumed to Know', p. 71.

46 Whitney Trettien, 'Media, Materiality, and Time in the History of Reading: The Case of the Little Gidding Harmonies', *PMLA*, 133.5 (2018), 1135–51 (p. 1142).

47 Quoted in Trettien, 'Media, Materiality, and Time', p. 1142.

48 Shakespeare and Bates, *Merchant of Venice*, p. iii.

49 Sarah Fielding and Candace Ward, *The Governess, or The Little Female Academy*, Broadview Editions (Peterborough: Broadview Press, 2005).

50 Kathryn Sutherland, 'Writings on Education and Conduct: Arguments for Female Improvement', in *Women and Literature in Britain, 1700–1800*, ed. Vivien Jones (Cambridge: Cambridge University Press, 2000), pp. 25–45.

51 Don Paul Abbott, '"A New Genus:" Mary Wollstonecraft and the Feminization of Elocution', *Rhetorica: A Journal of the History of Rhetoric*, 36.3 (2018), 269–95.

52 Jessica Wen Hui Lim, 'Barbauld's Lessons: The Conversational Primer in Late Eighteenth-Century British Children's Literature', *Journal for Eighteenth-Century Studies*, 43.1 (2020), 101–20.

53 Shakespeare and Clarke, *Shakespeare's Works*, p. vii.

54 C. E. Hughes and Betty T. Bennett, 'Clarke, Mary Victoria Cowden (1809–1898), Literary Scholar and Writer', in *Oxford Dictionary of National Biography* (Oxford: Oxford University Press, 2004), doi.org/10.1093/ref: odnb/5521.

55 Shakespeare and Clarke, *Shakespeare's Works*, p. xxiii.

56 William Shakespeare and Samuel Johnson, *The Plays of William Shakespeare, in Eight Volumes, with the Corrections and Illustrations of Various Commentators; to Which Are Added Notes by Sam. Johnson*, 8 vols (London: J. and R. Tonson, H. Woodfall, J. Rivington, R. Baldwin, L. Hawes, Clark and Collins, T. Longman, W. Johnston, T. Caslon, C. Corbet, T. Lownds, and the executors of B. Dodd, 1765), I, p. lxix; Samuel Johnson, 'Proposals for Printing the Dramatic Works of William Shakespeare (1756)', in *The Works of Samuel Johnson, LL.D.*, ed. Arthur Murphy, 2 vols (New York: George Dearborn, 1837), I, 467–69 (p. 468).

57 Shakespeare and Clarke, *Shakespeare's Works*, p. vii.

58 For more on this, see Suzanne Gossett, 'Emendations, Reconstructions, and the Uses of the Past', *Text*, 17 (2005), 35–54; Rasmussen, 'Editorial Memory'.

59 Emma Smith, *The Cambridge Introduction to Shakespeare* (Cambridge: Cambridge University Press, 2007), p. 50.

60 Bowers, 'Practical Texts and Definitive Editions', p. 419.

61 See chapter 5, 'Editing Her Story, Rewriting Hi/story: The Art of Female Self-Fashioning', in Daria Berg, *Women and the Literary World in Early Modern China, 1580–1700* (London: Routledge, 2013).

62 Sigrid Schottenius Cullhed, *Proba the Prophet: The Christian Virgilian Cento of Faltonia Betitia Proba*, Mnemosyne Supplements (Leiden: Brill, 2015), p. 2.

63 Seth Lerer, *Children's Literature: A Reader's History, from Aesop to Harry Potter* (Chicago, IL: University of Chicago Press, 2008), p. 46.

64 Fiona J. Griffiths, *The Garden of Delights: Reform and Renaissance for Women in the Twelfth Century*, The Middle Ages Series (Philadelphia: University of Pennsylvania Press, 2007).

65 Among many others, see Christie Carson and Peter Kirwan, *Shakespeare and the Digital World: Redefining Scholarship and Practice* (Cambridge: Cambridge

University Press, 2014); Laura Estill, 'Introduction: Special Issue, Digital Shakespeare Texts', *Renaissance & Reformation/Renaissance et Reforme*, 42.3 (2019), 167–70; Alan Galey and Rebecca Niles, 'Moving Parts: Digital Modeling and the Infrastructures of Shakespeare Editing', *Shakespeare Quarterly*, 68.1 (2017), 21–55; Sonia Massai, 'Editing Shakespeare in Parts', *Shakespeare Quarterly*, 68.1 (2017), 56–79; Paul Eggert, *The Work and the Reader in Literary Studies: Scholarly Editing and Book History* (Cambridge: Cambridge University Press, 2019); Hans Walter Gabler, *Text Genetics in Literary Modernism and Other Essays* (Open Book Publishers, 2018).

66 Gabler, *Text Genetics in Literary Modernism*, pp. 125, 138.

67 Sarah Neville, 'Rethinking Scholarly Commentary in the Age of Google', *Textual Cultures*, 12.1 (2019), 1–26 (p. 12).

CHAPTER 4

'This Story the World May Read in Me'
Biography and Bibliography

In 1996, Stephen Orgel asked readers to consider a deceptively simple question: 'What is an editor?' By exploring non-standard editorial roles and alternative forms of textual engagement, the previous chapters have offered some new answers to Orgel's original query. In this chapter, however, I wish to tweak his question somewhat in order to draw attention to an assumption that undergirds this entire book: *Who* is the editor?

Until now, I have implicitly asked you to accept the premise that these editors deserve study because they are women; in other words, that editorial identity offers insight into textual work. This assertion runs counter to much of twentieth-century editorial theory. In his classic work on editing, Philip Gaskell urged each editor to remember that 'his job is to convey the author's work to his readers, not to show off his own scholarship; and the readers are interested not in the editor but in the edition'.[1] This dictum developed during the late nineteenth and early twentieth centuries, when editorial practitioners managed to imbue bibliography and editing with an air of scientific discipline. If editing was a science, then editors increasingly had to position themselves as scientists – highly trained specialists applying an established set of technical procedures to raw data in order to produce new theories.

The objectivity and neutrality required of a scientist does not necessarily sit easily with the editorial task, because editing requires human beings to reckon with the products of human action. A. E. Housman stressed that 'textual criticism is not a branch of mathematics, nor indeed an exact science at all. It deals with a matter not rigid and constant, like lines and numbers, but fluid and variable; namely the frailties and aberrations of the human mind, and of its insubordinate servants, the human fingers'.[2] No human action or creation is truly neutral because human beings are not neutral. In fact, Carlo Bajetta asserts that 'editorial choice ... always overrules in some way both the authority of the writer and the desires of the reader, *no matter how candid, impersonal or apparently neutral this choice may seem*' (emphasis mine).[3] No editorial decision exists in a vacuum; as discussed regarding the amanuensis, the hand cannot be detached from the body and mind to which it belongs. Every edition reflects the lived experience of its editor.

Because every edition of Shakespeare reflects the cumulative effort of many agents as well as market forces, no single person is wholly responsible for any edition; however, Johnson's edition of Shakespeare is inextricably linked with Johnson's own name and importance, as are Pope's and Rowe's and Theobald's editions. The identity of the editor matters because, as D. F. McKenzie states so pithily, 'editors make, as well as mend'.[4] To fully understand an edition, the reader must recognise that an editor stands between the author and the text-in-hand, since, as Leah Marcus explains, 'the more aware we are of the processes of mediation to which a given edition has been subject, the less likely we are to be caught up in a constricting hermeneutic knot by which the shaping hand of the editor is mistaken for the intent of the author, or for some lost, "perfect" version of the author's creation'.[5]

But how does acknowledging the importance of the editor's identity affect textual criticism? How does the incorporation of biography into textual studies play out in practical terms? This chapter presents three case studies to demonstrate both the advantages and the risks of reading editions biographically. It focuses on student editions by three women editors, all produced for British users during the years 1909–27. Student editions are the simplest and most productive textual genre within which to demonstrate a biographical approach because, in most student editions, the editor's voice and perspective are unapologetically present.

Student editions tend to annihilate the fantasies of editorial invisibility and neutrality. Almost all student editions were expurgated to some degree, and, as discussed in Chapter 1, expurgation diminishes the user's sense of unmediated access to the text's original author. Moreover, in student editions, the presence of didactic commentary is a feature, not a bug. Editors of student editions adopted pedagogical tones and tactics, often drawing on their own experiences as teachers. And, like all teachers, their lessons were not confined strictly to their nominal subject matter. In her 1938 master's thesis surveying student editions of Shakespeare, Bessie Coat Wirth claimed that

> [s]ince it is the evident purpose of the editor to produce books that will meet the needs of the classroom he is missing his opportunity and failing in the part he contributes to the educational program if he neglects to emphasize those ethical values that will aid in the teaching of character.[6]

Since the presence of an authoritative, guiding – in Marcus's parlance, univocal – voice is crucial to this goal, the biases and influences that are present in all editions tend to be magnified in student editions. Like anything used in a classroom, a student edition of Shakespeare can have an enormous impact on a developing mind; however, while numerous modern critics have analysed Shakespeare adaptations such as the Lambs' *Tales* for hidden agendas and didactic undercurrents, student editions have yet to receive equivalent treatment.[7]

These specific editions were chosen based on nation of origin and publication date. Grouping editions in this way makes it possible to identify topical issues that were of national concern during the given period. During the 1880s, issues such as poverty, property ownership, reform, Irish unrest, and overseas military actions put pressure on social and political structures in England. One response to these anxieties came through an emphasis in education on 'Englishness' and national identity; this current is clearly evident in children's books produced during the early to mid-twentieth century.[8] As a central component of the developing national curriculum, Shakespeare played a key role in this project. The idea of the 'cultural nation' dependent on 'the deep ties of history, language, literature and religion' rather than political or civic allegiance became particularly significant in Europe during the nineteenth century.[9] Shakespeare's history plays in particular represented the ideal confluence of these factors for the developing English educational system – a writer promoted to national icon during the eighteenth century, whose use of the English language was considered emblematic, and who portrayed key moments of England's shared past.[10] Because the plays offered both engaging material and a recognisable version of English history, 'in the creation of the new curriculum, the ability to read and understand Shakespeare was tied to a sense of national identity'.[11] Expanding on Richard Schoch's connection between English national identity and the staging of medievalism in mid-nineteenth-century performances of Shakespeare's history plays, Kate Harvey demonstrates that fin-de-siècle retellings of Shakespeare's history plays for children served 'to foster a love of Shakespeare and also to cultivate a sense of pride in their nation's history and international status at a time when the future of Britain's international position was becoming increasingly insecure'.[12] Although Harvey focuses on narrative adaptations, similar motivations apply to the publication of student editions of the history plays and their accompanying commentary.

This context, however, simply offers a baseline awareness upon which to build more detailed, personalised assessments of individual editors' approaches to their work. To move beyond this, I take to heart Jill Levenson's assertion that 'often the notes reveal at least as much about the editor's temperament and scholarly aspirations as they do about Shakespeare's text'.[13] The voluminous and far-reaching paratextual materials associated with student editions offer wide scope for investigation. The three case studies that follow illustrate the ways in which I utilise these materials. The first details my process and results as I work backwards to see what an edition can tell us about its editor; the second demonstrates the dangers and difficulties of reading bibliography biographically; and the third lays out a case in which an editor's biography clearly illuminates her editorial work. In keeping with this chapter's goal of acknowledging personal bias and experience, I have applied Levenson's principle in both directions. This chapter is written in the first person and includes details of my research process as well as my thoughts and feelings about the research itself. Although I hope you, the reader, will find them useful, the conclusions I have drawn are my own, shaped by my own experience and perspectives. *Caveat emptor.*

Evelyn Smith

The majority of editor Evelyn Smith's life has been charted in some detail, thanks in large part to the efforts of biographer Hilary Clare.[14] The basic facts are as follows. Constance Evelyn Smith was born in Leamington Spa on 27 December 1885. Her mother was Eleanor Langford; her father, Henry Bartlett Smith, was the High Bailiff of Warwickshire Country Court. Evelyn was the oldest of three girls. All three attended the progressive Leamington High School. Evelyn excelled there and earned a scholarship to attend Royal Holloway College. She earned a first-class degree in English from Royal Holloway in 1907 as well as a scholarship to do postgraduate work. She left Royal Holloway c. 1909 to take up an appointment as Second English Mistress at Glasgow High School, where she remained until 1923.

In 1915, Evelyn found her father unconscious in his garden shed in Leamington Spa. He had shot himself. His suicide note explained that he had suffered from depression and anxiety exacerbated by trouble at work. Henry Smith died that evening in the hospital.

In 1923, Evelyn Smith resigned from Glasgow High School and became a full-time writer. She wrote a number of popular novels set in girls' schools and edited thirteen of Shakespeare's plays for Thomas Nelson and Sons. She owned a houseboat moored on Loch Lomond and shared her life with a woman named Dorothea 'Dodo' Mohr. On 23 March 1928, she died of pneumonia.[15]

Ultimately, when it came time to write about Smith, I found myself with an abundance of facts, but little insight into her inner life or experiences. In an attempt to fill this gap, I combed her Shakespeare editions and novels for anything that seemed relevant to her life or to the major issues of the period. Over the course of five years, Smith edited twelve of the plays for Thomas Nelson and Sons' Teaching of English Series, under the general editorship of Henry Newbolt. The series also employed Nora Ratcliff to edit *Othello* (1941) and *Antony and Cleopatra* (1947). Smith's editions are meticulous and well thought-out, with extensive questions aimed at both older and younger students. Smith's questions require students to actively engage with the text on a variety of levels, unlike many previous editions, which reflected the nineteenth-century curriculum's emphasis on rote memorisation. In this, they reflect both Smith's pedagogical talent and the goals espoused by series editor Henry Newbolt in the 1921 Newbolt Report on English education.[16] The Report advocated fewer annotations in student editions of Shakespeare in the belief that 'extensive annotation will not remove the impediments' to understanding archaic language; rather, it would 'actually add more'.[17] Correspondingly, the Teaching of English Series' preface explains that the series' overall goal is 'to make the reading of Shakespeare's plays as easy and straightforward as possible'.[18] The Report's recommendation for fewer notes did not mandate the erasure of *all* philological and grammatical notes in a student edition, however, and, judging from her other writing, Smith seemed to agree that some boring details were necessary. Smith's best-remembered works are novels set in a girls' school. These include *The First Fifth Form*, in which a teacher and her students have an exchange about the best way to learn Shakespeare. One student asks, 'Don't you think it *spoils* Shakespeare … learning all those dull old notes and dull meanings of words?' Her teacher wryly replies, 'Your powers of appreciation of Shakespeare's *Macbeth* won't be blasted forever because you know what the words he uses mean.'[19]

Therefore, while glossarial notes were 'reduced to the smallest compass', some on-page notation remained, and additional critical information and context were available in an introduction and appendices on Shakespeare, his career, and early modern drama. The introduction also included information on historical costumes and props that would be appropriate for staging. This was consistent with the priorities of the Newbolt Report, which included an entire section on the importance of incorporating reading, writing, and performing drama into the English curriculum. After all, the Report claimed, the most important function of a literary education is 'to teach young men and women the use of leisure', and 'the sooner a child becomes familiar with the best forms of theatrical amusement the less likely he is to be attracted by the worst'.[20] In other words, the sooner a child learns to enjoy Shakespeare, the less likely he is to get lured into burlesque shows and music halls as an adult. As a result, multiple questions in Smith's editions addressed classroom reading, performance, and creative writing, as well as performance history. In *Henry V*, for example, Smith explained Coleridge's idea of writing plays about every English king not covered by Shakespeare and establishing a national tradition of performing the complete sequence every year at Christmas.[21] In this vein, Smith directed students to choose a king, outline a play about his reign, and write an act or scene of the proposed drama.[22] Again, this was consistent with Smith's own pedagogy – her publications included volumes of abridged plays for classroom performance, and *The First Fifth Form* includes scenes of both classroom recitation and a form-room play assignment.

Smith's editions clearly draw on public and political issues. This is an area, however, in which Smith's private opinions are frustratingly opaque. In this instance, placing the editions within a national, rather than a personal context reveals some potential points of interest. One particular event stands out as a shared national trauma during the first decades of the twentieth century – First World War, or the Great War. Very little is known about Evelyn Smith's wartime experience. Salary records show that she remained employed at Glasgow High School during the war years. Her life on the home front would have been significantly touched by the conflict in Europe. Glasgow took in thousands of Belgian refugees, including children who were placed at GHS.[23] Some 2,500 students and graduates of GHS's affiliated boys' school served in the military. Glasgow's factories produced tanks, ordnance, and other vital war equipment, and the city was the site of several major anti-war and workers' rights protests, driven in large part by Glaswegian women.[24] Aside from all that, Smith's partner, Dorothea Mohr, was half German; although her father was relatively safe due to his age and status as a naturalised citizen, many German-born residents of Scotland were interned or repatriated during the war, and there were widespread anti-German riots in 1915.[25] Smith rarely mentioned the war in her fiction – the brutality of the Somme had no place in idyllic girls' school stories; however, Smith's 1927 edition of *Henry V* discusses the war directly and offers some oblique glimpses into the editor's mind.

Because of its singular and potent appeal, *Henry V* has often been appropriated to stir patriotism and emotion among English audiences. Catherine Alexander points to Charles Kean's 1859 production as an example of the play's use as a rallying cry in the wake of the Crimean War and other mid-century military mishaps, and to Laurence Olivier's Ministry of Information–sanctioned film, released prior to D-Day.[26] Emma Smith claims that

> [t]o stage the play has always been a political act, and most often consciously so. The politics to which the play has spoken have most commonly been British or, more specifically, English ones: no other Shakespeare play has been so ignored outside the English-speaking world, and it is both a cause and an effect of the insularity of its performance history that it has been seen to be so inescapably engaged with changing and contested definitions of English and British national identity.[27]

Obvious parallels between the Elizabethan and the Victorian periods provided easy fodder for analogy and allusion during the nineteenth and early twentieth centuries. Both were seen as golden ages under a long-lived female monarch, during which England expanded its power and influence, and the Elizabethan age was presented as an aspirational model for England's future.[28]

At the beginning of the First World War, many employed *Henry V* as a rallying cry to stir emotions and increase patriotic fervour. Actor Frank Benson performed several pieces from *Henry V*, including the St Crispin's Day speech, at recruitment rallies, and mounted a patriotic revival.[29] *The Times* and other newspapers reprinted the St Crispin's Day speech to inspire readers.[30] In the post-war years, however, attitudes towards the play began to shift. Discussing the rise of an anti-heroic view of the national past after the war, Raphael Samuel has suggested that 'debunking the past was a kind of national sport in the 1920s, a way perhaps of anaesthetizing the pain for those ... who had walked the fields of death, and for others, marking a break with their elders and betters'.[31] *Henry V*, with its stirring martial speeches and portrayal of a warrior king, became a target of this impulse. In a 1922 student edition, George Cowling employed a 'man of his time' argument to justify admiration of Shakespeare's Henry, admitting that '[Henry's] virtues perhaps are not ours. We live in a more sensitive and a more complex age, when the military virtues are not so highly prized. We must not forget that Henry lived in an age when war was lightly undertaken and fiercely waged.'[32] Others were less forgiving than Cowling. Poet and critic Gerald Gould, who had been employed in the propaganda department during the war, wrote an essay in 1919 contending that *Henry V* was 'a satire on monarchical government, on imperialism, on the baser kinds of "patriotism," and on war'.[33]

Published in 1927, Smith's edition of *Henry V* reflected both the influence of the Great War on the presentation of history plays and the benefit of a decade's distance from the war itself. The process of identifying a body of Great War literature began during the war, with the publication of books intended for both soldier and civilian audiences, and of collections such as George Herbert Clarke's *A Treasury of War Poetry* (1919), which offered overviews of the new canon in the immediate post-war period.[34] With the war's literary legacy becoming clear and distinct, Smith was able to pose questions connecting Shakespeare's portrayal of Henry's war in France with the recent war in Europe. Through the juxtaposition of contemporary war poetry and *Henry V*, Smith attempted not only to draw parallels between the play and modern events but also to foster in students a greater understanding of the recent conflict.

Smith structured many questions in accordance with the Newbolt Report's position that a good question 'itself offers a criticism and asks the candidate to refute or confirm it from the evidence of his own reading'.[35] Question 26 in *Henry V*, for example, demonstrates this critique–response format: 'It has been said that [*Henry V*] shows both the best and the worst of the English spirit. Discuss the truth of this.'[36] Although the critic remained anonymous in this instance, Smith often used quotes from specific authors to prompt responses. Rex Gibson, a modern editor of school editions, dismisses the practice of extensively citing critics as 'name-dropping … pseudo-scholarship' that privileges the thoughts of critics over both the play itself and the students' opinions and feelings.[37] While perhaps inconsistent with modern pedagogy, Smith made the best of her period's conventions by converting citations into provocative questions. According to the Newbolt Report's interpretation, an examiner's questions must necessarily 'ask for knowledge, but it must be knowledge which matters, which counts towards appreciation, towards seeing a work as a whole'.[38] Smith's wide-ranging, holistic questions put the Report's aspirations and pedagogical theories into practice; on a more personal level, examining the politics of her chosen citations allows us to better understand Smith herself. While Smith's questions were structurally designed to inspire insight in her readers, rather than to dictate interpretation, her choice of poets and critics might reflect an attempt to hint at anti-war sentiment while trying to avoid imposing ideology too directly.

Her first upper-level question immediately sets out her critical agenda, encouraging students to consider the play in terms of not just literary value, but political symbolism:

> On August 4, 1914, the day war was declared by Great Britain against Germany and Austria, an alteration was made in the programme of the Shakespearean festival season at Stratford-on-Avon, and *Henry V.* was played at the Memorial Theatre that night. From your knowledge of the play show fully why this choice was made.[39]

If this question is perhaps implicitly jingoistic, inviting essays on the power of the play to inspire heroism and nationalistic fervour, it nonetheless insists on the contemporary political force of Shakespeare's works and invites students to reflect on their institutional operations. It also leaves open the possibility for cynical, pragmatic answers. She begins introducing war poetry with an example of the war's earliest literary outputs:

> You may not remember what it was like to be a nation at war, but you are living with people who remember it well, and you have read poetry which was written by fighting men, and has all the value of sincerity. There is in all men a spirit which responds to the demand for superhuman exertion, to the promise of honour; a spirit which, in men who were poets, expresses itself as in those splendid last lines of Rupert Brooke's sonnet called *The Dead*:
>
> > 'Honour has come back, as a king, to earth,
> > And paid his subjects with a royal wage;
> > And Nobleness walks in our ways again;
> > And we have come into our heritage.'
>
> Where, in *Henry V.*, do you find the praise of honour, praise to which humanity can never remain unresponsive?[40]

Although Rupert Brooke's idealistic poems were popular, he gradually came to be seen to represent the naïveté and unthinking patriotism of the pre-Somme years.[41] Her description of the verse as possessing 'the value of sincerity' is carefully chosen – 'sincerity' implies a subjective, but not necessarily objective, truth.

In Brooke's defence, his idealism never had a chance to be tarnished; he died from an infected mosquito bite on his lip in 1915, having never engaged in the trench warfare that scarred so many of his fellow poets and soldiers.[42] Smith placed Brooke's call to glory alongside the work of poets who experienced the true horrors of the war:

> Read some of the war poetry that you will find in the third and fourth 'Georgian books' and elsewhere, and compare and contrast the attitude of the twentieth century man and the Elizabethan towards war. Read Wilfred Wilson Gibson's *Battle*, with its record of the little things that dwell in men's minds as they face great issues, of the pathos and the madness of war; read the poems of Siegfried Sassoon, with his savage irony for the complacency of the non-combatant, for the easy forgetfulness of peace, and his passionate desire for new beauty, for the colours that were his joy, for hours 'that move like a glitter of dancers.' Compare *The Assault*, by Robert Nichols, with Shakespeare's picture of the storming of Harfleur in *Henry V.*, Act III.[43]

Of these three, Sassoon in particular was known for his anger about the war, while Nichols and Gibson both attempted realistic 'trench lyrics'.[44] Gibson was unable to enlist due to poor eyesight, but Sassoon and Nichols were both treated for shell shock, and Sassoon wrote a well-publicised letter to Parliament protesting the war in 1917.[45] Their more experience-driven poetry provided a counterbalance to the emotive patriotism of Brooke's work.

Aside from standard Shakespeare editions and works of criticism – she favoured commentary by Coleridge, Hazlitt, and Johnson – Smith referenced numerous contemporary authors and critics whose political and intellectual activities leaned towards liberalism, pacifism, and socialism, and who may, collectively, give hints as to her reading habits. In *Henry V*, Smith quoted numerous writers who hated the play (e.g., George Bernard Shaw) or who defied simplistic conceptions of war, patriotism, and courage (e.g., Montaigne). She asked readers if they considered Hazlitt's description of Henry as a dissolute, cynical warmonger 'a fair description of the character of Henry'.[46] She excerpted Bertrand Russell at length, contrasting his concerns about how patriotism, when untempered by empathy for humanity as a whole, becomes 'a source of hatred for other countries' with Coleridge's denunciation of 'mock cosmopolitanism' which 'really implies nothing but a negation of, or indifference to, the particular love of our country'.[47]

Within *Henry V* alone, therefore, Smith cited three authors known for anti-war activities or pacifist beliefs: Siegfried Sassoon, Bertrand Russell, and George Bernard Shaw.[48] Other editions included references to pacifist and conscientious objector Gilbert Cannan and to John Drinkwater, who, while less explicitly anti-war, was perceived as having pacifist tendencies.[49]

Many of Smith's quoted writers ran in overlapping social and intellectual circles. John Drinkwater, Wilfrid Gibson, and Rupert Brooke were neighbours in the village of Dymock, earning them the moniker 'the Dymock poets'.[50] They, along with Nichols, Sassoon, and D. H. Lawrence, are also labelled 'Georgian poets' for their inclusion in the Georgian poetry anthologies. In *Coriolanus*, Smith contrasted a quote from Lawrence's book *The Plumed Serpent* with one from Arthur Clutton-Brock to prompt writing on the topic of tolerance.[51] Clutton-Brock, like Russell and Shaw, was a member of the Fabian Society. Given the significance of workers' rights actions in Glasgow during the war, it is suggestive that *Coriolanus* also included some particularly sharp liberal quotes from William Hazlitt and a reference to John Galsworthy's play *Strife*, which Smith describes as a 'labour play', to prompt thoughts on the play's politics. Galsworthy espoused causes ranging from prison reform and women's rights to animal welfare and free speech.

The combination of pacifism, socialism, and workers' rights reflected in Smith's citations fits logically within the context of wartime Glasgow, which was experiencing a period of radical political activity known as Red Clydeside, sparked by the 1911 strike at the Singer sewing machine factory.[52] Glasgow became the site of major anti-war activity, fuelled and organised by the oft-overlapping members of groups such as the militant local branch of the Women's Social and Political Union (WSPU), the Independent Labour Party, the Glasgow Women's Housing Association, the Peace Society, and the Women's International League. A 1914 anti-war demonstration drew 5,000 attendees to the Glasgow Green.[53] Major rent strikes overtook the city in 1915. In 1916, Glaswegian activist Helen Crawfurd formed the grassroots Women's Peace Crusade, which spread across the country. Over 100 local branches throughout England organised meetings and marches, and 14,000 people gathered for a 1917 demonstration in Glasgow.[54] Bertrand Russell, whom Smith cites at least four times in various editions, had to cancel the Glasgow stop in his 1916 lecture tour on political philosophy – the War Office banned him from entering certain parts of the country, including seaports, due to his vocal anti-war activities.[55] Smith may or may not have directly participated in these events, but she would certainly have been aware of them, and her reading habits suggest that she engaged with the thinkers and writers associated with these movements.

All of the preceding details, however, pertain to Smith's views on broad, societal issues. Her inner life remains frustratingly elusive, although several possible references to personal, emotional topics stand out. In *King Lear*, for example, she urged students to 'notice the persistence of one emotional idea, gaining strength until it overwhelms Lear's mind. (This is, of course, a characteristic of mental disease – to be observed in nervous breakdown and delirium as well as actual insanity.)'[56] In his suicide note, Hilary Clare explains, Smith's father blamed his depression on 'a decline in prestige [at work] as well as an increased work load'; he also expressed his fear of 'disability and perhaps mental derangement'. The inquiry into his death resulted in a verdict of 'suicide during temporary insanity'.[57] The connection between Henry Smith, fixated on loss of position and privileges, and Lear seems entirely plausible.

Like many historical same-sex couples, the nature of Evelyn and Dorothea Mohr's relationship remains ambiguous – starting around 1913–14, they shared a flat in Glasgow and vacationed together at Loch Lomond, on Evelyn's houseboat.[58] Dorothea was an art teacher. She attended evening classes in design at the Glasgow School of Art, likely in Charles Rennie MacKintosh's iconic building, during 1914–15, and is included in the school's Home Front Memorial.[59] In the wake of the Great War, attitudes towards close female friendships continued to evolve in response to changing demographics, increasing numbers of women in the workforce, and evolving sociological and psychological concepts, including the rise of Freud. During the post-war years, some women writers worked to valorise female friendships, framing them as genuine alternatives to marriage.[60] In her commentary on *As You Like It*, Smith argued that

> friendship between women has often been the subject of ridicule, but there are instances of it to be found in the greatest literature of the world – in the Bible and in Shakespeare. The Bible celebrates Ruth and Naomi as well as David and Jonathan.... Twice [Shakespeare] has shown a really vital friendship, like that which [George] Meredith believed could exist between two women.[61]

Other writers also cited Ruth and Naomi as a model for healthy female relationships, including Mary Scharlieb. In *The Bachelor Woman and Her Problems*, published three years after Smith's edition of *As You Like It*, Scharlieb argued that ideal female friendships could be 'instruments of tremendous uplift and sublimation'.[62]

By pairing Naomi and Ruth with David and Jonathan, Smith may have injected a subversive element into her argument. The story of David and Jonathan had long been used in reference to same-sex relationships, but by the end of the nineteenth century, it possessed increasingly erotic associations, particularly after Oscar Wilde cited the pair during his 1895 trial as a defence for his relationships with men.[63] As recently as 1918, Rose Allatini's novel *Despised and Rejected*, which portrayed both male and female homosexuality, was banned under the Defence of the Realm Act for, ostensibly, its discussion of pacifism; the novel's publisher protested his innocence regarding the sexual content, claiming that he 'was assured by the author that the love between the hero and his friend was analogous to that between David and Jonathan'.[64] That same year, the infamous 'Cult of the Clitoris' libel case connected female homosexuality, sedition, and dancer Maud Allan's performance of Oscar Wilde's *Salome*. Lord Alfred Douglas, Wilde's former lover and linchpin of the case against Wilde, even testified that Wilde had intended the play to be 'sodomitic'.[65] In 1921, some politicians attempted to make sexual relations between women a crime, although they were ultimately unsuccessful.[66] While Smith's note offers no concrete clues regarding her relationship with Dorothea, it does suggest that she felt the need to defend an important part of her life against outside censure.

To summarise, based on the combination of her biographical details and her published work, my impression of Evelyn Smith is as follows. Evelyn Smith was a well-educated Englishwoman from a reasonably well-off, though somewhat troubled, family. She loved her adopted home, Scotland, and the outdoors; one of her favourite places was her houseboat. She was a dynamic teacher who enjoyed her students and thought critically about pedagogy. When given the chance, however, she gave up teaching in favour of becoming a full-time writer. She produced work, as both an author and an editor, at a remarkable pace. During the Great War, as a single woman without brothers whose father committed suicide in 1915, her primary connection to the fighting came through the girls she continued to teach, many of whose fathers, brothers, uncles, cousins, friends, and sweethearts never returned. In Glasgow, however, she also lived at the centre of significant war industry and social unrest. Smith herself had pacifist tendencies which may have developed further during and after the war. She was sympathetic to labour movements and interested in socialist thought. She read modern authors as well as the classics and enjoyed attending the theatre. She cared deeply for her partner, Dorothea, and she appreciated the homosocial camaraderie she found in girls' schools, as both a student and a teacher. While some of this is supposition, it is deeply rooted in both Smith's own writing and available biographical facts and offers valuable, if qualified, insight into an under-appreciated woman editor.

Agnes Russell Weekes

My research into the next editor, Agnes Russell Weekes, did not produce such satisfying results. It did teach me a valuable lesson, however, about the dangers of approaching biographical research with preconceived notions or ideological goals.

Agnes Russell Weekes edited three plays for the University Tutorial Series: *As You Like It* (1909), *The Tempest* (1909), and *Cymbeline* (1919). This series, published by W. B. Clive, was aimed at Upper Form students preparing to take the University of London matriculation examinations. A slight confusion arises around how many editions Weekes edited for W. B. Clive, as her name also appears on editions of *As You Like It* (1912) and *The Tempest* (1914) in their Junior Shakespeare series. These editions, which are advertised for Lower and Middle Forms, seem to have been simplified for younger readers from Weekes's initial work by the co-editors listed on the title page. The books are undated; in the case of the Weekes editions of *As You Like It* (1909) and *The Tempest* (1909), the dates on the Cambridge University Library stamps are verifiably accurate within two years, as Weekes is advertised on the title page as having a BA from the University of London, which she received in 1907. She did not receive her MA until 1910. Each edition in the University Tutorial Shakespeare includes the same general introduction on the 'Life and Works of Shakespeare', followed by an introduction to the specific play in question, with sections on text, date, sources, character, metre, rhyme, and prose. The text appears next, followed by separate notes and a simple index of significant words.

Weekes was born in 1881 in Kent, the daughter of a Church of England clergyman.[67] Her father was the vicar of St John the Baptist in Sutton at Hone. She had two sisters, Rose Kirkpatrick and Helen Mary. In 1907, she took a first-class degree in modern languages from the University of London. She is listed as a private study student rather than a matriculated student, meaning that she studied at home without enrolling at one of the affiliated colleges.[68] She was awarded her MA in 1910, and the 1911 census finds her living with Rose at 9 Queen Anne Terrace, Cambridge. Agnes was employed as a tutor for the University Correspondence College, and Rose was an author. Both wrote 'unenfranchised' in the column labelled 'Infirmity'.[69] One suffragist argument held that in withholding the vote from women, the government placed them in the same category as other disenfranchised populations such as 'criminals' and 'lunatics', as illustrated in Figure 4.1.

Figure 4.1 'It's time I got out of this place', a suffrage poster designed by Emily Harding Andrews and printed by the Artists' Suffrage League (1908). Reproduced by kind permission of the Syndics of Cambridge University Library

In the lead-up to the 1911 census, which included new questions about marriage, infant mortality, and infirmity, some suffragists called for women to boycott the process by refusing to fill in their forms.[70] In part, they believed that the statistical information gathered could be used in arguments against women's suffrage and right to work, while on a more fundamental level, they objected to being 'counted' by a government that did not consider them equal to men. Some women 'evaders' hid from the census takers to avoid participation.[71] Others wrote messages to the government on their forms registering their protest, such as WSPU organiser Dorothy Bowker, who wrote, 'No Vote – No Census. I am Dumb politically. Blind to the Census. Deaf to Enumerators. Being classed with criminals lunatics & paupers I prefer to give no further particulars.'[72] The sisters' decision to classify themselves as 'unenfranchised' in a column meant to indicate deafness, blindness, or 'feeble-mindedness' was a response to the wider and more radical boycott movement.

This detail electrified me. As is the case with Evelyn Smith and many other women editors, I had very little personal material from which to glean insight into Weekes's personality and perspective. This left me with her published work and a few letters written between her and a publisher.

The census document, however, felt like an entry point into her life. The 1911 census was the first in which, rather than give their information to census takers, who recorded it in a book, people filled out and turned in forms themselves. Rose Weekes filled out the form for herself, Agnes, and a live-in servant named Emily Hutchings. Even in Rose's cramped hand-writing, 'unenfranchised' almost overran its allotted column, as seen in Figure 4.2. This declaration brought the Weekes sisters into the company of Emmeline and Christabel Pankhurst, Elizabeth Garrett Anderson, and other famous figures. It began to make Agnes a living person to me, rather than a name on the page.

A deeper dive into her fiction gave me additional reasons to suspect that Agnes had led an unconventional life. Both sisters worked as authors by 1911. Agnes might have published as early as 1899, but her first known novel was *Yarborough the Premier*, which appeared in 1904, the same year as Rose's first novel. The sisters wrote both in collaboration and alone, sometimes using their own names and some-times the nom de plume Anthony Pryde, a name chosen by their American publisher.[73] *Jenny Essenden*, published around 1916, contains a note explaining that 'This work, though it is by a well-known hand, is published anonymously for reasons of a domestic nature.'[74] Those 'reasons' were most likely related to reputation, as *Jenny Essenden* is deliciously scandalous.[75] A review of *Jenny Essenden* claims that 'the chief stock-in-trade of the book lies in a deliberate, rather repellent emphasis on the theme of sex'.[76] Given that Weekes was editing for the University Tutorial Series while receiving such reviews, a strong demar-cation of her two professional identities protected the domestic accept-ability of her textbooks. The safely asexual 'A. R. Weekes, MA', editor of Shakespeare, Lamb, and Keats, could remain self-contained, unsul-lied by association with the problematic novelist who displayed such a 'repellent emphasis' on sex.

Having uncovered these details, I was primed for Weekes's editions to be the blatantly 'feminist' editions I had dreamed of finding. As I said before, however, this is a story about disappointment, not triumph. Weekes's editions offer a cautionary reminder that holding radical views about one issue did not guarantee similar liberality regarding other topics – a suffragist could also be a supporter of Empire, and many of its racial underpinnings.[77] Weekes adopts an intensely charged stance on Caliban in her edition of *The Tempest*. Victorian and Edwardian children's books often deployed racial stereotypes conforming to a hierarchical categorisa-tion of 'other' races.[78] Stephen Heathorn has demonstrated that African and Australian aboriginal people were most frequently characterised as the

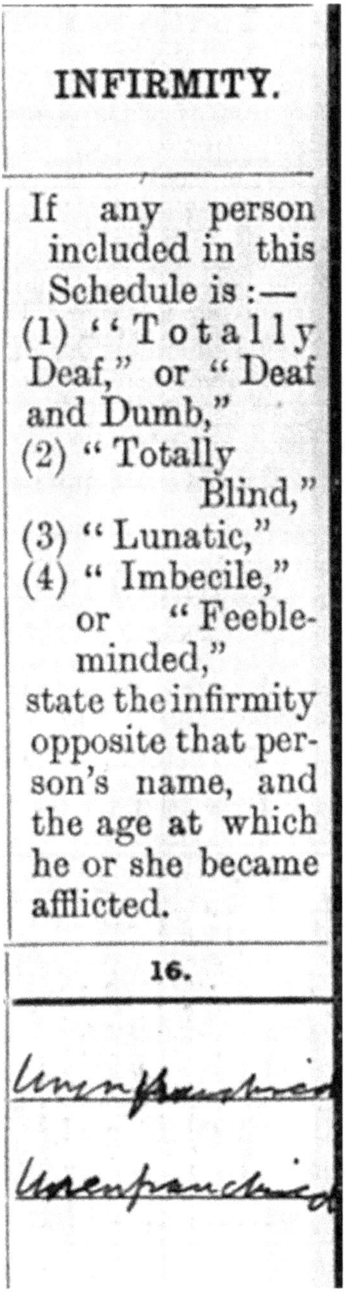

INFIRMITY.

If any person included in this Schedule is :—
(1) ''Totally Deaf," or " Deaf and Dumb,"
(2) " Totally
         Blind,"
(3) " Lunatic,"
(4) " Imbecile,"
    or   " Feeble-
    minded,"
state the infirmity opposite that person's name, and the age at which he or she became afflicted.

16.

Unenfranchised

Unenfranchised

Figure 4.2   Agnes and Rose Weekes's 1911 Census form. PRO RG 14/9141/153. Image used by permission of The National Archives of the UK

lowest, most 'debased' races, possessing no capacity for self-improvement and incapable of 'developing' to fit Western conceptions of advanced civilisation.[79] Some races, however, were seen as poetical in their simplicity, representing humanity in an idyllic, Edenic 'state of grace', or capable of improvement, given the proper assistance. Weekes's commentary on Ariel clearly states that 'for him there is no second servitude; once freed from the bondage to which he is reduced by Prospero's arts and his own sense of gratitude . . . he is free . . . Ariel is all but human'.[80] The implied contrast, of course, is with Caliban, who is nowhere near human. To Weekes, Ariel is the redeemable savage, civilised by colonisers to the point that he can be left to his own devices. Even so, she reminds us, 'he is not human, and we must not fall into the error of thinking him so. He, too, has a limited intelligence and has to be reminded of past benefits', that is, the improvements and kindnesses granted to him by colonisers.[81]

Caliban, on the other hand, has no such advantages in Weekes's interpretation:

> He thinks a great deal about food and drink, and takes kindly to Stephano's bottle, as savages generally do when the vices of civilisation come within their reach. His intelligence is limited; his aspirations are dwarfed; the utmost that he hopes for is not freedom, but an exchange of servitude. He frets under the yoke of Prospero, but give him a master to his taste – the drunken, pompous butler – and he will lick his foot in grovelling humility.[82]

In Weekes' reading, Caliban's natural state is that of subject and servant, and he cannot function without a master. The Romantic poets interpreted Caliban in light of Rousseau's and Montaigne's theories of the 'noble savage', as well as eighteenth-century revolutionary philosophies about the rights of individuals.[83] The influence of Darwin and the idea of the evolutionary 'missing link' also affected portrayals of Caliban. An 1894 edition by Elizabeth Lee reflects both the Romantic reading and the effects of Darwinian theory when she describes Caliban as 'a monster, half-man, half-beast, but for all that he is a poetical character . . . He is fully alive to the beauty of nature, and is acquainted with everything that she has placed upon the island.'[84] This reading of Caliban was common until the 1920s.[85] Contrary to mainstream interpretation, however, Weekes characterises Caliban as incapable of absorbing the effects of civilisation and lacking the natural poetry of the 'noble savage'.

Despite her possible suffragist leanings, Weekes proves little more modern on issues of gender than on race. In her novels, Weekes displays a fairly conventional attitude to her female characters. Her heroines are spunky but virtuous; 'wicked' women always get their just deserts by the end. A similar spirit prevails in her commentary on Shakespeare's plays. Although she restricts herself in *The Tempest* to a standard encomium on Miranda's virtue, *Cymbeline* and *As You Like It* prove more intriguing. In *As You Like It*, Weekes demonstrates her need for heroines to be almost entirely free of 'indelicacy'. Although unlike some critics, she retains Rosalind's comment about 'my child's father', despite the implied reference to sex and procreation, she does feel the need to excuse it, explaining that

> this is the reading of all the Folios, and its meaning is borne out by what follows ... It was only in the eighteenth century that commentators, who lived in an age of surface delicacy, altered the text to 'for my father's child'. The manner of speech belongs to the age of Shakespeare, not particularly to Shakespeare, and is no blemish on the character of Rosalind.[86]

A common thread in her introductions to both plays is the question of whether the men deserve the women they are paired with, given the female characters' self-evident virtues and the men's equally obvious flaws. In *Cymbeline* in particular, she takes issue with the behaviour of Posthumus, denouncing him as a weak-willed coward who doubts his wife even as he spends her money in Rome.[87] His greatest crime, in Weekes's eyes, is not uxoricide, but outsourcing – rather than kill his wife himself, he orders a servant to do so. 'One can feel for Othello when with his own hand he stifles the woman he loves', Weekes claims, '[b]ut to pass such a commission to a servant is unpardonable'.[88] Iachimo's behaviour fails to elicit any particular outrage from Weekes; she ultimately pronounces him to be 'not a thorough-paced villain, but a man of considerable artistic sensibility, who sins from want of moral principle but is reformed by the horror which the results of his own actions inspire'.[89]

Particularly interesting judgements emerge in her commentary on *Cymbeline* and the Queen. She dismisses attempts to blame Cymbeline's cruelty to his daughter on the Queen, pointing out that '[t]his is the excuse of a weak man – "The woman tempted me." Cymbeline should have been a constitutional and not an absolute monarch. But he would have done well enough if his wife had let him alone.'[90] The Queen she sums up as '[c]ruel, crafty, hypocritical', but not without 'some fine qualities', which she displays in her defiance of the Roman envoy.[91] In reference to the Queen's comment that 'I never do him wrong / But he does buy my injuries, to be friends; / Pays dear for my offences', Weekes, who herself never married, notes: 'Critics, apparently unmarried, stumble over these words.. . . . But is there any deeper meaning than that the Queen, like many wise wives, always "gets angry first" – flies into a temper before Cymbeline has time to do so, and frightens him into meekness?'[92] Here, remarkably, Weekes seems to support this chapter's premise, suggesting that a critic's life experience and, in this case, gender, affect their critical output. Although it is not the focus of the edition, her commentary on *Cymbeline* also touches on issues of race and colonialism. When Imogen wishes that Cloten and Posthumus could duel 'in Afric', without interference, Weekes specifies that in such a place, 'no gentleman would be at hand to intervene'; as to Imogen herself, Weekes considers it the highest praise to say that '[t]here is nothing of the helpless fine lady about Imogen. She would have made a firstrate colonist's wife.'[93]

I wanted Agnes Russell Weekes to be someone that she was not – someone who did not consider calling someone 'a firstrate colonist's wife' to be high praise. I built an identity around her participation in the census protest, and, had the evidence in the editions been less blatant, I might have written about her in that light. A single emotive detail could have derailed me entirely.[94] As it is, Weekes remains a sore subject for me, as this section makes clear, and I must acknowledge that these emotions cloud my critical perspective about her work. Rather than resent her, I try to treat Agnes as part of a lesson learned. Bio-bibliography must be undertaken carefully and within limits. A fact without context is easily misconstrued. And, as a twenty-first-century feminist, to become invested in the women of the past is often to invite disappointment. Agnes may not have been what I wanted her to be, but that does not negate her contribution to Shakespearean editorial history.

Dorothy Macardle

As a corrective to the equivocation of the Smith case and the lingering irritation at Weekes, the final case study describes a situation which clearly demonstrates how biography can illuminate textual work.

In the past few decades, it has become increasingly commonplace to consider Shakespeare's plays through a postcolonial lens, with particular attention paid to the relationships between England, Scotland, Ireland, and Wales – as Willy Maley puts it, 'the make-up and break-up of the United Kingdom'.[95] The often-contentious nature of these relationships over the last four centuries has resulted in an extremely fruitful transhistorical examination of the reception of Shakespeare's plays. While performance and criticism are the most obvious targets of this sort of investigation, editorial history can contribute in sometimes unexpected ways, as Leah Marcus has recently demonstrated.[96]

Amongst leading Irish nationalists, many of whom came from literary or theatrical backgrounds (or at least possessed ambitions in that direction), the consumption of Shakespeare involved a division of loyalties.[97] Such a potent symbol of English culture could not be uncomplicatedly enjoyed by many Irish thinkers and artists who struggled to assert their own nation's independence in both politics and cultural identity. W. B. Yeats, the most famous example of an Irish artist who publicly renounced Shakespeare's cultural centrality, wrote that Shakespeare inhibited Irish cultural development because '[the Irish] are not content to dig our own potato patch in peace. We peer over the wall at our neighbour's garden instead of making our own garden green and beautiful.'[98] This contradiction is given physical manifestation in an anecdote about Patrick Pearse, a teacher and writer who led, and was executed in the wake of, the 1916 Easter Rising: 'He loved his books [especially] his many editions of Shakespeare, all of which he watched in the booksellers' windows, nobly renounced, entered, fingered, steeled himself, fled whole streets away, lingered, wavered, turned back and purchased, radiant and ashamed until he saw the next.'[99] This furtive book-buying ran counter to Pearse's goals of educating Irish children in their own culture and language, rather than those of England.[100] For Pearse, the editions were a guilty pleasure, their temptation great enough to overcome his ideological stance towards English literature. Murphy suggests that in response to this dual call, Pearse and other nationalists 'refashioned Shakespeare, drawing on his work ... to stage actual plays of their own and also a public spectacle of political resistance'.[101]

The editor Dorothy Macardle's background reflects this see-sawing of cultural loyalties, and her editions demonstrate a less blatant, but potentially more effective, method by which Irish nationalists could refashion Shakespeare. She was born in 1889 in Dundalk, a town very close to the future partition line, the daughter of an Irish brewer who supported Home Rule and a fiercely patriotic Englishwoman. Macardle described her mother, whose father died in action in the Sudan, as 'a little soldier, every fragile inch of her', and recounted an incident in which her Irish father came home to find that the patriotic decorations had crept out of the nursery, which was always hung with pictures of the Queen and military heroes, into the front hallway, which had been newly decorated with Union Jacks.[102] Macardle later expressed her sense that the wealthy Irish class to which her family belonged was overly invested in maintaining the

Victorian status quo, an attitude that impelled its daughters to embrace republicanism as a domestic as well as a political rebellion.[103] In 1905, Macardle moved to Dublin to attend Alexandra College and joined the intellectual and political discussion about Ireland's future. During that time, she met Maud Gonne MacBride, revolutionary and Yeats's muse, and joined the Gaelic League. After completing a teacher training course in 1914, she moved to Stratford-upon-Avon, where she lived for several years. Her biographer Nadia Clare Smith suggests that her time in Stratford was 'clouded by her growing disillusionment with England, which she once viewed as the champion of liberty and democracy'.[104]

Macardle likely met Carmelite Shakespeare series editor Clara Linklater Thomson at a conference for English teachers in Stratford organised by Macardle in 1914, at which Thomson delivered a paper on 'The Appreciation of Poetry'.[105] The Carmelite Shakespeare series, published by Horace Marshall and Son c. 1905–25, is unusual for both its female series editor and its large proportion of texts edited by women.[106] Macardle's first edition for Carmelite was *The Merchant of Venice* (c. 1915), but her most intriguing was *The Tempest* (c. 1917).[107] Macardle remained in Stratford until 1917, when she returned to Dublin in the wake of the Easter Rising. Based on these dates, and the estimated date of the edition's publication, she likely prepared the edition as her time in Stratford was drawing to a close. Carmelite editions did not include introductions or extensive direct commentary on plots or characters. Instead, each edition offered questions at the end of every act and at the end of the play. Within this format, as discussed in the context of Smith's editions, the voice of the editor becomes subliminal and suggestive rather than direct and authoritative. Like Smith, Macardle never states her own opinions outright, but they lurk within her questions.

The editions' title pages identify their editor as 'D. M. Macardle, BA'. Although the surname is Irish, this moniker provides little other information about the editor. He or she is probably Irish and has a bachelor's degree. At this point in her life, Macardle had yet to publish any of her best-known works. Her name and background might have been known by teachers who attended the Stratford conference that she had organised, but overall, Macardle had no distinctive public identity at the time her editions were published. Macardle's editions were probably not intended to deliberately advance a 'Celtic' Shakespeare. Rather, during this transitional period in her life, as an Irishwoman living in England, moving farther away from the politics inculcated by her English mother, Macardle's treatment of characters who embody the 'other' shows her growing nationalist views inserting themselves into her work on the great icon of English culture. The relevance of her questions in *The Tempest* becomes evident largely in hindsight, but they contribute to an understanding of her developing worldview and provide a fascinating example of how Shakespeare for children could act as a subversive vehicle.

One strand of thought in Macardle's edition of *The Tempest* related to the question of what happens to a country when its oppressors leave. Prior to Prospero's departure, Ariel and Caliban were not allies, but they did share common ground in being ruled by the same master. Facing a seismic shift in the island's power structure, it is unclear in the play how these two dramatically different beings will exist in relation to one another. Several questions Macardle asks point to the challenge of defining freedom, as she prompts students to consider Gonzalo's and Caliban's ideas of freedom, and to write an essay on 'True Freedom'.[108] She encouraged them to write accounts of how Caliban lived after Prospero left, and what Ariel 'did and thought and felt on his first day of freedom'.[109] Although Macardle poses the questions without offering her own suggested answers, other Irish writers and thinkers had turned their thoughts to these issues. Establishing a coherent system of government is the first challenge faced by a newly emancipated citizenry, and long prior to any successful moves towards Irish independence, internecine struggles over governance and political ideology created serious rifts among various Irish factions; Richard English makes the point that sectarianism predated partition.[110] Limited consensus existed in the decades prior to the publication of Macardle's edition as to the shape of the theoretical Irish state. Macardle's involvement with Yeats's circle, particularly her friendship with Maud Gonne, make it likely that she was familiar with Yeats's brand of cultural nationalism. In the questions about Act II, Macardle posed a more focused question about politics and governance: 'Do you think Gonzalo's Commonwealth would prosper? Prepare a debate on the ideal Commonwealth.'[111] Gonzalo's vision for the island is a pre-lapsarian utopia modelled on Montaigne, a more extreme version of the pre-Industrial Eden that Yeats painted Ireland to be in comparison with England. Yeats wrote that

> Ireland will always be in the main an agricultural country. Industries we may have, but we will not have, as England has, a very rich class nor whole districts blackened with smoke like what they call in England their 'Black Country'. . . . Wherever men have tried to imagine a perfect life, they have imagined a place where men plow and sow and reap, not a place where there are great wheels turning and great chimneys vomiting smoke.[112]

Macardle also addresses the human element of governance when exploring the relationship between Prospero and Caliban. When Stephano and Trinculo encounter Caliban for the first time, she asks, 'Can you learn anything from this scene about the way in which the Elizabethan explorers treated the inhabitants of the lands they discovered?'[113] She later poses a whole series of more direct questions about Prospero and Caliban:

> 6. Is Prospero a person by whom we would willingly be ruled?
> 7. Was it wrong of Prospero to subdue the spirits of the island to his will?
> . . .
> 9. Could Prospero have done without the services of Caliban?
> 10. Was Prospero justified in forcing Caliban to work for him?[114]

These are, at best, leading questions. Taken together like this, the implied answers seem very clear – no, yes, no, and no. The last two questions in particular point to a strand of socialist thought that was significant in the ideology of some Irish nationalists, such as the Easter Rising leader James Connolly, but that was inconsistent with the goals of many nationalists, whose grievances often involved property ownership.[115]

Compare Agnes Russell Weekes's characterization of Caliban as incapable of absorbing the effects of civilisation and lacking the natural poetry of the 'noble savage' with the questions posed by Macardle:

> Discuss the justice of Prospero's treatment of Caliban.
> Is Caliban a very dangerous creature? Is there real danger of his injuring Prospero?[116]

> When does Caliban try to judge of character and distinguish beauty? Are his judgments intelligent?
>   Discover, if possible, from his words about himself whether Caliban has self-respect of any kind.
> Is it true that without his books Prospero would be no more powerful than Caliban?[117]

> 'In some respects Caliban is a noble being' (Coleridge). Refer to any traces of nobility shown by his words or actions.
>   Discuss whether Caliban ever shows intelligence.[118]

Macardle's writing displays empathy for Caliban, while Weekes's harsh characterisation was extreme compared with that of other commentators from the period. Both Macardle and Weekes inject their own, opposing attitudes into their school editions. While Macardle questions the morality of colonisation, Weekes condemns Caliban to a state of permanent servanthood.[119] The juxtaposition of these two editions demonstrates how fundamentally an editor's background and biases can shape the presentation of a text. Where Weekes's tone is dictatorial, holding forth on 'what Shakespeare meant' without offering opportunity for dissent, Macardle's use of the Carmelite format creates opportunities for counter-readings, and reflects, in many ways, the editor's position as an outsider.

Macardle did more than simply explore her questions about freedom and governance in writing. After her return to Dublin in 1917, she fought and suffered for her nationalist beliefs. A final edition for the Carmelite Shakespeare, *Twelfth Night*, appeared by 1922, but her political activities precluded further editorial work. An edition of *Coriolanus* was advertised in 1924, but I have found no evidence that it was ever published.[120] Instead, Macardle joined Cumann na mBan, the women's corps of the Irish Volunteers, and was arrested during the War of Independence.[121] Like most Cumann na mBan members, she opposed the Anglo-Irish Treaty, siding with the republicans, as a result of which she was fired from her teaching position at Alexandra College and was again arrested, this time at Maud Gonne MacBride's house, in 1922. Imprisoned at Kilmainham and Mountjoy Gaols, she joined her fellow female inmates in hunger strikes and wrote a short story collection entitled *Earth-Bound*, dedicated to her fellow prisoners and highlighting the role of women in the Irish struggle.[122] She became a supporter of Éamon de Valera and wrote a significant history of the period between 1919 and 1937, entitled *The Irish Republic*. She lived until 1958, long enough to become disillusioned with her country's treatment of women's rights.

***

'Intimate' is not always a word associated with textual studies; however, it is certainly a word that characterises this research. Throughout this process, I have learned about the most intimate aspects of these women's lives – marriages, friendships, fights, pregnancies, miscarriages, arrests, illnesses, and deaths. This type of work, as Henry Woudhuysen has pointed out, is vulnerable to the charge of being literary gossip rather than serious study – just 'chatter about Shelley', as some nineteenth-century critics complained.[123] Ultimately, I find myself in agreement with Jerome McGann, who writes that

> like cells or thunderstorms (and unlike a triangle, or time), texts are empirical phenomena ... But because texts – like revolutions and families, but unlike cells and thunderstorms – are social rather than natural phenomena, our textual knowledge is deepest when it is most personal and most historical.[124]

The merging of the biographical and the bibliographical can produce compelling results, although it must always be approached with a degree of caution in order to avoid imposing bias or preconceived notions upon the evidence. Through a judicious application of this method, however, it is possible to recover the humanity in this branch of humanism, and to develop a richer, more holistic understanding of editorial history.

Notes

1 Gaskell, *From Writer to Reader*, p. 7.
2 A. E. Housman, 'The Application of Thought to Textual Criticism', in *The Classical Papers of A. E. Housman, 1915–1936*, 3 vols (Cambridge: Cambridge University Press, 1972), III, 1058–69 (pp. 1058–59).
3 Carlo Bajetta, 'The Authority of Editing: Thoughts on the Function(s) of Modern Textual Criticism', *Textus*, 19 (2006), 305–22 (pp. 312–13).
4 D. F. McKenzie, *Bibliography and the Sociology of Texts* (Cambridge: Cambridge University Press, 1986), p. 39.
5 Marcus, *Unediting the Renaissance*, p. 3.
6 Bessie Coat Wirth, 'The Ethical Values of Shakespeare as Presented to the High-School Student of *Julius Caesar*, *Macbeth*, and *Hamlet*' (master's thesis, Loyola University, 1938), p. 195.
7 For discussion of adaptations, see work by Janet Bottoms, Erica Hateley, Felicity James, Jean I. Marsden, Susan J. Wolfson, Kate Harvey, and Velma Bourgeois Richmond, among others.
8 John M. MacKenzie, *Propaganda and Empire: The Manipulation of British Public Opinion, 1880–1960* (Manchester: Manchester University Press, 1984), p. 179; Linda Colley, *Shakespeare and the Limits of National Culture* (Egham: Royal Holloway, University of London, 1999); Stephen Heathorn, '"Let Us Remember That We, Too, Are English": Constructions of Citizenship and National Identity in English Elementary School Reading Books, 1880–1914', *Victorian Studies*, 38.3 (1995), 395–427; Stephen Heathorn, *For Home, Country, and Race: Gender, Class, and Englishness in the Elementary School, 1880–1914* (Toronto: University of Toronto Press, 2000); Peter Yeandle, 'Lessons in Englishness and Empire, c. 1880–1914: Further Thoughts on the English/British Conundrum', in *History, Nationhood and the Question of Britain*, ed. Helen Brocklehurst and Robert Phillips (Basingstoke: Palgrave Macmillan, 2004), pp. 274–88.
9 Krishan Kumar, *The Making of English National Identity*, Cambridge Cultural Social Studies (Cambridge: Cambridge University Press, 2003), p. 24.
10 For more on this, see Michael Dobson, *The Making of the National Poet: Shakespeare, Adaptation and Authorship, 1660–1769* (Oxford: Oxford University Press, 1994); Mark G. Hollingsworth, 'Nineteenth-Century Shakespeares: Nationalism and Moralism' (DPhil dissertation, University of

Nottingham, 2007); Dobson, 'Bowdler and Britannia'; Gary Taylor, *Reinventing Shakespeare: A Cultural History from the Restoration to the Present* (London: Hogarth Press, 1990); Emma Depledge, *Shakespeare's Rise to Cultural Prominence: Politics, Print and Alteration, 1642–1700* (Cambridge: Cambridge University Press, 2018); Enrico Scaravelli, *The Rise of Bardolatry in the Restoration: Paratexts of Shakespearean Adaptations and Other Texts 1660–1737* (Bern, Switzerland: Peter Lang CH, 2015); *This England, That Shakespeare: New Angles on Englishness and the Bard*, ed. Margaret Tudeau-Clayton and Willy Maley (Farnham: Ashgate, 2010).

11 Kate Harvey, 'Shakespeare's History Plays and Nationhood in Children's Literature and Education', in *Children's Literature on the Move: Nations, Translations, Migrations*, ed. Nora Maguire and Beth Rodgers (Dublin: Four Courts Press, 2013), p. 58.

12 Harvey, 'Shakespeare's History Plays and Nationhood in Children's Literature and Education', p. 53; Richard W. Schoch, *Shakespeare's Victorian Stage: Performing History in the Theatre of Charles Kean* (Cambridge: Cambridge University Press, 1998).

13 Jill L. Levenson, 'Framing Shakespeare: Introductions and Commentary in Critical Editions of the Plays', in *Shakespeare and Textual Studies*, ed. Margaret Jane Kidnie and Sonia Massai (Cambridge: Cambridge University Press, 2015), pp. 377–90 (p. 382).

14 I am deeply grateful to Hilary Clare for helping me fill in some of the blanks with unpublished material gathered for her biography of Smith.

15 All of this information is drawn from Hilary Clare, 'Evelyn Smith, Part 1', *Folly*, November 1995, pp. 1–5; Hilary Clare, 'Evelyn Smith, Part 2', *Folly*, March 1996, pp. 6–11.

16 Other members of the commission included Shakespeareans Frederick Boas, Arthur Quiller-Couch, Caroline Spurgeon, and J. Dover Wilson.

17 *The Teaching of English in England. Report of the Departmental Committee Appointed by the President of the Board of Education to Inquire into the Position of English in the Educational System of England* (London: Board of Education, 1921), p. 312.

18 William Shakespeare and Evelyn Smith, *Shakespeare's King Henry V*, Teaching of English Series, 114 (London: Thomas Nelson & Sons, 1927), p. v.

19 Evelyn Smith, *The First Fifth Form* (London: Blackie & Son, 1926), pp. 57–59.

20 *The Newbolt Report*, p. 315.

21 The mind boggles.

22 William Shakespeare and Evelyn Smith, *Shakespeare's King Henry V*, Teaching of English Series, 114 (London: Thomas Nelson & Sons, 1927), p. 192.

23 Jacqueline Jenkinson, 'Refugees Welcome Here: Caring for Belgian Refugees in Scotland during the First World War', *History Scotland*, May–June 2018, 35–42 (p. 39).

24 Maggie Craig, *When the Clyde Ran Red: A Social History of Red Clydeside* (Edinburgh: Birlinn, 2018).

25 For details on the experiences of Germans in Glasgow during the war, see Ben Braber, 'Within Our Gates: A New Perspective on Germans in Glasgow during the First World War', *Journal of Scottish Historical Studies*, 29.2 (2009), 87–105.

26 Catherine Alexander, 'Shakespeare and War: A Reflection on Instances of Dramatic Production, Appropriation, and Celebration', *Exchanges: The Warwick Research Journal*, 1.2 (2014), 279–96 (pp. 285–86); see also Schoch, *Shakespeare's Victorian Stage*.

27 William Shakespeare and Emma Smith, *King Henry V*, Shakespeare in Performance (Cambridge: Cambridge University Press, 2002), pp. 1–2.

28 Lynne W. Hinojosa, *The Renaissance, English Cultural Nationalism, and Modernism, 1860–1920* (Basingstoke: Palgrave Macmillan, 2009), p. 193.

29 Paul Brown, 'Stealing Soldiers' Hearts: Appropriating *Henry V* and Marching Shakespeare's Boys off to the Great War', *Vides*, 3 (2015), 33–43; Alexander, 'Shakespeare and War', pp. 288–89.

30 Hinojosa, *Renaissance, English Cultural Nationalism, and Modernism*, p. 168.

31 Raphael Samuel, *Island Stories: Unravelling Britain, vol. II: Theatres of Memory*, ed. Alison Light, Sally Alexander, and Gareth Stedman Jones (London: Verso, 1998), p. 211.

32 William Shakespeare and George H. Cowling, *The Life of King Henry the Fifth*, Methuen's English Classics (London: Methuen & Co., 1922), p. 15.

33 Gerald Gould, 'A New Reading of *Henry V*', *The English Review*, 1919, 42–55 (p. 44); Brown, 'Stealing Soldiers' Hearts', p. 35.

34 Santanu Das, 'Reframing First World War Poetry: An Introduction', in *The Cambridge Companion to the Poetry of the First World War*, ed. Santanu Das, Cambridge Companions to Literature (Cambridge: Cambridge University Press, 2013), pp. 7–8.

35 *The Newbolt Report*, p. 305.

36 Shakespeare and Smith, *Henry V*, p. 182.

37 Gibson, 'Editing Shakespeare for School Students', p. 197.

38 *The Newbolt Report*, p. 308.

39 Shakespeare and Smith, *Henry V*, p. 171.

40 Shakespeare and Smith, *Henry V*, pp. 172–73.

41 Elizabeth Vandiver, 'Early Poets of the First World War', in *The Cambridge Companion to the Poetry of the First World War*, ed. Santanu Das (Cambridge: Cambridge University Press, 2013), pp. 69–80.

42 Adrian Caesar, 'Brooke, Rupert Chawner (1887–1915), Poet', in *Oxford Dictionary of National Biography* (Oxford: Oxford University Press, 2017), doi.org/10.1093/ref:odnb/32093.

43 Shakespeare and Smith, *Henry V*, p. 173.

44 Sarah Cole, 'Siegfried Sassoon', in *The Cambridge Companion to the Poetry of the First World War*, ed. Santanu Das (Cambridge: Cambridge University Press, 2013), pp. 94–104; Mark Rawlinson, 'Later Poets of the First World War', in *The Cambridge Companion to the Poetry of the First World War*, ed. Santanu Das (Cambridge: Cambridge University Press, 2013), pp. 81–93.

45 R. N. Currey and Sayoni Basu, 'Gibson, Wilfrid Wilson (1878–1962), Poet', in *Oxford Dictionary of National Biography* (Oxford: Oxford University Press, 2009), doi.org/10.1093/ref:odnb/33392; Edmund Blunden and Sayoni Basu, 'Nichols, Robert Malise Bowyer (1893–1944), Poet and Playwright', in *Oxford Dictionary of National Biography* (Oxford: Oxford University Press, 2016), doi.org/10.1093/ref:odnb/35223.

46 Shakespeare and Smith, *Henry V*, pp. 176–77.

47 Bertrand Russell: 'A world full of patriots may be a world full of strife. The more intensely a nation believes in its patriotism, the more fanatically indifferent it will become to the damage suffered by other nations.' Quoted in Shakespeare and Smith, *Henry V*, pp. 174–75.

48 Shaw's actual attitude towards war was complex, but his opposition to First World War garnered him an anti-war reputation. Lagretta Tallent Lenker, 'Shaw: The Bellicose Pacifist', *SHAW: The Annual of Bernard Shaw Studies*, 28.1 (2008), 1–10.

49 William Shakespeare and Evelyn Smith, *Shakespeare's Tragedy of Coriolanus*, Teaching of English Series (London: Thomas Nelson & Sons, 1926), pp. 198–99; William Shakespeare and Evelyn Smith, *Shakespeare's King Henry IV. Part I*, Teaching of English Series, 33 (London: Thomas Nelson & Sons, 1925), p. 145.

50 The most famous of the Dymock poets was Robert Frost. Guy Cuthbertson, 'Dymock Poets (Act. 1913–1915)', in *Oxford Dictionary of National Biography* (Oxford: Oxford University Press, 2009), doi.org/10.1093/ref:odnb/100255.

51 Shakespeare and Smith, *Shakespeare's Tragedy of Coriolanus*, p. 178.

52 Craig, *When the Clyde Ran Red*.

53 Jill Liddington, *The Road to Greenham Common: Feminism and Anti-Militarism in Britain since 1820* (Syracuse, NY: Syracuse University Press, 1991), p. 114.

54 Liddington, *The Road to Greenham Common*, pp. 115–16.

55 Liddington, *The Road to Greenham Common*, p. 118.

56 William Shakespeare and Evelyn Smith, *Shakespeare's Tragedy of King Lear*, Teaching of English Series, 96 (London: Thomas Nelson & Sons, 1926), p. 174.

57 Clare, 'Evelyn Smith, Part 1', p. 4.

58 Clare, 'Evelyn Smith, Part 2', p. 7.

59 'The Glasgow School of Art Home Front Memorial', *Glasgow School of Art: Archives & Collections*, https://gsaarchives.net/collections/index.php/nmc-1721.

60 Lesley Hall, '"Sentimental Follies" or "Instruments of Tremendous Uplift"? Reconsidering Women's Same-Sex Relationships in Interwar Britain', *Women's History Review*, 25.1 (2016), 124–42 (p. 133).

61 William Shakespeare and Evelyn Smith, *Shakespeare's Comedy of As You Like It*, Teaching of English Series (London: Thomas Nelson & Sons, 1926), p. 151.

62 Quoted in Hall, '"Sentimental Follies" or "Instruments of Tremendous Uplift"?', p. 134.

63 For an overview, see chapter 4 in James E. Harding, *The Love of David and Jonathan: Ideology, Text, Reception*, BibleWorld (Abingdon, Oxon: Routledge, 2014); for Oscar Wilde's use of David and Jonathan, see pp. 344–50.

64 George Simmers, 'Despised and Rejected', *Great War Fiction*, 2009, https://greatwarfiction.wordpress.com/2009/12/05/despised-and-rejected; for a discussion of the novel, see Deborah Cohler, 'Sapphism and Sedition: Producing Female Homosexuality in Great War Britain', *Journal of the History of Sexuality*, 16.1 (2007), 68–94.

65 Cohler, 'Sapphism and Sedition', p. 89.

66 Gill Rossini, *Same Sex Love, 1700–1957: A History and Research Guide* (South Yorkshire: Pen & Sword History, 2017), p. 90.

67 '1901 England Census – Agnes Russell Weekes', National Archives of the UK, PRO RG 13/708, Folio 18, Page 27; www.ancestry.com.

68 *The Historical Record (1836–1912) Being a Supplement to the Calendar Completed to September 1912* (London: University of London Press, 1912), p. 395.

69 '1911 England Census – "Agnes Russell Weekes"', National Archives of the UK, PRO RG 14/9121 Sch 153; www.ancestry.com.

70 Jill Liddington and Elizabeth Crawford, '"Women Do Not Count, Neither Shall They Be Counted": Suffrage, Citizenship and the Battle for the 1911 Census', *History Workshop Journal*, 71.1 (2011), 98–127 (p. 110).

71 Liddington and Crawford, 'Women Do Not Count', p. 115.

72 Liddington and Crawford, 'Women Do Not Count', p. 122.

73 Sandra Kemp, Charlotte Mitchell, and David Trotter, 'Weekes, A. R. [Agnes Russell Weekes] and Weekes, R. K. [Rose Kirkpatrick Weekes]', in *Edwardian Fiction: An Oxford Companion* (Oxford: Oxford University Press, 1997), pp. 410–11; 'Books and Authors', *New York Times* (New York, 3 June 1923), p. BR18.

74 Agnes Russell Weekes, *Jenny Essenden* (London: Andrew Melrose, 1916).

75 Its subtitle, 'A Romance of the Other Woman', gives a hint as to its contents. Mark Sturt, a veteran of the Great War recently returned to London from an expedition in the Southern Andes, marries Maisie Archdale in secret, but begins an affair with the dashing, disreputable Jenny Essenden. Much drama ensues before Mark and Maisie eventually reunite.

76 'The Splendid Folly', *The Bookman: A Review of Books and Life*, April 1921, 177–78.

77 For a discussion of suffragists and empire, see Deirdre David, *Rule Britannia: Women, Empire, and Victorian Writing* (Ithaca, NY: Cornell University Press, 1995). For more on women and empire, see Lucy Delap, 'The Superwoman: Theories of Gender and Genius in Edwardian Britain', *The Historical Journal*, 47.1 (2004), 101–26; Philippa Levine, ed., *Gender and Empire* (Oxford University Press, 2007); Paula M. Krebs, *Gender, Race, and the Writing of Empire: Public Discourse and the Boer War* (Cambridge: Cambridge University

Press, 2004); Clare Midgley, 'Bringing the Empire Home: Women Activists in Imperial Britain, 1790s–1930s', in *At Home with the Empire: Metropolitan Culture and the Imperial World*, ed. Catherine Hall and Sonya O. Rose (Cambridge: Cambridge University Press, 2006), pp. 230–50; Jane Rendall, 'The Condition of Women, Women's Writing and the Empire in Nineteenth-Century Britain', in *At Home with the Empire: Metropolitan Culture and the Imperial World*, ed. Catherine Hall and Sonya O. Rose (Cambridge: Cambridge University Press, 2006), pp. 101–21.

78 Heathorn, *For Home, Country, and Race*, p. 122.
79 Heathorn, *For Home, Country, and Race*, p. 122.
80 William Shakespeare and Agnes Russell Weekes, *The Tempest*, University Tutorial Series (London: W. B. Clive, University Tutorial Press, 1909), p. xxiii.
81 Shakespeare and Weekes, *The Tempest*, p. xxiii.
82 Shakespeare and Weekes, *The Tempest*, p. xxii.
83 Alden T. Vaughan and Virginia Mason Vaughan, *Shakespeare's Caliban: A Cultural History* (Cambridge: Cambridge University Press, 1991), p. 102.
84 William Shakespeare and Elizabeth Lee, *The Tempest*, Blackie's Junior School Shakespeare (London: Blackie and Son, 1894), p. 10. For more on Lee, see Chapter 2.
85 Vaughan and Vaughan, *Shakespeare's Caliban*, pp. 112–13.
86 William Shakespeare and Agnes Russell Weekes, *As You Like It*, University Tutorial Series (London: W. B. Clive, University Tutorial Press, 1909), p. 93.
87 William Shakespeare and Agnes Russell Weekes, *Cymbeline*, University Tutorial Series (London: W. B. Clive, University Tutorial Press, 1919), p. xxviii.
88 Shakespeare and Weekes, *Cymbeline*, p. 145.
89 Shakespeare and Weekes, *Cymbeline*, p. xxxii.
90 Shakespeare and Weekes, *Cymbeline*, p. xxvii.
91 Shakespeare and Weekes, *Cymbeline*, p. xxviii.
92 Shakespeare and Weekes, *Cymbeline*, pp. 122–23.
93 Shakespeare and Weekes, *Cymbeline*, pp. 124, xxx.
94 Perhaps more than a *single* detail. Later in their lives, after their sister Helen was widowed, Agnes, Rose, and Helen lived together in the village of Slindon, in Sussex. They occupied Gaston Cottage (formerly Gassons), previously owned by Bessie Rayner Parkes Belloc, a renowned feminist and campaigner for women's rights, the first editor of the *English Women's Journal*, the founder of the female-staffed Victoria Printing Press – in summary, one of the founders of the first organised women's movement in Britain. She also happened to be the mother of writers Hilaire Belloc and Marie Belloc Lowndes. Lowndes wrote mystery and crime novels; Agnes and Rose wrote in related genres during the same period. Coincidence? Almost certainly. Tantalising? Definitely.
95 Willy Maley, 'British Ill Done?: Recent Work on Shakespeare and British, English, Irish, Scottish and Welsh Identities', *Literature Compass*, 3.3 (2006), 487–512 (pp. 487–88).

96 Marcus, *How Shakespeare Became Colonial.*
97 Andrew Murphy, 'Shakespeare's Rising: Ireland and the 1916 Tercentenary', in *Celebrating Shakespeare: Commemoration and Cultural Memory*, ed. Clara Calvo and Coppélia Kahn (Cambridge: Cambridge University Press, 2015), pp. 161–81 (p. 164).
98 Quoted in Philip Edwards, *Threshold of a Nation: A Study in English and Irish Drama* (Cambridge: Cambridge University Press, 1979), p. 199; Andrew Murphy, 'An Irish Catalysis: W. B. Yeats and the Uses of Shakespeare', *Shakespeare Survey*, 64 (2011), 208–19; for more on Yeats and Shakespeare, see Oliver Hennessey, *Yeats, Shakespeare, and Irish Cultural Nationalism* (Lanham, MD: Fairleigh Dickinson University Press, 2014); Andrew Murphy has also interestingly charted other Irish writers' appropriations of Shakespeare's biography. Andrew Murphy, 'Shakespeare's Irish Lives: The Politics of Biography', *Shakespeare Survey*, 68 (2015), 267–81.
99 Quoted in Murphy, 'Shakespeare's Rising', p. 167; for more on Shakespeare and the Easter Rising, see Willy Maley, 'Shakespeare, Easter 1916, and the Theatre of the Empire of Great Britain', *Studies in Ethnicity and Nationalism*, 16.2 (2016), 189–205.
100 Brendan Walsh, *The Pedagogy of Protest: The Educational Thought and Work of Patrick H. Pearse* (Oxford: Peter Lang, 2007).
101 Murphy, 'Shakespeare's Rising', p. 180.
102 Nadia Clare Smith, *Dorothy Macardle: A Life* (Dublin: Woodfield Press, 2007), pp. 7–8.
103 Nadia Clare Smith, 'From Dundalk to Dublin: Dorothy Macardle's Narrative Journey on Radio Éireann', *The Irish Review*, 42 (2010), 27–42 (p. 32).
104 Smith, *Dorothy Macardle*, p. 21.
105 'News and Notes: The Stratford Conferences', *English Journal*, 3 (1914), 521–22 (p. 522).
106 The series is difficult to track and appears not to have been completed, but of the eleven editions I have found, only two were edited by men (*Henry V* by A. Foster Watson and *2 Henry IV* by J. W. B. Adams.). All books in the Carmelite series use the editors' initials instead of first names, obscuring their genders.
107 These editions are undated, so the publication dates are estimates. See the sidenote 'A Primer on Early Student Editions of Shakespeare' for dating procedures.
108 William Shakespeare and D. M. Macardle, *The Tempest*, The Carmelite Shakespeare (London: Horace Marshall and Son, 1917), pp. 46, 89.
109 Shakespeare and Macardle, *The Tempest*, pp. 87–88.
110 Richard English, *Irish Freedom: The History of Nationalism in Ireland* (London: Pan, 2007), p. 242.
111 Shakespeare and Macardle, *The Tempest*, p. 46.
112 Murphy, 'An Irish Catalysis', p. 217.
113 Shakespeare and Macardle, *The Tempest*, p. 47.

114 Shakespeare and Macardle, *The Tempest*, p. 87.
115 English, *Irish Freedom*, p. 264.
116 Shakespeare and Macardle, *The Tempest*, p. 28.
117 Shakespeare and Macardle, *The Tempest*, p. 60.
118 Shakespeare and Macardle, *The Tempest*, p. 88.
119 Shakespeare and Weekes, *The Tempest*, p. xxx.
120 Advertisement in William Shakespeare and C. L. Thomson, *A Midsummer Night's Dream*, The Carmelite Shakespeare (London: Horace Marshall and Son, 1924).
121 Caitriona Clear, 'Cumann Na MBan', in *The Oxford Companion to Irish History* (Oxford: Oxford University Press, 2002).
122 Jennifer Molidor, 'Dying for Ireland: Violence, Silence, and Sacrifice in Dorothy Macardle's *Earth-Bound: Nine Stories of Ireland* (1924)', *New Hibernia Review/Iris Éireannach Nua*, 12.4 (2008), 43–61.
123 Woudhuysen, 'Some Women Editors of Shakespeare', p. 80.
124 McGann, *The Textual Condition*, p. 177.

CHAPTER 5

'We Few, We Happy Few'
Women and the New Bibliography

Establishing the role of women editors in the context of mid-twentieth-century scholarship requires a re-examination of the intellectual movement that shaped it – the New Bibliography – and the early twentieth-century environment that nurtured its creation. Although the label 'New Bibliographers' has been criticised by Honigmann, Werstine, and others for creating a false sense of homogeneity, it remains a convenient and recognizable identifier for a group of scholars who had many disagreements, but whose work, in concert, produced certain effects.[1] The early to mid-twentieth century presents a peculiar paradox in understanding the trends related to women's involvement in editing. As previous chapters have discussed, women edited a significant number of school editions prior to 1940. After 1940, however, there appears to be a major decrease in the number of new editions prepared by women. The number remains low until the mid-1970s, when they gradually begin to rise once more. At the time of writing, I am aware of only thirteen editions by women published between 1940 and 1970. During the thirty years prior, between 1910 and 1940, women edited at least eighty-one published editions. Clearly this is a statistically significant decrease, and it is probably the result of multiple factors, including a levelling-off of the demand for new school editions after the initial rush around the turn of the century and decreased production during and in the immediate aftermath of the war years.[2] This chapter, however, will focus specifically on the changes in the editorial profession that resulted from the rise to prominence of the New Bibliography, and will explore how those changes affected women editors.[3]

The central figures of the New Bibliography are very emphatically a collection of founding *fathers*, as Laurie Maguire has emphasised; among the most celebrated were the famed triumvirate of W. W. Greg, R. B. McKerrow, and A. W. Pollard in the first wave, and John Dover Wilson, Fredson Bowers, and Charlton Hinman in the next. The members of this male cohort do not appear to have been consciously hostile to female scholars. Pollard and McKerrow both worked closely with female collaborators.[4] Still, it is observable that only a few women were involved in the great editorial projects of the early to mid-twentieth century. This chapter will discuss four of the most important: Grace Trenery, Una Ellis-Fermor, Alice Walker, and Evelyn Spearing Simpson. Trenery, Ellis-Fermor, and Walker all worked on Shakespeare; Simpson worked on Jonson and Donne. Although she is the only non-Shakespearean editor discussed at length in this book, the prestige of Simpson's projects within the scholarly community and the detail that her experience allows us to add to the overall picture of women's positions in the editorial world argue strongly for her inclusion. The commonalities in these women's experiences indicate that their appointments to those editorial roles almost always resulted from personal connections with well-placed male colleagues. This is not to say that they did not deserve these jobs on their own merits; however, it does suggest that, as has almost always been the case, both in academia and beyond, many well-qualified, talented women were probably overlooked simply for not being in the right place, knowing the right person, at the right time.

The New Bibliography

Pollard, Greg, and McKerrow envisioned bibliography as a scholarly discipline to be practised with scientific rigour and accuracy. English literature's place as a standard academic discipline in England dates back only to the late nineteenth century. Even as newer institutions such as University College London incorporated it into their programmes, more traditional universities like Oxford and Cambridge remained bastions of the classical curriculum. In order to convince the schools that English should be studied alongside Latin and Greek, that literary studies were more than just 'chatter about Shelley', its advocates shaped their practices to resemble the methods used to study and teach the classics and the Bible, incorporating in particular the philological work emerging from German universities.[5] At the same time, the Victorian ethos of a 'popular', accessible Shakespeare faded as educational reforms enshrined him in new curricula, requiring students to read and study the plays from an early age, to analyse them as 'literature' rather than to enjoy them as entertainment.[6] Gradually, Shakespeare became the property of the academy, the tent-pole author supporting the legitimisation of a new discipline. In other words, as Gary Taylor has summed up, 'by making the study of English literature difficult, they made it respectable'.[7]

And indeed, the products of that study were often ostentatiously difficult, self-consciously attempting to demonstrate that literary work required discipline and erudition. As James Turner has illustrated, literary studies as a discipline grew 'from the confluence of two ancient, historically related fields of knowledge: philology and rhetoric'.[8] The influence of these fields can be seen in student editions of Shakespeare, which often included questions that prompted students to memorise extensively, recite aloud, identify examples of parts of speech and rhetorical devices, and analyse etymology. These impulses carried through into adult literary work as well. Although the New Bibliographers evinced a certain amount of scorn for the methods of the preceding generation, their search for quantifiable, verifiable truth owed a great deal to the work of Furnivall and the New Shakspere Society, which was founded with the goal of determining the order of the plays' composition.[9] Some of the Society's members employed metrical analysis, statistics, and mathematics in their studies. F. G. Fleay became particularly notorious for his metrical analysis, which Algernon Charles Swinburne caricatured as 'the weak-ending test, the light-ending test, the double-ending test, the triple-ending test, the heavy-monosyl-labic-eleventh-syllable-of-the-double-ending test, the run-on-line test, and the central-pause test', all carried out under the auspices of the 'Polypseudocriticopantodapomorosophisticometricoglossematographico-maniacal Company for the Confusion of Shakespeare and Diffusion of Verbiage Unlimited'.[10] This was parodic hyperbole, but not by much; Fleay claimed that critics employing his tests needed 'a thorough training in the Natural Sciences, especially in Mineralogy, classificatory Botany, and above all, in Chemical Analysis'.[11]

As English literature became institutionalised, a new distinction arose around the status of 'professional' scholars of literature. Defining 'professional' as a category required the establishment of an oppositional label, that of the 'amateur'. Discussing the status of the professional historian, which underwent a similar shift, Bonnie Smith suggests that 'the distinction between these juxtaposed terms was crucial to the ability of the professionals to fashion themselves as part of the elite power structure, discrete from the untutored views of ordinary people'.[12] The professional/amateur paradigm is critical to understanding the decrease in numbers of women editors that began after 1940. To impose the illusion of objectivity on what might be thought a subjective topic, scholars created a new set of standards, to the detriment of the amateur:

the insistence upon accuracy lent itself to the new academic culture; creativity could not be routinely measured, but correctness could ... Amateur scholars could not be trusted, because they were careless. 'Armchair' editors could not be trusted, because they neglected their fieldwork, relying on other people's transcriptions, other people's proofreading, other people's eyes.[13]

Taylor focuses on the rapid expansion of the English department during this period, and the increasing number of people employed to 'do Shakespeare'; while true on the larger level of Shakespeare studies as a whole, this analysis ignores the brief contraction that resulted when the supply of editors trained according to the new scientific principles failed to meet the demand of publishers.[14] Many scholars, including men such as those involved with the New Shakspere Society, were classed as amateurs, particularly if they did not hold a university post. These developments also prompted another shift in editorial authority, from the dispersed, multi-vocal authority of the nineteenth century back to a more monolithic, centralised power. Grace Ioppolo, characterising Greg as the 'patriarch' of the New Bibliography, explains that as the new standards of editing became entrenched,

> those who quibbled with [them] were summarily dismissed or excommunicated from a field which had begun to emerge as a scientific discipline if not a sanctified religion. The more elitist the membership, the more mysterious the discipline became to outsiders ... Greg and his followers made bibliography so arcane and specialized that they were allowed to act incontestably and incontrovertibly.[15]

As early as 1901, A. W. Pollard complained in a letter that 'it [was] becoming increasingly difficult to find any one man (or woman) able to combine the gift of literary exposition with the very high knowledge of philology now insisted on' for an academic post in English.[16] This suggests that fewer *people*, not just fewer women, met the new qualifications for academic posts and editorial positions; and this was a problem that intensified in the early decades of the twentieth century.

This is not to say that women did not have additional challenges to overcome in order to enter the ranks of the new and improved editorial profession.[17] English as a taught subject had strongly 'feminine' roots to 'overcome' as it moved into the universities.[18] Although it benefitted from the demand created by women students, its popularity among women, traditionally considered less capable of academic rigour, worked against the public perception of English as a serious topic of study.[19] English was seen as the 'soft' alternative to the traditionally 'hard' classics curriculum, suitable primarily for women, children, and the working classes – that tripartite subordinate grouping. And although, as the previous chapters discussed, women were editing Shakespeare during the rise of the New Bibliography, almost all of those editions were domestic texts. Smith (again, regarding historians) writes that women were seen as 'the quintessential amateurs, who dealt with the market; men, the appropriate professionals, who served more lofty ends'.[20] So how did Trenery, Ellis-Fermor, Walker, and Simpson manage to reach the upper echelons of professional scholarly editing? Chapters 2 and 3 detailed some of the ways that women leveraged personal and professional connections to become involved with editorial work. The stories of these four women suggest that well into the twentieth century, women editors' successes still relied in part on finding a way into the primarily male network of editors via male colleagues.

The Arden Shakespeare: Grace Trenery and Una Ellis-Fermor

As discussed in the introduction to student editions, the first series of the Arden Shakespeare demonstrates the direct links between nineteenth-century student editions and modern critical editions. Arden1 employed Grace Trenery to edit *Much Ado About Nothing*, and her edition was published in 1924.[21] *Much Ado* was the final volume of Arden1 to be published, twenty-five years after Edward Dowden's *Hamlet* had initiated it. Dowden, W. J. Craig, and Robert Hope Case served as the general editors in succession, with Case overseeing most of the series after Craig's death in 1906.[22] Methuen hired twenty volume editors for the series, with several completing multiple editions. Trenery was the only woman among the twenty. She was most likely chosen by Case, given that they both worked in the University of Liverpool's English department. But the employment of a woman editor was also fairly consistent with the Methuen publishing house's wider practices. In her history of the list, Maureen Duffy points out that the first book published under the Methuen name was written by a woman and suggests that this initiated a consistent pattern of hiring women and publishing work by women authors.[23]

Trenery's edition of *Much Ado* demonstrates the degree to which New Bibliographical ideas had entered mainstream editing by the 1920s. Because Arden1 used the Globe/Cambridge edition as a base text, Trenery was not responsible for preparing an entirely original text; however, the first series editors did occasionally depart from the Globe text.[24] Trenery notes in the introduction that 'the present edition keeps throughout to the Quarto as closely as possible'.[25] She bases this decision on Pollard's hypothesis in *Shakespeare's Fight with the Pirates* that the Quarto text (1600) was set from a prompt book in Shakespeare's own handwriting. She also engages with Arthur Quiller-Couch and John Dover Wilson's theory, as set out in the New Cambridge edition (1923), that signs exist of an earlier version of the play that underwent revision.[26] In a *Times Literary Supplement* review, John Middleton Murry praised the editor and her edition, describing it as 'conservative: [and] all the better for it' and hailing it as 'a worthy conclusion' to the Arden1 series.[27]

Although Trenery as editor survives in her Arden edition, like many women editors, Trenery as a person remains somewhat shrouded in mystery. She was born in 1886 in a suburb of Liverpool; according to her baptismal records, her father, John, was a master mariner.[28] She attended Liverpool University and was the 'Lady President' of the Guild of Students in 1912–13.[29] She then went on to teach at Liverpool, and her Arden edition was published in 1924. Her only other publication seems to be a 1915 article in the *Modern Language Review* entitled 'Ballad Collections of the Eighteenth Century', examining the practices of eighteenth-century editors of ballads.[30] Like many women editors, including Agnes Russell Weekes and Flora Masson, Trenery had a literary sister: Gladys Trenery wrote horror stories under the pen name G. G. Pendarves.[31] Passenger manifests reveal that Grace travelled extensively right up to the beginning of the Second World War, reaching locales as distant as Japan, Burma, and Indonesia.[32] It is unusual to find surviving images of women editors who have no alternative claim to fame, but thanks to her travels, Trenery is an exception. Buried in the archives of the *Gleaner* newspaper, published in Kingston, Jamaica, sits a grainy photo (Figure 5.1), next to an article entitled 'Lecturer Leaves'. It reads:

> Leaving Hotel Manchester with much regret was Miss Grace Robarts Trenery, lecturer in English and Education at Liverpool University.
>
> 'My Cornish heritage served me well on the trip down to Jamaica,' said she as she superintended the disposal of her luggage in the Kingston-bound car. 'Our Atlantic crossing was so rough that I was the only woman passenger up during the first few days after we left England.'
>
> Miss Trenery said that she was induced to come to Jamaica because she loves the warmth and had heard that Jamaica is the only island that combines temperate climate with beautiful scenery and lovely gardens.
>
> 'Mandeville has fulfilled all that I had hoped for in this perfect holiday. I've had more actually than I'd expect because no one told me what wonderful voices Jamaican people possess. Why, even the peasantry had such musical inflexions that I marvel that you have not produced more

REGRETTED TO LEAVE MANDEVILLE

Miss Grace Roberts Trenery, lecturer in English Literature, and
Education at Liverpool University, was on the verge of departure
for Kingston to catch her homeward bound boat when our roving
reporter arrived at Manchester Hotel where Miss Trenery spent
a delightful fortnight.

Figure 5.1   Grace Trenery in the Kingston *Gleaner* (22 March 1939), p. 10. Image used
by permission of the Gleaner Company (Media) Limited.

professional singers. Probably the island's distances from the greater musical
centres makes it difficult for the very obvious talent to be trained and
exploited.'

More praise Miss Trenery had for Jamaica too.

'Everyone here is so friendly without being in the least aggressive. I think
that without knowing anyone at all in Jamaica the casual visitor could arrive
here and not be lonely or depressed. Certainly mine has been a perfect
fortnight.'[33]

During the war, Trenery evacuated to the Cambrian coast with some of
the students and other lecturers. A student reminiscing about that period
remembers her offering the literary witticism that 'there are streaks of
Bacon in it', although unfortunately he offers no context or explanation
for the statement.[34] In 1942, she took up the position of Warden of
Women Students at University College Bangor, not far from where she

and the Liverpool students resided during evacuation.[35] She died in a Worcester nursing home in 1950, leaving the bulk of her estate to her friend Lilian Knight Barrie, who was a headmistress in Birmingham as well as J. M. Barrie's niece.[36] She does not appear to have published any work after 1924, but the reasons for this are unclear. Trenery's edition remained the sole Arden *Much Ado* for fifty-seven years, until A. R. Humphreys' edition was finally released in 1981.

Around 1945–47, Methuen commissioned Una Ellis-Fermor, a professor at Bedford College, to look at the Arden1 volumes, some of which were nearly fifty years old, in order to assess possibilities for the series' future. Impressed by her report detailing the rationale for a new series, Methuen hired Ellis-Fermor as the general editor for the enterprise.[37] She oversaw it until her death in 1958, during which time fourteen volumes were completed.[38] She also undoubtedly had a hand in commissioning and overseeing editions that appeared after her death.[39] The origins of Ellis-Fermor's role in Arden2 remain somewhat murky, but they appear, like Trenery, to have involved Arden1 general editor R. H. Case. In 1930, Methuen released *The Life and Works of Christopher Marlowe*, for which Case served as general editor. Una Ellis-Fermor was the only woman hired for the series; she prepared both parts of *Tamburlaine the Great*. The edition was well-reviewed, and the British Academy awarded her the Rose Mary Crawshay Prize for the edition and her other work on Marlowe.[40] She went on to publish a number of books with Methuen throughout the 1930s, including *The Jacobean Drama* (1936), which remained in print in revised editions through to the 1960s.[41] It seems likely that Case approved of Ellis-Fermor's work. From Methuen's point of view, when looking for someone to assess the Arden series in 1946, Ellis-Fermor was already a known quantity and an established scholar who had earned the confidence of the previous series editor.

Unfortunately, the Arden archives appear to have been lost during the past few decades, during which the list has changed hands multiple times.[42] Evidence of Ellis-Fermor's work as general editor, therefore, is either buried in an unwitting publisher's files or has been destroyed. A few traces remain in other archives, however. Letters to Arden2 *Winter's Tale* editor J. H. P. Pafford indicate that Ellis-Fermor commissioned Pafford's edition prior to her death, although the edition was not published until 1963. In one letter discussing an editorial appointment for the *Cymbeline* volume, Ellis-Fermor sets out some of her doubts about the multiple-volume edition:

I am not sure that it isn't time we stopped having whole books on simple plays: it tempts young scholars or critics to oversubtle and sometimes slightly parochial commentary. Or perhaps we should assign a lower limit in age, so as to let in Dover Wilson, Granville Barker, and the otherwise mature! I am inclined to think such tendencies make a man dangerous as an editor: one does not want unbalanced editing in a general edition like the Arden.[43]

In a reply to Pafford's letter suggesting J. H. Walter as a potential editor, Ellis-Fermor enthuses, 'He seems the very person to tackle one of our tiresome problematic texts and I am writing to him this weekend to ask whether he would care for one of the five or six most formidable. A Malone Society editor is the very man for that kind of job.'[44] Despite Ellis-Fermor's use of the male pronoun, women did edit for the Malone Society as early as 1927; however, even under Ellis-Fermor's stewardship, Arden2 turned out to be an almost entirely male affair. The only Arden2 volume completed by a woman was *As You Like It* (1975), prepared by Agnes Latham; however, the Arden2 prefaces reveal that Latham was not the only woman editor selected for Arden2. Beatrice White, a professor at Westfield College, University of London, and a frequent editor of texts for the Early English Text Society, was commissioned to edit *Troilus and Cressida*, but for unknown reasons Roy Walker took over from her, followed by Kenneth Palmer, who eventually finished the edition.[45] The timeline does suggest that White could have been one of Ellis-Fermor's hires. Agnes Latham's situation is similarly suggestive. Although Latham was a decade younger than Ellis-Fermor, both had attended Somerville College, Oxford, and both had taught in the English department at Bedford College, where their employment overlapped for nearly twenty years. Ellis-Fermor died seventeen years before the publication of *As You Like It*, but given the infamously long preparation time allowed to (or taken by) Arden editors, it is quite possible that Ellis-Fermor commissioned Latham's edition at some point before her death in 1958. Without further documentary evidence, however, these remain unconfirmed but tantalising hints at an embryonic network of women editors in the UK.

Ultimately, Arden2 as a whole garnered a mixed legacy, some of which critics tend to attribute to Ellis-Fermor. Ellis-Fermor's original plan had called for new editors to produce minor revisions to stereotyped versions of the Arden1 text, but this scheme was carried out only for the first two editions in the series, after which the editors prepared new texts. As Egan points out, even once the strategy had shifted, a miscellaneous approach persisted, and Egan attributes this to Ellis-Fermor's decision not to 'impose uniformity on the series'.[46] Some editors reused large portions of their predecessors' texts or took their texts from other publishers. In Murphy's view, Ellis-Fermor, 'though a sound scholar and critic, was not a textual specialist and many of the volume editors also lacked extensive experience of editing', resulting in 'something of an uneven affair'.[47]

There is a possible counter-narrative here, however. Ellis-Fermor had not edited Shakespeare prior to taking up the role of general editor, but she was by no means a textual neophyte – her edition of *Tamburlaine* was well-regarded, and although the rest of her work did have a more critical bent, she acknowledges and takes into account the ongoing work of textual scholars.[48] Ellis-Fermor's reference to the Malone Society, which had a well-established reputation for bibliographical exactitude and high editorial standards, suggests that even early in the process, Ellis-Fermor sought qualified editors for Arden2. The original, oft-derided plan to make only minimal corrections to bring the Arden1 editions up to date was almost certainly developed with an awareness of the publishers' bottom line. Methuen may not have been willing to invest in an entirely new series in the mid 1940s. Frank Kermode recalled that Methuen

> warned [the editors] that they were merely doing a service to the scholarly public, that there was no money in the project; they couldn't afford to reset text and commentary and would have to go on using the ancient stereotypes. This meant that if we changed anything ... we had to replace it with exactly the same number of characters as we had deleted. One had visions of printers close to mutiny, chiselling away at the plates and laboriously soldering on the substituted letters.[49]

The series' success, he says, came as a surprise to everyone involved. Had they anticipated how profitable the series would become, Methuen might have made different choices during Arden2's initial stages, including commissioning new editions from the start. They might even have chosen a better-known scholar than Ellis-Fermor to serve as general editor. Either way, it seems unjust to lay the entire burden for Arden2's shortcomings at Ellis-Fermor's feet. Arguably, Ellis-Fermor's replacements, Harold Brooks and Harold Jenkins, did not have significantly more published Shakespearean editorial work to their names when starting their tenures as general editors, but Jenkins had been taught by McKerrow, Greg, and C. J. Sisson, conferring upon him an editorial lineage that Ellis-Fermor lacked.

The narrative that blames Ellis-Fermor for Arden2's lack of 'uniformity' may even have originated with her successors, Brooks and Jenkins. In 1979, Jenkins wrote to *Much Ado* editor Arthur Humphreys that 'fuller and better instructions' had not been established from the commencement of the series in part due to 'Miss Ellis-Fermor's wish to give individual editors a freer hand than in the result has seemed altogether desirable', and he marvelled at 'how much better the general editors could do if they were starting all over again now!'[50] Ellis-Fermor is an easy scapegoat for the Arden2's flaws: she died long before the completion of the series and was, therefore, unable to defend her decisions; she was a woman with a primarily non-Shakespearean scholarly focus at the helm of a Shakespeare series; and while she may have had Case's support before his death in 1944, she lacked connections to the highest-ranking members of the editorial Old Boys' Club. Although the next two editors I consider had their own struggles to contend with, the lack of direct connection to elite male editors was certainly not one of them.

The Editorial and the Personal: Evelyn Spearing Simpson and Alice Walker

Both Alice Walker and Evelyn Spearing Simpson are among the select group of women discussed in this book who have previously been the subjects of critical attention. Laurie Maguire and Chanita Goodblatt have written about Walker and Simpson, respectively, in rich detail.[51] Walker's student T. H. Howard-Hill contributed biographies on his teacher to both the *ODNB* and a series on twentieth-century bibliographers.[52] Both of their best-known projects have been discussed elsewhere in detail: Walker's Oxford Shakespeare by Andrew Murphy, and Simpson's Oxford Ben Jonson by Martin Butler.[53] While these are excellent sources on Walker and Simpson individually, this section examines both women's lives in conversation with one another, and with the lives of other women editors, in order to reveal commonalities in their experiences.

Changing editorial standards were not the only issue facing women editors heading into the mid-century. Various socioeconomic factors also affected women's participation in scholarship and the professionalised university. Carol Dyhouse suggests that the periods following both world wars, particularly the 1930s and 1950s, represented a period of increased precarity for women in universities.[54] Women's enrolment for higher degrees decreased after both wars.[55] There is some debate over the question of whether a conservative backlash after the Great War significantly decreased opportunity for women.[56] Certainly, even if political victories such as the right to vote and the Sex Disqualification (Removal) Act immediately followed the war, major roadblocks remained. Because

Oxford did not allow married women tutors until after 1945, the editor Evelyn Spearing gave up a post at Oxford in order to marry Percy Simpson in 1921. The 'marriage bar' was a common unofficial prohibition in universities – married women were no longer considered primary bread-winners, so there was no reason for them to be working.[57] According to the universities' logic, the money spent on their salaries would be better off used on an unmarried woman's salary, or (a portion of) a man's salary, and the 'profession' of wife, and its attendant responsibilities, was seen as incompatible with an academic post.[58] Resignation was 'expected' but not officially required, for the most part.

An exception came when Liverpool University, in the 1930s, attempted to institute a rule mandating that women's employment be automatically terminated upon marriage, after which they would have to reapply for their old jobs; women's groups vociferously objected, and after a protracted battle, the university rescinded the ruling. Nevertheless, the woman at the centre of the fight, Margaret Miller, still lost her job.[59] Isabel Bisson, the first woman president of the Association of University Teachers, was also an editor of Shakespeare. During the Miller controversy, she addressed the Association, calling for patience, compromise, and a 'quiet unspectacular exploration, without fear or rivalry, of what is our common problem as men and women university teachers'. The days of straightforward battles for access to education were over, she said, and new, more nuanced issues were emerging.[60] Bisson herself held a post in the Department of Education at the University of Birmingham before her marriage in 1933, at the height of the marriage bar controversy, to fellow Birmingham lecturer Laurence Adolphus Bisson.[61] Laurence subsequently took up a post at Oxford, where Isabel, disqualified by her marriage from holding an official university post, found work as a tutor and examiner, as well as editing *As You Like It* (1941) for the New Clarendon Shakespeare.[62]

Women like Bisson and Evelyn Spearing Simpson attempted to main-tain a commitment to academic life, even if it could no longer take the form of a full-time, university-sanctioned career. Evelyn and Percy completed the monumental *Works of Ben Jonson* for Oxford University Press in 1952.[63] Evelyn then took on a ten-volume edition of Donne's sermons, which she was forced to finish alone since her collaborator, George R. Potter, died in 1954, just after the release of the first volume. At one point during the preparation of the Donne edition, she attempted to secure a grant to pay a domestic to assist her during her research. She was doubtful about her chances of success because, as she complained to a friend:

> I don't believe a [grant] committee composed of men can ever be brought
> to understand that it is impossible to do proper research work of a high
> quality if one has continuously to interrupt it to cook a joint and 2
> vegetables, make gravy & the like, make an apple tart, & when the meal
> is finished, wash up, etc, etc. answer the door-bell, dust the sitting-room, &
> all the hundred & one other jobs you know so well. One can do some
> research work, such as checking proofs & answering queries about doubtful
> points, but the main task of sitting down to survey all the sermons for a
> volume and write the Introduction, and then deal with problems of date
> and historical background, requires that one should be able to concentrate
> for hours at a time, & have all one's books & papers around one.[64]

Although Evelyn proved particularly skilled at this juggling act – so much
so that scholar F. P. Wilson, who, probably not coincidentally, also
collaborated with his wife, Joanna, wrote to Evelyn that 'how you manage
to combine the duties of a wife, a housekeeper, and a scholar, as you have
done for years astonishes all your admirers' – the tension between academic achievement and domestic responsibilities disrupted the lives of
many scholarly women.[65] When their partnership began, Alice Walker
told R. B. McKerrow that her time was hers to spend as she desired, except
in the case of 'domestic crises', as when her mother became ill and she had
to run the household.[66] Money and job security were perennial problems.
When she agreed to assist McKerrow, Walker was unemployed, living with
her parents or friends after the conclusion of a temporary assistant lecture-
ship at Royal Holloway College. She was nominally unemployed for eight
years, until she returned to Royal Holloway as the college librarian in
1939.[67] Walker struggled to discuss money with McKerrow, who, to his
credit, was insistent that she be paid fairly for her work on the Oxford
Shakespeare. At one point, after several years of intensive labour, she
suggested that she would be happy for McKerrow to supplement her salary
(which he considered inadequate) by giving her any duplicate books he
had in his library.[68]

Lacking the security of an academic post, Alice Walker remained busy
during the 1930s, becoming half of one of the most significant male-
female partnerships among the New Bibliographers. During the preparation of his Oxford old-spelling Shakespeare, R. B. McKerrow asked
Walker to check over the text, notes, and collations for each play as he
completed them. What seems to have first been envisioned as assistance
with checking collations quickly grew to something more like co-
editorship. In addition to reviewing the pre-existing critical work on
Walker, this discussion draws on a significant primary source that has

not previously received extensive attention. Walker gave instructions that her papers should be destroyed upon her death; luckily, her editorial partner R. B. McKerrow left *his* papers, including over 160 letters and documents from Walker, to Trinity College, Cambridge. Rather less luckily, his papers did suffer the depredations of his son's oversight and editing before they were handed over to the library. It is unclear how much was lost in this process, although the son claimed to have removed only letters that had nothing to do with Shakespeare or editing. While A. C. Green has mined this unpublished correspondence extensively, he did so with a focus on McKerrow rather than Walker.[69] Turning the focus onto Walker deepens the portrait of their editorial partnership and personal friendship. Their always respectful relationship did not preclude 'Dr McKerrow', as Walker always addressed her letters, from addressing her as 'Miss Walker', despite the fact that she had earned her doctorate almost a decade before.[70] In these letters, written between 1935 and 1939, during which time Walker was unemployed and living with her parents or various friends, Walker reveals a relentlessly detail-oriented, exacting mind, and a willingness to challenge and question her senior, male colleague – after one particularly long exchange, she admitted to the ailing McKerrow that 'I expect . . . that what you really long for is not an antidote for yourself, but poison for me'.[71]

In order to better understand McKerrow's editorial method, and thus to better correct his work, Walker began querying McKerrow about the nuts and bolts of his editorial principles. Walker and McKerrow developed a collegial relationship, frequently exchanging jokes and personal details. In one letter, after a long exchange of disagreements over a misunderstood point, Walker offered the kind of humour only truly funny between two deeply engaged textual editors, and indicative of some of the tensions that could develop in a long-term editorial endeavour, as well as in a scholarly collaboration:

> When you told me on one of the *Romeo & Juliet* slips the other day that you saw no harm in recording a reading of Rowe's because it showed he was a good guesser, with the strict notion of what was proper in your collations & what was not (derived from the F2–Camb. rejected reading) in mind, I felt that if you had said that to me on the edge of a cliff I should certainly have pushed you over![72]

The letters reveal that Walker was deeply involved in the final version of McKerrow's *Prolegomena to the Oxford Shakespeare* (or 'Treatment of the Text', as they called it), carefully hammering out McKerrow's arguments with him, pointing out weaknesses, and suggesting improvements. Walker's greatest contribution to McKerrow's work seems to have been consistency. McKerrow acknowledged that editing required a mix of method and intuition, writing that the final leaps necessary to achieve as full an understanding of the author as possible required 'an informed and disciplined imagination'.[73] Walker maintained a version of this view throughout her career, admitting in 1953 that 'an editor can, I think, only trust to his judgment'; however, she was deeply aware of the contradictions between that pragmatic understanding and the strict, detailed rules that McKerrow was attempting to set out.[74]

In an effort to alleviate that problem, she questioned him carefully on perceived inconsistencies, such as the decision mentioned in the letter above to collate a reading of Rowe's 'because it showed he was a good guesser', a reasoning not aligned with McKerrow's stated policy of not collating variant readings from later editors that 'have no merit whatever except that they make sense'.[75] During this process, Walker seemed to realise that she had, in her view, crossed the line and irritated McKerrow:

> By putting to you my own doubts and doubts that it seemed to me might occur to readers at either end of the scale I thought I was doing what you wanted me to do. It would have been far easier to write a panegyric. I should have enjoyed it far more, as (contrary to your belief) I don't enjoy criticising what you have done. Nor do I (as you suppose) always think that what you do is wrong. I know you are far oftener right than I am.
>
> I hope this will have made my attitude clearer. The last thing I wish to do is to obstruct in any way. That would be not only ungrateful but inconsiderate. I dare say I have on occasions put things in a manner that was more strong than seemly.... I expect I have been far too anxious in my capacity as watch-dog, and that I have barked when there was no need.[76]

Walker worried that McKerrow's and Oxford University Press's visions for the text were too muddled and contradictory, and that by striving to appeal to both specialist and non-specialist audiences, they would end up with a text suited to no one. McKerrow's text, if completed, would have been the first assembled entirely according to the principles developed by the New Bibliographers, and Walker understood that this, as well as his choice to produce an old-spelling edition, needed explication:

> I'm horrified to hear that the O.U.P. doesn't want a long introduction. I should have thought the last thing they would want would be to run the risk of readers (and reviewers) failing to understand what you are doing. It's most unfair to you to expect you to be willing to stand up to the inevitable fire of criticism without first having had the opportunity of saying what you

are doing and why, and it's also most inconsiderate to readers to expect them to worry out for themselves all the problems to which you could have supplied an answer if you had been allowed to. Most people who will read your edition will, I feel sure, have little notion of the kind of difficulty that besets anyone who is neither producing a facsimile reprint nor modernising an Elizabethan text. They will probably imagine it is all plain sailing! And if you have given thought to the various problems that occur it's only reasonable that you should want to state the problems and offer what seems to you the proper solution. To want to cut down the Introduction to a new venture of this kind seems to me suicidal. If I were a publisher, I should – in the circumstances – publish the Introduction as a separate work at a good stiff price and make what I could myself out of it! Anyone who intended to use the works themselves seriously would have to buy it![77]

At this point, no comprehensive, practical guide to editing along New Bibliographical principles had been produced. Out of the original triumvirate, only McKerrow ever attempted to edit Shakespeare's complete works – Pollard and Greg restricted themselves to theoretical bibliographic work and the editing of other early modern texts, primarily, although Greg did edit a parallel-text edition of *The Merry Wives of Windsor*.[78]

When McKerrow learned that Greg was planning to deliver the 1939 Clark lectures on 'The Editorial Problem in Shakespeare', he feared that his long labour on the Oxford text was about to be pre-empted by his friend, who had seen early drafts of his 'Treatment of the Text'.[79] Walker mentioned the issue in a letter to McKerrow:

I hope you are really taking a holiday and that you aren't always slinking off to quiet corners with your Shakespeare Introduction. That seems to me a lamentable waste of a holiday, though I know of course that you want to get your oar in before Dr. Greg starts paddling around.[80]

Ultimately, Oxford University Press decided that Walker's commercial instincts were sound and chose to publish 'Treatment of the Text' in a separate volume, which was hastily produced and released in May 1939 under the title *A Prolegomena to the Oxford Shakespeare*. In the introduction, McKerrow anxiously took pains to make clear how long his work had been in progress, and that Greg had read early drafts.[81] McKerrow's fears proved unfounded, though, since Greg's lectures covered material different from that treated in the *Prolegomena*.

Despite the extensive work done by both McKerrow and Walker, their old-spelling edition never appeared – the first Oxford Shakespeare actually published was Stanley Wells and Gary Taylor's *Complete Works* in 1986. Andrew Murphy and Laurie Maguire have identified a possible reason for the project's abandonment in Walker's 'loss of faith' in the principles of the old-spelling edition.[82] Walker's letters reveal that she had questioned some of McKerrow's editorial principles, including those relating to punctuation, spelling, and the treatment of stage directions and names, from the beginning of her involvement with the work. McKerrow acknowledged in a letter to Kenneth Sisam at the Press that while Walker understood his ideas better than anyone, she did not always agree with them.[83] Advocates for old-spelling editions argue that modernisation irons out the puns, rhymes, and ambiguities of the original spelling while imposing anachronistic meanings on words.[84] To Walker, an old-spelling edition was 'necessary as a prelude to one in modern spelling', but she recognised the limited value of old-spelling editions for many readers, and tended to advocate for modern spelling.[85] Her only published editions were in a modern spelling series, the New Cambridge Shakespeare.[86]

Although she brought up and argued her points with McKerrow, she deferred to his decisions concerning editorial principles. Considering how much work had already been done by McKerrow's death, it is certainly possible that Walker preferred not to continue such an epic task within guidelines with which she did not agree. Additionally, she may have been concerned that the Press would appoint a senior male scholar to take over as full editor, leaving her in the position of assistant. Despite her central role in the project, McKerrow informed Walker in 1939 that although Oxford University Press had agreed to keep her on as assistant editor in the event of his death, 'they would probably wish to appoint a professor or someone of that kind as Editor in Chief'. Upon McKerrow's death in 1940, Walker assumed day-to-day responsibility for the Oxford Shakespeare, with E. K. Chambers, W. W. Greg, and David Nichol Smith serving as an advisory board, at her request.[87] Howard-Hill notes that her lack of published bibliographical work at the time of McKerrow's death argued against her assuming sole responsibility for the edition, and finds no evidence she was ever officially given the role of general editor before the Second World War interrupted the work; rather, she assumed the post on a somewhat de facto basis.[88] After the war, the Press chose G. I. Duthie to head up the revitalised project. Walker signed on as coeditor in 1955, becoming the sole editor again when Duthie became ill two years later.[89] She never completed the edition; Howard-Hill reports that, when he approached her in 1972, 'she simply did not want to talk about the edition'.[90] The Oxford Shakespeare project languished until the hiring of Stanley Wells in 1978.

Walker's later work on compositor studies and her editions of *Troilus and Cressida* and *Othello* for the New Cambridge Shakespeare explain her oft-awarded title of 'most important female editor of the twentieth century'.[91] Whether she deserves that title is a separate question. Objectively, Charlotte Porter and Helen Clarke completed a larger body of published editorial work. They had, however, been largely forgotten, relegated to the dustbins of editorial history with many other 'amateurs', until Roberts's 2006 article rescued them from obscurity.[92] Walker's distinction can be explained in several ways. First, she engaged closely with New Bibliographical theories, making her part of the mainstream and 'significant' editorial currents of the twentieth century. In 1960, she became a Reader in Bibliography and Textual Criticism at Oxford, which conferred upon her a substantial level of institutional authority and prestige. Finally, her position as McKerrow's assistant and protégé essentially grandfathered her into the all-male New Bibliographical cohort. Walker, like Evelyn Simpson, began her editorial career as the adjunct, junior member of a male-led team, brought on to support the male editor in illness, old age, or exhaustion.

Both Walker and Simpson tended to be deferential to their male partners, who had ultimate authority over the project. Percy Simpson signed on to the Oxford Ben Jonson edition in 1903, agreeing to a 1907 completion date. That date came and went, and over twenty years later, Evelyn wrote to R. W. Chapman at Oxford University Press suggesting that she be brought on to edit the final volumes. Percy had refused to accept additional collaborators several times before, and in deference to her husband's feelings, Evelyn 'warned Chapman that the suggestion would have to be made as if on the Press's initiative: Percy would not contemplate the idea if she put it forward herself'.[93] Once she was officially added to the project, Evelyn remained aware of her husband's possible sensitivities regarding her involvement with the project and was fiercely protective of him. In 1937, Evelyn wrote a brief note to W. W. Greg informing him that Percy had finally accepted a D.Litt. from Oxford. 'If you are reviewing Vol. V', she wrote pointedly, 'you may be glad to know – please don't trouble about any congratulations'.[94] Five years later, in a letter to Greg responding to his harsh critiques of the Jonson edition, she wrote:

> There is a minor point which my husband would not like me to mention, but it irritates me. He has been D.Litt. of Oxford for the last 6 or 7 years, but you always refer to him as 'Mr Simpson', though we always describe you as Dr Greg. You could ascertain his degree from the cover of the number of R.E.S. in which your review appeared, or from Who's Who.

> I prefer to be called 'Mrs Simpson', except in American publications, where
> I wish to be known as 'Dr Evelyn Simpson' when I write on Donne. 'Dr &
> Mrs Simpson' should be the form of reference to us in our joint work on
> Jonson.[95]

Simpson downgraded her own authority even as she championed her
husband's, deliberately positioning herself as the subordinate member of
their partnership.

The contradictory mix of deference and assertiveness displayed in these
instances is consistent with how her daughter, Mary Fleay, described her
parents' attitudes:

> She was not a strong feminist – she was certainly never a suffragette –
> though she upheld the view that women should be highly educated & able
> to use their abilities. In this she was not in conflict with my father, who, for
> a Victorian, held extremely liberal opinions. Of the two my mother was the
> more brilliant & my father always acknowledged this.[96]

Percy may have deferred to his wife's brilliance in private, but the public
perception of their partnership skewed more towards the traditional framing of male-female partnerships. Evelyn, ever sensitive to her husband's
feelings, seems to have encouraged that, explaining in that same letter to
Greg that, although she could not say so publicly, 'certain of your criti-
cisms represent, in a stronger form, my own ideas about the presentation
of our edition'; however, 'he is nearly seventy-seven, & I do not like to
press opposition on matters which seem to me trivial'.[97] Although Evelyn
ultimately took over primary responsibility for the edition and completed
it after Percy's death, Martin Butler points out that their contemporaries
relegated Evelyn to an ancillary role of 'editorial polisher', with Greg
writing in his review of volumes 9 and 10 that he would 'speak throughout
of Dr. Simpson in the singular. It is manifest that the substance of the
work is Dr. Percy's, and it may be assumed without disparagement that
Dr. Evelyn's part has been mainly one of consultation and revision.'[98]
After relegating her to a limited role in the edition's creation, Greg adds
insult to injury by complaining that she could have done a better job of
polishing the final product.[99] This type of criticism of the female member
of an editorial team had already occurred almost a century before, when
the anonymous critic 'Jaques' insisted that 'lady editor' Mary Cowden
Clarke was to blame for 'the numberless alterations, mutilations, corruptions, or whatever we may choose to call them, which deface these noble
dramas'.[100] Cowden Clarke, Simpson, and Walker all experienced the
phenomenon described by Thompson and Roberts, in which the female

half of a male-female partnership becomes the ancillary 'helpmate' and the scapegoat for any shortcomings in the final product.[101]

Additionally, despite its usefulness in bringing her into the editorial fold, Walker's connection with McKerrow became a double-edged sword after his death. Greg, as the longest-lived of the triumvirate, had the longest time in which to formulate his editorial ideas, and to refute those of his deceased friends. Greg framed the beginning of *The Editorial Problem in Shakespeare* as a response to McKerrow's *Prolegomena*, arguing with and expanding upon McKerrow's principles. Gradually, the deceased McKerrow became perceived as a proponent of 'conservative' editorial theory, in opposition to the more 'radical', up-to-date work produced by the still-living Greg. Setting aside the question of whether this assessment is fair or accurate, Walker's close connection to McKerrow was an inextricable part of her editorial identity. Chained to the old-spelling edition, a concept growing increasingly obsolete, Walker's opportunities to innovate in her work for the Oxford Shakespeare were limited, while both her reviews and her New Cambridge editions demonstrate that Walker possessed a capacity and desire for editorial innovation. Maguire suggests that her final 'Prospero-like' act of requesting that her papers be destroyed after her death 'ranks as one of Walker's clearest textual statements'.[102] Undoubtedly, it was a dramatic full stop to a life unusually focused on punctuation – one could even say a substantive one.

Given the somewhat arbitrary nature of this chapter's 1950 cut-off date, this is undoubtedly an incomplete picture of the mid-century editorial world. Further archival work should be done in order to fill in the details of how women bibliographers and editors interacted with their male colleagues. In addition to seeking out women's archival remains, male editors' archives should be mined more carefully for traces of women whose papers were not centrally preserved. The Arden Shakespeare archives may yet resurface, and personal interviews with surviving Arden2 editors and publishing-house employees would undoubtedly provide more details. Moreover, the archival material that has survived provides some evidence of changing tides within the scholarly world. As in Chapter 3, American universities once again offer an enormous amount of untapped material. Archives at institutions such as Yale and the University of Chicago demonstrate that while they might not always have been successful, as in the case of Ellis-Fermor and the Arden2, women continued to quietly assemble networks of fellow female scholars during the early to mid-twentieth century. Henrietta Bartlett, Belle da Costa Greene, and other female scholars and bibliophiles banded together to form the Hroswitha Club.

Twenty-five years after McKerrow hired Walker to check his collations, Evelyn Simpson hired Mary Holtby as her assistant. Like Walker, Holtby's competence gradually earned her a large role in the preparation of Evelyn's Donne edition. Moreover, after Evelyn's original co-editor, George Potter, died, his widow insisted upon helping to complete the edition, often to Evelyn's irritation – although Mabel Harrington Potter held a BA from Mt. Holyoke and an MA from Columbia, she had studied music, not Donne.[103] Edith Rickert, with John Manly, employed at least twenty-seven women in America and England during the sixteen-year process of assembling their Chaucer edition.[104]

On the whole, however, the details gathered thus far indicate how vital the support of male colleagues could be in the increasingly insular, male-dominated world of professional editing. In this sense, it seems that little had changed since the late nineteenth century, when female scholars relied on men like Frederick Furnivall for contacts and backing. But while they may have needed men to unlock doors for them, women editors like Grace Trenery, Una Ellis-Fermor, Alice Walker, and Evelyn Spearing Simpson moved commandingly through those opened doors. Editing, like so many things, is not and has never been purely a meritocracy, and to say that they needed the men around them for this kind of assistance in no way downgrades their achievements or casts doubts on their talents or scholarly merit. It simply acknowledges the pragmatic reality that access matters, and when playing a rigged game, success hinges on seizing opportunities when they present themselves.

Notes

1 E. A. J. Honigmann, 'The New Bibliography and Its Critics', in *Textual Performances: The Modern Reproduction of Shakespeare's Drama*, ed. Lukas Erne and Margaret Jane Kidnie* (Cambridge: Cambridge University Press, 2004), pp. 77–93; Paul Werstine, 'Housmania: Episodes in Twentieth-Century "Critical" Editing of Shakespeare', in *Textual Performances: The Modern Reproduction of Shakespeare's Drama*, ed. Lukas Erne and Margaret Jane Kidnie (Cambridge: Cambridge University Press, 2004), pp. 49–62; A. C. Green, 'The Difference between McKerrow and Greg', *Textual Cultures*, 4.2 (2009), 31–53.

2 For trends in educational publishing, see chapter 5 in Weedon, *Victorian Publishing*.

3 For a wider overview of the New Bibliography, see Laurie E. Maguire, *Shakespearean Suspect Texts: The 'Bad' Quartos and Their Contexts* (Cambridge: Cambridge University Press, 1996); Egan, *The Struggle for Shakespeare's Text*; Murphy, *Shakespeare in Print*.

4 McKerrow collaborated with Alice Walker, as discussed below. In 1916, Pollard and Henrietta C. Bartlett published *A Census of Shakespeare's Plays in Quarto 1594–1709*. For Bartlett, see the sidenote 'On Women Editing Not-Shakespeare (or Not Editing)', above.

5 D. C. Greetham, 'A History of Textual Scholarship', in *The Cambridge Companion to Textual Scholarship*, ed. Neil Fraistat and Julia Flanders (Cambridge: Cambridge University Press, 2013), pp. 16–41 (p. 35); Jo McMurtry, *English Language, English Literature: The Creation of an Academic Discipline* (Hamden, CT: Archon Books, 1985), pp. 13–17; Dabbs, 'Shakespeare and the Department of English', pp. 89–91; Gerald Graff, 'Is There a Conversation in This Curriculum? Or, Coherence without Disciplinarity', in *English as a Discipline, or Is There a Plot in This Play?*, ed. James C. Raymond (Tuscaloosa: University of Alabama Press, 1996), pp. 11–28 (pp. 15–17). On the gendering of the discipline of philology in Germany, see Walter Erhart, 'The Gender of Philology – A Genealogy of *Germanistik*', in *Gendered Academia: Wissenschaft und Geschlechterdifferenz, 1890–1945*, ed. Miriam Kauko, Sylvia Mieszkowski, and Alexandra Tischel (Gottingen: Wallstein Verlag, 2005), pp. 41–64 (p. 46).

6 Dabbs, 'Shakespeare and the Department of English', pp. 84–85, 89.

7 Taylor, *Reinventing Shakespeare*, p. 246.

8 Turner, *Philology*, p. 254.

9 For details on the founding of the NSS, see chapter 1 in Kahan, *Quest for Shakespeare*.

10 Murphy, *Shakespeare in Print*, p. 211.

11 Quoted in Turner, *Philology*, p. 263.

12 Smith, *The Gender of History*, p. 7.

13 Taylor, *Reinventing Shakespeare*, p. 254.

14 Taylor, *Reinventing Shakespeare*, pp. 255–56.

15 Grace Ioppolo, '"Much They Ought Not to Have Attempted": Editors of Collected Editions of Shakespeare from the Eighteenth to the Twentieth Centuries', in *The Culture of Collected Editions*, ed. Andrew Nash (Basingstoke: Palgrave Macmillan, 2003), pp. 157–71 (p. 164).

16 Quoted in Tatiana Wolff, 'English', in *Bedford College, University of London: Memories of 150 Years*, ed. J. Mordaunt Crook (London: Royal Holloway and Bedford New College, 2001), pp. 95–108 (p. 98).

17 For more on the involvement of women in the development of English as a discipline, see Ben Knights, 'Reading as a Man: Women and the Rise of English Studies in England', and Ina Schabert, 'A Double-Voiced Discourse: Shakespeare Studies by Women in the Early 20th Century', both in *Gendered Academia: Wissenschaft und Geschlechterdifferenz 1890–1945*, ed. Miriam Kauko, Sylvia Mieszkowski, and Alexandra Tischel (Gottingen: Wallstein Verlag, 2005).

18 Graff, 'Is There a Conversation in This Curriculum?', p. 15. For more on the connections between Shakespeare, English literature, and education for women and the working class, see Bottoms, 'Doing Shakespeare'; Murphy,

Shakespeare for the People; Richard D. Altick, *The English Common Reader: A Social History of the Mass Reading Public, 1800–1900*, 2nd ed. (Columbus: Ohio State University Press, 1998); Dinah Birch, *Our Victorian Education* (Oxford: Blackwell, 2008); Rosemary O'Day, 'Women and Education in Nineteenth Century England', in *Women, Scholarship and Criticism: Gender and Knowledge c. 1790–1900*, ed. Joan Bellamy, Anne Laurence, and Gill Perry (Manchester: Manchester University Press, 2000), pp. 91–109; Dinah Birch, 'Education', in *The Cambridge History of Victorian Literature*, ed. Kate Flint (Cambridge: Cambridge University Press, 2012), pp. 329–49; Ziegler, 'Introducing Shakespeare'; Franklin E. Court, *Institutionalizing English Literature: The Culture and Politics of Literary Study, 1750–1900* (Stanford, CA: Stanford University Press, 1992); Juliette Dor, 'Caroline Spurgeon (1869–1942) and the Institutionalisation of English Studies as a Scholarly Discipline', *Philologie Im Netz*, Supplement 4 (2009), 55–66; Alexandra Lawrie, *The Beginnings of University English: Extramural Study, 1885–1910* (Basingstoke: Palgrave Macmillan, 2014).

19 McMurtry, *English Language, English Literature*, p. 13.

20 Smith, *The Gender of History*, p. 7.

21 William Shakespeare and Grace Trenery, *Much Ado About Nothing*, The Arden Shakespeare (London: Methuen & Co., 1924).

22 Craig was best known as one of the editors for the seminal Cambridge/ Globe editions.

23 Maureen Duffy, *A Thousand Capricious Chances: A History of the Methuen List, 1889–1989* (London: Methuen, 1989), p. 2. *Much Ado* is one of two plays have been edited twice by women over the course of the Arden's publication, as Clare McEachern edited it for Arden3 (2007). The other play edited twice by women for Arden is *As You Like It* (Agnes Latham, 1975, and Juliet Dusinberre, 2006).

24 Egan, *The Struggle for Shakespeare's Text*, p. 241.

25 Shakespeare and Trenery, *Much Ado About Nothing*, p. xi.

26 Shakespeare and Trenery, *Much Ado About Nothing*, pp. xvi–xi.

27 John Middleton Murry, 'Much Ado', *Times Literary Supplement*, 1165 (1924), 293.

28 *Liverpool, England, Church of England Baptisms, 1813–1917*, digital images, entry for Grace Robarts Trenery, 1887, citing Liverpool Record Office, 283 JWD/2/2; www.ancestry.com.

29 'Past Guild Officers @ Liverpool Guild of Students', www.liverpoolguild.org/ main-menu/about-us/history-of-the-guild/past-guild-officers.

30 Grace R. Trenery, 'Ballad Collections of the Eighteenth Century', *The Modern Language Review*, 10.3 (1915), 283–303; she was also thanked for her help with the preparation of a volume of Keats after the editor was killed in the First World War. John Keats and W. T. Young, *Poems of Keats: Endymion: The Volume of 1820 and Other Poems* (Cambridge: Cambridge University Press, 1917).

31 Terence E. Hanley, 'G. G. Pendarves (1885–1938)', http://tellersofweirdtales
   .blogspot.com/2016/05/gg-pendarves-1885-1938.html.
32 'UK, Incoming Passenger Lists, 1878–1960; Port of Departure: Batavia,
   Indonesia', 1930, National Archives of the UK, BT26/948/62; www
   .ancestry.com; 'UK, Incoming Passenger Lists, 1878–1960; Port of
   Departure: Rangoon, Burma', 1933, TNA, BT26/1017/56, www.ancestry
   .com; 'UK, Incoming Passenger Lists, 1878–1960; Port of Departure:
   Yokohama, Japan', 1939, TNA, BT26/ 1179/122; www.ancestry.com.
33 'Lecturer Leaves', *Kingston Gleaner* (Kingston, Jamaica, 22 March 1939),
   p. 10.
34 Paul Edward Hedley Hair, *Arts, Letters, Society: A Miscellany Commemorating
   the Centenary of the Faculty of Arts at the University of Liverpool* (Liverpool:
   Liverpool University Press, 1996), p. 54.
35 *Universities Review, Volumes 13–16* (Bristol: J. W. Arrowsmith, 1942),
   pp. 39, 76.
36 'Probate Record and Last Will and Testament of Grace Robartes Trenery',
   1950, Principal Probate Registry; https://probatesearch.service.gov.uk.
37 Duffy, *A Thousand Capricious Chances*, p. 134.
38 'Dr. Una Ellis-Fermor', *The Times* (London, 25 March 1958), p. 10.
39 The editions published during Ellis-Fermor's life were *Macbeth* (ed. Kenneth
   Muir, 1951), *Love's Labour's Lost* (ed. Richard David, 1951), *King Lear* (ed.
   Kenneth Muir, 1952), *Titus Andronicus* (ed. J. C. Maxwell, 1953), *The
   Tempest* (ed. Frank Kermode, 1954), *Antony and Cleopatra* (ed. M.R.
   Ridley, 1954), *Henry V* (ed. J. H. Walter, 1954), *King John* (ed. E. A.
   J. Honigmann, 1954), *The Merchant of Venice* (ed. John Russell Brown,
   1955), *Julius Caesar* (ed. T. S. Dorsch, 1955), *Cymbeline* (ed. J. M.
   Nosworthy, 1955), *Richard II* (ed. Peter Ure, 1956), *2 Henry VI* (ed.
   Andrew S. Cairncross, 1957), and *Henry VIII* (ed. R. A. Foakes, 1957).
40 M. Hope Dodds, Review of *Tamburlaine the Great*, by Christopher Marlowe
   and U. M. Ellis-Fermor, *The Modern Language Review*, 26.2 (1931), 188–89;
   'Rose Mary Crawshay Prize', *The British Academy*, www.thebritishacademy.ac
   .uk/rose-mary-crawshay-prize.
41 Una Ellis-Fermor, *The Jacobean Drama* (London: Methuen & Co., 1936).
42 Duffy mentions a 'carefully maintained' archive and file room in her 1989
   book. Duffy, *A Thousand Capricious Chances*, p. ix. Some Methuen records
   are held in the University of Reading Special Collections, within the
   Routledge archives. Arden Publisher Margaret Bartley (Bloomsbury
   Publishing) says that the Arden Shakespeare records are not in the current
   list-owner's possession. (personal communication) The Harold Jenkins Papers
   at Queen Mary, University of London, include drafts and correspondence
   from his work on Arden2, but these date from after Ellis-Fermor's death.
43 Una Ellis-Fermor, 'Letter to J. H. P. Pafford', 28 May 1948, Senate House
   Library, Archives and Manuscripts, John Henry Pyle Pafford Papers, MS 780/
   17.

44 Ellis-Fermor, 'Letter to J. H. P. Pafford'. Walter eventually edited *Henry V* (1954) for Arden2.

45 William Shakespeare and Kenneth Palmer, *Troilus and Cressida*, Arden Shakespeare, Second Series (London: Methuen, 1982), p. vii.

46 Egan, *The Struggle for Shakespeare's Text*, p. 252.

47 Murphy, *Shakespeare in Print*, p. 237.

48 Dodds, Review of *Tamburlaine the Great*, p. 188.

49 Frank Kermode, 'In the Forest of Arden', *The Independent* (London, 18 March 1995), section Culture: Books, www.independent.co.uk/arts-enter tainment/books/in-the-forest-of-arden-1611731.html.

50 Harold Jenkins, 'Letter to Arthur Humphreys', 16 January 1979, Queen Mary University of London Archives: Harold Jenkins Papers, HJ/9/12.

51 Maguire, 'Alice Walker'; Chanita Goodblatt, '"The University Is a Paradise, Rivers of Knowledge Are There": Evelyn Mary Spearing Simpson', in *Women Editing/Editing Women: Early Modern Women Writers and the New Textualism*, ed. Ann Hollinshead Hurley and Chanita Goodblatt (Newcastle: Cambridge Scholars, 2009), pp. 257–84.

52 T. H. Howard-Hill, 'Walker, Alice (1900–1982)', in *Oxford Dictionary of National Biography* (Oxford: Oxford University Press, 2004), doi.org/10.1093/ref:odnb/60296; T. H. Howard-Hill, 'Alice Walker', in *Twentieth-Century British Book Collectors and Bibliographers*, ed. William Baker and Kenneth Womack, The Dictionary of Literary Biography, 201 (Detroit, MI: Gale Research, 1999), pp. 297–305.

53 Murphy, *Shakespeare in Print*, pp. 223–29; Martin Butler, 'The Making of the Oxford "Ben Jonson"', *The Review of English Studies*, 62.257 (2011), 738–57.

54 Carol Dyhouse, 'The British Federation of University Women and the Status of Women in Universities, 1907–1939', *Women's History Review*, 4.4 (1995), 465–85 (p. 469).

55 Jennifer Jones and Josephine Castle, 'Women in UK Universities, 1920–1980', *Studies in Higher Education*, 11.3 (1986), 289–97 (p. 294).

56 For an overview of the positions, see Adrian Bingham, '"An Era of Domesticity"? Histories of Women and Gender in Interwar Britain', *Cultural and Social History*, 1.2 (2004), 225–33.

57 Although it was unofficial in academia, it was official in other fields, such as teaching and the Civil Service. For a brief overview of marriage bars, see Kate Murphy, 'A Marriage Bar of Convenience? The BBC and Married Women's Work 1923–39', *Twentieth Century British History*, 25.4 (2014), 533–61.

58 Unsurprisingly, women earned less than men, particularly in co-educational settings. See Dyhouse, *No Distinction of Sex?*, pp. 149–51.

59 Dyhouse, *No Distinction of Sex?*, pp. 163–67.

60 'Notes and Announcements', *Bulletin of the American Association of University Professors (1915–1955)*, 21.6 (1935), 462–72 (p. 467); Dyhouse, *No Distinction of Sex?*, p. 168.

61 'Marriages', *The Times* (London, 6 September 1933), p. 1; A.E., 'Laurence Adolphus Bisson, 1897–1965', *French Studies*, 20.1 (1966), 114–15.

62 '1939 England and Wales Register – Isabella J. Bisson', National Archives of the UK, PRO RG 101/2180E/283/2; www.ancestry.com; William Shakespeare and Isabel J. Bisson, *As You Like It*, New Clarendon Shakespeare (Oxford: Oxford University Press, 1941).

63 C. H. Herford was also involved with the project, but died in 1931, long before its completion.

64 Evelyn Simpson, quoted in Goodblatt, '"The University Is a Paradise"', p. 276.

65 F. P. Wilson, 'Letter to Evelyn Spearing Simpson', 21 January 1962, Evelyn Simpson Papers. James Marshall and Marie-Louise Osborn Collection, Beinecke Rare Book and Manuscript Library, Yale University, Series I, Box 3, Folder 83; see editor Fanny Johnson's references to this problem in her novel, discussed in Chapter 2. Johnson, *In statu pupillari*, I, pp. 98–99.

66 Alice Walker, 'Letter to R. B. McKerrow', 5 March 1936, Trinity College Library, Cambridge: MCKW, A4/3.

67 Howard-Hill, 'Walker, Alice (1900–1982)'.

68 Alice Walker, 'Letter to R. B. McKerrow', 28 March 1939, MCKW, A4/162.

69 Green, 'The Difference between McKerrow and Greg'. I am deeply grateful to Mr. Green for providing me with the transcripts of the McKerrow–Walker letters, along with his careful annotations.

70 McKerrow did refer to Walker by her full title in the preface of the *Prolegomena*.

71 Alice Walker, 'Letter to R. B. McKerrow', 15 September 1937, MCKW, A4/109.

72 The 'slips' Walker refers to were part of her system for noting remarks or corrections for McKerrow's attention. Alice Walker, 'Letter to R. B. McKerrow', 15 February 1937, MCKW, A4/79.

73 McKerrow, *Prolegomena for the Oxford Shakespeare*, p. viii.

74 Alice Walker, *Textual Problems of the First Folio* (Cambridge: Cambridge University Press, 1953), p. 89; Maguire, 'Alice Walker', p. 334.

75 McKerrow, *Prolegomena for the Oxford Shakespeare*, p. 68.

76 Alice Walker, 'Letter to R. B. McKerrow', 26 September 1937, MCKW, A4/118.

77 Alice Walker, 'Letter to R. B. McKerrow', 18 December 1937, MCKW, A4/138.

78 William Shakespeare and W. W. Greg, *Shakespeare's Merry Wives of Windsor* (Oxford: Clarendon Press, 1910).

79 Green, 'The Difference between McKerrow and Greg', pp. 39–42.

80 Alice Walker, 'Letter to R. B. McKerrow', 14 November 1938, MCKW, A4/155.

81 McKerrow, *Prolegomena for the Oxford Shakespeare*, pp. ix–x.

82 Maguire, 'Alice Walker', p. 331; Murphy, *Shakespeare in Print*, p. 229.

83 Murphy, *Shakespeare in Print*, p. 226.

84 Stanley Wells, 'Old and Modern Spelling', in *Re-editing Shakespeare for the Modern Reader*, Oxford Shakespeare Studies (Oxford: Clarendon Press, 1984), pp. 5–31 (p. 8).

85 Maguire, 'Alice Walker', p. 332.

86 William Shakespeare and Alice Walker, *Troilus and Cressida*, New Cambridge Shakespeare (Cambridge: Cambridge University Press, 1969); William Shakespeare, Alice Walker, and J. Dover Wilson, *Othello*, New Cambridge Shakespeare (Cambridge: Cambridge University Press, 1957).

87 Maguire, 'Alice Walker', p. 343.

88 Howard-Hill, 'Alice Walker', pp. 300–301.

89 Murphy, *Shakespeare in Print*, p. 228.

90 Murphy, *Shakespeare in Print*, p. 229.

91 For Walker's legacy, see Thompson, 'Feminist Theory and the Editing of Shakespeare'; Valerie Wayne, 'Remaking the Texts: Women Editors of Shakespeare, Past and Present', in *Women Making Shakespeare: Text, Performance and Reception*, ed. Gordon McMullan, Lena Cowen Orlin, and Virginia Mason Vaughan (London: Bloomsbury Arden Shakespeare, 2014), pp. 57–67; I am very grateful to Claire M. L. Bourne for her fascinating paper on Walker, given in our SAA seminar. Claire M. L. Bourne, '"Typographical Distinction": Alice Walker's Edward Capell's Shakespeare', in the Women and Book History seminar (Shakespeare Association of America, Los Angeles, 2018); for a sampling of Walker's published work, see Alice Walker, 'Principles of Annotation: Some Suggestions for Editors of Shakespeare', *Studies in Bibliography*, 9 (1957), 95–105; Alice Walker, 'Compositor Determination and Other Problems in Shakespearian Texts', *Studies in Bibliography*, 7 (1955), 3–15; Alice Walker, 'The Textual Problem of "Troilus and Cressida"', *The Modern Language Review*, 45.4 (1950), 459–64; Alice Walker, 'The Text of *Measure for Measure*', *The Review of English Studies*, 34.133 (1983), 1–20; Walker, *Textual Problems of the First Folio*.

92 Roberts, 'Women Edit Shakespeare', p. 146.

93 Butler, 'The Making of the Oxford "Ben Jonson"', p. 748.

94 Evelyn Spearing Simpson, 'Letter to W. W. Greg', 25 May 1937, Walter Wilson Greg Papers, James Marshall and Marie-Louise Osborn Collection, Beinecke Rare Book and Manuscript Library, Series XI, Box 9.

95 Butler, 'The Making of the Oxford "Ben Jonson"', p. 752.

96 Mary Fleay, quoted in Goodblatt, '"The University Is a Paradise"', p. 261.

97 Evelyn Spearing Simpson, 'Letter to W. W. Greg', 15 August 1942, Walter Wilson Greg Papers. Series XI, Box 9.

98 W. W. Greg, 'Reviewed Work(s): Ben Jonson. Vol. IX. An Historical Survey of the Text: The Stage History of the Plays: Commentary on the Plays by C. H. Herford, Evelyn Simpson, Percy Simpson and Ben Jonson; Ben Jonson. Vol. X. Play Commentary: Masque Commentary by C. H. Herford, Percy Simpson, Evelyn Simpson and Ben Jonson', *The Review of English Studies*, 2.7 (1951), 275–80; quoted in Butler, 'The Making of the Oxford "Ben Jonson"', p. 752.

99 Greg, 'Reviewed Work(s)', p. 276.

100 Quoted in Thompson and Roberts, 'Mary Cowden Clarke', p. 179.

101 Thompson and Roberts, 'Mary Cowden Clarke', p. 178.
102 Maguire, 'Alice Walker', p. 344.
103 These details are all drawn from correspondence in the Evelyn Simpson Papers, part of the James Marshall and Marie-Louise Osborn Collection, held in the Beinecke Rare Book and Manuscript Library at Yale University.
104 Yarn, 'Rickert's Network of Women Editors'.

Epilogue

Here are the facts. From 1800 until the present day, the play most frequently edited by women has been *As You Like It*, with thirty-seven editions prepared by women either alone or in collaboration. It is closely followed by *Twelfth Night* and *A Midsummer Night's Dream* with thirty-two each, *The Merchant of Venice, Julius Caesar,* and *Macbeth* with thirty, *Hamlet* with twenty-nine, *The Taming of the Shrew, Othello,* and *The Tempest* with twenty-eight, and *King Lear* with twenty-seven. The plays least-edited by women have been *Titus Andronicus, 2 Henry 6, 3 Henry 6,* and *Two Noble Kinsmen*, each with twelve, followed by *Timon of Athens* with thirteen, and *Pericles* with fourteen. Although these numbers do somewhat bear out the generalisation that when women were hired to edit, they were primarily assigned to less textually complex comedies, the more important correlation may be with the popularity of certain plays within the educational publishing market.[1] The plays most commonly edited by women were frequently taught in schools beginning in the late nineteenth century. *Hamlet* and *Othello* certainly cannot be accused of being textually simple, but they have been edited by women twenty-nine and twenty-eight times, respectively; *King Lear* lags just behind with twenty-seven editions. Similarly, the plays least-edited by women have traditionally been unpopular in schools (*2* and *3 Henry VI*) or have not always been included in the main canon of Shakespeare's plays due to disputed attribution (*Titus Andronicus, Two Noble Kinsmen, Timon of Athens, Pericles*). Gender may have played a role in editorial assignments, particularly beginning in the mid-twentieth century, but the market forces influencing demand were at least equally powerful. More editions of certain plays were needed; therefore, there were more opportunities for women to edit those plays.

In total, I have found sixty-nine women who edited Shakespeare prior to 1950 in the UK and the US. As I said in the Prologue, the only things all sixty-nine of these people have in common are their gender and the fact that they edited at least one edition of Shakespeare prior to 1950; however, some similarities can be teased out of their biographies. Many worked as teachers in jobs ranging from elementary- to university-level. The majority attained at least a bachelor's degree, and the ranks of women editors include many 'firsts' relating to women's higher education. Agnes Knox Black and Helen Gray Cone were the first women awarded the title of 'professor' at their institutions. Flora Masson and Charlotte Stopes were two of the first three women to attend Edinburgh, although they did so before the university granted degrees to women. Some of the first women to receive PhDs from elite institutions in the US and the UK became editors of early modern texts, including Laura Wylie and Elizabeth Deering Hanscom (Yale), and Evelyn Spearing Simpson (Oxford). Louise Pound was the first female president of the Modern Language Association. Most women editors also produced other kinds of literary work. Many were novelists, playwrights, or poets, including Agnes Russell Weekes, Fanny Johnson, Evelyn Smith, Dorothy Margaret Stuart, Dorothy Macardle, Nora Ratcliff, Katharine Lee Bates, and Helen Gray Cone.

In regard to their personal lives, twenty of the sixty-eight that I have been able to identify married.[2] Of those nineteen, even fewer had children. Agnes Knox Black seems to have assisted her husband with their edition of *Othello* near the end of his life, and Adeliza Green took on her edition of *Henry V* when her husband, the series editor, died. Cecily Boas and Nora Ratcliff both edited for series for which their husbands also edited – in Boas's case, her husband was the series editor. Mary Cowden Clarke and Lois G. Hufford both edited and wrote with their husbands throughout their lives. Fathers or brothers influenced the literary and academic careers of Emma Gollancz, Elizabeth Lee, Fanny Johnson, Flora Masson, and Henrietta Bowdler. Some of those who did not marry lived their entire lives with their mothers or unmarried sisters, including Flora Masson, Grace Trenery, and Agnes Russell Weekes. All three had sisters who also worked in the literary world. Others had long-term, dedicated relationships with women, the best-documented being Katharine Lee Bates, Charlotte Porter and Helen Clarke, Laura Wylie, and Martha Hale Shackford.

As I mentioned in Chapter 4, in his discussion of the editorial task, Philip Gaskell downplayed editorial identity in favour of textual primacy. When Gaskell wrote his classic work on textual studies, however, there was little need to be interested in the identity of the editor – the singular 'him'

of whom Gaskell spoke could be taken largely for granted. The editor was
a white man. Anything else was an aberration.

When the statistics enumerated in this book are factored into the larger
picture of editorial history, however, it becomes clear that Gaskell was
writing in the final days of a particular trend in editing, and that those
levels of homogeneity and singularity in editorial identity have not always
been the standards in Shakespeare editing, although they were well-
entrenched by the mid-twentieth century. The nature of editorial authority swings back and forth between singularity and plurality, depending on
societal pressures and larger intellectual trends. On one side of the pendu-
lum is a concentrated, univocal editorial presence, reflecting a singular,
'monolithic' vision of the text, in Leah Marcus's description; on the other
is a more dispersed authority, offering the possibility of multiple texts,
multiple voices, and less dogmatic textual solutions. The starting position
in the seventeenth century was plurality. As has been widely documented,
the atmosphere and methods of work in the printing- and play-houses
created a collaborative product in which the work of individual hands was
difficult to discern.[3] The beginning of the eighteenth century, at which
point most date the birth of Shakespearean editorial history, represented a
turn towards the concentration and distillation of editorial power.[4]
Individual men of letters, most well-known to the public for other literary
or theatrical endeavours, undertook the task of editing monumental editions of the complete works. Their 'right' to do so, and to be taken
seriously, came primarily from two sources: their own reputations and
their sanctified status as the chosen delegates of the Tonson publishing
house.[5] Tonson's long-lived monopoly on the publication of Shakespeare
restricted the role of editor to a chosen few. They conferred that consol-
idated authority, based, in John Thompson's Bourdieu-inspired formulation, largely on their intellectual and symbolic capital, upon each editor in
turn.[6] However, when Tonson's stranglehold was broken in 1774 by the
House of Lords decision ending perpetual copyright, the tide began to
turn.[7] Publishers of Shakespeare multiplied exponentially; correspondingly, so did editors. At the same time, growing literacy rates and increased
popularity led to greater demand for a cheaper, more egalitarian
Shakespeare, one available to and affordable for working-class readers,
women, and children.

At the beginning of the twentieth century, the New Bibliography
ushered in a new era of singularity, during which an aura of 'hard science'
enveloped the editorial profession, restricting the ranks of those qualified
to edit, and investing those who did edit according to the new principles

'with a prestige and control that could not be questioned'.[8] During the eighteenth century, the Tonson house was the source of editorial/textual authority; during the twentieth century, that authority shifted to research universities. The development of English as a university discipline during the late nineteenth century created a new generation of officially accredited scholars able to parlay degrees and university posts into editorial work. It became common for editors to be listed on title pages and advertisements with their university affiliations. John Jowett has also identified instability and fear of 'disintegration' as a motive for creating a monolithic textual Shakespeare during this period.[9] The most recent shift took place as the century drew to a close, when the dramatic evolution of criticism associated with postmodern intellectual movements was accompanied by a new wave of textual/editorial theory. The merging of the textual and the critical, spearheaded by critics such as Jerome McGann and D. F. McKenzie, reinvigorated scholarly editing, opening it up to 'non-specialist' editors, whose alternative viewpoints were seen as both intellectually valuable and increasingly marketable, creating a new demand for multiplicity. When embarking on a series of Shakespeare editions, most modern publishing houses now attempt to think more strategically about variety in the roster of editors.[10] This desire for diversity is predicated on the understanding that the editor brings their own experiences and viewpoint to the text, and that these things shape the resulting edition.[11]

Both shifts toward multiplicity have occurred with the advent of new technologies – inexpensive new methods of printing, papermaking, and bookbinding in the nineteenth century and digital technology in the twentieth and twenty-first centuries. Both shifts also coincided with a significant increase in the number of women editing Shakespeare. Multiplicity enables diversity. The digital age has transformed editing and publishing and created the field of digital humanities, and women have been involved in developing literary-studies applications for computers since the field's inception. Although Roberto Busa is most often credited as the founder of computational method in the humanities, beginning in 1951, Josephine Miles headed up a largely female team that employed machine methods to create a concordance of the poetical works of John Dryden. The resulting concordance was published in 1957, seventeen years before the first volumes of Busa's monumental Aquinas concordance made it into print.[12] Within the Shakespeare subfield, Dolores Marie Burton wrote the first monograph describing computer-assisted literary-critical study in 1973.[13] Both Burton and Sally Yeates Sedelow focused on stylistic studies.[14] In the early 1960s, Patricia Fell prepared the program that would be used for Trevor Howard-Hill's *Oxford Shakespeare Concordances*, based on Alice Walker's unfinished Oxford Shakespeare – one imagines Walker wistfully comparing this process with her early years of painstaking collation work, which relied on carbon copies, countless handwritten slips of papers, and many miles of coloured parcel tape.[15] Bernice Kliman's *Enfolded Hamlet*, Teena Rochfort Smith's four-text *Hamlet*, and Ann Thompson and Neil Taylor's multi-text Arden3 edition comprise a fascinating mini-history of women's involvement in innovative textual presentations of *Hamlet*. And imagine – this brief list does not even begin to consider the countless (usually unacknowledged) women who worked as typists, card-feeders, and others on the early large-scale computer projects.

In the twenty-first century, contending with entirely new demands and opportunities, publishers and editors are radically rethinking what an edition looks like and how it is produced. The Internet Shakespeare Editions project, and its successor, LEMDO, have been experimenting with the preparation and presentation of open-access, peer-reviewed editions since 1996. Bloomsbury's Drama Online offers Arden3 in a custom-formatted platform to allow easy access to textual and critical notes, and the next series of Arden, currently in the making, will likely integrate digital elements more fully, in every stage of the editorial process. Norton3 textual editor Gordon McMullan remarked that the new Norton digital platform offers endless possibilities to implement the last three decades' worth of editorial theory and practice.[16] Only time will tell how new technologies will reshape the form and substance of a Shakespeare edition. Moving forward, however, it seems wise to look backward, to redefine more clearly what being an editor of Shakespeare has meant at each phase of the role's evolution, and to better understand the people who filled those roles. Focusing on a small subset of editors paradoxically requires consideration of editorship as a whole; therefore, a study of women editors, in addition to the obvious goal of reinstating forgotten women in the literary record, offers insight into the larger trends of editorial history.

Perhaps the most pressing lesson to take from this history is that the previous phase of dispersed editorial authority was *temporary*. As we push towards greater diversity in the editorial field, it is vital to consider how to institute lasting change, not just immediate demographic improvements. The Norton3 textual editors were justifiably pleased with their final gender breakdown – twenty-one women editors to nineteen male editors. The Arden Publisher expects at least 50 per cent of the Arden4 editors to be women.[17] The next series of the Cambridge Shakespeare will be led by an all-female team of general editors.[18] As McMullan acknowledged regarding Norton3, however, certain demographic biases persist, including those favouring scholars employed by major research institutions and those based in the UK and the United States.[19] Looking forward to, say, Norton4 or Arden5 – horribile dictu! – we must continue to actively engage with expanding diversity beyond binary gender to engage with questions of race, sexual orientation, gender identity, gender expression, nationality, and institutional affiliation.

Setting aside those broad, practical implications, however, I hope this book also demonstrates that editorial history still contains many undiscovered treasures, many stories yet untold. These stories range from the mundane, such as Katharine Lee Bates's struggle with severe dental pain while finishing her edition of *Merchant*, to the sublime, like the realisation that Dorothy Macardle was writing short stories from a cell in Kilmanhain Gaol while on a hunger strike instead of editing *Coriolanus*. While these details might not affect modern textual practices, they can transform and humanise our understanding of the editorial tradition. Moreover, these editors and their stories deserve to be remembered for their own sakes. By challenging traditional textual hierarchies and embracing the value of, in McGann's words, the personal and the historical, it is possible to reach a dynamic, multidimensional understanding of Shakespearean editorial history that reflects both the products and processes of textual labour.

Notes

1 Taylor, 'Textual and Sexual Criticism', p. 197; Thompson, 'Feminist Theory and the Editing of Shakespeare', p. 86.
2 As of this writing, I have been unable to unearth details on one: Edith M. Ward.
3 Massai, *Shakespeare and the Rise of the Editor*; *The Cambridge History of the Book in Britain, vol. 4: 1557–1695*, ed. John Barnard and D. F. McKenzie (Cambridge: Cambridge University Press, 2002).
4 Massai, *Shakespeare and the Rise of the Editor*; for editing in the eighteenth century, see Andrew Murphy, 'The Birth of the Editor', in *Concise Companion to Shakespeare and the Text*, ed. Andrew Murphy (Chichester: Wiley-Blackwell, 2010), pp. 93–108; Colin Franklin, *Shakespeare Domesticated: The Eighteenth-Century Editions* (Aldershot: Scholar Press, 1991); Walsh, *Shakespeare, Milton, and Eighteenth-Century Literary Editing*; De Grazia, *Shakespeare Verbatim*.

5 For a detailed history of Shakespeare and the Tonson house, see chapters 3 and 4 in Murphy, *Shakespeare in Print*; Harry M. Geduld, *Prince of Publishers: A Study of the Work and Career of Jacob Tonson* (Bloomington: Indiana University Press, 1969).

6 John B. Thompson, *Merchants of Culture: The Publishing Business in the Twenty-First Century*, 2nd ed. (Cambridge: Polity Press, 2015), pp. 7–8.

7 Murphy, *Shakespeare in Print*, p. 137; Ronan Deazley, *On the Origin of the Right to Copy: Charting the Movement of Copyright Law in Eighteenth Century Britain (1695–1775)* (London: Hart Publishing, 2004).

8 Ioppolo, '"Much They Ought Not to Have Attempted"', p. 159.

9 John Jowett, 'Disintegration, 1924', *Shakespeare*, 10.2 (2014), 171–87.

10 Gordon McMullan, 'Reflections on the Politics of Editing a Complete Works of Shakespeare', *Contemporary Theatre Review*, 25.1 (2015), 76–79; John Jowett, 'Editing Shakespeare's Plays in the Twentieth Century', *Shakespeare Survey*, 59 (2006), 1–19.

11 Suzanne Gossett, 'Why Should a Woman Edit a Man?', in *Women Editing/ Editing Women: Early Modern Women Writers and the New Textualism*, ed. Ann Hollinshead Hurley and Chanita Goodblatt (Newcastle: Cambridge Scholars, 2009), pp. 25–34; Thompson, 'Feminist Theory and the Editing of Shakespeare'; Suzanne Gossett, '"To Foster Is Not Always to Preserve": Feminist Inflections in Editing *Pericles*' and Lois Potter, 'Editing Desdemona', both in *In Arden: Editing Shakespeare: Essays in Honour of Richard Proudfoot*, ed. Ann Thompson and Gordon McMullan (London: Arden Shakespeare, 2003), pp. 65–80 and pp. 81–94; Wayne, 'The Gendered Text and Its Labour'; Valerie Wayne, 'The Sexual Politics of Textual Transmission', in *Textual Formations and Reformations*, ed. Laurie E. Maguire and Thomas L. Berger (Newark: University of Delaware Press, 1998); Laurie E. Maguire, 'Feminist Editing and the Body of the Text', in *A Feminist Companion to Shakespeare*, ed. Dympna Callaghan (Oxford: Oxford University Press, 2000), pp. 59–79.

12 Rachel Sagner Buurma and Laura Heffernan, 'Search and Replace: Josephine Miles and the Origins of Distant Reading', *Modernism/Modernity Print Plus*, 3.1 (2018). https://modernismmodernity.org/forums/posts/search-and-replace.

13 John Lavagnino, *Shakespeare and the Digital World: Redefining Scholarship and Practice*, ed. Christie Carson and Peter Kirwan (Cambridge: Cambridge University Press, 2014), p. 14; Dolores Burton, *Shakespeare's Grammatical Style: A Computer-Assisted Analysis of Richard II and Anthony and Cleopatra*, Dan Danciger Publication Series (Austin: University of Texas Press, 1973).

14 Sally Yeates Sedelow, 'The Computer in the Humanities and Fine Arts', *ACM Computing Surveys (CSUR)*, 2.2 (1970), 89–110.

15 Dolores M. Burton, 'Automated Concordances and Word Indexes: The Early Sixties and the Early Centers', *Computers and the Humanities*, 15.2 (1981), 83–100 (p. 85). Walker frequently mentioned said parcel tape in her accompanying letters to McKerrow. For example, on 15 June 1936, she wrote:

The green tape is giving out. Worse is to follow. You have been warned! I have some perfectly vile pink tape I am proposing to use up on your parcels. When I asked my sister to get me some quiet coloured sealing wax to tone it down and showed her what wanted toning she ejaculated 'Christ!' and brought me a stick of tar-black. The combination will look awful. Probably the post-office will confiscate the parcel as looking too sinister. The only other way I can think of for using up the material is to get a pair of shoe socks and make a surréaliste picture like one I saw in Venice a few years ago – it's a pity I am a bit late for the exhibition! (Alice Walker, 'Letter to R. B. McKerrow', 15 June 1936, Trinity College Library, Cambridge: MCKW, A4/33)

16 McMullan, 'Reflections on the Politics of Editing', p. 78.
17 Margaret Bartley, personal communication.
18 M. J. Kidnie, Sonia Massai, and Gill Woods.
19 McMullan, 'Reflections on the Politics of Editing', p. 78.

Appendices

This section consists of two appendices. The first is a quick reference guide to women who prepared editions of Shakespeare between 1800 and 1950. In order to be concise, extensive biographies have not been written for women whose lives are discussed in this book, or those who are well-known in their own rights. If, for example, an *Oxford Dictionary of National Biography* or *American National Biography* entry exists, or a substantial biography has been written, its citation is included, and I refer you there for more information. Many lesser-known women editors could not be included in the book, however, and brief biographies of those I have been able to identify can be found here. Because this appendix is essentially an annotated bibliography, the citations of editions and sources in this section have not been included in the bibliography unless they also appear in the main text of the book. Entries are listed alphabetically by the editor's first name.

The second section is a list of every edition that has been prepared by a woman editor since 1800 of which I am currently aware.[1] The information offered includes male co-editors (when applicable), date of publication, the publisher, and the series or edition title (when applicable). The primary identifier is always the woman editor; any male collaborators have been included in a separate column. When texts were reprinted or re-packaged under different names by the publisher (as with Laura Valentine's many Warne editions), only the date of the first printing has been given. Any dates that are uncertain have been marked with 'c.'. The lists include some editions that were commissioned but never completed. These are marked 'NP' for 'never published'; editions still in preparation are marked 'FC' for 'forthcoming'. As with the dates, only the first published series/edition title is listed. Women who served as general editors of a series, without editing individual volumes/plays in that series, are not included; however, the names of multi-volume, multi-editor series (such as Arden2) overseen by at least one female general editor are marked with asterisks. Although it

206

includes the Sonnets, it does not include the other poems, *Edward III*, or *Sir Thomas More*. This collection is meant as a starting point. In addition to the likelihood of human error, many more women editors could be hiding under gender-neutral initials or ambiguous first names. The continuing digitisation of library catalogues will no doubt unearth more forgotten editions. It is most thorough up to 1950; past this point, I have no illusions whatsoever that it is complete. This book is in itself a case study of how difficult it can be to parse out who did what on any given edition or series. To anyone who has been excluded, I apologise unreservedly, and invite you to get in touch to make sure your edition is added to future versions of the list. By the same token, if I have unintentionally misgendered anyone or used a dead name, I am immensely sorry and would be happy to correct any mistakes in digital or future print editions. I respect every person's right to self-identify. If you would like to be added to this list, or if you would prefer to be listed under a different name or removed entirely, please feel free to contact me.

Women Editors of Shakespeare, 1800–1950

Ada Rehan (1857–1916)

Irish-born actress Ada Rehan earned great acclaim as a member of Augustin Daly's theatrical company, particularly for her performance as Katharine in *The Taming of the Shrew*. She wrote the introduction for a 'Player's Edition', published by Doubleday, Page.

Editions

William Shakespeare and Ada Rehan, *The Taming of the Shrew* (New York: Doubleday, Page, 1900)

Sources

Melissa Vickery-Bareford, 'Rehan, Ada (1857–1916), Actress', *American National Biography* (Oxford: Oxford University Press, 2000), doi.org/10.1093/anb/9780198606697.article.1800976

Adeliza Norman Johnston Green (1877–1956)

The daughter of a Manchester councillor, Adeliza Norman Johnston was a lecturer in the department of education at the University College of North Wales, Bangor, when she met her future husband, John Alfred Green. The Greens had six children and settled in Sheffield when John Green took a position as professor of education at Sheffield University. During this time, John edited a number of Shakespeare editions for the Companion Shakespeare series, published by Christopher's, but the series was left unfinished when he died in 1922. Adeliza relocated for a job as a lecturer in the department of education at University College, Southampton, and took up her husband's work, doing the majority of the editorial work on an edition of *Henry V*.

Editions

William Shakespeare and A. N. Green, *King Henry V*, The Companion Shakespeare (London: Christopher's, 1923)

Sources

'1881 England Census – Adeliza N. Johnston', National Archives of the UK, PRO RG1/3885, Folio 62, Page 8, www.ancestry.com

Gary McCulloch, 'Green, John Alfred (1867–1922), Educationist', in *Oxford Dictionary of National Biography* (Oxford: Oxford University Press, 2004), doi.org/10.1093/ref:odnb/63808

Agnes Knox Black (1864–1945)

Ontario-born Agnes Knox was a well-known elocutionist during the late nineteenth century. In 1894, she married Ebenezer Charlton Black, with whom she had three children. They moved to Boston, where Agnes worked as a teacher of elocution at the New England Conservatory of Music before taking a job at Boston University (BU). In 1908, she became the first woman awarded the title of 'professor' at BU. Her husband Ebenezer was hired by publisher Ginn & Co. to re-edit the famous Hudson School Shakespeare for a revised series, called the New Hudson Shakespeare. Ebenezer died in 1927; *Othello*, the volume he co-edited with Agnes, was published in 1926, and was the last volume completed. It therefore seems likely that Agnes helped Ebenezer complete the edition near the end of his life.

Editions

William Shakespeare, W. H. Hudson, Ebenezer Charlton Black, and Agnes Knox Black, *Othello*, New Hudson Shakespeare (Boston: Ginn & Co., 1926)

Sources

'The Goddess of Reason – Agnes Knox Black | Book Lives', https://booklives.ca/islandora/object/booklives:499

Agnes Russell Weekes (1881–1940)

The daughter of a clergyman, Agnes Russell Weekes received her BA and MA from the University of London. Agnes and her sister Rose were prolific novelists, both separately and together, sometimes publishing under their own names and sometimes under the nom de plume 'Anthony Pryde'. See Chapter 4.

Editions

William Shakespeare and Agnes Russell Weekes, *As You Like It*, University Tutorial Series (London: W.B. Clive, University Tutorial Press, 1909)
William Shakespeare and Agnes Russell Weekes, *Cymbeline*, University Tutorial Series (London: W. B. Clive, University Tutorial Press, 1919)
William Shakespeare and Agnes Russell Weekes, *The Tempest*, University Tutorial Series (London: W. B. Clive, University Tutorial Press, 1909)

Sources

Agnes Russell Weekes, 'Probate Record and Last Will and Testament', 1940, Principal Probate Registry, https://probatesearch.service.gov.uk
Sandra Kemp, Charlotte Mitchell, and David Trotter, 'A. R. Weekes and R. K. Weekes', in *The Oxford Companion to Edwardian Fiction* (Oxford: Oxford University Press, 1997)

Alice Meynell (1847–1922)

A well-known poet and journalist, Alice Meynell worked at the centre of the London literary world around the turn of the century. See Chapter 1.

Editions

William Shakespeare, Alice Meynell, and Sidney Lee, *The Taming of the Shrew*, Renaissance Shakespeare (New York: George D. Sproul, 1907)

Sources

June Badeni, 'Meynell [née Thompson], Alice Christiana Gertrude', in *Oxford Dictionary of National Biography* (Oxford: Oxford University Press, 2004), doi.org/10.1093/ref:odnb/35008

Alice Walker (1900–1982)

Born in Manchester, Alice Walker attended Royal Holloway, eventually becoming one of the most significant women editors of the twentieth century. See Chapter 5.

Editions

William Shakespeare and Alice Walker, *Troilus and Cressida*, New Cambridge
Shakespeare (Cambridge: Cambridge University Press, 1957)
William Shakespeare, Alice Walker, and J. Dover Wilson, *Othello*, New
Cambridge Shakespeare (Cambridge: Cambridge University Press, 1957)

Sources

T. H. Howard-Hill, 'Walker, Alice (1900–1982)', in *Oxford Dictionary of National
Biography* (Oxford: Oxford University Press, 2004), doi.org/10.1093/ref:
odnb/60296

Anna Patricia Butler (1887–1973)

Anna Patricia Butler was born in Cambridge, Massachusetts. Her parents,
Elizabeth and Matthew, were Irish immigrants; Matthew worked as a baker
in a cracker factory. Anna attended Trinity College in Washington, DC, the
country's first Catholic liberal arts women's college, then returned to Cambridge
to teach high school. While teaching, she earned her MA from Boston
University. She then went on to complete her doctorate at Boston College.

Editions

William Shakespeare, Anna P. Butler, and M. A. Feehan, *Macbeth*, Loyola
English Classics (Chicago: Loyola University Press, 1935)

Sources

1910 US Census, Middlesex County, MA, pop. sch., city of Cambridge, ED 756,
p. 7A, dwell. 82, fam. 151, Anna P. Butler, NARA microfilm publication
T624, roll 595, www.ancestry.com
Anna Patricia Butler, 'Christian Hope as Found in the Poems of Francis
Thompson' (doctoral dissertation, Boston College, 1931).
'Massachusetts, USA, Boston Archdiocese Roman Catholic Sacramental Records,
1789–1900', digital images, citing *St. Mary of the Annunciation (Cambridge)*
Baptisms, 1878–1896, Anna Patricia Butler, 6 April 1887, vol. 58453, p. 96,
www.ancestry.com

Cecily Boas (1898–1973)

Born Augusta Alice Cecilia Whitehead in Germany, Cecily, as she was
known, spent part of her youth abroad due to her father's position with

the British diplomatic services; when Cecily was eight, J. Beethom Whitehead was appointed envoy to Serbia. In 1923, she married Guy Boas, whose father, F. S. Boas, was one of the most significant British Shakespeare critics of the late nineteenth century. Guy Boas, who also wrote on Shakespeare and was general editor of the New Eversley Shakespeare, served as headmaster of the Sloane School in Chelsea for several decades. The school's yearbook noted that during that time, Cecily was 'well-known for her devotion to the school' and 'held in the greatest affection' by the students and staff. During the Second World War, she ran the school's Scout Troop. In 1948, she reviewed fellow New Eversley editor Dorothy Margaret Stuart's book *The English Abigail* for the English Association's journal.

Editions

William Shakespeare and Cecily Boas, *As You Like It*, New Eversley Shakespeare (London: Macmillan, 1936)

Sources

'1911 England Census – Cecilia Whitehead', National Archives of the UK, PRO RG14/5800 Sch 7, www.ancestry.com

Cicely Boas, 'The English Abigail, by Dorothy Margaret Stuart (Book Review)', *English*, 7 (1948), p. 85

'Court Circular', *The Times* (London, 9 April 1923), p. 15

'England & Wales, Civil Registration Death Index, 1916–2007', digital images, entry for Augusta Alice C. Boas, 1973, citing General Register Office, London, England, *England and Wales Civil Registration Indexes*, vol. 5d, p. 1152, www.ancestry.com

'Mr. Guy Boas', *The Cheynean: Sloane School Magazine*, December 1961, pp. 2–10

Charlotte Carmichael Brown Stopes (1840–1929)

Pioneering archivist and historian Charlotte Stopes fought for many causes, including suffrage, women's rights, rational dress, and education. Her daughter, Marie Stopes, became an advocate for birth control. See Chapter 2.

Editions

William Shakespeare and C. C. Stopes, *Shakespeare's Sonnets*, King's Classics (London: Alexander Moring, De la More Press, 1904)

Sources

Kathleen E. McLuskie, 'Remembering Charlotte Stopes', in *Women Making Shakespeare: Text, Performance and Reception*, ed. Gordon McMullan, Lena Cowen Orlin, and Virginia Mason Vaughan (London: Bloomsbury Arden Shakespeare, 2014), pp. 195–205
Stephanie Green, *The Public Lives of Charlotte and Marie Stopes*, Dramatic Lives (London: Pickering & Chatto, 2013)

Charlotte Endymion Porter (1857–1942)

An American poet, literary critic, and editor. See Chapter 3.

Editions

William Shakespeare, Helen Archibald Clarke, and Charlotte Endymion Porter, *Shakespeare's Complete Works*, Pembroke Edition, 12 vols (New York: Thomas Y. Crowell & Co, 1903)
William Shakespeare, Helen Archibald Clarke, and Charlotte Endymion Porter, *Shakespeare: First Folio Edition*, 40 vols (New York: T. Y. Crowell, 1903)

Sources

Elaine Oswald, 'Porter, Charlotte Endymion (1857–1942), Editor and Publisher, Dramatist, and Translator', in *American National Biography* (Oxford: Oxford University Press, 2000), doi.org/10.1093/anb/9780198606697.article.1602368

Charlotte Mary Yonge (1823–1901)

A remarkably prolific novelist, Charlotte Yonge also edited periodicals, school texts, and entries for the letter 'N' in the *Oxford English Dictionary*. See 'A Primer on Early Student Editions'.

Editions

William Shakespeare and Charlotte Mary Yonge, *The First Part of Henry IV*, Shakespeare's Plays for Schools (Westminster: National Society's Depository, 1883)
William Shakespeare and Charlotte Mary Yonge, *Julius Caesar*, Shakespeare's Plays for Schools (Westminster: National Society's Depository, 1885)
William Shakespeare and Charlotte Mary Yonge, *The Second Part of Shakespeare's King Henry IV* (Westminster: National Society's Depository, 1883)
William Shakespeare and Charlotte Mary Yonge, *Shakespeare's King Henry V* (Westminster: National Society's Depository, 1885)

William Shakespeare and Charlotte Mary Yonge, *Shakespeare's King Richard the Second* (Westminster: National Society's Depository, 1885)

Sources

Elisabeth Jay, 'Yonge, Charlotte Mary (1823–1901), Novelist', in *Oxford Dictionary of National Biography* (Oxford: Oxford University Press, 2004), doi.org/10.1093/ref:odnb/37065

Charlotte Whipple Underwood (1870–1937)

Charlotte Whipple Underwood grew up in Wisconsin before attending the University of Michigan. She graduated in 1892 and began teaching in Chicago high schools. She married Lewis H. Williams, a mechanical engineer, in 1902. They had two daughters.

Editions

William Shakespeare and Charlotte Whipple Underwood, *Shakespeare's The Merchant of Venice*, Macmillan's Pocket Classics (New York: Macmillan Company, 1899)

Sources

1900 US Census, Cook County, IL, pop. sch., City of Chicago, ED 332, p. 3, dwell. 42, fam. 52, Charlotte Underwood, NARA microfilm publication T623, roll 1854, www.ancestry.com

1910 US Census, Lake County, IL, pop. sch., City of Waukegan, ED 115, p. 5B, dwell. 101, fam. 121, Charlotte W. Williams, NARA microfilm publication T624, roll 302, www.ancestry.com

US School Yearbooks, 1900–1990, digital images, citing 'University of Michigan Yearbook, 1921', p. 97, www.ancestry.com

Clara Linklater Thomson (1867–1934)

Somerville-educated Clara Thomson taught at multiple girls' schools and wrote children's books and educational literature for Horace Marshall and Son. She appears to have been the first woman to serve as the general editor for a multi-volume Shakespeare series.

Editions

William Shakespeare and C. L. Thomson, *Julius Caesar*, The Carmelite Shakespeare (London: Horace Marshall and Son, 1914)

William Shakespeare and C. L. Thomson, *Macbeth*, The Carmelite Shakespeare (London: Horace Marshall and Son, 1916)
William Shakespeare and C. L. Thomson, *A Midsummer Night's Dream*, The Carmelite Shakespeare (London: Horace Marshall and Son, 1924)

Sources

'1891 England Census – Clara Thomson', National Archives of the UK, PRO RG12/2836, Folio 71, Page 2, www.ancestry.com
'1901 England Census – Clara Thomson', National Archives of the UK, PRO RG13/2913, Folio 7, Page 5, www.ancestry.com
'1911 England Census – Clara Thomson', National Archives of the UK, PRO RG14/7806, Sch 23, www.ancestry.com
Clara Thomson, 'Probate Record and Last Will and Testament', 1935, Principal Probate Registry, https://probatesearch.service.gov.uk
'Somerville Hall Register 1889–1896 – Clara Thomson', Somerville College Archives, Oxford

Clara Longworth Chambrun (1873–1954)

Clara Longworth was born to a wealthy and well-connected American family; her brother Nicholas was a member of the House of Representatives and married Alice, daughter of President Theodore Roosevelt. Clara married the Count de Chambrun, a descendant of the Marquis de Lafayette, eventually settling with him in Paris, where she remained throughout the Nazi occupation during the Second World War. After having two children, she earned a doctorate from the Sorbonne at the age of forty-eight. She was a Chevalier of the French Legion of Honor. Editor Alice Walker once described her arguments as having a 'childish, monkey-like slipperiness', and suggested that she would fit in well amongst the Baconians.

Editions

William Shakespeare and Clara Longworth Chambrun, *The Sonnets of William Shakespeare: New Light and Old Evidence* (New York: G. P. Putnam & Sons, 1913)

Sources

Alice Walker, 'Letter to R. B. McKerrow', 6 December 1938, Trinity College Library, Cambridge: MCKW, A4/156

Mary Niles Maack, '"I Cannot Get Along without the Books I Find Here": The American Library in Paris during the War, Occupation, and Liberation, 1939–1945', *Library Trends*, 55.3 (2007), 490–512

'Mme. de Chambrun Dies in Paris at 80', *New York Times* (New York, 2 June 1954), p. 31

Dorothy Margaret Callan Macardle (1889–1958)

Irish nationalist, rebel, historian, and playwright. See Chapter 4.

Editions

William Shakespeare and D. M. Macardle, *The Merchant of Venice*, The Carmelite Shakespeare (London: Horace Marshall and Son, 1915)

William Shakespeare and D. M. Macardle, *The Tempest*, The Carmelite Shakespeare (London: Horace Marshall and Son, 1917)

William Shakespeare and D. M. Macardle, *Twelfth Night*, The Carmelite Shakespeare (London: Horace Marshall and Son, 1922)

Sources

Nadia Clare Smith, *Dorothy Macardle: A Life* (Dublin: Woodfield Press, 2007)

Leanne Lane, *Dorothy Macardle* (Dublin: UCD Press, 2019)

Dorothy Margaret Stuart (1889–1963)

English poet Dorothy Margaret Stuart won a silver medal for Great Britain in the International Literary Contest of the Eighth Olympiad (1924) for *Sword Songs*. She wrote novels and books on history for both children and adults. She was deeply involved with the English Association and reviewed books for their journal for over twenty years.

Editions

William Shakespeare, E. V. Davenport, and Dorothy Margaret Stuart, *The Life of King Henry the Fifth*, New Eversley Shakespeare (London: Macmillan, 1935)

Sources

G.B., 'Dorothy Margaret Stuart', *English: Journal of the English Association*, 14.84 (1963), 225

Edith May Penney (1878–1974)

Edith May Penney grew up in Minnesota and attended the University of Minnesota. Her yearbook claimed, 'There's no companion like the Penney.' She became an English high school teacher, eventually moving to New York, where she taught at the Bronxville School and the Teachers' College at Columbia University. She lived to be ninety-six years old.

Editions

William Shakespeare and Edith M. Penney, *The Tempest*, Winston Companion Classics (Philadelphia: John C. Winston Company, 1927)

Sources

'North Carolina, Death Certificates, 1909–1976', digital images, entry for Edith M. Penney, 1974, no. 14507, citing *North Carolina Death Certificates*, microfilm S.123, www.ancestry.com

Percival M. Symonds and Edith M. Penney, 'The Increasing of English Vocabulary in the English Class', *The Journal of Educational Research*, 15.2 (1927), 93–103

University of Minnesota, Gopher Board of Editors, *The Gopher, Volume 11, 1898*, University of Minnesota Libraries, University Archives, p. 102, umedia.lib. umn.edu/item/p16022coll339:15493

Edith M. Ward (dates unknown)

Editions

William Shakespeare and Edith M. Ward, *Julius Caesar*, Stratford Classics (Chicago, IL: Lyons & Carnahan, 1934)

Edith Rickert (1871–1938)

Best known for her monumental edition of Chaucer, produced with John Matthews Manly, University of Chicago professor Edith Rickert was also active on the London literary scene in the 1890s and early 1900s, recording her interactions in journals and letters. See Chapter 3.

Editions

William Shakespeare, Edith Rickert, and E. K. Chambers, *A Midsummer Night's Dream*, The Arden Shakespeare, revised edition (Boston: D. C. Heath, 1916)

Appendices

Sources

Elizabeth Scala, 'Scandalous Assumptions: Edith Rickert and the Chicago Chaucer Project', *Medieval Feminist Forum: A Journal of Gender and Sexuality*, 30.1 (2000), 27–37

'Guide to the Edith Rickert Papers 1858–1960', www.lib.uchicago.edu/e/scrc/ findingaids/view.php?eadid=ICU.SPCL.RICKERTE

Molly G. Yarn, 'Rickert's Network of Women Editors', *Collaborative Humanities Research and Pedagogy: The Networks of John Matthews Manly and Edith Rickert* (Basingstoke: Palgrave, forthcoming)

William Snell, 'A Woman Medievalist Much Maligned: A Note in Defense of Edith Rickert (1871–1938)', *Philologie Im Netz*, Supplement 4 (2009), 41–54

Elizabeth Deering Hanscom (1865–1960)

After completing her bachelor's and master's degrees at Boston University, Elizabeth Hanscom became, along with Laura Wylie, one of the first seven women to receive PhDs from Yale in 1894. She then took up a post at Smith College, where she remained until retirement. Hanscom was an early advocate for including American literature in the English curriculum.

Editions

William Shakespeare and Elizabeth Deering Hanscom, *The Second Part of Henry the Fourth*, The Tudor Shakespeare (New York: Macmillan Company, 1912)

Sources

'Biographies of Yale's First Women Ph.D.'s | Women Faculty Forum', http://wff .yale.edu/biographies-yales-first-women-phds

Elizabeth Inchbald (1753–1821)

During the late eighteenth century, Elizabeth Inchbald, née Simpson, leveraged a fairly average acting career into a significantly more successful career as a writer, becoming particularly popular for her plays and novels.

Editions

William Shakespeare and Elizabeth Inchbald, *The British Theatre*, 25 vols (London: Longman, Hurst, Rees, and Orme, 1808), I–V

Sources

Annibel Jenkins, *I'll Tell You What: The Life of Elizabeth Inchbald* (Lexington: University Press of Kentucky, 2003)
Jane Spencer, 'Inchbald [née Simpson], Elizabeth (1753–1821), Writer and Actress', in *Oxford Dictionary of National Biography* (Oxford: Oxford University Press, 2004), doi.org/10.1093/ref:odnb/14374

Elizabeth Lee (1857–1920)

Teacher, translator, editor, and biographer. See Chapter 2.

Editions

William Shakespeare and Elizabeth Lee, *The Tempest*, Blackie's Junior School Shakespeare (London: Blackie and Son, 1894)
William Shakespeare and Elizabeth Lee, *Twelfth Night, or What You Will*, Blackie's Junior School Shakespeare (London: Blackie and Son, 1895)

Sources

Gillian Fenwick, 'Lee, Elizabeth (1857/8–1920), Biographer and Translator', in *Oxford Dictionary of National Biography* (Oxford: Oxford University Press, 2004), doi.org/10.1093/ref:odnb/41160

Emma Gollancz (1856–1929)

Emma Gollancz was born into a well-off Jewish family in London. She attended Newnham College, but left without completing her degree in order to care for her parents. She worked with her brother Israel on various literary endeavours. See Chapter 2.

Editions

William Shakespeare and Israel Gollancz, *The Temple Shakespeare* (London: J. M. Dent, 1894–97)

Sources

'Miss Emma Gollancz', *The Times* (London, 13 September 1929), p. 14
Ruth Dudley Edwards, *Victor Gollancz: A Biography* (London: Faber & Faber, 2012)

Essie Chamberlain (1888–1988)

Illinois-born Essie Chamberlain attended Illinois State Normal College. The Normal College yearbook in 1908 included a poem about the graduates, in which the stanza about Chamberlain read 'Essie Chamberlain is teaching / These young Seniors how to read. / Macbeth first, then 'tis Hamlet. / Splendid teaching, all's agreed.' She taught at Oak Park and River Forest Township High School in the Chicago area and was an active member of the National Council of Teachers of English, eventually becoming its president. She was hired by multiple publishers to edit Shakespeare, and also wrote actively on topics related to education theory.

Editions

William Shakespeare and Essie Chamberlain, *Julius Caesar*, Riverside Literature Series, 67 (Boston: Houghton Mifflin, 1929)

William Shakespeare and Essie Chamberlain, *Shakespeare's Taming of the Shrew*, Academy Classics for Junior High Schools, ed. Stella S. Center (Boston: Allyn and Bacon, 1926)

William Shakespeare, Essie Chamberlain, and G. B Harrison, *The Merchant of Venice*, New Reader's Shakespeare (New York: Holt, 1932)

William Shakespeare, Essie Chamberlain, G. B. Harrison, and F. H. Pritchard, *As You Like It*, New Reader's Shakespeare (New York: Holt, 1932)

William Shakespeare, Essie Chamberlain, G. B. Harrison, and F. H. Pritchard, *The Tragedy of Hamlet, Prince of Denmark*, New Reader's Shakespeare (New York: Holt, 1932)

William Shakespeare, Essie Chamberlain, G. B. Harrison, and F. H. Pritchard, *The Tragedy of Macbeth*, New Reader's Shakespeare (New York: Holt, 1932)

Sources

1920 US Census, Cook County, IL, pop. sch., City of Oak Park, ED 156, p. 3A, dwell. 48, fam. 53, Essie Chamberlain, NARA microfilm publication T625, roll 361, image 1091, www.ancestry.com

1940 US Census, Cook County, IL, pop. sch., City of Oak Park, ED 16-364, p. 5A, dwell. 427, fam. 118, Essie Chamberlain, NARA microfilm publication T627, roll 785, www.ancestry.com

'Blast from the Past: We've Come a Long Way', www.ncte.org/centennial/blastfrompast/womenpresidents

US School Yearbooks, 1880–2012, digital images, citing 'The Index', Illinois State Normal College, 1908, p. 99, www.ancestry.com

Esther Walker Wood (1866–1952/3)

Esther Walker, a journalist and art critic, was an early member of the Fabian Society, serving on the executive committee in 1902, and the Independent Labour Party. In 1893, she married J. W. Wood, after which she joined the Social Democratic Federation. She also wrote on the Pre-Raphaelites and edited the works of George Eliot. After divorcing her husband, she lived with writer and Fabian Gertrude Dix.

Editions

William Shakespeare, Esther Wood, Goldwin Smith, and William H. Fleming, *The Personal Shakespeare*, 15 vols (New York: Doubleday, Page, 1904). N.B.: This edition used the Porter-Clarke Pembroke Text.

Sources

The Labour Annual (London: Clarion, 1896), p. 238
Sheila Rowbotham, *Rebel Crossings: New Women, Free Lovers, and Radicals in Britain and the United States* (New York: Verso Books, 2016)

Evelyn Smith (1885–1928)

Best known for her fiction set in girls' schools, based on her own experiences as a pupil and teacher, Evelyn Smith also edited thirteen Shakespeare plays in eight years for Thomas Nelson and Sons. Born in England, she spent most of her adult life in Scotland, living on a houseboat. She died unexpectedly of pneumonia in 1928. See Chapter 4.

Editions

William Shakespeare and Evelyn Smith, *Shakespeare's Comedy of A Midsummer Night's Dream*, Teaching of English Series (London: Thomas Nelson & Sons, 1925)
William Shakespeare and Evelyn Smith, *Shakespeare's Comedy of As You Like It*, Teaching of English Series (London: Thomas Nelson & Sons, 1926)
William Shakespeare and Evelyn Smith, *Shakespeare's Comedy of The Merchant of Venice*, Teaching of English Series (London: Thomas Nelson & Sons, 1926)
William Shakespeare and Evelyn Smith, *Shakespeare's Comedy of Much Ado About Nothing*, Teaching of English Series (London: Thomas Nelson & Sons, 1926)
William Shakespeare and Evelyn Smith, *Shakespeare's Comedy of Twelfth Night*, Teaching of English Series (London: Thomas Nelson & Sons, 1926)

William Shakespeare and Evelyn Smith, *Shakespeare's King Henry IV. Part I*, Teaching of English Series (London: Thomas Nelson & Sons, 1925)

William Shakespeare and Evelyn Smith, *Shakespeare's King Henry V*, Teaching of English Series (London: Thomas Nelson & Sons, 1927)

William Shakespeare and Evelyn Smith, *Shakespeare's King Henry the Eighth*, Teaching of English Series (London: Thomas Nelson & Sons, 1928)

William Shakespeare and Evelyn Smith, *Shakespeare's Tragedy of Coriolanus*, Teaching of English Series (London: Thomas Nelson & Sons, 1926)

William Shakespeare and Evelyn Smith, *Shakespeare's Tragedy of King Lear*, Teaching of English Series (London: Thomas Nelson & Sons, 1926)

William Shakespeare and Evelyn Smith, *Shakespeare's Tragedy of King Richard the Third*, Teaching of English Series (London: Thomas Nelson & Sons, 1923)

William Shakespeare and Evelyn Smith, *Shakespeare's Tragedy of Macbeth*, Teaching of English Series (London: Thomas Nelson & Sons, 1925)

Sources

Hilary Clare, 'Evelyn Smith', *Folly*, 22

Fanny Eliza Johnson (1855–1943)

Fanny Johnson grew up in a family devoted to education. Her parents operated a school in Cambridge, and she ultimately became a teacher, then the headmistress of Bolton High School. She retired rather early due to health problems and returned to Cambridge, where, among other literary work, she edited Shakespeare for a series overseen by her brother, literary scholar R. Brimley Johnson. An active suffragist and supporter of women's education, although she did not herself attend university, Fanny served as the Press Secretary for the Cambridge Women's Suffrage Association. She lived to be nearly ninety years old.

Editions

William Shakespeare and Fanny Johnson, *King Henry V*, Blackwood's School Shakespeare (Edinburgh: William Blackwood and Sons, 1901)

William Shakespeare and Fanny Johnson, *Macbeth*, Blackwood's School Shakespeare (Edinburgh: William Blackwood and Sons, 1903)

William Shakespeare and Fanny Johnson, *Twelfth Night*, Blackwood's School Shakespeare (Edinburgh: William Blackwood and Sons, 1904)

Sources

Veronica Millington, *Fanny Eliza Johnson: A Thoroughly Modern Victorian Headmistress, Bolton High School for Girls, 1888–1893* (Hebden Bridge: Royd House, 2008)

Flora Masson (1856–1937)

Decorated for her service as a nurse during First World War, Flora Masson grew up in the world of English literature. Her father was David Masson, professor at Edinburgh and pioneer in teaching English in the universities. Her childhood memories included numerous literary luminaries visiting her family's home. Masson took full advantage of the opportunities available to her – she, alongside Charlotte Stopes, was one of the first three women to earn the equivalent of Edinburgh degrees for their work in the women's extension programme that her father had helped to create. During her professional life as a nurse, she became friends with Florence Nightingale. She and her sister Rosaline, a historian, lived together in Edinburgh for most of their lives, both engaged in literary pursuits.

Editions

William Shakespeare and Flora Masson, *As You Like It*, Dent's Shakespeare for Schools (London: J. M. Dent, 1903)

Sources

Flora Masson, *Victorians All* (London and Edinburgh: W. & R. Chambers, 1931)
Professor Basil Williams, 'Miss Flora Masson', *The Times* (London, 5 October 1937), p. 9

Gertrude Blanche Sellon (1871–1940)

Gertrude Blanche Sellon emigrated from New Zealand to England with her mother and two sisters sometime before 1891. She worked as a teacher in London. When she died, her estate totalled £26,102; however, the source of her wealth is unclear.

Editions

William Shakespeare and G. B. Sellon, *Hamlet*, The Carmelite Shakespeare (London: Horace Marshall and Son, 1922)
William Shakespeare and G. B. Sellon, *King Lear*, The Carmelite Shakespeare (London: Horace Marshall and Son, 1925)

Sources

'1891 England Census – Gertrude Sellon', National Archives of the UK, PRO RG12/1249, Folio 86, Page 30, www.ancestry.com

'1901 England Census – Gertrude Sellon', National Archives of the UK, PRO RG13/115, Folio 38, Page 15, www.ancestry.com

'1911 England Census – Gertrude Sellon', National Archives of the UK, PRO RG14/570, Sch 203, www.ancestry.com

Gertrude Blanche Sellon, 'Probate Record and Last Will and Testament', 1940, Principal Probate Registry, https://probatesearch.service.gov.uk

Gertrude Eleanor Hollingworth (1892–1936)

Born in London, the daughter of a travelling piano salesman, Gertrude Eleanor Hollingworth attended East London College on scholarship, eventually receiving her BA in Modern and Medieval Languages from the University of London in 1913, followed by her MA in 1915. She edited numerous student editions of Shakespeare and other authors. She lived in Cambridge.

Editions

William Shakespeare, A. J. F. Collins, and G. E. Hollingworth, *King Henry V*, The Tutorial Shakespeare (London: W. B. Clive, 1929)

William Shakespeare and G. E. Hollingworth, *Coriolanus*, Matriculation Shakespeare (London: University Tutorial Press, 1924)

William Shakespeare and G. E. Hollingworth, *King Henry IV, Part I*, Matriculation Shakespeare (London: W. B. Clive, 1925)

William Shakespeare and G. E. Hollingworth, *King Henry VIII*, The Tutorial Shakespeare (London: W. B. Clive, University Tutorial Press Ltd, 1929)

William Shakespeare and G. E. Hollingworth, *Macbeth*, The Tutorial Shakespeare (London: W. B. Clive, 1927)

William Shakespeare and G. E. Hollingworth, *The Tragedy of Hamlet, Prince of Denmark* The Tutorial Shakespeare (London: W. B. Clive, 1926)

William Shakespeare, G. E. Hollingworth, and Henry Charles Duffin, *Twelfth Night, or What You Will* Matriculation Shakespeare (London: University Tutorial Press, 1936)

William Shakespeare, G. E. Hollingworth, and A. F. Watt, *Julius Caesar*, The Tutorial Shakespeare (London: W. B. Clive; University Tutorial, 1928)

William Shakespeare, A. F. Watt, and G. E. Hollingworth, *King Richard the Second*, The Tutorial Shakespeare (London: W. B. Clive, 1929)

William Shakespeare, A. F. Watt, and G. E. Hollingworth, *A Midsummer Night's Dream*, Matriculation Shakespeare (London: University Tutorial Press, 1929)

Sources

Gertrude Eleanor Hollingworth, 'Grant of Letters of Administration', 1936, https://probatesearch.service.gov.uk

'London, England, School Admissions and Discharges, 1840–1911 – Gertrude Eleanor Hollingworth, Highbury County School', London Metropolitan Archives, London, England, *School Admission and Discharge Registers*, reference: LCC/EO/DIV03/HIG/AD/001, www.ancestry.com

'Master of Arts: Honours and Higher Degrees: Internal Students', in *University of London: The Historical Record (1836–1926)* (British History Online), pp. 147–53, www.british-history.ac.uk/no-series/london-university-graduates

Grace Robartes Trenery (1886–1950)

Grace Trenery attended the University of Liverpool, after which she took up a teaching position in their English faculty. She was one of several staff members who oversaw students when the university evacuated during Second World War. See Chapter 5.

Editions

William Shakespeare and Grace Trenery, *Much Ado About Nothing*, The Arden Shakespeare (London: Methuen, 1924)

Sources

Grace Robartes Trenery, 'Probate Record and Last Will and Testament', 1950, Principal Probate Registry, https://probatesearch.service.gov.uk

'Past Guild Officers @ Liverpool Guild of Students', www.liverpoolguild.org/main-menu/about-us/history-of-the-guild/past-guild-officers

Paul Edward Hedley Hair, *Arts, Letters, Society: A Miscellany Commemorating the Centenary of the Faculty of Arts at the University of Liverpool* (Liverpool: Liverpool University Press, 1996), p. 54

Hallie Devalance Walker (1882–1963)

Hallie Walker was born in Missouri and received her master's degree from the University of Texas in 1914 for a dissertation on George Eliot. She went on to teach journalism in public schools in Dallas, Texas.

Editions

William Shakespeare and Hallie D. Walker, *As You Like It*, Lippincott's Classics (Philadelphia: J. B. Lippincott, 1929)

Sources

Hallie D. Walker, 'The Interpretation of Humble Life in the Novels of George Eliot' (master's thesis, University of Texas, 1914)

'Texas, Death Certificates, 1903–1982', digital images, entry for Hallie Devalance Walker, 1963, no. 36388, citing Texas Department of State Health Services, www.ancestry.com

University of Texas Bulletin: Directory of the University of Texas for the Long Session of 1917–1918 (University of Texas, Austin, 1 November 1917), p. 21

Helen Archibald Clarke (1860–1926)

American poet, composer, and editor. See Chapter 3.

Editions

William Shakespeare, Helen Archibald Clarke, and Charlotte Endymion Porter, *Shakespeare's Complete Works*, Pembroke Edition, 12 vols (New York: Thomas Y. Crowell & Co, 1903)

William Shakespeare, Helen Archibald Clarke, and Charlotte Endymion Porter, *Shakespeare: First Folio Edition*, 40 vols (New York: T. Y. Crowell, 1903)

Sources

Jeanne Addison Roberts, 'Women Edit Shakespeare', *Shakespeare Survey*, 59 (2006), 136–46

Helen Elizabeth Harding (1873–?)

Helen Harding was born in Somerville, MA, in 1873. Her educational background is unknown – one census record indicates that she did not attend school – but she took up a teaching post at English High School in Somerville in 1901 and remained there until at least 1904. By 1910, she had moved to the Bronx. She taught in the public school system until at least 1940.

Editions

William Shakespeare, Helen Elizabeth Harding, and Maxwell Anderson, *Julius Caesar and Elizabeth the Queen*, Noble's Comparative Classics (New York: Noble and Noble, 1932)

William Shakespeare, Sophocles, Eugene O'Neill, and Helen Elizabeth Harding, *Comparative Tragedies, Old and New – Hamlet, Electra, Beyond the Horizon*, Noble's Comparative Classics (New York: Noble and Noble, 1939)

Sources

1900 US Census, Middlesex County, MA, pop. sch., city of Cambridge, ED 679, p. 3, dwell. 68, fam. 77, Helen E. Harding, NARA microfilm publication T623, roll 1854, www.ancestry.com

1920 US Census, Kings County, NY, pop. sch., city of Brooklyn, ED 482, p. 4B, dwell. 71, fam. 78, Helen E. Harding, NARA microfilm publication T625, roll 1157, www.ancestry.com

City of Somerville, Massachusetts, Annual Reports (Somerville, MA: Somerville Journal Print, 1903)

Helen Gray Cone (1859–1934)

Helen Cone attended Hunter College in New York City and remained to teach after graduating, becoming the first woman to hold a professorship at the all-female college. She achieved some fame as a poet with collections like *Soldiers of the Light* (1911) and *Oberon and Puck* (1885). See Chapter 3.

Editions

William Shakespeare and Helen Gray Cone, *Merchant of Venice*, English Classics: Star Series (New York: Globe School Book Company, 1900)

William Shakespeare, Helen Gray Cone, and Richard Grant White, *Hamlet*, The Riverside Literature Series, 116 (Boston: Houghton Mifflin, 1897)

William Shakespeare, Helen Gray Cone, and Richard Grant White, *Macbeth*, The Riverside Literature Series, 106 (Boston: Houghton Mifflin, 1897)

William Shakespeare, Helen Gray Cone, and Richard Grant White, *Twelfth Night; or What You Will*, Riverside Literature Series, 149 (Boston: Houghton Mifflin, 1901)

Sources

Julio L. Hernandez-Delgado, 'The Helen Gray Cone Collection, 1859–1934, Finding Aid', https://library.hunter.cuny.edu/sites/default/files/documents/archives/finding_aids/Helen_Gray_Cone_1859_1934.pdf

Henrietta Bowdler (1750–1830)

Best known during her own life for her writing on religious subjects, Henrietta Bowdler anonymously edited *The Family Shakespeare*, which became the most famous expurgated edition of the plays of Shakespeare. The verb 'to bowdlerise' was coined from her name.

Editions

William Shakespeare and Henrietta Maria Bowdler, *The Family Shakespeare*, 4 vols (Bath: R. Cruttwell, 1807)

Sources

M. Clare Loughlin-Chow, 'Bowdler, Henrietta Maria [Harriet] (1750–1830), Writer and Literary Editor', *Oxford Dictionary of National Biography* (Oxford: Oxford University Press, 2004) doi.org/10.1093/ref:odnb/3028

Ida E. Melson (1878–1958)

Georgian Ida Melson was the head of the English department at Girls' High School in Atlanta, Georgia. In her free time, she campaigned for suffrage and wrote short stories.

Editions

William Shakespeare and Ida E. Melson, *Twelfth Night*, Winston Companion Classics (Philadelphia: John C. Winston Company, 1927)

Sources

'Georgia, Death Index, 1919–1998', digital images, entry for Ida E. Melson, 1958, no. 15457, citing *Indexes of Vital Records for Georgia: Deaths, 1919–1998*, www.ancestry.com

'Miss Ida Melson Will Read Two of Her Short Stories Which Have Been Accepted by Harper's Magazine', *The Atlanta Constitution* (25 February 1923), p. 2

'Politics and Tea', *The Atlanta Constitution* (6 September 1914), p. 2

Isabel Jane Bisson (1895–1986)

Aberdeen native Isabel Jane Maitland Smith was a faculty member at the University of Birmingham when she met and married fellow lecturer

Laurence Adolphus Bisson. At the time of her marriage, she was the president of the Association of University Teachers. They moved to Oxford, where Laurence took up a post. Although Isabel could not hold a post at Oxford as a married woman, she tutored and served as an examiner, as well as editing *As You Like It*. The Bissons later moved to Belfast. See Chapter 5.

Editions

William Shakespeare and Isabel J. Bisson, *As You Like It*, New Clarendon
    Shakespeare (Oxford: Oxford University Press, 1941)

Sources

'1939 England and Wales Register – Isabella J. Bisson', National Archives of the
    UK, PRO RG 101/2180E, www.ancestry.com
A.E., 'Laurence Adolphus Bisson, 1897–1965', *French Studies*, 20.1 (1966),
    114–15
Isabel Bisson, 'Five Years in the Universities', *The Political Quarterly*, 7.4, 551–64
'Marriages', *The Times* (London, 6 September 1933), p. 1

Jane Lee (1850–1895)

Polyglot Jane Lee was the first Vice-Principal of Old Hall at Newnham College, Cambridge. See Chapter 2.

Sources

E. H. Lyster, 'The Late Miss Jane Lee', in *Cambridge Letters, Etc, 1895*
    (London: Women's Printing Society, 1895), pp. 27–30, Newnham
    College Archives
'Newnham College Registry Card for Jane Lee', Newnham College Archives

Jennie Ellis Burdick (1882–?)

Not much is known about Jennie Ellis Burdick. Born in Rhode Island, she was employed by New York–based publisher Bigelow Smith to prepare the Aldus Shakespeare, which combined materials by various well-known scholars such as Israel Gollancz, Henry Hudson, and C. H. Herford. Burdick wrote a synopsis for each play and seems to have been responsible for compiling the volume, as she signed the editor's preface. Burdick married Walter J. Webster, a dentist. She appears to have been a keen amateur ornithologist.

Editions

William Shakespeare, Jennie Ellis Burdick, et al., *The Aldus Shakespeare, with Copious Notes and Comments* (New York: Bigelow Smith, 1909)

Sources

1900 US Census, Essex County, NJ, pop. sch., city of East Orange, ED 172, p. 11A, dwell. 113, fam. 186, Jennie Ellis Burdick, NARA microfilm publication T623, roll 968, www.ancestry.com
1910 US Census, Hudson County, NJ, pop. sch., city of Jersey City, ED 163, p. 8B, dwell. 81, fam. 208, Jennie E. B. Webster, NARA microfilm publication T624, roll 891, www.ancestry.com
T. S. Palmer, 'Thirty-Fifth Stated Meeting of the American Ornithologists' Union', *The Auk*, 35.1 (1918), 65–73

Jennie F. Chase (1859–1943)

Jennie Chase lived and taught in her native St. Louis, Missouri, for her entire life. She edited a variety of books for Macmillan, as well as writing poetry.

Editions

William Shakespeare and Jennie F. Chase, *The Tragedy of Romeo and Juliet*, Macmillan Pocket American and English Classics (New York: Macmillan Company, 1917)

Sources

'Funeral Service Tomorrow for Miss Jennie F. Chase', *St. Louis Post-Dispatch* (St. Louis, Missouri, 13 December 1943), p. 15

Katharine Lee Bates (1859–1929)

Poet and professor who spent her career at Wellesley College. Most famous for writing the lyrics to 'America the Beautiful'. See Chapter 3.

Editions

William Shakespeare and Katharine Lee Bates, *Shakespeare's Comedy of As You Like It*, The Students' Series of English Classics (Boston: Leach, Shewell, & Sanborn, 1896)
William Shakespeare and Katharine Lee Bates, *Shakespeare's Comedy of the Merchant of Venice*, The Students' Series of English Classics (Boston: Leach, Shewell, & Sanborn, 1894)
William Shakespeare and Katharine Lee Bates, *Shakespeare's Comedy of A Midsummer-Night's Dream*, The Students' Series of English Classics (Boston: Leach, Shewell, & Sanborn, 1895)
William Shakespeare, Katharine Lee Bates, and Frederick S. Boas, *The Tempest*, The Arden Shakespeare, revised edition (Boston: D. C. Heath, 1916)

Sources

Lillian S. Robinson, 'Bates, Katharine Lee (1859-1929), Educator and Writer', in *American National Biography* (Oxford: Oxford University Press, 1999)
Melinda M. Ponder, *From Sea to Shining Sea: The Story of the Poet of 'America the Beautiful'* (Chicago: Windy City Publishers, 2017)

Laura Emma Lockwood (1863–1956)

Laura Emma Lockwood attended the University of Kansas before earning her PhD at Yale in 1898. She taught at Wellesley College, where she developed a rivalry with fellow English professor Sophie Hart. According to a student's recollections, she enjoyed leading her students up the hills around Wellesley, making them recite *Paradise Lost* from memory. A passport application reveals that she was travelling in Germany at the outbreak of the First World War, obtaining a passport to leave Berlin on 5 August 1914, the day England declared war on Germany. See Chapter 3.

Editions

William Shakespeare, Laura Emma Lockwood, and Richard Grant White, *A Midsummer-Night's Dream*, Riverside Literature Series (Boston: Houghton Mifflin, 1911)

Sources

Patricia Ann Palmieri, *In Adamless Eden: The Community of Women Faculty at Wellesley* (New Haven, CT: Yale University Press, 1995), p. 165

'US Passport Applications, 1795–1925', NARA microfilm publication M1372, roll 1604, application of Laura Emma Lockwood, 1921, no. 33314, www .ancestry.com

Laura J. Wylie (1855–1932)

Alongside Tudor Shakespeare editor Hanscom, Laura Wylie was one of the first seven women to receive PhDs from Yale. After graduating, she took up a post at her alma mater Vassar College, and was quickly promoted to head of the department of English. An active suffragist, she and her partner Gertrude Buck are remembered at Vassar for championing theatre, in both the college and the surrounding community. When she died, the college published a memorial book, for which Eleanor Roosevelt wrote the final chapter. See Chapter 3.

Editions

William Shakespeare and Laura J. Wylie, *The Winter's Tale*, The Tudor Shakespeare (New York: Macmillan Company, 1912)

Sources

'Biographies of Yale's First Women Ph.D.'s | Women Faculty Forum', http://wff .yale.edu/biographies-yales-first-women-phds
Elisabeth Woodbridge Morris, *Miss Wylie of Vassar. Published for the Laura J. Wylie Memorial Associates.* (New Haven, CT: Yale University Press, 1934)
'Laura Johnson Wylie – Vassar College Encyclopedia – Vassar College', https:// vcencyclopedia.vassar.edu/faculty/prominent-faculty/laura-wylie.html

Laura Jewry Valentine (1814–1899)

Writer of children's books and editor for Frederick Warne. See the Prologue.

Editions

William Shakespeare and Laura Jewry Valentine, *The Works of William Shakespeare*, Chandos Classics (London: Frederick Warne, 1868)

Sources

See the Prologue.

Lilian Winstanley (1876–1960)

Described as a 'frail, wraith-like personality', Lilian Winstanley came to the University College of Wales, Aberystwyth, after studying with C. H. Herford at Owens College, now the University of Manchester. She was an early owner of a safety bicycle while at Manchester. She taught English at Aberystwyth for the rest of her life, writing several well-regarded books on the connections between Shakespeare's plays and contemporary politics.

Editions

William Shakespeare and L. Winstanley, *The Second Part of Henry the Fourth*, The Arden Shakespeare (London: D. C. Heath, 1918)

Sources

Dorothea Waley Singer, *Margrieta Beer, 1871–1951: A Memoir* (Manchester University Press, 1955), p. 17
Lillian Winstanley, 'Probate Record and Last Will and Testament', 1960, Principal Probate Registry, https://probatesearch.service.gov.uk
'Reviews – "The Praise of Wales"', *Welsh Outlook*, 20.12 (1933), 350–51

Lois Grosvenor Hufford (1845–1937)

Massachusetts-born Lois Hufford was a teacher in Indianapolis, Indiana. She edited extensively, both alone and with her husband George Hufford. They also wrote *Shakespeare in Tale and Verse* (1901) together.

Editions

William Shakespeare, George W. Hufford, and Lois G. Hufford, *Shakespeare's Julius Caesar*, New Pocket Classics (New York: Macmillan, 1900)

Sources

'Indiana, Death Certificates, 1899–2011', digital images, entry for Lois Grosvenor Hufford, 1937, no. 35708, citing *Indiana State Board of Health. Death Certificates, 1900–2011*, roll 12, www.ancestry.com

Louise Pound (1872–1958)

Nebraskan Louise Pound attended the University of Nebraska, where she became lifelong friends with author Willa Cather. In college, she was well-known as a champion athlete. She earned a PhD at Heidelberg and returned to teach at Nebraska. Her main focus of study was American folklore. In 1955, she became the first woman president of the Modern Language Association. See Chapter 3.

Editions

William Shakespeare and Louise Pound, *The First Part of Henry the Sixth, Henry the Sixth*, The Tudor Shakespeare (New York: Macmillan, 1911)

Sources

Robert Cochran, *Louise Pound: Scholar, Athlete, Feminist Pioneer* (Lincoln: University of Nebraska Press, 2009)
Robert B. Cochran, 'Pound, Louise (1872–1958), Folklorist', in *American National Biography* (Oxford: Oxford University Press, 2000), doi.org/10.1093/anb/9780198606697.article.0900606

Louise Wetherbee (1872–1953)

Louise Wetherbee was born in Massachusetts. She taught English and advised the drama club at Newton High School in Newton, MA.

Editions

William Shakespeare, Louise Wetherbee, and Samuel Thurber, *As You Like It*, Academy Classics (Boston: Allyn and Bacon, 1922)

Sources

1920 US Census, Middlesex County, MA, pop. sch., city of Newton, ED 361, p. 7A, dwell. 119, fam. 145, Louise M. Wetherbee, NARA microfilm publication T625, roll 716, www.ancestry.com
Graduation Exercises: Newton High School, Newton North High School (Newton Free Library, 1942), http://archive.org/details/graduationexerci1942unse

Mabel Abbott Bessey (1885–1943)

Educated at Cornell (BA, 1906), Mabel Abbott Bessey became a teacher at Bay Ridge High School, New York City. She was hired by Houghton Mifflin to edit several plays for the Riverside student editions in the 1930s.

Editions

William Shakespeare and Mabel A. Bessey, *The Tempest*, Riverside Literature Series (Boston: Houghton Mifflin, 1934)
William Shakespeare, Mabel A. Bessey, and Joseph Quincy Adams, *Hamlet*, The Riverside Literature Series (Boston: Houghton Mifflin, 1931)

Sources

1925 NY State Census, Kings County, NY, pop. sch., city of Brooklyn, ED 28, p. 7, dwell. 64, line 43, Mabel A. Bessey, *New York, US State Census, 1925*, www.ancestry.com
US School Yearbooks, 1900–1990, digital images, citing 'The Cornellian Yearbook', Cornell University, 1906, p. 340, www.ancestry.com

Magdalene Marie Weale (1890–1961)

Born in New South Wales, Magdalene Weale emigrated with her family to England and settled in London, where she became a teacher. In addition to her edition of *Love's Labour's Lost*, she prepared an edition of *The Quatrefoil of Love* for the Early English Text Society.

Editions

William Shakespeare and Magdalene Marie Weale, *Love's Labour's Lost*, Tutorial Shakespeare (London: University Tutorial Press, 1924)

Sources

'1911 England Census – Magdalene Marie Weale', National Archives of the UK, PRO RG14/2306, Sch. 275, www.ancestry.com

Margaret Cameron Coss Flower (1907–1998)

Born in America to moderately well-off parents, Margaret Coss attended Bryn Mawr College, earning her BA in 1928. Shortly after, she moved to

Cambridge to study at Newnham College where she met Desmond Flower, then a student at King's College. She married Flower, heir to the Cassell publishing company, in 1931. According to family legend, Margaret gave him a cloak owned by Alfred, Lord Tennyson, as a wedding gift. Their son Nicholas was born in 1935. Desmond enlisted in the Royal Artillery during Second World War, eventually serving at Normandy, while Margaret and Nicholas took a ship to New York from Galway five days before the Battle of Britain began. Although she returned to London to help at short-staffed Cassell in 1943, Desmond and Margaret's marriage was dissolved in 1952. Her son explains that 'six years of life in different worlds had changed [them] in ways which a new life together could not repair'. Margaret continued to teach, write, and publish with Cassell on topics from Victorian jewellery to Yugoslavian for travellers, eventually emigrating to Australia to live near her son and his family. Her portrait, done by Percy Wyndham Lewis, hangs in the National Portrait Gallery.

Editions

William Shakespeare and Margaret Flower, *The Sonnets of William Shakespeare* (London: Cassell, 1933)

Sources

Nicholas Flower, 'Query – Margaret Flower', 23 March 2016, email to author

Margaret Hill McCarter (1860–1938)

Margaret Hill was raised a Quaker in Indiana. After attending the State Normal School in Terre Haute, she began a career teaching English. She married, had three children, and became a prominent Kansas novelist. In 1920, McCarter was the first woman to speak at the Republican National Convention.

Editions

William Shakespeare and Margaret Hill McCarter, *Shakespeare's Julius Caesar*, Twentieth Century Classics and School Readings (Topeka, KS: Crane, 1900)
William Shakespeare and Margaret Hill McCarter, *Shakespeare's Macbeth*, Twentieth Century Classics and School Readings (Topeka, KS: Crane, 1900)
William Shakespeare and Margaret Hill McCarter, *Shakespeare's The Merchant of Venice*, Crane Classics (Topeka, KS: Crane, 1902)

William Shakespeare and Margaret Hill McCarter, *Shakespeare's Tragedy of King Lear*, Crane Classics (Topeka, KS: Crane, 1905)

Sources

'Margaret Hill McCarter, Topeka Novelist', https://washburn.edu/reference/cks/mapping/mccarter/index.html

Martha Foote Crow (1854–1924)

Martha Foote attended Syracuse University, where she was a founder of the sorority Alpha Phi. She eventually earned her PhD at Syracuse. She married John Crow and they both took up jobs at Iowa (now Grinnell) College. After John's death, she became a professor at the University of Chicago before accepting the post of dean of women at Northwestern University. She was commissioned to edit *King Lear* for D. C. Heath's Arden Shakespeare, but she was replaced as editor by David Nichol Smith for unknown reasons. See Chapter 3.

Sources

'Martha Foote Crow Papers: An Inventory of Her Papers at Syracuse University', https://library.syr.edu/digital/guides/print/crow_mf_prt.htm
William Shakespeare and J. C. Smith, *As You Like It*, Heath's English Classics (Boston: D. C. Heath, 1902)

Martha Hale Shackford (1875–1963)

Wellesley graduate Martha Hale Shackford attended Yale for her PhD before returning to Wellesley as a faculty member. She taught at Wellesley for forty-two years, alongside colleagues and fellow-editors Katharine Lee Bates and Laura Emma Lockwood. She spent her life with Margaret Sherwood, a Wellesley professor and novelist. Wellesley students gossiped that Shackford had 'stolen' Sherwood from another English professor, Sophie Jewett. See Chapter 3.

Editions

William Shakespeare and Martha Hale Shackford, *As You Like It*, The Tudor Shakespeare (New York: Macmillan Company, 1911)

Sources

'Martha Hale Shackford, Age 97, Wellesley College Professor, Poet, and Author', *Shackford Family History*, 2013, http://shackfordgenealogy.weebly.com/1/post/2013/12/sundays-obituary-martha-hale-shackford-age-97-wellesley-college-professor-poet-and-author-blog-98.html

Patricia Ann Palmieri, *In Adamless Eden: The Community of Women Faculty at Wellesley* (New Haven, CT: Yale University Press, 1995)

Mary Atkinson Maurice (1797–1858)

Teacher and education reformer. See Chapter 1.

Editions

William Shakespeare and Mary Atkinson Maurice, *Readings from the Plays of Shakespeare, in Illustration of His Characters* (London: John W. Parker, 1848)

Sources

Elaine Kaye, 'Maurice, Mary Atkinson (1797–1858)', in *Oxford Dictionary of National Biography* (Oxford: Oxford University Press, 2004), doi.org/10.1093/ref:odnb/51769

Mary Elizabeth Adams (1865–1944(?))

Mary Elizabeth Adams grew up in Ohio and attended Vassar College, earning her BA in 1884. She taught in Massachusetts, Kentucky, and New York before moving back to Cleveland, where she lived with her siblings.

Editions

William Shakespeare, Samuel Thurber, and Mary Elizabeth Adams, *Twelfth Night*, Academy Classics (Boston: Allyn and Bacon, 1925)

Sources

1900 US Census, Cuyahoga County, OH, pop. sch., city of Cleveland, ED 77, p. 5, dwell. 91, fam. 108, Mary E. Adams, NARA microfilm publication T623, roll 1854, www.ancestry.com

'US School Catalogs, 1765–1935', digitised images, citing *General Catalogue of the Officers and Graduates of Vassar College, 1861–1890*, p. 52, www.ancestry .com

Mary Cowden Clarke (1809–1898)

Often identified as the first woman editor of Shakespeare, Mary Cowden Clarke was a well-known Shakespeare critic during the nineteenth century.

Editions

William Shakespeare and Mary Cowden Clarke, *Shakespeare's Works. Edited, with a Scrupulous Revision of the Text, by M. Cowden Clarke* (New York: D. Appleton, 1860)

William Shakespeare, Mary Cowden Clarke, and Charles Cowden Clarke, *The Plays of Shakespeare*, Cassell's Illustrated Shakespeare, 3 vols (London: Cassell, 1864)

Sources

C. E. Hughes and Betty T. Bennett, 'Clarke, Mary Victoria Cowden (1809–1898), Literary Scholar and Writer', in *Oxford Dictionary of National Biography* (Oxford: Oxford University Press, 2004), doi.org/ 10.1093/ref:odnb/5521

Gail Marshall and Ann Thompson, 'Mary Cowden Clarke', in *Jameson, Cowden Clarke, Kemble, Cushman*, ed. Gail Marshall, Great Shakespeareans (London: Bloomsbury Arden Shakespeare, 2011), VII, 58–91

Mary Cowden Clarke, *My Long Life: An Autobiographic Sketch* (London: T. Fisher Unwin, 1896)

Maud Elma Kingsley (1865–1922)

Maud Kingsley attended Colby College and took a job as a schoolteacher. She started writing textbooks for the Boston-based Palmer Company and continued to do so prolifically her entire life.

Editions

William Shakespeare, Maud Elma Kingsley, and Frank Herbert Palmer, *Shakespeare's Comedy of As You Like It*, The Kingsley English Texts (Boston: Palmer Company, 1914)

William Shakespeare, Maud Elma Kingsley, and Frank Herbert Palmer, *Shakespeare's The Merchant of Venice*, The Kingsley English Texts (Boston: Palmer Company, 1911)

William Shakespeare, Maud Elma Kingsley, and Frank Herbert Palmer, *Shakespeare's Tragedy of Julius Caesar*, The Kingsley English Texts (Boston: Palmer Company, 1908)

William Shakespeare, Maud Elma Kingsley, and Frank Herbert Palmer, *Shakespeare's Tragedy of Macbeth*, The Kingsley English Texts (Boston: Palmer Company, 1909)

Sources

Colby College, 'Colby College Catalogue 1884–1885', 1884, 11, https://digitalcommons.colby.edu/catalogs/11

'Maine, US Death Records, 1761–1922', digital images, entry for Maud Elma Kingsley, 1922, citing *Maine, Death Records, 1761–1922*, 1908–1922 Vital Records, roll 30, www.ancestry.com

May McKitrick (1871–1937)

May McKitrick completed her undergraduate degree at the University of Wisconsin, after which she became an English teacher in Cleveland, Ohio. In 1928, she took a job as an assistant professor in the School of Education at Case Western Reserve University, where she remained until her death. She wrote about the practical teaching of English in high schools.

Editions

William Shakespeare and May McKitrick, *The Merchant of Venice*, Winston Companions (Philadelphia: John C. Winston Company, 1926)

Sources

May McKitrick, 'The Adaptation of the Work in English to the Actual Needs and Interests of the Pupils', *The English Journal*, 2.7 (1913), 405–16

May McKitrick, 'Creative Writing in the New Era', *The English Journal*, 23.4 (1934), 298

Yearbook (University of Wisconsin, Madison, 1891), p. 47, *US School Yearbooks, 1880–2012*, www.ancestry.com

Muriel St Clare Byrne (1895–1983)

Tudor historian Muriel St Clare Byrne attended Somerville College during the same period as Dorothy L. Sayers, Vera Brittain, and Una Ellis-

Fermor. She and Sayers remained friends throughout their lives and co-wrote the play that Sayers later turned into *Busman's Honeymoon*. Byrne was a governor of the Royal Shakespeare Company and OBE. She worked for fifty years on a six-volume edition of Lord Lisle's letters. See the sidenote 'On Women Editing Not-Shakespeare (or Not Editing)'.

Editions

William Shakespeare and Muriel St Clare Byrne, *Henry VIII*, New Eversley Shakespeare (London: Macmillan, 1937)

Sources

'Special Collections – Somerville College Oxford', www.some.ox.ac.uk/library-it/special-collections/special-collections

Nora Ratcliff (1900–1981)

Born Nora Everatt, Nora and her husband Arthur James John Ratcliff both edited volumes for Newbolt's Teaching of English Series. Nora Ratcliff was also a playwright and wrote about village drama.

Editions

William Shakespeare and Nora Ratcliff, *Shakespeare's Tragedy of Antony and Cleopatra*, Teaching of English Series (London: Thomas Nelson & Sons, 1947)
William Shakespeare and Nora Ratcliff, *Shakespeare's Tragedy of Othello*, Teaching of English Series (London: Thomas Nelson & Sons, 1941)

Sources

'1939 England and Wales Register – Nora Ratcliff', National Archives of the UK, PRO RG101/3840G, www.ancestry.com
'England & Wales, Civil Registration Marriage Index, 1916–2005 – Nora Everatt', 1925, General Register Office, United Kingdom, *England and Wales Civil Registration Indexes*, Yorkshire West Riding, Vol. 9a, Page 194, www.ancestry.com
Nora Ratcliff, *Rude Mechanicals: A Short Review of Village Drama* (London: Thomas Nelson & Sons, 1938)

Pauline Gertrude Wiggin Leonard (1869–1948)

Pauline Wiggin attended Smith, Radcliffe, and the New York State Library School, and taught at both Vassar and Wellesley alongside Laura Wylie, Katharine Lee Bates, and Martha Hale Shackford. She then took up a post as a librarian at West Virginia University. She married William Leonard, an instructor at WVU, and had one son. In addition to Shakespeare, she wrote about her great passion for gardening.

Editions

William Shakespeare and Pauline Gertrude Wiggin, *Shakespeare's The Merchant of Venice*, Golden Key Series (Boston: D. C. Heath, 1931)
William Shakespeare and Pauline Gertrude Wiggin, *Shakespeare's Midsummer Night's Dream*, Golden Key Series (Boston: D. C. Heath, 1929)

Sources

Stewart Plein, 'Pauline Gertrude Wiggin Leonard, the Scholar Librarian', West Virginia University Libraries, 2015, https://news.lib.wvu.edu/2015/09/16/pauline-gertrude-wiggin-leonard-the-scholar-librarian

Phoebe Sheavyn (1865–1968)

Forthright literary scholar Phoebe Sheavyn struggled from a young age until her retirement against the subordinate positions allowed to women teachers, particularly in universities. This earned her a 'prickly' reputation at Manchester University, where she taught and served as warden to the women students. She wrote extensively on the inequities and difficulties faced by women students and academics. Her best-known work was *The Literary Profession in the Elizabethan Age*. She lived to be 102 years old.

Editions

William Shakespeare and Phoebe Sheavyn, *King Lear*, Black's School Shakespeare (London: Adam and Charles Black, 1898)

Sources

Enid Huws Jones, 'Sheavyn, Phoebe Ann Beale (1865–1968), Literary Scholar and Feminist', in *Oxford Dictionary of National Biography* (Oxford: Oxford University Press, 2009), doi.org/10.1093/ref:odnb/52388

Rosa Baughan (1829–1911)

Rosa Baughan grew up in a 'dame school' operated in Marylebone by her mother. The 1841 census, taken when Baughan was twelve, shows that seventeen girls between the ages of five and nineteen boarded in her home as 'pupils'. Ten years later, with both Rosa and her sister Clara grown and assisting their mother, the number of pupils remained steady, but they were also employing at least four other teachers, suggesting that perhaps they taught day students as well as boarders. Baughan was best known for her books on palmistry, astronomy, physiognomy, and graphology. See Chapter 1.

Editions

Rosa Baughan, *Shakespeare's Plays Abridged and Revised for the Use of Girls*, 2 vols (London: T. J. Allman, 1863 and 1871)

Sources

'1841 England Census – Rosa Baughan', National Archives of the UK, PRO HO107/681/2, Folio 50, Page, 31, Line 25, www.ancestry.com
'1851 England Census – Rosa Baughan', National Archives of the UK, PRO HO107/1491, Folio 412, Page 20, www.ancestry.com
'1871 England Census – Rosa Baughan', National Archives of the UK, PRO RG10/188, Folio 27, Page 47, www.ancestry.com

Rose Adelaide Witham (1873–?)

After attending Smith College and Radcliffe, Rose Witham taught at schools in Massachusetts, Rhode Island, and Kansas. Her supervisor at Radcliffe was Tudor Shakespeare general editor William Allan Neilson.

Editions

William Shakespeare, Samuel Thurber, and R. Adelaide Witham, *Macbeth*, Academy Classics (Boston: Allyn and Bacon, 1922)
William Shakespeare and R. Adelaide Witham, *As You like It*, Riverside Literature Series (Boston: Houghton Mifflin, 1931)
William Shakespeare and Rose Adelaide Witham, *The Merchant of Venice* Riverside Literature Series (Boston: Houghton Mifflin, 1929)

Sources

R. Adelaide Witham, *English and Scottish Popular Ballads* (Boston: Houghton Mifflin, 1937)

US School Catalogs, 1765–1935, digital images, *Ancestry.com*, citing 'Official Circular, No. 19', Smith College, 1892, p. 39, www.ancestry.com

Sarah Willard Hiestand (1857–1929)

Sarah Willard Hiestand lived in Chicago with her husband, Henry, and five children. She was a founding member of the Rogers Park Women's Club. She and Henry retired to utopian cooperative Fairhope, Alabama, where she directed Shakespeare plays for the community.

Editions

William Shakespeare and Sarah Willard Hiestand, *The Comedy of Errors*, The Beginner's Shakespeare (Boston: D. C. Heath, 1901)

William Shakespeare and Sarah Willard Hiestand, *The Comedy of The Tempest*, The Beginner's Shakespeare (Boston: D. C. Heath, 1900)

William Shakespeare and Sarah Willard Hiestand, *The Comedy of The Winter's Tale*, The Beginner's Shakespeare (Boston: D. C. Heath, 1901)

William Shakespeare and Sarah Willard Hiestand, *A Midsummer-Night's Dream*, The Beginner's Shakespeare (Boston: D. C. Heath, 1900)

Sources

Cathalynn Donelson, *Fairhope* (Mount Pleasant, SC: Arcadia Publishing, 2005), p. 108

Mary Beth Klatt, *Chicago's Fashion History: 1865–1945* (Mount Pleasant, SC: Arcadia Publishing, 2010), p. 80

Teena Rochfort Smith (1861–1883)

Literary scholar who planned a four-text edition of *Hamlet*. See Chapter 2.

Sources

Ann Thompson, 'Teena Rochfort Smith, Frederick Furnivall, and the New Shakspere Society's Four-Text Edition of Hamlet', *Shakespeare Quarterly*, 49 (1998), 125–39

Virginia Gildersleeve (1877–1965)

Dean of Barnard College and diplomat. See Chapter 3.

Editions

William Shakespeare and Virginia Gildersleeve, *The Tragedy of King Lear*, The Tudor Shakespeare (New York: Macmillan Company, 1912)

Sources

Cynthia Farr Brown, 'Gildersleeve, Virginia Crocheron (1877–1965), College Administrator and International Affairs Expert', in *American National Biography* (Oxford: Oxford University Press, 2000), doi.org/10.1093/anb/9780198606697.article.0900297

Virginia Crocheron Gildersleeve, *Many a Good Crusade: Memoirs* (New York: Macmillan, 1954)

Shakespeare Editions Prepared by Women, 1800–2021

Play and editor(s)	Male editor(s)	Publication date	Publisher	Series
All's Well That Ends Well (19 total)				
Mary Cowden Clarke		1860	Appleton	
Mary Cowden Clarke	Charles Cowden Clarke	1864–68	Cassell	Cassell's Illustrated Shakespeare
Laura Jewry Valentine		1868	Frederick Warne	Chandos Classics
Emma Gollancz	Israel Gollancz	1899–1902	J. M. Dent	Temple Shakespeare
Charlotte E. Porter and Helen A. Clarke		1903	Thomas Y. Crowell	Pembroke
Esther Wood		1904	Doubleday, Page	The Personal Shakespeare
Charlotte E. Porter and Helen E. Clarke		1909	Thomas Y. Crowell	First Folio
Jennie Ellis Burdick		1909	Bigelow Smith	Aldus Shakespeare
Barbara Everett		1970	Penguin	New Penguin
Marie Edel & Anne Barton	G. Blakemore Evans et al.	1974	Houghton Mifflin	Riverside Shakespeare
Susan Snyder		1993	Clarendon	Oxford Shakespeare
Jean E. Howard and Katharine Eisaman Maus	Stephen Greenblatt, Walter Cohen	1997	W. W. Norton	Norton1
Barbara Mowat	Paul Werstine	2001	Simon & Schuster	Folger Shakespeare Library
Claire McEachern		2001	Penguin	Pelican
Elizabeth Huddleston and Sheila Innes		2001	Cambridge University Press	Cambridge School Shakespeare
Kathleen Kalpin Smith		2012	Hackett	New Kittredge
Suzanne Gossett and Helen Wilcox		2018	Arden Bloomsbury	Arden3*
Helen Ostovich	Andrew Griffith	2019		Internet Shakespeare Editions*
Melissa Aaron	Jay Halio, John A. Quintus	FC	Texas A&M	New Variorum*

(cont.)

Play and editor(s)	Male editor(s)	Publication date	Publisher	Series
Antony and Cleopatra (23)				
Elizabeth Inchbald		1808	Longman, Hurst, Rees, & Orme	British Theatre
Mary Cowden Clarke		1860	Appleton	
Mary Cowden Clarke	Charles Cowden Clarke	1864–68	Cassell	Cassell's Illustrated Shakespeare
Laura Jewry Valentine		1868	Frederick Warne	Chandos Classics
Emma Gollancz	Israel Gollancz	1899–1902	J. M. Dent	Temple Shakespeare
Charlotte E. Porter and Helen E. Clarke		1903	Thomas Y. Crowell	Pembroke
Esther Wood		1904	Doubleday, Page	The Personal Shakespeare
Charlotte E. Porter and Helen E. Clarke		1909	Thomas Y. Crowell	First Folio
Jennie Ellis Burdick		1909	Bigelow Smith	Aldus Shakespeare
Nora Ratcliff		1947	Thomas Nelson & Sons	Teaching of English
Barbara Everett		1964	New American Library	Signet Classics
Marie Edel	G. Blakemore Evans et al.	1974	Houghton Mifflin	Riverside Shakespeare
Jan McKeith		1984	Macmillan	Macmillan Shakespeare
Jean E. Howard and Katharine Eisaman Maus	Stephen Greenblatt, Walter Cohen	1997	W. W. Norton	Norton1
Roma Gill		1997	Oxford University Press	Oxford School Shakespeare
Barbara Mowat	Paul Werstine	1999	Simon & Schuster	Folger Shakespeare Library
Janet Suzman	Barry Gaines	2001	Applause Theatre Books	Applause Shakespeare

Editor		Year	Publisher	Series
Mary Berry		2002	Cambridge University Press	Cambridge School Shakespeare
Sarah Hatchuel		2008	Hackett	New Kittredge
Ania Loomba		2011	W. W. Norton	Norton Critical Editions
Virginia Mason Vaughan		2015	W. W. Norton	Norton3*
Terri Bourus		2016	Oxford University Press	New Oxford
Molly G. Yarn	Jonathan Bate, Eric Rasmussen, Ian De Jong	FC	Bloomsbury	RSC2

As You Like It (37)

Editor		Year	Publisher	Series
Henrietta Bowdler		1807	R. Crutwell for J. Hatchard, London	The Family Shakespeare
Elizabeth Inchbald		1808	Longman, Hurst, Rees, & Orme	British Theatre
Mary Atkinson Maurice		1848	John W. Parker	
Mary Cowden Clarke		1860	Appleton	
Mary Cowden Clarke	Charles Cowden Clarke	1864–68	Cassell	Cassell's Illustrated Shakespeare
Laura Jewry Valentine		1868	Frederick Warne	Chandos Classics
Rosa Baughan		1871	T. J. Allman	
Katharine Lee Bates		1896	Leach, Sewell, & Sanborn	
Emma Gollancz	Israel Gollancz	1899–1902	J. M. Dent	Temple Shakespeare
Flora Masson		1903	J. M. Dent	Dent's School Shakespeare
Charlotte E. Porter and Helen A. Clarke		1903	Thomas Y. Crowell	Pembroke

Play and editor(s)	Male editor(s)	Publication date	Publisher	Series
Esther Wood		1904	Doubleday, Page	The Personal Shakespeare
Charlotte E. Porter and Helen E. Clarke		1906	Thomas Y. Crowell	First Folio
Agnes Russell Weekes		1909	W. B. Clive	University Tutorial Series
Jennie Ellis Burdick		1909	Bigelow Smith	Aldus Shakespeare
Martha Hale Shackford		1911	Macmillan	Tudor Shakespeare
Louise Wetherbee	Samuel Thurber	1922	Allyn & Bacon	Academy Classics*
Evelyn Smith		1926	Thomas Nelson & Sons	Teaching of English
Hallie D. Walker		1929	J. B. Lippincott Company	Lippincott's Classics
Essie Chamberlain	G. B. Harrison, F. H. Pritchard	1932	Holt	New Reader's
Cicely Boas		1936	Macmillan	New Eversley
Isabel Bisson		1941	Clarendon	New Clarendon
Marie Edel and Anne Barton	G. Blakemore Evans et al.	1974	Houghton Mifflin	Riverside Shakespeare
Agnes Latham		1975	Methuen	Arden2*
Roma Gill		1994	Oxford University Press	Oxford School Shakespeare*
Barbara Mowat	Paul Werstine	1995	Simon & Schuster	Folger Shakespeare Library
Jean E. Howard and Katharine Eisaman Maus	Stephen Greenblatt, Walter Cohen	1997	W. W. Norton	Norton1
Frances E. Dolan		2000	Penguin	Pelican2
Cynthia Marshall		2004	Cambridge University Press	Shakespeare in Production*

Juliet Dusinberre		2006	Thomson Learning	Arden3*
Patricia Lennox		2010	Hackett	New Kittredge
Leah Marcus		2011	W. W. Norton	Norton Critical Editions
Pamela Brown and Jean E. Howard		2014	Bedford-St. Martin's	Texts & Contexts
Linzy Brady		2015	Cambridge University Press	Cambridge School Shakespeare*
Leah S. Marcus		2015	W. W. Norton	Norton3*
Molly G. Yarn	Jonathan Bate, Eric Rasmussen, Ian De Jong	FC	Bloomsbury	RSC2
Nora J. Williams		FC	Arden Bloomsbury	Arden Performance Editions*

The Comedy of Errors (18)

Elizabeth Inchbald		1808	Longman, Hurst, Rees, & Orme	British Theatre
Mary Cowden Clarke		1860	Appleton	
Rosa Baughan		1871	T. J. Allman	
Mary Cowden Clarke		1864–68	Cassell	Cassell's Illustrated Shakespeare
Laura Jewry Valentine		1868	Frederick Warne	Chandos Classics
Emma Gollancz	Israel Gollancz	1899–1902	J. M. Dent	Temple Shakespeare
Sarah Willard Hiestand		1901	D. C. Heath	Beginner's Shakespeare
Charlotte E. Porter and Helen A. Clarke		1903	Thomas Y. Crowell	Pembroke
Charlotte E. Porter and Helen E. Clarke		1903	Thomas Y. Crowell	First Folio
Esther Wood		1904	Doubleday, Page	The Personal Shakespeare

(cont.)

Play and editor(s)	Male editor(s)	Publication date	Publisher	Series
Jennie Ellis Burdick		1909	Bigelow Smith	Aldus Shakespeare
Marie Edel and Anne Barton	G. Blakemore Evans et al.	1974	Houghton Mifflin	Riverside Shakespeare
Barbara Mowat	Paul Werstine	1996	Simon & Schuster	Folger Shakespeare Library
Jean E. Howard and Katharine Eisaman Maus	Stephen Greenblatt, Walter Cohen	1997	W. W. Norton	Norton1
Frances E. Dolan		1999	Penguin	Pelican2
Laury Magnus		2011	Hackett	New Kittredge
Sarah Neville		2016	Oxford University Press	New Oxford*
Marissa Greenberg and Jayme Yeo		FC		Internet Shakespeare Editions*

Coriolanus (19)

Elizabeth Inchbald		1808	Longman, Hurst, Rees, & Orme	British Theatre
Mary Cowden Clarke		1860	Appleton	
Rosa Baughan		1863	T. J. Allman	
Mary Cowden Clarke	Charles Cowden Clarke	1864–68	Cassell	Cassell's Illustrated Shakespeare
Laura Jewry Valentine		1868	Frederick Warne	Chandos Classics
Emma Gollancz	Israel Gollancz	1899–1902	J. M. Dent	Temple Shakespeare
Charlotte E. Porter and Helen A. Clarke		1903	Thomas Y. Crowell	Pembroke
Esther Wood		1904	Doubleday, Page	The Personal Shakespeare
Charlotte E. Porter and Helen E. Clarke		1908	Thomas Y. Crowell	First Folio

Jennie Ellis Burdick		1909	Bigelow Smith	Aldus Shakespeare
Dorothy M. Macardle		NP	Horace Marshall & Sons	Carmelite Shakespeare*
Gertrude Eleanor Hollingworth		1924	W. B. Clive	University Tutorial Series
Evelyn Smith		1926	Thomas Nelson & Sons	Teaching of English
Marie Edel	G. Blakemore Evans et al.	1974	Houghton Mifflin	Riverside Shakespeare
Jean E. Howard and Katharine Eisaman Maus	Stephen Greenblatt, Walter Cohen	1997	W. W. Norton	Norton1
Roma Gill		1999	Oxford University Press	Oxford School Shakespeare*
Barbara Mowat		2009	Simon & Schuster	Folger Shakespeare Library
Cathy Shrank		2015	W. W. Norton	Norton3*
Molly G. Yarn	Jonathan Bate, Eric Rasmussen, Ian De Jong	FC	Bloomsbury	RSC2

Cymbeline (20)

Henrietta Bowdler		1807	R. Crutwell for J. Hatchard, London	The Family Shakespeare
Elizabeth Inchbald		1808	Longman, Hurst, Rees, & Orme	British Theatre
Mary Cowden Clarke		1860	Appleton	
Mary Cowden Clarke	Charles Cowden Clarke	1864–68	Cassell	Cassell's Illustrated Shakespeare
Laura Jewry Valentine		1868	Frederick Warne	Chandos Classics
Emma Gollancz	Israel Gollancz	1899–1902	J. M. Dent	Temple Shakespeare
Charlotte E. Porter and Helen A. Clarke		1903	Thomas Y. Crowell	Pembroke
Esther Wood		1904	Doubleday, Page	The Personal Shakespeare

(cont.)

Play and editor(s)	Male editor(s)	Publication date	Publisher	Series
Jennie Ellis Burdick		1909	Bigelow Smith	Aldus Shakespeare
Charlotte E. Porter and Helen A. Clarke		1910	Thomas Y. Crowell	First Folio
Agnes Russell Weekes		1919	W. B. Clive	University Tutorial Series
Cicely Boas		1936	Macmillan	New Eversley
Marie Edel	G. Blakemore Evans et al.	1974	Houghton Mifflin	Riverside Shakespeare
Jean E. Howard and Katharine Eisaman Maus	Stephen Greenblatt, Walter Cohen	1997	W. W. Norton	Norton1
Barbara Mowat	Paul Werstine	2003	Simon & Schuster	Folger Shakespeare Library
Ann Thompson		2015	W. W. Norton	Norton3*
Valerie Wayne		2017	Arden Bloomsbury	Arden3*
Jennifer Forsyth		2019		Internet Shakespeare Editions*
Molly G. Yarn	Jonathan Bate, Eric Rasmussen, Ian De Jong	FC	Bloomsbury	RSC2
Grace Tiffany	Maurice Hunt, Christopher P. Baker, Gabriel Egan	FC	Texas A&M	New Variorum*
Hamlet (29)				
Henrietta Bowdler		1807	R. Crutwell for J. Hatchard, London	The Family Shakespeare
Elizabeth Inchbald		1808	Longman, Hurst, Rees, & Orme	British Theatre
Mary Atkinson Maurice		1848	John W. Parker	

	Appleton	1860		Mary Cowden Clarke
	T. J. Allman	1863		Rosa Baughan
Cassell's Illustrated Shakespeare	Cassell	1864–68	Charles Cowden Clarke	Mary Cowden Clarke
Chandos Classics	Frederick Warne	1868		Laura Jewry Valentine
		NP		Teena Rochfort Smith
Riverside Literature Series	Houghton Mifflin	1897	Richard Grant White	Helen Gray Cone
Temple Shakespeare	J. M. Dent	1899–1902	Israel Gollancz	Emma Gollancz
Pembroke	Thomas Y. Crowell	1903		Charlotte E. Porter and Helen A. Clarke
The Personal Shakespeare	Doubleday, Page	1904		Esther Wood
First Folio	Thomas Y. Crowell	1905		Charlotte E. Porter and Helen A. Clarke
Aldus Shakespeare	Bigelow Smith	1909		Jennie Ellis Burdick
Carmelite Shakespeare*	Horace Marshall & Son	c. 1922		Gertrude Blanche Sellon
University Tutorial Series	W. B. Clive	1926		Gertrude Eleanor Hollingworth
New Reader's	Holt	1932	G. B. Harrison, F. H. Pritchard	Essie Chamberlain
Noble's Comparative Classics	Noble & Noble	1939	G. Blakemore Evans et al.	Helen E. Harding
Riverside Shakespeare	Houghton Mifflin	1974		Marie Edel
Three Text Hamlet*	AMS	1991	Paul Bertram	Bernice Kliman
Oxford School Shakespeare*	Oxford University Press	1992		Roma Gill
Folger Shakespeare Library	Simon & Schuster	1992	Paul Werstine	Barbara Mowat
Norton1	W. W. Norton	1997	Stephen Greenblatt, Walter Cohen	Jean E. Howard and Katharine Eisaman Maus
New Cambridge Early Quartos	Cambridge University Press	1998		Kathleen O. Irace

Play and editor(s)	Male editor(s)	Publication date	Publisher	Series
Ann Thompson	Neil Taylor	2006–7	Thomson Learning	Arden3*
Terri Bourus		2007	Bloomsbury	Sourcebooks Shakespeare
Bernice Kliman	James W. Lake	2009	Hackett	New Kittredge
Abigail Rokison-Woodall		2017	Arden Bloomsbury	Arden Performance Editions*
Laury Magnus	Eric Rasmussen, Hardin Aasand, Frank N. Clary, Marvin W. Hunt	FC	Texas A&M	New Variorum*

Henry IV, Part 1 (22)

Play and editor(s)	Male editor(s)	Publication date	Publisher	Series
Henrietta Bowdler		1807	R. Crutwell for J. Hatchard, London	The Family Shakespeare
Elizabeth Inchbald		1808	Longman, Hurst, Rees, & Orme	British Theatre
Mary Cowden Clarke		1860	Appleton	
Rosa Baughan		1863	T. J. Allman	
Mary Cowden Clarke	Charles Cowden Clarke	1864–68	Cassell	Cassell's Illustrated Shakespeare
Laura Jewry Valentine		1868	Frederick Warne	Chandos Classics
Charlotte Mary Yonge		c. 1883	National Society's Depository	Shakespeare's Plays for Schools
Emma Gollancz	Israel Gollancz	1899–1902	J. M. Dent	Temple Shakespeare
Charlotte E. Porter and Helen A. Clarke		1903	Thomas Y. Crowell	Pembroke

Esther Wood		1904	Doubleday, Page	The Personal Shakespeare
Jennie Ellis Burdick		1909	Bigelow Smith	Aldus Shakespeare
Charlotte E. Porter		1911	Thomas Y. Crowell	First Folio
Gertrude Eleanor Hollingworth		1925	W. B. Clive	University Tutorial Series
Evelyn Smith		1925	Thomas Nelson & Sons	Teaching of English
Marie Edel	G. Blakemore Evans et al.	1974	Houghton Mifflin	Riverside Shakespeare
Roma Gill		1984	Oxford University Press	Oxford School Shakespeare*
Barbara Mowat	Paul Werstine	1994	Simon & Schuster	Folger Shakespeare Library
Judith Weil	Herbert Weil	1997	Cambridge University Press	New Cambridge
Jean E. Howard and Katharine Eisaman Maus	Stephen Greenblatt, Walter Cohen	1997	W. W. Norton	Norton1
Barbara Hodgdon		1997	Bedford	Texts & Contexts
Rosemary Gaby		2013		Internet Shakespeare Editions
Anna Pruitt		2016	Oxford University Press	New Oxford*

Henry IV, Part 2 (20)

Henrietta Bowdler		1807	R. Crutwell for J. Hatchard, London	The Family Shakespeare
Elizabeth Inchbald		1808	Longman, Hurst, Rees, & Orme	British Theatre
Mary Cowden Clarke		1860	Appleton	
Rosa Baughan		1863	T. J. Allman	
Mary Cowden Clarke	Charles Cowden Clarke	1864–68	Cassell	Cassell's Illustrated Shakespeare
Laura Jewry Valentine		1868	Frederick Warne	Chandos Classics

Play and editor(s)	Male editor(s)	Publication date	Publisher	Series
Charlotte Mary Yonge		c. 1883	National Society's Depository	Shakespeare's Plays for Schools
Emma Gollancz	Israel Gollancz	1899–1902	J. M. Dent	Temple Shakespeare
Charlotte E. Porter and Helen A. Clarke		1903	Thomas Y. Crowell	Pembroke
Esther Wood		1904	Doubleday, Page	The Personal Shakespeare
Jennie Ellis Burdick		1909	Bigelow Smith	Aldus Shakespeare
Charlotte E. Porter		1911	Thomas Y. Crowell	First Folio
Elizabeth Deering Hanscom		1912	Macmillan	Tudor Shakespeare
Lilian Winstanley		1918	D. C. Heath	Heath's Arden
Marie Edel	G. Blakemore Evans et al.	1974	Houghton Mifflin	Riverside Shakespeare
Jean E. Howard and Katharine Eisaman Maus	Stephen Greenblatt, Walter Cohen	1997	W. W. Norton	Norton1
Barbara Mowat	Paul Werstine	1999	Simon & Schuster	Folger Shakespeare Library
Line Cottegnies		2015	W. W. Norton	Norton3*
Claire McEachern		2017	Penguin	Pelican2
Rosemary Gaby		FC		Internet Shakespeare Editions*

Henry V (26)

Play and editor(s)	Male editor(s)	Publication date	Publisher	Series
Elizabeth Inchbald		1808	Longman, Hurst, Rees, & Orme	British Theatre
Mary Cowden Clarke		1860	Appleton	
Rosa Baughan		1863	T. J. Allman	
Mary Cowden Clarke	Charles Cowden Clarke	1864–68	Cassell	Cassell's Illustrated Shakespeare

Laura Jewry Valentine		1868	Frederick Warne	Chandos Classics
Charlotte Mary Yonge		c. 1885	National Society's Depository	Shakespeare's Plays for Schools
Emma Gollancz	Israel Gollancz	1899–1902	J. M. Dent	Temple Shakespeare
Fanny Johnson		1901	William Blackwood & Son	Blackwood's School Shakespeare
Charlotte E. Porter and Helen A. Clarke		1903	Thomas Y. Crowell	Pembroke
Esther Wood		1904	Doubleday, Page	The Personal Shakespeare
Charlotte E. Porter and Helen A. Clarke		1906	Thomas Y. Crowell	First Folio
Jennie Ellis Burdick		1909	Bigelow Smith	Aldus Shakespeare
A. N. Green (Mrs. J. A. Green)		1923	Christopher's	Companion Shakespeare
Evelyn Smith		1927	Thomas Nelson & Sons	Teaching of English
Gertrude Eleanor Hollingworth	A. J. F. Collins	1929	W. B. Clive	University Tutorial Series
Dorothy Margaret Stuart	E. V. Davenport	1935	Macmillan	New Eversley
Virginia Freund	Louis B. Wright	1957	Penguin	Pelican
Marie Edel	G. Blakemore Evans et al.	1974	Houghton Mifflin	Riverside Shakespeare
Roma Gill		1995	Oxford University Press	Oxford School Shakespeare*
Barbara Mowat	Paul Werstine	1995	Simon & Schuster	Folger Shakespeare Library
Jean E. Howard and Katharine Eisaman Maus	Stephen Greenblatt, Walter Cohen	1997	W. W. Norton	Norton1
Marilyn Bell		2001	Cambridge University Press	Cambridge School Shakespeare
Emma Smith		2002	Cambridge University Press	Shakespeare in Production*

Play and editor(s)	Male editor(s)	Publication date	Publisher	Series
Annalisa Castaldo		2011	Hackett	New Kittredge
Claire McEachern		2017	Penguin	Pelican2
M. J. Kidnie		FC	Texas A&M	New Variorum*
Henry VI, Part 1 (16)				
Mary Cowden Clarke		1860	Appleton	
Mary Cowden Clarke	Charles Cowden Clarke	1864–68	Cassell	Cassell's Illustrated Shakespeare
Laura Jewry Valentine		1868	Frederick Warne	Chandos Classics
Emma Gollancz	Israel Gollancz	1899–1902	J. M. Dent	Temple Shakespeare
Charlotte E. Porter and Helen A. Clarke		1903	Thomas Y. Crowell	Pembroke
Esther Wood		1904	Doubleday, Page	The Personal Shakespeare
Jennie Ellis Burdick		1909	Bigelow Smith	Aldus Shakespeare
Louise Pound		1911	Macmillan	Tudor Shakespeare
Charlotte E. Porter		1912	Thomas Y. Crowell	First Folio
Marie Edel	G. Blakemore Evans et al.	1974	Houghton Mifflin	Riverside Shakespeare
Jean E. Howard and Katharine Eisaman Maus	Stephen Greenblatt, Walter Cohen	1997	W. W. Norton	Norton1
Barbara Mowat	Paul Werstine	2008	Simon & Schuster	Folger Shakespeare Library
Michèle Willems		2012	Hackett	New Kittredge
Jennifer Forsyth		2015	W. W. Norton	Norton3*

Sarah Neville		2016	Oxford University Press	New Oxford*
Molly G. Yarn	Jonathan Bate, Eric Rasmussen, Ian De Jong	FC	Bloomsbury	RSC2

Henry VI, Part 2 (13)

Mary Cowden Clarke		1860	Appleton	
Mary Cowden Clarke	Charles Cowden Clarke	1864–68	Cassell	Cassell's Illustrated Shakespeare
Laura Jewry Valentine		1868	Frederick Warne	Chandos Classics
Jane Lee		NP		
Emma Gollancz	Israel Gollancz	1899–1902	J. M. Dent	Temple Shakespeare
Charlotte E. Porter and Helen A. Clarke		1903	Thomas Y. Crowell	Pembroke
Esther Wood		1904	Doubleday, Page	The Personal Shakespeare
Jennie Ellis Burdick		1909	Bigelow Smith	Aldus Shakespeare
Charlotte E. Porter		1912	Thomas Y. Crowell	First Folio
Marie Edel	G. Blakemore Evans et al.	1974	Houghton Mifflin	Riverside Shakespeare
Jean E. Howard and Katharine Eisaman Maus	Stephen Greenblatt, Walter Cohen	1997	W. W. Norton	Norton1
Barbara Mowat	Paul Werstine	2008	Simon & Schuster	Folger Shakespeare Library
Molly G. Yarn	Jonathan Bate, Eric Rasmussen, Ian De Jong	FC	Bloomsbury	RSC2

Henry VI, Part 3 (13)

Mary Cowden Clarke		1860	Appleton	
Mary Cowden Clarke	Charles Cowden Clarke	1864–68	Cassell	Cassell's Illustrated Shakespeare

Play and editor(s)	Male editor(s)	Publication date	Publisher	Series
Laura Jewry Valentine		1868	Frederick Warne	Chandos Classics
Jane Lee		NP		
Emma Gollancz	Israel Gollancz	1899–1902	J. M. Dent	Temple Shakespeare
Charlotte E. Porter and Helen A. Clarke		1903	Thomas Y. Crowell	Pembroke
Esther Wood		1904	Doubleday, Page	The Personal Shakespeare
Jennie Ellis Burdick		1909	Bigelow Smith	Aldus Shakespeare
Charlotte E. Porter		1912	Thomas Y. Crowell	First Folio
Marie Edel	G. Blakemore Evans et al.	1974	Houghton Mifflin	Riverside Shakespeare
Jean E. Howard and Katharine Eisaman Maus	Stephen Greenblatt, Walter Cohen	1997	W. W. Norton	Norton1
Barbara Mowat	Paul Werstine	2009	Simon & Schuster	Folger Shakespeare Library
Molly G. Yarn	Jonathan Bate, Eric Rasmussen, Ian De Jong	FC	Bloomsbury	RSC2
Henry VIII (18)				
Henrietta Bowdler		1807	R. Crutwell for J. Hatchard, London	The Family Shakespeare
Elizabeth Inchbald		1808	Longman, Hurst, Rees, & Orme	British Theatre
Mary Cowden Clarke		1860	Appleton	
Mary Cowden Clarke	Charles Cowden Clarke	1864–68	Cassell	Cassell's Illustrated Shakespeare
Laura Jewry Valentine		1868	Frederick Warne	Chandos Classics

Emma Gollancz	Israel Gollancz	1899–1902	J. M. Dent	Temple Shakespeare
Charlotte E. Porter and Helen A. Clarke		1903	Thomas Y. Crowell	Pembroke
Esther Wood		1904	Doubleday, Page	The Personal Shakespeare
Jennie Ellis Burdick		1909	Bigelow Smith	Aldus Shakespeare
Charlotte E. Porter		1912	Thomas Y. Crowell	First Folio
Evelyn Smith		1928	Thomas Nelson & Sons	Teaching of English
Gertrude Eleanor Hollingworth		1929	W. B. Clive	University Tutorial Series
Muriel St. Clare Byrne	Guy Boas	1937	Macmillan	New Eversley
Marie Edel	G. Blakemore Evans et al.	1974	Houghton Mifflin	Riverside Shakespeare
Jean E. Howard and Katharine Eisaman Maus	Stephen Greenblatt, Walter Cohen	1997	W. W. Norton	Norton1
Barbara Mowat	Paul Werstine	2007	Simon & Schuster	Folger Shakespeare Library
Pascale Drouet		2015	W. W. Norton	Norton3*
Diane Jacacki		FC		Internet Shakespeare Editions*

Julius Caesar

Henrietta Bowdler		1807	R. Crutwell for J. Hatchard, London	The Family Shakespeare
Elizabeth Inchbald		1808	Longman, Hurst, Rees, and Orme	British Theatre
Mary Cowden Clarke		1860	Appleton	
Rosa Baughan		1863	T.J. Allman	
Mary Cowden Clarke	Charles Cowden Clarke	1864–68	Cassell	Cassell's Illustrated Shakespeare
Laura Jewry Valentine		1868	Frederick Warne	Chandos Classics

(cont.)

Play and editor(s)	Male editor(s)	Publication date	Publisher	Series
Charlotte Mary Yonge		c. 1885	National Society's Depository	Shakespeare's Plays for Schools
Emma Gollancz	Israel Gollancz	1899–1902	J.M. Dent	Temple Shakespeare
Lois G. Hufford	George W. Hufford	1900	Macmillan	New Pocket Classics
Margaret Hill McCarter		1900	Crane & Co.	20th Century Classics and School Readings
Charlotte E. Porter and Helen A. Clarke		1903	Thomas Y. Crowell	Pembroke
Esther Wood		1904	Doubleday, Page	The Personal Shakespeare
Charlotte E. Porter and Helen A. Clarke		1904	Thomas Y. Crowell	First Folio
Jennie Ellis Burdick		1909	Bigelow Smith	Aldus Shakespeare
Maud Elma Kingsley	Frank Herbert Palmer	1911	The Palmer Company	Kingsley English Texts*
Clara Linklater Thomson		c. 1915	Horace Marshall & Son	Carmelite Shakespeare*
Gertrude Eleanor Hollingworth	A.F. Watt	1928	W.B. Clive	University Tutorial Series
Essie Chamberlain		1929	Houghton Mifflin	Riverside Literature Series
Helen E. Harding		1932	Noble and Noble	Noble's Comparative Classics
Edith M. Ward		1934	Lyons & Carnahan	Stratford Classics
Barbara Rosen	William Rosen	1963	Penguin	Signet
Marie Edel	G. Blakemore Evans et al.	1974	Houghton Mifflin	Riverside Shakespeare
Barbara Mowat	Paul Werstine	1992	Simon & Schuster	Folger Shakespeare Library
Roma Gill		1989	Oxford University Press	Oxford School Shakespeare*

Jean E. Howard & Katharine Eisaman Maus	Stephen Greenblatt, Walter Cohen	W.W. Norton	1997	Norton1
Sarah Hatchuel		Hackett	2008	New Kittredge
Vicki Wienand	Robert Smith	Cambridge University Press	2014	Cambridge School Shakespeare*
Sarah Neville		Oxford University Press	2016	New Oxford*
Molly G. Yarn	Jonathan Bate, Eric Rasmussen, Ian De Jong	Bloomsbury	FC	RSC2
Sarah K. Scott	M.L. Stapleton	Texas A&M	FC	New Variorum*

King John (16)

Henrietta Bowdler		R. Crutwell for J. Hatchard, London	1807	The Family Shakespeare
Elizabeth Inchbald		Longman, Hurst, Rees, & Orme	1808	British Theatre
Mary Atkinson Maurice		John W. Parker	1848	
Mary Cowden Clarke		Appleton	1860	
Rosa Baughan		T. J. Allman	1863	
Mary Cowden Clarke	Charles Cowden Clarke	Cassell	1864–68	Cassell's Illustrated Shakespeare
Laura Jewry Valentine		Frederick Warne	1868	Chandos Classics
Emma Gollancz	Israel Gollancz	J. M. Dent	1899–1902	Temple Shakespeare
Charlotte E. Porter and Helen A. Clarke		Thomas Y. Crowell	1903	Pembroke
Esther Wood		Doubleday, Page	1904	The Personal Shakespeare

Play and editor(s)	Male editor(s)	Publication date	Publisher	Series
Jennie Ellis Burdick		1909	Bigelow Smith	Aldus Shakespeare
Charlotte E. Porter		1910	Thomas Y. Crowell	First Folio
Marie Edel	G. Blakemore Evans et al.	1974	Houghton Mifflin	Riverside Shakespeare
Jean E. Howard and Katharine Eisaman Maus	Stephen Greenblatt, Walter Cohen	1997	W. W. Norton	Norton1
Barbara Mowat	Paul Werstine	2000	Simon & Schuster	Folger Shakespeare Library
Claire McEachern		2000	Penguin	Pelican2

King Lear (27)

Play and editor(s)	Male editor(s)	Publication date	Publisher	Series
Henrietta Bowdler		1807	R. Crutwell for J. Hatchard, London	The Family Shakespeare
Elizabeth Inchbald		1808	Longman, Hurst, Rees, & Orme	British Theatre
Mary Atkinson Maurice		1848	John W. Parker	
Mary Cowden Clarke		1860	Appleton	
Rosa Baughan		1863	T. J. Allman	
Mary Cowden Clarke	Charles Cowden Clarke	1864–68	Cassell	Cassell's Illustrated Shakespeare
Laura Jewry Valentine		1868	Frederick Warne	Chandos Classics
Phoebe Sheavyn		1898	A&C Black	Black's School Shakespeare
Martha Foote Crowe		NP	D. C. Heath	Heath's Arden
Emma Gollancz	Israel Gollancz	1899–1902	J. M. Dent	Temple Shakespeare

Charlotte E. Porter and Helen A. Clarke		1903	Thomas Y. Crowell	Pembroke
Esther Wood		1904	Doubleday, Page	The Personal Shakespeare
Charlotte E. Porter and Helen A. Clarke		1905	Thomas Y. Crowell	First Folio
Margaret Hill McCarter		1905	Crane & Co.	First Folio
Jennie Ellis Burdick		1909	Bigelow Smith	Aldus Shakespeare
Virginia Gildersleeve		1912	Macmillan	Tudor Shakespeare
Gertrude Blance Sellon		c. 1925	Horace Marshall & Son	Carmelite Shakespeare*
Evelyn Smith		1926	Thomas Nelson & Sons	Teaching of English
Marie Edel	G. Blakemore Evans et al.	1974	Houghton Mifflin	Riverside Shakespeare
Barbara Mowat	Paul Werstine	1993	Simon & Schuster	Folger Shakespeare Library
Roma Gill		1994	Oxford University Press	Oxford School Shakespeare*
Jean E. Howard, Katharine Eisaman Maus, and Barbara K. Lewalski	Stephen Greenblatt, Walter Cohen	1997	W. W. Norton	Norton1
Grace Ioppolo		2008	W. W. Norton	Norton Critical Editions
Elspeth Bain	Nic Amy	2015	Cambridge University Press	Cambridge School Shakespeare*
Grace Ioppolo		2015	W. W. Norton	Norton3*
Paula Glatzer	Richard Knowles, Kevin Donovan	FC	Texas A&M	New Variorum*
Sarah Hatchuel		2008	Hackett	New Kittredge
Vicki Wienand	Robert Smith	2014	Cambridge University Press	Cambridge School Shakespeare*
Sarah Neville		2016	Oxford University Press	New Oxford*

(cont.)

Play and editor(s)	Male editor(s)	Publication date	Publisher	Series
Molly G. Yarn	Jonathan Bate, Eric Rasmussen, Ian De Jong	FC	Bloomsbury	RSC2
Sarah K. Scott	M. L. Stapleton	FC	Texas A&M	New Variorum*
Love's Labour's Lost (16)				
Mary Cowden Clarke		1860	Appleton	
Mary Cowden Clarke	Charles Cowden Clarke	1864–68	Cassell	Chandos Classics
Laura Jewry Valentine		1868	Frederick Warne	Cassell's Illustrated Shakespeare
Rosa Baughan		1871	T. J. Allman	Temple Shakespeare
Emma Gollancz	Israel Gollancz	1899–1902	J. M. Dent	Temple Shakespeare
Charlotte E. Porter and Helen A. Clarke		1903	Thomas Y. Crowell	Pembroke
Charlotte E. Porter and Helen A. Clarke		1903	Thomas Y. Crowell	First Folio
Esther Wood		1904	Doubleday, Page	The Personal Shakespeare
Jennie Ellis Burdick		1909	Bigelow Smith	Aldus Shakespeare
Magdalen Marie Weale		1924	University Tutorial Press	Tutorial Shakespeare
Marie Edel and Anne Barton	G. Blakemore Evans et al.	1974	Houghton Mifflin	Riverside Shakespeare
Barbara Mowat	Paul Werstine	1996	Simon & Schuster	Folger Shakespeare Library
Jean E. Howard and Katharine Eisaman Maus	Stephen Greenblatt, Walter Cohen	1997	W. W. Norton	Norton1

268

Editor	General editor	Year	Publisher	Series
Roma Gill		2002	Oxford University Press	Oxford School Shakespeare*
Jill P. Ingram		2012	Hackett	New Kittredge
Jane Kingsley-Smith		2015	W. W. Norton	Norton3*

Macbeth (30)

Editor	General editor	Year	Publisher	Series
Henrietta Bowdler		1807	R. Crutwell for J. Hatchard, London	The Family Shakespeare
Elizabeth Inchbald		1808	Longman, Hurst, Rees, & Orme	British Theatre
Mary Atkinson Maurice		1848	John W. Parker	
Mary Cowden Clarke		1860	Appleton	
Rosa Baughan		1863	T. J. Allman	
Mary Cowden Clarke	Charles Cowden Clarke	1864–68	Cassell	Cassell's Illustrated Shakespeare
Laura Jewry Valentine		1868	Frederick Warne	Chandos Classics
Helen Gray Cone	Richard Grant White	1897	Houghton Mifflin	Riverside Literature Series
Emma Gollancz	Israel Gollancz	1899–1902	J. M. Dent	Temple Shakespeare
Margaret Hill McCarter		1900	Crane & Co.	
Fanny Johnson		c. 1903	William Blackwood & Son	Blackwood's School Shakespeare
Charlotte E. Porter and Helen A. Clarke		1903	Thomas Y. Crowell	Pembroke
Esther Wood		1904	Doubleday, Page	The Personal Shakespeare
Charlotte E. Porter and Helen A. Clarke		1904	Thomas Y. Crowell	First Folio
Jennie Ellis Burdick		1909	Bigelow Smith	Aldus Shakespeare
Clara Linklater Thomson		c. 1916	Horace Marshall & Son	Carmelite Shakespeare*

Play and editor(s)	Male editor(s)	Publication date	Publisher	Series
Rose Adelaide Witham		1922	Allyn & Bacon	Academy Classics*
Evelyn Smith		1925	Thomas Nelson & Sons	Teaching of English
Gertrude Eleanor Hollingworth	S. E. Goggin	1927	W. B. Clive	University Tutorial Series
Essie Chamberlain	G. B. Harrison, F. H. Pritchard	1932	Holt	New Reader's
Anna P. Butler	M. A. Feehan	1935	Loyola University Press	Loyola English Classics
Marie Edel	G. Blakemore Evans et al.	1974	Houghton Mifflin	Riverside Shakespeare
Roma Gill		1977	Oxford University Press	Oxford School Shakespeare*
Barbara Mowat	Paul Werstine	1992	Simon & Schuster	Folger Shakespeare Library
Jean E. Howard and Katharine Eisaman Maus	Stephen Greenblatt, Walter Cohen	1997	W. W. Norton	Norton1
Annalisa Castaldo		2008	Hackett	New Kittredge
Sandra Clark and Pamela Mason		2015	Arden Bloomsbury	Arden3*
Linzy Brady	David James	2015	Cambridge University Press	Cambridge School Shakespeare*
Katherine Steele Brokaw		2019	Arden Bloomsbury	Arden Performance Editions*
Molly G. Yarn	Jonathan Bate, Eric Rasmussen, Ian De Jong	FC	Bloomsbury	RSC2

Measure for Measure (21)

Elizabeth Inchbald		1808	Longman, Hurst, Rees, & Orme	British Theatre
Mary Cowden Clarke		1860	Appleton	

Edition	Publisher	Year		Editor(s)
Cassell's Illustrated Shakespeare	Cassell	1864–68	Charles Cowden Clarke	Mary Cowden Clarke
Chandos Classics	Frederick Warne	1868		Laura Jewry Valentine
Temple Shakespeare	J. M. Dent	1899–1902	Israel Gollancz	Emma Gollancz
Pembroke	Thomas Y. Crowell	1903		Charlotte E. Porter and Helen A. Clarke
The Personal Shakespeare	Doubleday, Page	1904		Esther Wood
First Folio	Thomas Y. Crowell	1909		Charlotte E. Porter and Helen A. Clarke
Aldus Shakespeare	Bigelow Smith	1909		Jennie Ellis Burdick
Riverside Shakespeare	Houghton Mifflin	1974	G. Blakemore Evans et al.	Marie Edel and Anne Barton
Shakespearean Originals	Routledge	1996		Grace Ioppolo
Folger Shakespeare Library	Simon & Schuster	1997	Paul Werstine	Barbara Mowat
Norton1	W. W. Norton	1997	Stephen Greenblatt, Walter Cohen	Jean E. Howard and Katharine Eisaman Maus
Oxford School Shakespeare*	Oxford University Press	2001		Roma Gill
Applause Shakespeare	Applause Theatre Books	2001	Leon Rubin	Grace Ioppolo
Cambridge School Shakespeare	Cambridge University Press	2002		Jane Coles
Texts & Contexts	Bedford-St. Martin's	2004	Ivo Kamps	Karen Raber
Norton Critical Editions	W. W. Norton	2009		Grace Ioppolo
New Kittredge	Hackett	2012		Bernice Kliman and Laury Magnus
New Oxford*	Oxford University Press	2016		Terri Bourus
Internet Shakespeare Editions*		FC	James Mardock	Kristin Lucas

The Merchant of Venice (30)

Play and editor(s)	Male editor(s)	Publication date	Publisher	Series
Elizabeth Inchbald		1808	Longman, Hurst, Rees, & Orme	British Theatre
Mary Atkinson Maurice		1848	John W. Parker	
Mary Cowden Clarke		1860	Appleton	
Mary Cowden Clarke	Charles Cowden Clarke	1864–68	Cassell	Cassell's Illustrated Shakespeare
Laura Jewry Valentine		1868	Frederick Warne	Chandos Classics
Rosa Baughan		1871	T. J. Allman	
Katherine Lee Bates		1894	Leach, Sewell, & Sanborn	Teaching of English
Charlotte Whipple Underwood		1899	Macmillan	Macmillan Pocket Classics
Emma Gollancz	Israel Gollancz	1899–1902	J. M. Dent	Temple Shakespeare
Helen Gray Cone		1900	Globe School Book Company	English Classics: Star Series
Margaret Hill McCarter		1902	Crane & Co.	Crane Classics
Charlotte E. Porter and Helen A. Clarke		1903	Thomas Y. Crowell	Pembroke
Charlotte E. Porter and Helen A. Clarke		1904	Thomas Y. Crowell	First Folio
Esther Wood		1904	Doubleday, Page	The Personal Shakespeare
Maud Elma Kingsley	Frank Herbert Palmer	1908	The Palmer Company	Kingsley English Texts
Jennie Ellis Burdick		1909	Bigelow Smith	Aldus Shakespeare

Dorothy M. Macardle	c. 1915	Horace Marshall & Son	Carmelite Shakespeare
Evelyn Smith	1926	Thomas Nelson & Sons	Teaching of English
May McKitrick	1926	John C. Winston	Winston Companions
Rose Adelaide Witham	1929	Houghton Mifflin	Riverside Literature Series
Pauline Gertrude Wiggin	1931	D. C. Heath	Golden Key Series
Essie Chamberlain	1932	Holt	New Reader's
G. B. Harrison, F. H. Pritchard			
Marie Edel and Anne Barton; G. Blakemore Evans et al.	1974	Houghton Mifflin	Riverside Shakespeare
Roma Gill	1979	Oxford University Press	Oxford School Shakespeare*
Molly Mahood	1987	Cambridge University Press	New Cambridge
Barbara Mowat; Paul Werstine	1992	Simon & Schuster	Folger Shakespeare Library
Stephen Greenblatt, Walter Cohen; Jean E. Howard and Katharine Eisaman Maus	1997	W. W. Norton	Norton[1]
M. Lindsay Kaplan	2002	Bedford/St. Martin's	Texts & Contexts
Leah Marcus	2006	W. W. Norton	Norton Critical Editons
Janelle Jenstad; Stephen Wittek	FC		Internet Shakespeare Editions

The Merry Wives of Windsor (15)

Elizabeth Inchbald	1808	Longman, Hurst, Rees, & Orme	British Theatre
	1860	Appleton	
Mary Cowden Clarke; Charles Cowden Clarke	1864–68	Cassell	Cassell's Illustrated Shakespeare
Mary Cowden Clarke	1868	Frederick Warne	Chandos Classics
Laura Jewry Valentine			
Emma Gollancz; Israel Gollancz	1899–1902	J. M. Dent	Temple Shakespeare

Play and editor(s)	Male editor(s)	Publication date	Publisher	Series
Charlotte E. Porter and Helen A. Clarke		1903	Thomas Y. Crowell	Pembroke
Esther Wood		1904	Doubleday, Page	The Personal Shakespeare
Charlotte E. Porter and Helen A. Clarke		1909	Thomas Y. Crowell	First Folio
Jennie Ellis Burdick		1909	Bigelow Smith	Aldus Shakespeare
Marie Edel and Anne Barton	G. Blakemore Evans et al.	1974	Houghton Mifflin	Riverside Shakespeare
Jean E. Howard and Katharine Eisaman Maus	Stephen Greenblatt, Walter Cohen	1997	W. W. Norton	Norton1
Barbara Mowat	Paul Werstine	2004	Simon & Schuster	Folger Shakespeare Library
Helen Ostovich		2015	W. W. Norton	Norton3*
Sarah Neville		2016	Oxford University Press	New Oxford*
Helen Ostovich		FC		Internet Shakespeare Editions*

A Midsummer Night's Dream (32)

Henrietta Bowdler		1807	R. Crutwell for J. Hatchard, London	The Family Shakespeare
Mary Cowden Clarke		1860	Appleton	
Mary Cowden Clarke	Charles Cowden Clarke	1864–68	Cassell	Cassell's Illustrated Shakespeare
Laura Jewry Valentine		1868	Frederick Warne	Chandos Classics
Rosa Baughan		1871	T. J. Allman	
Katherine Lee Bates		1895	Leach, Sewell & Sanborn	

Emma Gollancz	Israel Gollancz	1899–1902	J. M. Dent	Temple Shakespeare
Sarah Willard Hiestand		1900	D. C. Heath	Beginner's Shakespeare
Charlotte E. Porter and Helen A. Clarke		1903	Thomas Y. Crowell	Pembroke
Charlotte E. Porter and Helen A. Clarke		1903	Thomas Y. Crowell	First Folio
Esther Wood		1904	Doubleday, Page	The Personal Shakespeare
Jennie Ellis Burdick		1909	Bigelow Smith	Aldus Shakespeare
Laura Emma Lockwood		1911	Houghton Mifflin	Riverside Shakespeare
Edith Rickert	E.K. Chambers	1916	D. C. Heath	Heath's Arden
Clara Linklater Thomson		c. 1924	Horace Marshall & Sons	Carmelite Shakespeare*
Evelyn Smith		1925	Thomas Nelson & Sons	Teaching of English
Gertrude Eleanor Hollingworth	A.F. Watt	1929	University Tutorial Press	Matriculation Shakespeare
Pauline Gertrude Wiggin		1929	D. C. Heath	Golden Key
Madeleine Doran		1959	Penguin	Pelican
Marie Edel and Anne Barton	G. Blakemore Evans et al.	1974	Houghton Mifflin	Riverside Shakespeare
Roma Gill		1977	Oxford University Press	Oxford School Shakespeare*
Barbara Mowat	Paul Werstine	1993	Simon & Schuster	Folger Shakespeare Library
Jean E. Howard and Katharine Eisaman Maus	Stephen Greenblatt, Walter Cohen	1997	W. W. Norton	Norton1
Gail Kern Paster	Skiles Howard	1999	Bedford-St. Martin's	Texts & Contexts
Terri Bourus		2007	Bloomsbury	Sourcebooks Shakespeare
Linda Buckle		2014	Cambridge University Press	Cambridge School Shakespeare*

Play and editor(s)	Male editor(s)	Publication date	Publisher	Series
Terri Bourus		2016	Oxford University Press	New Oxford*
Abigail Rokison-Woodall		2017	Arden Bloomsbury	Arden Performance Editions*
Grace Ioppolo		2018	W. W. Norton	Norton Critical Editions
Molly G. Yarn	Jonathan Bate, Eric Rasmussen, Ian De Jong	FC	Bloomsbury	RSC2
Suzanne Westfall and Diane Jacacki		FC		Internet Shakespeare Editions*
Judith Kennedy, Susan May, Roberta Barker	Richard Kennedy, David Nichol	FC	Texas A&M	New Variorum*

Much Ado About Nothing (23)

Play and editor(s)	Male editor(s)	Publication date	Publisher	Series
Henrietta Bowdler		1807	R. Crutwell for J. Hatchard, London	The Family Shakespeare
Elizabeth Inchbald		1808	Longman, Hurst, Rees, & Orme	British Theatre
Mary Cowden Clarke		1860	Appleton	
Mary Cowden Clarke	Charles Cowden Clarke	1864–68	Cassell	Cassell's Illustrated Shakespeare
Laura Jewry Valentine		1868	Frederick Warne	Chandos Classics
Rosa Baughan		1871	T. J. Allman	
Emma Gollancz	Israel Gollancz	1899–1902	J. M. Dent	Temple Shakespeare
Charlotte E. Porter and Helen A. Clarke		1903	Thomas Y. Crowell	Pembroke

Esther Wood		1904	Doubleday, Page	The Personal Shakespeare
Charlotte E. Porter and Helen A. Clarke		1907	Thomas Y. Crowell	First Folio
Jennie Ellis Burdick		1909	Bigelow Smith	Aldus Shakespeare
Grace R. Trenery		1924	Methuen	Arden1
Evelyn Smith		1926	Thomas Nelson & Sons	Teaching of English
Josephine Waters Bennett		1958	Penguin	Pelican
Marie Edel and Anne Barton	G. Blakemore Evans et al.	1974	Houghton Mifflin	Riverside Shakespeare
Jean E. Howard and Katharine Eisaman Maus	Stephen Greenblatt, Walter Cohen	1997	W. W. Norton	Norton1
Roma Gill		1999	Oxford University Press	Oxford School Shakespeare*
Barbara Mowat	Paul Werstine	2005	Simon & Schuster	Folger Shakespeare Library
Claire McEachern		2005	Arden Bloomsbury	Arden3*
Trudi L. Darby		2015	W. W. Norton	Norton3*
Anna Pruitt		2016	Oxford University Press	New Oxford*
Anna Kamaralli		2018	Arden Bloomsbury	Arden Performance Editions*
Gretchen Minton	Cliff Werier	FC		Internet Shakespeare Editions*

Othello (28)

Henrietta Bowdler	1807	R. Crutwell for J. Hatchard, London	The Family Shakespeare
Elizabeth Inchbald	1808	Longman, Hurst, Rees, & Orme	British Theatre
Mary Atkinson Maurice	1848	John W. Parker	
Mary Cowden Clarke	1860	Appleton	

Play and editor(s)	Male editor(s)	Publication date	Publisher	Series
Mary Cowden Clarke	Charles Cowden Clarke	1864–68	Cassell	Cassell's Illustrated Shakespeare
Laura Jewry Valentine		1868	Frederick Warne	Chandos Classics
Emma Gollancz	Israel Gollancz	1899–1902	J. M. Dent	Temple Shakespeare
Charlotte E. Porter and Helen A. Clarke		1903	Thomas Y. Crowell	Pembroke
Esther Wood		1904	Doubleday, Page	The Personal Shakespeare
Charlotte E. Porter and Helen A. Clarke		1908	Thomas Y. Crowell	First Folio
Jennie Ellis Burdick		1909	Bigelow Smith	Aldus Shakespeare
Agnes Knox Black	E. C. Black	1926	Ginn & Co.	New Hudson
Nora Ratcliff		1941	Thomas Nelson & Sons	Teaching of English
Alice Walker	J. Dover Wilson	1957	Cambridge University Press	New Cambridge
Marie Edel	G. Blakemore Evans et al.	1974	Houghton Mifflin	Riverside Shakespeare
Celia Hilton	R. T. Jones	1984	Macmillan	Macmillan Shakespeare
Roma Gill		1989	Oxford University Press	Oxford School Shakespeare*
Barbara Mowat	Paul Werstine	1993	Simon & Schuster	Folger Shakespeare Library
Jean E. Howard and Katharine Eisaman Maus	Stephen Greenblatt, Walter Cohen	1997	W. W. Norton	Norton1
Julie Hankey		2005	Cambridge University Press	Shakespeare in Production*
Kim F. Hall		2007	Bedford-St. Martin's	Texts & Contexts
Gretchen Schulz		2011	Hackett	New Kittredge

Editor	Other editor(s)	Year	Publisher	Series
Jane Coles		2014	Cambridge University Press	Cambridge School Shakespeare*
Clare McManus		2015	W. W. Norton	Norton3*
Ayanna Thompson	E. A. J. Honigmann	2016	Arden Bloomsbury	Arden3*
Molly G. Yarn	Jonathan Bate, Eric Rasmussen, Ian De Jong	FC	Bloomsbury	RSC2
Jessica Slights		FC		Internet Shakespeare Editions*
Jill Levenson	Joseph Porter, Christopher E. McGee	FC		New Variorum*
Pericles (15)				
Mary Cowden Clarke		1860	Appleton	
Mary Cowden Clarke	Charles Cowden Clarke	1864–68	Cassell	Cassell's Illustrated Shakespeare
Laura Jewry Valentine		1868	Frederick Warne	Chandos Classics
Emma Gollancz	Israel Gollancz	1899–1902	J. M. Dent	Temple Shakespeare
Charlotte E. Porter and Helen A. Clarke		1903	Thomas Y. Crowell	Pembroke
Esther Wood		1904	Doubleday, Page	The Personal Shakespeare
Jennie Ellis Burdick		1909	Bigelow Smith	Aldus Shakespeare
Charlotte E. Porter and Helen A. Clarke		1910	Thomas Y. Crowell	First Folio
Marie Edel	G. Blakemore Evans et al.	1974	Houghton Mifflin	Riverside Shakespeare
Jean E. Howard and Katharine Eisaman Maus	Stephen Greenblatt, Walter Cohen	1997	W. W. Norton	Norton1
Doreen Delvecchio	Antony Hammond	1998	Cambridge University Press	New Cambridge

(cont.)

Play and editor(s)	Male editor(s)	Publication date	Publisher	Series
Suzanne Gossett		2004	Thomson	Arden3*
Barbara Mowat	Paul Werstine	2005	Simon & Schuster	Folger Shakespeare Library
Lois Potter		2015	W. W. Norton	Norton3*
Deanne Williams	Tom Bishop	FC		Internet Shakespeare Editions*
Richard II (20)				
Henrietta Bowdler		1807	R. Crutwell for J. Hatchard, London	The Family Shakespeare
Mary Cowden Clarke		1860	Appleton	
Rosa Baughan		1863	T. J. Allman	
Mary Cowden Clarke	Charles Cowden Clarke	1864–68	Cassell	Cassell's Illustrated Shakespeare
Laura Jewry Valentine		1868	Frederick Warne	Chandos Classics
Charlotte M. Yonge		c. 1885	National Society's Deposity	Shakespeare's Plays for Schools
Emma Gollancz	Israel Gollancz	1899–1902	J. M. Dent	Temple Shakespeare
Charlotte E. Porter and Helen A. Clarke		1903	Thomas Y. Crowell	Pembroke
Esther Wood		1904	Doubleday, Page	The Personal Shakespeare
Jennie Ellis Burdick		1909	Bigelow Smith	Aldus Shakespeare
Charlotte E. Porter		1910	Thomas Y. Crowell	First Folio
Gertrude Eleanor Hollingworth	A. F. Watt	1929	W. B. Clive	University Tutorial Series
Marie Edel	G. Blakemore Evans et al.	1974	Houghton Mifflin	Riverside Shakespeare

Editor	Editor	Publisher	Series	Year
Barbara Mowat	Paul Werstine	Simon & Schuster	Folger Shakespeare Library	1992
Jean E. Howard and Katharine Eisaman Maus	Stephen Greenblatt, Walter Cohen	W. W. Norton	Norton1	1997
Roma Gill		Oxford University Press	Oxford School Shakespeare*	1998
Jacquelyn Kilpatrick		Hackett	New Kittredge	2011
Anna Pruitt		Oxford University Press	New Oxford*	2016
Frances E. Dolan		Penguin	Pelican2	2017
Catherine Lisak			Internet Shakespeare Editions*	FC

Richard III (17)

Editor	Editor	Publisher	Series	Year
Henrietta Bowdler		R. Crutwell for J. Hatchard, London	The Family Shakespeare	1807
Elizabeth Inchbald		Longman, Hurst, Rees, & Orme	British Theatre	1808
Mary Cowden Clarke		Appleton		1860
Rosa Baughan		T. J. Allman		1863
Mary Cowden Clarke	Charles Cowden Clarke	Cassell	Cassell's Illustrated Shakespeare	1864–68
Laura Jewry Valentine		Frederick Warne	Chandos Classics	1868
Emma Gollancz	Israel Gollancz	J. M. Dent	Temple Shakespeare	1899–1902
Charlotte E. Porter and Helen A. Clarke		Thomas Y. Crowell	Pembroke	1903
Esther Wood		Doubleday, Page	The Personal Shakespeare	1904
Jennie Ellis Burdick		Bigelow Smith	Aldus Shakespeare	1909
Charlotte E. Porter		Thomas Y. Crowell	First Folio	1910
Evelyn Smith		Thomas Nelson & Sons	Teaching of English	1924
Marie Edel	G. Blakemore Evans et al.	Houghton Mifflin	Riverside Shakespeare	1974

Play and editor(s)	Male editor(s)	Publication date	Publisher	Series
Barbara Mowat	Paul Werstine	1996	Simon and Schuster	Folger Shakespeare Library
Jean E. Howard and Katharine Eisaman Maus	Stephen Greenblatt, Walter Cohen	1997	W. W. Norton	Norton1
Janis Lull		1999	Cambridge University Press	New Cambridge
Linzy Brady and Jane Coles		2015	Cambridge University Press	Cambridge School Shakespeare*
Romeo and Juliet (21)				
Elizabeth Inchbald		1808	Longman, Hurst, Rees, & Orme	British Theatre
Mary Atkinson Maurice		1848	John W. Parker	
Mary Cowden Clarke		1860	Appleton	
Rosa Baughan		1863	T. J. Allman	
Mary Cowden Clarke	Charles Cowden Clarke	1864–68	Cassell	Cassell's Illustrated Shakespeare
Laura Jewry Valentine		1868	Frederick Warne	Chandos Classics
Emma Gollancz	Israel Gollancz	1899–1902	J. M. Dent	Temple Shakespeare
Charlotte E. Porter and Helen A. Clarke		1903	Thomas Y. Crowell	Pembroke
Esther Wood		1904	Doubleday, Page	The Personal Shakespeare
Charlotte E. Porter and Helen A. Clarke		1907	Thomas Y. Crowell	First Folio
Jennie Ellis Burdick		1909	Bigelow Smith	Aldus Shakespeare

Jennie F. Chase		1917	Macmillan	Macmillan Pocket Classics
Marie Edel	G. Blakemore Evans et al.	1974	Houghton Mifflin	Riverside Shakespeare
Barbara Mowat	Paul Werstine	1992	Simon & Schuster	Folger Shakespeare Library
Jean E. Howard and Katharine Eisaman Maus	Stephen Greenblatt, Walter Cohen	1997	W. W. Norton	Norton1
Jill L. Levenson		2000	Oxford University Press	Oxford Shakespeare
Roma Gill		2001	Oxford University Press	Oxford School Shakespeare*
Dympna Callaghan		2003	Bedford-St. Martin's	Texts & Contexts
Bernice Kliman and Laury Magnus		2008	Focus Publishing	New Kittredge
Hester Lees-Jeffries		FC	Cambridge University Press	New Cambridge
Erin A. Sadlack		FC		Internet Shakespeare Editions*

Sonnets (15)

Mary Cowden Clarke		1860	Appleton	
Laura Jewry Valentine		1868	Frederick Warne	Chandos Classics
Emma Gollancz	Israel Gollancz	1899–1902	J. M. Dent	Temple Shakespeare
Charlotte E. Porter and Helen A. Clarke		1903	Thomas Y. Crowell	Pembroke
Charlotte Carmichael Brown Stopes		1904	Alexander Moring/ De la More Press	King's Classics
Esther Wood		1904	Doubleday, Page	The Personal Shakespeare
Jennie Ellis Burdick		1909	Bigelow Smith	Aldus Shakespeare
Charlotte E. Porter		1912	Thomas Y. Crowell	First Folio
Clara L. Chambrun		1913	G. P. Putnam & Sons	

Play and editor(s)	Male editor(s)	Publication date	Publisher	Series
Margaret Flower		1933	Cassell & Co.	
Marie Edel	G. Blakemore Evans et al.	1974	Houghton Mifflin	Riverside Shakespeare
Jean E. Howard and Katharine Eisaman Maus	Stephen Greenblatt, Walter Cohen	1997	W. W. Norton	Norton1
Katherine Duncan-Jones		1997	Cengage	Arden3*
Barbara Mowat	Paul Werstine	2004	Simon & Schuster	Folger Shakespeare Library
Lynne Magnusson		2015	W. W. Norton	Norton3*

The Taming of the Shrew (28)

Play and editor(s)	Male editor(s)	Publication date	Publisher	Series
Mary Cowden Clarke	Charles Cowden Clarke	1860	Appleton	
Mary Cowden Clarke	Charles Cowden Clarke	1864–68	Cassell	Cassell's Illustrated Shakespeare
Laura Jewry Valentine		1868	Frederick Warne	Chandos Classics
Rosa Baughan		1871	T. J. Allman	
Emma Gollancz	Israel Gollancz	1899–1902	J. M. Dent	Temple Shakespeare
Ada Rehan		1900	Doubleday, Page	
Charlotte E. Porter and Helen A. Clarke		1903	Thomas Y. Crowell	Pembroke
Esther Wood		1904	Doubleday, Page	The Personal Shakespeare
Alice Meynell		1907	George D. Sproul	Renaissance Shakespeare
Charlotte E. Porter and Helen A. Clarke		1908	Thomas Y. Crowell	First Folio
Jennie Ellis Burdick		1909	Bigelow Smith	Aldus Shakespeare
Essie Chamberlain		1928	Allyn & Bacon	Academy Classics*

Editor(s)	Editor(s)	Publisher	Year	Series
Marie Edel and Anne Barton	G. Blakemore Evans et al.	Houghton Mifflin	1974	Riverside Shakespeare
Ann Thompson		Cambridge University Press	1984	New Cambridge
Roma Gill		Oxford University Press	1990	Oxford School Shakespeare*
Barbara Mowat	Paul Werstine	Simon & Schuster	1992	Folger Shakespeare Library
Frances E. Dolan		St. Martin's Press	1996	Texts & Contexts
Jean E. Howard and Katharine Eisaman Maus	Stephen Greenblatt, Walter Cohen	W. W. Norton	1997	Norton1
Elizabeth Schafer		Cambridge University Press	2003	Shakespeare in Production*
Antonia Forster		Bloomsbury	2008	Sourcebooks Shakespeare
Dympna Callaghan		W. W. Norton	2009	Norton Critical Editions
Barbara Hodgdon		Arden Bloomsbury	2010	Arden3*
Laury Magnus		Focus Publishing	2010	New Kittredge
Linzy Brady		Cambridge University Press	2014	Cambridge School Shakespeare*
Sarah Werner		W. W. Norton	2015	Norton3*
Anna Pruitt		Oxford University Press	2016	New Oxford*
Erin Kelly			FC	Internet Shakespeare Editions
Antonia Forster	Keir Elam, Fernando Cioni	Texas A&M	FC	New Variorum*

The Tempest (28)

Editor(s)	Publisher	Year	Series
Henrietta Bowdler	R. Crutwell for J. Hatchard, London	1807	The Family Shakespeare
Elizabeth Inchbald	Longman, Hurst, Rees, & Orme	1808	British Theatre

(cont.)

Play and editor(s)	Male editor(s)	Publication date	Publisher	Series
Mary Atkinson Maurice		1848	John W. Parker	
Mary Cowden Clarke		1860	Appleton	
Mary Cowden Clarke	Charles Cowden Clarke	1864–68	Cassell	Cassell's Illustrated Shakespeare
Laura Jewry Valentine		1868	Frederick Warne	Chandos Classics
Rosa Baughan		1871	T. J. Allman	
Elizabeth Lee		1884	Blackie & Son	
Sarah Willard Hiestand		1900	D. C. Heath	Beginner's Shakespeare
Emma Gollancz	Israel Gollancz	1899–1902	J. M. Dent	Temple Shakespeare
Charlotte E. Porter and Helen A. Clarke		1893	Thomas Y. Crowell	Pembroke
Esther Wood		1904	Doubleday, Page	The Personal Shakespeare
Charlotte E. Porter and Helen A. Clarke		1908	Thomas Y. Crowell	First Folio
Agnes Russell Weekes		1909	W. B. Clive	University Tutorial Series
Jennie Ellis Burdick		1909	Bigelow Smith	Aldus Shakespeare
Dorothy M. Macardle		c. 1916	Horace Marshall & Sons	Carmelite Shakespeare*
Edith M. Penney		1927	John C. Winston	Winston Companions
Mabel A. Bessey		1934	Houghton Mifflin	Riverside Literature
Anne Righter/Barton		1968	Penguin	New Penguin
Marie Edel	G. Blakemore Evans et al.	1974	Houghton Mifflin	Riverside Shakespeare
Barbara Mowat	Paul Werstine	1994	Simon & Schuster	Folger Shakespeare Library

Jean E. Howard and Katharine Eisaman Maus	Stephen Greenblatt, Walter Cohen	1997	W. W. Norton	Norton1
Roma Gill		1998	Oxford University Press	Oxford School Shakespeare*
Virginia Mason Vaughan	A.T. Vaughan	1999	Nelson	Arden3*
Christine Dymkowski		2000	Cambridge University Press	Shakespeare in Production*
Linzy Brady	David James	2014	Cambridge University Press	Cambridge School Shakespeare
Christine Dymkowski	Andrew Gurr, Christopher Wilson, Christopher Hardman	FC	Texas A&M	New Variorum*
Miranda Fay Thomas		FC	Arden Bloomsbury	Arden Performance Editions*

Timon of Athens (14)

Mary Cowden Clarke		1860	Appleton	
Mary Cowden Clarke	Charles Cowden Clarke	1864–68	Cassell	Cassell's Illustrated Shakespeare
Laura Jewry Valentine		1868	Frederick Warne	Chandos Classics
Emma Gollancz	Israel Gollancz	1899–1902	J. M. Dent	Temple Shakespeare
Charlotte E. Porter and Helen A. Clarke		1903	Thomas Y. Crowell	Pembroke
Esther Wood		1904	Doubleday, Page	The Personal Shakespeare
Charlotte E. Porter and Helen A. Clarke		1909	Thomas Y. Crowell	First Folio

Play and editor(s)	Male editor(s)	Publication date	Publisher	Series
Jennie Ellis Burdick		1909	Bigelow Smith	Aldus Shakespeare
Marie Edel	G. Blakemore Evans et al.	1974	Houghton Mifflin	Riverside Shakespeare
Jean E. Howard and Katharine Eisaman Maus	Stephen Greenblatt, Walter Cohen	1997	W. W. Norton	Norton1
Frances E. Dolan		2000	Penguin	Pelican2
Barbara Mowat	Paul Werstine	2001	Simon & Schuster	Folger Shakespeare Library
Gretchen E. Minton	Anthony B. Dawson	2008	Arden Bloomsbury	Arden3*
Molly G. Yarn	Jonathan Bate, Eric Rasmussen, Ian De Jong	FC	Bloomsbury	RSC2

Titus Andronicus (12)

Play and editor(s)	Male editor(s)	Publication date	Publisher	Series
Mary Cowden Clarke		1860	Appleton	
Laura Jewry Valentine		1868	Frederick Warne	Chandos Classics
Emma Gollancz	Israel Gollancz	1899–1902	J. M. Dent	Temple Shakespeare
Charlotte E. Porter and Helen A. Clarke		1903	Thomas Y. Crowell	Pembroke
Esther Wood		1904	Doubleday, Page	The Personal Shakespeare
Charlotte E. Porter and Helen A. Clarke		1909	Thomas Y. Crowell	First Folio
Jennie Ellis Burdick		1909	Bigelow Smith	Aldus Shakespeare
Marie Edel	G. Blakemore Evans et al.	1974	Houghton Mifflin	Riverside Shakespeare

Jean E. Howard and Katharine Eisaman Maus	Stephen Greenblatt, Walter Cohen	1997	W.W. Norton	Norton1
Sonia Massai	Jacques Berthoud	2001	Penguin	New Penguin
Barbara Mowat	Paul Werstine	2005	Simon & Schuster	Folger Shakespeare Library
Catherine Silverstone		2015	W. W. Norton	Norton3*

Troilus and Cressida (15)

Mary Cowden Clarke		1860	Appleton	
Mary Cowden Clarke	Charles Cowden Clarke	1864–68	Cassell	Cassell's Illustrated Shakespeare
Laura Jewry Valentine		1868	Frederick Warne	Chandos Classics
Emma Gollancz	Israel Gollancz	1899–1902	J. M. Dent	Temple Shakespeare
Charlotte E. Porter and Helen A. Clarke		1903	Thomas Y. Crowell	Pembroke
Esther Wood		1904	Doubleday, Page	The Personal Shakespeare
Jennie Ellis Burdick		1909	Bigelow Smith	Aldus Shakespeare
Charlotte E. Porter and Helen A. Clarke		1910	Thomas Y. Crowell	First Folio
Beatrice White		NP		
Alice Walker		1957	Cambridge University Press	New Cambridge
Marie Edel	G. Blakemore Evans et al.	1974	Houghton Mifflin	Riverside Shakespeare
Jean E. Howard and Katharine Eisaman Maus	Stephen Greenblatt, Walter Cohen	1997	W. W. Norton	Norton1

Play and editor(s)	Male editor(s)	Publication date	Publisher	Series
Frances A. Shirley		2005	Cambridge University Press	Shakespeare in Production*
Barbara Mowat	Paul Werstine	2007	Simon & Schuster	Folger Shakespeare Library
Gretchen E. Minton		2015	W. W. Norton	Norton3*
Twelfth Night (32)				
Henrietta Bowdler		1807	R. Crutwell for J. Hatchard, London	The Family Shakespeare
Elizabeth Inchbald		1808	Longman, Hurst, Rees, & Orme	British Theatre
Mary Cowden Clarke		1860	Appleton	
Mary Cowden Clarke	Charles Cowden Clarke	1864–68	Cassell	Cassell's Illustrated Shakespeare
Laura Jewry Valentine		1868	Frederick Warne	Chandos Classics
Rosa Baughan		1871	T. J. Allman	
Elizabeth Lee		1885	Blackie & Sons	
Emma Gollancz	Israel Gollancz	1899–1902	J. M. Dent	Temple Shakespeare
Helen Gray Cone		1901	Houghton Mifflin	Riverside Literature
Charlotte E. Porter and Helen A. Clarke		1903	Thomas Y. Crowell	Pembroke
Esther Wood		1904	Doubleday, Page	The Personal Shakespeare
Fanny Johnson		c. 1904	William Blackwood & Sons	Blackwood's School Shakespeare
Charlotte E. Porter and Helen A. Clarke		1906	Thomas Y. Crowell	First Folio

Editor(s)	General Editor(s)	Year	Publisher	Series/Edition
Jennie Ellis Burdick		1909	Bigelow Smith	Aldus Shakespeare
Dorothy M. Macardle		c. 1922	Horace Marshall & Sons	Carmelite Shakespeare*
Mary Elizabeth Adams		1925	Allyn & Bacon	Academy Classics*
Evelyn Smith		1926	Thomas Nelson & Sons	Teaching of English
Ida E. Melson		1927	John C. Winston	Winston's Companions
Gertrude Eleanor Hollingworth	Henry Charles Duffin	1936	University Tutorial Press	Matriculation Shakespeare
Molly Mahood		1968	Penguin	New Penguin
Marie Edel and Anne Barton	G. Blakemore Evans et al.	1974	Houghton Mifflin	Riverside Shakespeare
Elizabeth Story Donno		1985	Cambridge University Press	New Cambridge
Roma Gill		1986	Oxford University Press	Oxford School Shakespeare
Barbara Mowat	Paul Werstine	1993	Simon & Schuster	Folger Shakespeare Library
Laurie E. Osborne		1995	Prentice Hall	Shakespearean Originals
Jean E. Howard and Katharine Eisaman Maus	Stephen Greenblatt, Walter Cohen	1997	W. W. Norton	Norton1
Elizabeth Schafer		2009	Cambridge University Press	Shakespeare in Production*
Gayle Gaskill		2012	Hackett	New Kittredge
Gail Kern Paster		2015	W. W. Norton	Norton3*
Gretchen E. Minton		2020	Arden Bloomsbury	Arden Performance Editions*
Molly G. Yarn	Jonathan Bate, Eric Rasmussen, Ian De Jong	FC	Bloomsbury	RSC2
Gayle Gaskill and Dorothy Boerner	James M. Schiffer, Walter Cannon, Duncan Salkeld	FC	Texas A&M	New Variorum*

Play and editor(s)	Male editor(s)	Publication date	Publisher	Series
The Two Gentlemen of Verona (18)				
Mary Cowden Clarke		1860	Appleton	
Mary Cowden Clarke	Charles Cowden Clarke	1864–68	Cassell	Cassell's Illustrated Shakespeare
Laura Jewry Valentine		1868	Frederick Warne	Chandos Classics
Rosa Baughan		1871	T. J. Allman	
Emma Gollancz	Israel Gollancz	1899–1902	J. M. Dent	Temple Shakespeare
Charlotte E. Porter and Helen A. Clarke		1903	Thomas Y. Crowell	Pembroke
Esther Wood		1904	Doubleday, Page	The Personal Shakespeare
Charlotte E. Porter and Helen A. Clarke		1908	Thomas Y. Crowell	First Folio
Jennie Ellis Burdick		1909	Bigelow Smith	Aldus Shakespeare
Marie Edel and Anne Barton	G. Blakemore Evans et al.	1974	Houghton Mifflin	Riverside Shakespeare
Jean E. Howard and Katharine Eisaman Maus	Stephen Greenblatt, Walter Cohen	1997	W. W. Norton	Norton1
Barbara Mowat	Paul Werstine	1999	Simon & Schuster	Folger Shakespeare Library
Susan Leach	Rex Gibson	1994	Cambridge University Press	Cambridge School Shakespeare
Mary Beth Rose		2000	Penguin	Pelican2
Nathalie Rivere de Carles		2015	W. W. Norton	Norton3*
Sarah Neville		2016	Oxford University Press	New Oxford*

Editor	Co-editor(s)	Year	Publisher	Edition
Patricia Derrick	Dana E. Aspinall, Gabriel Egan	FC	Texas A&M	New Variorum*
Melissa Walter		FC		Internet Shakespeare Editions*
The Two Noble Kinsmen (12)				
Mary Cowden Clarke		1860	Appleton	
Mary Cowden Clarke	Charles Cowden Clarke	1864–68	Cassell	Cassell's Illustrated Shakespeare
Laura Jewry Valentine		1868	Frederick Warne	Chandos Classics
Charlotte E. Porter and Helen A. Clarke		1893	Thomas Y. Crowell	Pembroke
Esther Wood		1904	Doubleday, Page	The Personal Shakespeare
Charlotte E. Porter and Helen A. Clarke		1909	Thomas Y. Crowell	First Folio
Jennie Ellis Burdick		1999	Bigelow Smith	Aldus Shakespeare
Marie Edel	G. Blakemore Evans et al.	1974	Houghton Mifflin	Riverside Shakespeare
Lois Potter		1997	Thomson	Arden3*
Jean E. Howard and Katharine Eisaman Maus	Stephen Greenblatt, Walter Cohen	1997	W. W. Norton	Norton1
Barbara Mowat	Paul Werstine	2010	Simon & Schuster	Folger Shakespeare Library
Hannah Crawforth		2015	W. W. Norton	Norton3*
The Winter's Tale (21)				
Henrietta Bowdler		1807	R. Crutwell for J. Hatchard, London	The Family Shakespeare
Elizabeth Inchbald		1808	Longman, Hurst, Rees, & Orme	British Theatre
Mary Cowden Clarke		1860	Appleton	

Play and editor(s)	Male editor(s)	Publication date	Publisher	Series
Mary Cowden Clarke	Charles Cowden Clarke	1864–68	Cassell	Cassell's Illustrated Shakespeare
Laura Jewry Valentine		1868	Frederick Warne	Chandos Classics
Emma Gollancz	Israel Gollancz	1899–1902	J. M. Dent	Temple Shakespeare
Sarah Willard Hiestand		1901	D. C. Heath	Beginner's Shakespeare
Charlotte E. Porter and Helen A. Clarke		1903	Thomas Y. Crowell	Pembroke
Esther Wood		1904	Doubleday, Page	The Personal Shakespeare
Charlotte E. Porter and Helen A. Clarke		1908	Thomas Y. Crowell	First Folio
Jennie Ellis Burdick		1909	Bigelow Smith	Aldus Shakespeare
Laura J. Wylie		1912	Macmillan	Tudor Shakespeare
Marie Edel	G. Blakemore Evans et al.	1974	Houghton Mifflin	Riverside Shakespeare
Roma Gill		1996	Oxford University Press	Oxford School Shakespeare*
Jean E. Howard and Katharine Eisaman Maus	Stephen Greenblatt, Walter Cohen	1997	W. W. Norton	Norton1
Barbara Mowat	Paul Werstine	1998	Simon & Schuster	Folger Shakespeare Library
Frances E. Dolan		1999	Penguin	Pelican2
Sheila Innes		2002	Cambridge University Press	Cambridge School Shakespeare
Virginia Westling Haas	Robert Kean Turner	2005	Modern Language Association	New Variorum
Terri Bourus		2016	Oxford University Press	New Oxford*

Note: * denotes the names of multi-volume, multi-editor series overseen by at least one female general editor. FC, forthcoming; NP, never published.

Note

1 As I mentioned in the Prologue, this list excludes performance editions, by which I mean editions abridged or adapted for performance, often in schools, or editions reflecting the texts used in historical productions, including prompt books. I based this decision on the fact that these texts were designed for a particular use and were never advertised as reflecting Shakespeare's 'complete' text, making them adaptations rather than editions. The point is, undoubtedly, debatable. For anyone interested in pursuing this topic, I suggest researching Elsie Fogerty, Belle Cumming Kennedy, Mary Anderson, and Maude Adams.

Works Cited

Archival Documents and Primary Sources

'1841 England Census – Laura Jewry', National Archives of the UK, PRO HO 107/970/15/16/25, www.ancestry.com.

'1851 England Census – Charlotte Lyndon', National Archives of the UK, PRO HO 107/1664, Folio 27, Page 21, www.ancestry.com.

'1851 England Census – Laura Jewry', National Archives of the UK, PRO HO 107/1659, Folio 832, Page 8, www.ancestry.com.

'1861 England Census – Laura B.C. Valentine', National Archives of the UK, PRO RG 9/451, Folio 81, Page 30, www.ancestry.com.

'1861 Wales Census – Charlotte Lyndon', National Archives of the UK, PRO RG 9/4348, Folio 34, Page 14, www.ancestry.com.

'1891 England Census – Laura B. C. Valentine', National Archives of the UK, PRO RG 12/33, Folio 122, Page 25, www.ancestry.com.

'1901 England Census – Agnes Russell Weekes', National Archives of the UK, PRO RG 13/708, Folio 18, Page 27, www.ancestry.com.

'1911 England Census – "Agnes Russell Weekes"', National Archives of the UK, PRO RG 14/9121 Sch 153, www.ancestry.com.

'1911 England Census – "Emma Gollancz"', National Archives of the UK, PRO RG 14/634 Sch 19, www.ancestry.com.

'1939 England and Wales Register – Isabella J. Bisson', National Archives of the UK, PRO RG 101/2180E/283/2, www.ancestry.com.

A.E., 'Laurence Adolphus Bisson, 1897–1965', *French Studies*, 20.1 (1966), 114–15.

'Advertisement', *The Athenaeum* (London, 20 June 1868), p. 849.

'Advertisement for the Caxton Edition of the Complete Works of Shakespeare' (Caxton Publishing Company, undated), David Nichol Smith Papers. Osborn Collection, Beinecke Rare Book and Manuscript Library, Yale University, Box 2, Folder 11.

Bartlett, Henrietta C., and Alfred W. Pollard, *A Census of Shakespeare's Plays in Quarto, 1594–1709* (New Haven, CT: Yale University Press, 1916).

Bates, Katharine Lee, 'Diary, 1893–1897', Wellesley College Archives, Katharine Lee Bates Papers, Box 2, Folder: Diaries (1893–97, 1894).

'Letter to Cornelia Bates', 8 July 1894, Wellesley College Archives, Katharine Lee Bates Papers, Box 4.

'Letter to Cornelia Bates', 23 July 1894, Wellesley College Archives, Katharine Lee Bates Papers, Box 4.

'Letter to Cornelia Bates', 12 August 1894, Wellesley College Archives, Katharine Lee Bates Papers, Box 4.

'Letter to Edith Rickert', 8 March 1900, Edith Rickert Papers, Special Collections Research Center, University of Chicago Library, Box 1, Folder 6.

'Letter to Edith Rickert', 19 July 1910, Edith Rickert Papers, Special Collections Research Center, University of Chicago Library, Box 1, Folder 7.

'Letter to George P. Brett', 12 November 1897, Macmillan Company Records, Manuscripts and Archives Division, New York Public Library, Box 34.

'Letter to Jane Bates', 6 July 1894, Wellesley College Archives, Katharine Lee Bates Papers, Box 4.

'Letter to Jane Bates', 12 July 1894, Wellesley College Archives, Katharine Lee Bates Papers, Box 4.

'Books and Authors', *New York Times* (3 June 1923), p. BR18.

'Books and Authors: The Bankside Shakespeare. List of Editions of Shakespeare for Critical Students', *Christian Union (1870–1893)*, 3 October 1889, 396.

British Academy Archives, 'Miscellaneous Correspondence and Papers: 1908', BAA/SEC/1/34/6a-c.

Butler, H., 'Letters Regarding Miss Lyndon', 9 June 1860, Boston Public Library, Thomas Pennant Barton Shakespeare Collection, No. 15 in G39.30.15.

Cambridge Letter, &c., 1889 (London: Women's Printing Society, 1889), Newnham College Archives.

Castell, J. C., and C. F. W. Mead, 'Memories of F. J. Furnivall, V', in *Frederick James Furnivall: A Volume of Personal Record* (London: Henry Frowde, Oxford University Press, 1911), pp. 16–25.

Chapman, John, ed., 'History and Biography', *Westminster Review*, 33.1 (1868), 264–84.

Chapman, R. W., 'Letter to David Nichol Smith', 4 April 1907, David Nichol Smith Papers. Osborn Collection, Beinecke Rare Book and Manuscript Library, Yale University, Box 2, Folder 8.

Clarke, James Stanier, and John McArthur, *The Naval Chronicle: Volume 34, July–December 1815: Containing a General and Biographical History of the Royal Navy of the United Kingdom with a Variety of Original Papers on Nautical Subjects* (Cambridge: Cambridge University Press, 2010).

Crosby, Joseph, 'Miss Teena Rochfort-Smith', *Shakespeariana; A Critical and Contemporary Review of Shakespearian Literature*, April 1884, 173.

Dent, J. M., *The House of Dent, 1888–1938; Being the Memoirs of J. M. Dent, with Additional Chapters Covering the Last 16 Years by Hugh R. Dent*, revised edition (London: J. M. Dent & Sons, 1938).

Dodds, M. Hope, Review of Tamburlaine the Great, by Christopher Marlowe and U. M. Ellis-Fermor, *The Modern Language Review*, 26.2 (1931), 188–89.

'Dr. Una Ellis-Fermor', *The Times* (London, 25 March 1958), p. 10.

Ellis-Fermor, Una, *The Jacobean Drama* (London: Methuen & Co., 1936).

    'Letter to J. H. P. Pafford', 28 May 1948, Senate House Library, Archives and Manuscripts, John Henry Pyle Pafford Papers, MS 780/17 .

Evans, Mary Ann, 'Letter to Mrs. R. Valentine', 7 July 1867, Special Collections, University of Iowa Libraries, Iowa City, MsL E927 va.

Fleay, F. G., 'Letter to Katharine Lee Bates', 14 July 1902, Wellesley College Archives, Katharine Lee Bates Papers, Box 24.

Furness, Horace Howard, 'Letter to Katharine Lee Bates', 27 March 1895, Wellesley College Archives, Katharine Lee Bates Papers, Box 24.

Furnivall, Frederick James, 'Letter to J. M. Manly', 18 August 1894, John Matthews Manly Papers, Special Collections Research Center, University of Chicago Library, Box 1, Folder 2.

    'Second Report', in *The New Shakspere Society's Transaction, 1877–79* (London: Publisht for the Society by Trübner & Co., 1879).

    Teena Rochfort-Smith: A Memoir (London, 1883).

Gildersleeve, Virginia, 'Convocation Hour', 1919, Virginia Crocheron Gildersleeve papers, Rare Book and Manuscript Library, Columbia University Library, Series IV, Box 58.

    'War Time Education for Girls', 1918, Virginia Crocheron Gildersleeve papers, Rare Book and Manuscript Library, Columbia University Library, Series IV, Box 58.

Gildersleeve, Virginia Crocheron, *Many a Good Crusade: Memoirs* (New York: Macmillan, 1954).

Gollancz, Emma, 'Letter to J. M. Dent', 6 January 1898, J. M. Dent and Sons Records #11043, Rare Book Literary and Historical Papers, Wilson Library, University of North Carolina at Chapel Hill, Series 4.2, Folder 5139.

    'Letter to J. M. Dent', 19 August 1898, J. M. Dent and Sons Records #11043, Rare Book Literary and Historical Papers, Wilson Library, University of North Carolina at Chapel Hill, Series 4.2, Folder 5139.

    'Letter to J. M. Dent', 5 January 1899, J. M. Dent and Sons Records #11043, Rare Book Literary and Historical Papers, Wilson Library, University of North Carolina at Chapel Hill, Series 4.2, Folder 5139.

Gomme, Alice B., 'Memories of F. J. Furnivall, XIV', in *Frederick James Furnivall: A Volume of Personal Record* (London: Henry Frowde, Oxford University Press, 1911), pp. 62–64.

Gould, Gerald, 'A New Reading of Henry V', *The English Review*, 1919, 42–55.

'Grant of Letters of Administration for Jane Lee', 1896, Principal Probate Registry, https://probatesearch.service.gov.uk.

Graves, R. P., 'Letter to Eliza Adams', 6 February 1883, St John's College Library, Papers of John Crouch Adams, 26/4/3.

Greg, W. W., *The Calculus of Variants: An Essay on Textual Criticism* (Oxford: Clarendon Press, 1927).

    'Reviewed Work(s): Ben Jonson. Vol. IX. An Historical Survey of the Text: The Stage History of the Plays: Commentary on the Plays by C. H. Herford,

Evelyn Simpson, Percy Simpson and Ben Jonson; Ben Jonson. Vol. X. Play
Commentary: Masque Commentary by C. H. Herford, Percy Simpson,
Evelyn Simpson and Ben Jonson', *The Review of English Studies*, 2.7
(1951), 275–80.

Hill, Ellen Louise, 'Letter to Katharine Lee Bates', Wellesley College Archives,
Katharine Lee Bates Papers, Box 24.

*The Historical Record (1836–1912) Being a Supplement to the Calendar Completed to
September 1912* (London: University of London Press, 1912).

Holmes, Frank R., *A Complete Index: Volumes 1–25 of Poet-Lore* (Boston: Richard
G. Badger, Gorham Press, 1916).

Hubbard, James Mascarene, *Catalogue of the Barton Collection, Boston Public
Library. In Two Parts: Part I, Shakespeare's Works and Shakespeariana; Part
II, Miscellaneous*, 2 vols (Bostons: Published by the Trustees, 1880), 1.

'Indenture between Laura Belinda Charlotte Valentine and Frederick Warne,
Armand William Duret and Edward James Dodd', 1874, Frederick Warne
Archive, University of Reading Special Collections, Ledger, p. 557.

Iris, 'Letter to Frederick Furnivall', n.d., King's College London College Archives,
Frederick Furnivall Collection, Group 1/2/7.

Jaggard, William, *Shakespeare Bibliography*, reprint (London: Dawsons of Pall
Mall, 1971).

Jenkins, Harold, 'Letter to Arthur Humphreys', 16 January 1979, Queen Mary
University of London Archives: Harold Jenkins Papers, HJ/9/12.

J. M. Dent and Co., 'Letter to Emma Gollancz', 4 January 1898, J. M. Dent and
Sons Records #11043, Rare Book Literary and Historical Papers, Wilson
Library, University of North Carolina at Chapel Hill, Series 4.2, Folder
5139.

Johnson, Charles F., 'Shakespeare as a Text-Book', *Shakespeariana: A Critical and
Contemporary Review of Shakespearian Literature*, 1 November 1887, p. 487.

Johnson, Fanny, *In statu pupillari*, ed. Anna Bogen, Women's University
Narratives, 1890–1945, 4 vols (London: Pickering & Chatto, 2015), 1.

Johnson, Samuel, 'Proposals for Printing the Dramatic Works of William
Shakespeare (1756)', in *The Works of Samuel Johnson, LL.D.*, ed. Arthur
Murphy, 2 vols (New York: George Dearborn, 1837), 1, 467–69.

Kellner, Anna, 'Postcard to Frederick Furnivall', n.d., King's College London
College Archives, Frederick Furnivall Collection, Group 1/2/7.

King, Arthur, and A. F. Stuart, *The House of Warne: One Hundred Years of
Publishing* (London: Frederick Warne & Co., 1965).

Knox, Kathleen, 'On the Study of Shakespeare for Girls', *Journal of Education*,
1895, 222–23.

Lady Cornwallis, 'Letter to Thomas Cautley Newby', 29 June 1854, British
Library, Western Manuscripts, Royal Literary Fund, Case Files 1790s–
1970s, Loan 96 RLF 1/1351/4.

'Lawyer's Notes', Unknown, J. M. Dent and Sons Records #11043, Rare Book
Literary and Historical Papers, Wilson Library, University of North Carolina
at Chapel Hill, Series 4.2, Folder 5141.

'Lecturer Leaves', *Kingston Gleaner* (Kingston, Jamaica, 22 March 1939), p. 10.

Lee, Jane, 'On the Authorship of the Second and Third Parts of *Henry VI*, and Their Originals, *The Contention* and *The True Tragedy*', in *Transactions of the New Shakspere Society, 1877–79*, ed. Frederick James Furnivall (London: Publisht for the Society by Trübner & Co., 1879), pp. 219–92.

Lee, Sidney, 'Letter to Katharine Lee Bates', 5 April 1913, Wellesley College Archives, Katharine Lee Bates Papers, Box 23.

'Shakespeare's Stage: England's Debt to the Burbages', *The Times Literary Supplement*, 610 (1913), 385.

'The Linacre Professorship', *The Times* (London, 26 August 1881), p. 10.

'Literary Gossip', *The Athenaeum*, 23 December 1899, p. 866.

Liverpool, England, Church of England Baptisms, 1813–1917, digital images, Ancestry, entry for Grace Robarts Trenery, 1887, citing Liverpool Record Office, 283 JWD/2/2 www.ancestry.com.

Lupton, Margaret, 'Letter to Frederick Furnivall', 11 February 1900, King's College London College Archives, Frederick Furnivall Collection, Group 1/2/7.

Lyndon, Charlotte, *A Concordance to Select Quotations from the Plays of Shakespeare: Alphabetically Arranged with Full References* (London: Simpkin, Marshall, 1850).

Lyster, E. H., 'The Late Miss Jane Lee', in *Cambridge Letters, Etc., 1895* (London: Women's Printing Society, 1895), pp. 27–30.

Mais, S. P. B., *Rebellion* (London: Grant Richards, 1917).

'Marriages', *The Times* (London, 6 September 1933), p. 1.

Marx, Jenny, 'Shakespearian Studies in England: London, End of December 1876', in *Marx, Engels on Literature and Art*, by Friedrich Engels and Karl Marx (Moscow: Progress Publishers, 1976).

'Membership List', in *The New Shakspere Society's Transactions, 1874–75* (London: Trübner & Co., 1875).

Milford, H. S., 'Letter to David Nichol Smith', 26 July 1905, David Nichol Smith Papers, Osborn Collection, Beinecke Rare Book and Manuscript Library, Yale University, Box 2, Folder 9.

'Miss Elizabeth Lee', *The Times* (London, 13 July 1920), p. 14.

'Miss Emma Gollancz', *The Times* (London, 13 September 1929), p. 14.

Morshead, E. D. A., '*Faust*', *The Academy*, 752 (1886), 215–16.

'Mr. Frederick Warne', *The Athenaeum*, 16 November 1901, p. 663.

Murry, John Middleton, 'Much Ado', *Times Literary Supplement*, 1165 (1924), 293.

Neilson, W. A., 'Letter to Doris H. Taylor', 24 June 1922, Smith College Archives, William Allan Neilson Personal Papers, Box 47, Folder 1081.

Nelson, A. H., 'Letter to William A. Neilson', 23 December 1921, William Allan Neilson Personal Papers, Box 47, Smith College Archives, Folder 1081.

'News and Notes: The Stratford Conferences', *English Journal*, 3 (1914), 521–22.

'Notes and Announcements', *Bulletin of the American Association of University Professors (1915–1955)*, 21.6 (1935), 462–72.

'Notes on Books', *Notes and Queries*, s11-IV.81 (1911), 59–60.

'Past Guild Officers @ Liverpool Guild of Students', www.liverpoolguild.org/main-menu/about-us/history-of-the-guild/past-guild-officers.

Peet, Wm. H., 'Laura Jewry, Afterwards Mrs. R. Valentine', *Notes and Queries*, s11-XII.301 (1915), 266-a.

'Poetry and Verse', *The Critic: A Weekly Review of Literature and the Arts*, 14 August 1897, 88.

Porter, Charlotte Endymion, 'Letter to Richard Gilder', 12 March 1908, New York Public Library Archives and Manuscripts, Richard Watson Gilder Papers, Box 13, Folder 8.

'Probate Record and Last Will and Testament of Grace Robartes Trenery', 1950, Principal Probate Registry, https://probatesearch.service.gov.uk.

'Rational Dress', *Saturday Review of Politics, Literature, Science and Art*, 61.1587 (1886), 433.

Rickert, Edith, 'Diary, 1896' (London, 1896), Edith Rickert Papers, Special Collections Research Center, University of Chicago Library, Box 1, Folder 14.

'Diary, 1896–97' (London, 1896), Edith Rickert Papers, Special Collections Research Center, University of Chicago Library, Box 2, Folder 1.

'Diary, 1898–99' (Poughkeepsie, NY, 1898), Edith Rickert Papers, Special Collections Research Center, University of Chicago Library, Box 2, Folder 5.

'Political Propaganda and Satire in "A Midsummer Night's Dream" (To Be Continued)', *Modern Philology*, 21.1 (1923), 53–87.

'Political Propaganda and Satire in "A Midsummer Night's Dream." II', *Modern Philology*, 21.2 (1923), 133–54.

Rolfe, W. J., 'A School of Shakespeare: School Courses in Shakespeare', *Shakespeariana: A Critical and Contemporary Review of Shakespearian Literature*, 1 July 1887, p. 313.

Scudder, Vida Dutton, 'Letter to Dr. George N. Shuster', 31 January 1945, Hunter College Archives, Helen Gray Cone Papers, Box 1, Folder 5.

'Shakespeare Bibliography', *Saturday Review of Politics, Literature, Science and Art; London*, 111.2904 (1911), 782.

Simpson, Evelyn Spearing, 'Letter to W. W. Greg', 25 May 1937, Walter Wilson Greg Papers, James Marshall and Marie-Louise Osborn Collection, Beinecke Rare Book and Manuscript Library, Series XI, Box 9.

'Letter to W. W. Greg', 15 August 1942, Walter Wilson Greg Papers, James Marshall and Marie-Louise Osborn Collection, Beinecke Rare Book and Manuscript Library, Series XI, Box 9.

'The Splendid Folly', *The Bookman: A Review of Books and Life*, April 1921, 177–178.

Smith, Evelyn, *The First Fifth Form* (London: Blackie & Son, 1926).

Stopes, Charlotte Carmichael, 'Memories of F. J. Furnivall, XLV', in *Frederick James Furnivall: A Volume of Personal Record* (London: Oxford University Press, 1911), pp. 188–92.

Taylor, Doris H., 'Letter to W. A. Neilson', 21 June 1922, Smith College Archives, William Allan Neilson Personal Papers, Box 47, Folder 1081.

The Teaching of English in England. Report of the Departmental Committee Appointed by the President of the Board of Education to Inquire into the Position of English in the Educational System of England (London: Board of Education, 1921).

Toulmin Smith, Lucy, 'Letter to J. M. Manly', 12 June 1896, John Matthews Manly Papers, Special Collections Research Center, University of Chicago Library, Box 1, Folder 4.

Trenery, Grace R., 'Ballad Collections of the Eighteenth Century', *The Modern Language Review*, 10.3 (1915), 283–303.

'UK, Incoming Passenger Lists, 1878–1960; Port of Departure: Batavia, Indonesia', 1930, National Archives of the UK, BT26/948/62 www.ancestry.com.

'UK, Incoming Passenger Lists, 1878–1960; Port of Departure: Rangoon, Burma', 1933, National Archives of the UK, BT26/1017/56 www.ancestry.com.

'UK, Incoming Passenger Lists, 1878–1960; Port of Departure: Yokohama, Japan', 1939, National Archives of the UK, BT26/1179/122 www.ancestry.com.

Universities Review, vols. 13–16 (Bristol: J. W. Arrowsmith, 1942).

Valentine, Laura Belinda Charlotte, 'Letter to the Committee of the Literary Fund', 28 June 1854, British Library, Western Manuscripts, Royal Literary Fund, Case Files 1790s–1970s, Loan 96 RLF 1/1351/2.

Valentine, Laura Jewry, *The Cup and the Lip: A Novel*, 3 vols (London: T. C. Newby, 1851), I.

Walker, Alice, 'Compositor Determination and Other Problems in Shakespearian Texts', *Studies in Bibliography*, 7 (1955), 3–15.

'Letter to R. B. McKerrow', 2 March 1936, Trinity College Library, Cambridge: Papers of R. B. McKerrow (MCKW), A4/2.

'Letter to R. B. McKerrow', 5 March 1936, Trinity College Library, Cambridge: MCKW, A4/3.

'Letter to R. B. McKerrow', 28 March 1939, Trinity College Library, Cambridge: MCKW, A4/162.

'Letter to R. B. McKerrow', 15 September 1937, Trinity College Library, Cambridge: MCKW, A4/109.

'Letter to R. B. McKerrow', 15 February 1937, Trinity College Library, Cambridge: MCKW, A4/79.

'Letter to R. B. McKerrow', 26 September 1937, Trinity College Library, Cambridge: MCKW, A4/118.

'Letter to R. B. McKerrow', 18 December 1937, Trinity College Library, Cambridge: MCKW, A4/138.

'Letter to R. B. McKerrow', 14 November 1938, Trinity College Library, Cambridge: MCKW, A4/155.

'Principles of Annotation: Some Suggestions for Editors of Shakespeare', *Studies in Bibliography*, 9 (1957), 95–105.

'The Text of *Measure for Measure*', *The Review of English Studies*, 34.133 (1983), 1–20.

'The Textual Problem of "Troilus and Cressida"', *The Modern Language Review*, 45.4 (1950), 459–64.
Textual Problems of the First Folio (Cambridge: Cambridge University Press, 1953).
Wallace, Charles William, 'Letter to Katharine Lee Bates', 25 July 1910, Wellesley College Archives, Katharine Lee Bates Papers, Box 23.
Weekes, Agnes Russell, *Jenny Essenden* (London: Andrew Melrose, 1916).
White, Richard Grant, 'The Lady Gruach's Husband', *Massachusetts Ploughman and New England Journal of Agriculture*, 23 April 1870, 3.
Studies in Shakespeare (Boston: Houghton Mifflin, 1885).
Wiggin, Pauline G., *An Inquiry into the Authorship of the Middleton-Rowley Plays* (Boston: Ginn & Co., 1897).
Williams, Professor Basil, 'Miss Flora Masson', The Times (London, 5 October 1937), p. 9.
Wilson, F. P., 'Letter to Evelyn Spearing Simpson', 21 January 1962, Evelyn Simpson Papers. James Marshall and Marie-Louise Osborn Collection, Beinecke Rare Book and Manuscript Library, Yale University, Series I, Box 3, Folder 83.
Wilson, J. Dover, 'Letter to Henrietta C. Bartlett', 13 November 1937, Henrietta C. Bartlett Papers. General Collection. Beinecke Rare Book and Manuscript Library, Yale University, Series I, Box 5, Folder 264.
'Letter to Henrietta C. Bartlett', 17 December 1937, Henrietta C. Bartlett Papers. General Collection. Beinecke Rare Book and Manuscript Library, Yale University, Series I, Box 5, Folder 264.
Winsor, Justin, 'A Choice of Shakespeares', *The Literary World; A Monthly Review of Current Literature*, 8.10 (1878), 179.
Wirth, Bessie Coat, 'The Ethical Values of Shakespeare as Presented to the High-School Student of *Julius Caesar*, *Macbeth*, and *Hamlet*' (master's thesis, Loyola University, 1938).

Editions Cited

Baughan, Rosa, *Shakespeare's Plays Abridged and Revised for the Use of Girls*, 2 vols (London: T. J. Allman, 1863), 1.
Chaucer, Geoffrey, John Matthews Manly, and Edith Rickert, *The Text of the Canterbury Tales* (Chicago, IL: University of Chicago Press, 1940).
Dunn, Esther Cloudman, ed., *Eight Famous Elizabethan Plays* (New York: Modern Library, 1932).
Eliot, George, *Middlemarch: A Study of Provincial Life*, 8 vols (London: William Blackwood and Sons, 1871), 1.
Fielding, Sarah, and Candace Ward, *The Governess, or The Little Female Academy*, Broadview Editions (Broadview Press, 2005).
Goethe, Johann Wolfgang von, and Jane Lee, *Faust. Part I. With Introduction and Notes, and an Appendix on Part II*, Macmillan's Foreign School Classics (London: Macmillan, 1886).

Heywood, Thomas, and Madeleine Doran, *If You Know Not Me You Know Nobody*, Malone Society Reprints (London: Printed for the Malone Society by J. Johnson at the Oxford University Press, 1935).

Keats, John, and W. T. Young, *Poems of Keats: Endymion: The Volume of 1820 and Other Poems* (Cambridge: Cambridge University Press, 1917).

Lamb, Mary, and Charles Lamb, *Tales from Shakespeare: Illustrated with Paintings of Scenes from Shakespeare by Various Artists*, ed. Katherine Duncan-Jones (London: Folio Society, 2003).

Shakespeare, William, and Katharine Lee Bates, *Shakespeare's Comedy of As You Like It*, The Students' Series of English Classics (Boston: Sibley & Ducker, 1896).

Shakespeare's Comedy of A Midsummer-Night's Dream, The Students' Series of English Classics (Boston: Sibley & Ducker, 1895).

Shakespeare's Comedy of the Merchant of Venice, The Students' Series of English Classics (Boston: Sibley & Ducker, 1894).

Shakespeare, William, and Isabel J. Bisson, *As You Like It*, New Clarendon Shakespeare (Oxford: Oxford University Press, 1941).

Shakespeare, William, and Henrietta Maria Bowdler, *The Family Shakespeare*, 4 vols (Bath: R. Cruttwell, 1807).

Shakespeare, William, and Rosa Baughan, *Shakespeare's Plays Abridged and Revised for the Use of Girls*, 2 vols (London: T. J. Allman, 1863).

Shakespeare, William, Helen Archibald Clarke, and Charlotte Endymion Porter, *The Complete Works of William Shakespeare*, reprinted from the First Folio (London: George G. Harrap, 1906), i.

Shakespeare: First Folio Edition, 40 vols (New York: T. Y. Crowell & Co., 1903–13), IV.

Shakespeare's Complete Works, Pembroke Edition, 12 vols (New York: Thomas Y. Crowell & Co., 1903).

Shakespeare, William, and Mary Cowden Clarke, *Shakespeare's Works. Edited, with a Scrupulous Revision of the Text, by M. Cowden Clarke* (New York: D. Appleton & Co., 1860).

Shakespeare, William, Mary Cowden Clarke, and Charles Cowden Clarke, *The Plays of Shakespeare*, Cassell's Illustrated Shakespeare, 3 vols (London: Cassell & Co., 1864), III.

Shakespeare, William, Helen Gray Cone, and Richard Grant White, *Macbeth*, The Riverside Literature Series, 106 (Boston: Houghton Mifflin and Company, 1897).

Shakespeare, William, and George H. Cowling, *The Life of King Henry the Fifth*, Methuen's *English Classics* (London: Methuen & Co., 1922).

Shakespeare, William, John D. Cox, and Eric Rasmussen, *King Henry VI, Part 3*, Arden Shakespeare, Third Series (London: Bloomsbury Arden Shakespeare, 2001).

Shakespeare, William, and Benjamin Dawson, *King Henry the Fifth*, The University Shakespeare (London: Simpkin, Marshall & Co.; Hamilton, Adams & Co., 1888).

Shakespeare, William, and Katherine Duncan-Jones, *Shakespeare's Sonnets*, Arden Shakespeare, Third Series, revised edition (London: Arden Shakespeare, 2010).

Shakespeare, William, and Israel Gollancz, *Shakespeare's First Part of King Henry VI: With Preface, Glossary, &c*, The Temple Shakespeare (London: J. M. Dent and Co., 1898).

Shakespeare, William, and W. W. Greg, *Shakespeare's Merry Wives of Windsor* (Oxford: Clarendon Press, 1910).

Shakespeare, William, and Samuel Johnson, *The Plays of William Shakespeare, in Eight Volumes, with the Corrections and Illustrations of Various Commentators; to Which Are Added Notes by Sam. Johnson*, 8 vols (London: J. and R. Tonson, H. Woodfall, J. Rivington, R. Baldwin, L. Hawes, Clark and Collins, T. Longman, W. Johnston, T. Caslon, C. Corbet, T. Lownds, and the executors of B. Dodd, 1765), I.

Shakespeare, William, and Ronald Knowles, *King Henry VI Part 2*, Arden Shakespeare, Third Series (London: Bloomsbury Arden Shakespeare, 1999).

Shakespeare, William, and Elizabeth Lee, *The Tempest*, Blackie's Junior School Shakespeare (London: Blackie and Son, 1894).

Shakespeare, William, and D. M. Macardle, *The Tempest*, The Carmelite Shakespeare (London: Horace Marshall and Son, 1917).

Shakespeare, William, and Flora Masson, *As You Like It*, Dent's Shakespeare for Schools (London: J. M. Dent & Co., 1903).

Shakespeare, William, and Mary Atkinson Maurice, *Readings from the Plays of Shakespeare, in Illustration of His Characters* (London: John W. Parker, 1848).

Shakespeare, William, Alice Meynell, and Sidney Lee, *The Taming of the Shrew*, Renaissance Shakespeare (New York: George D. Sproul, 1907), VII.

Shakespeare, William, and Kenneth Palmer, *Troilus and Cressida*, Arden Shakespeare, Second Series (London: Methuen, 1982).

Shakespeare, William, Edith Rickert, and E. K. Chambers, *A Midsummer Night's Dream*, The Arden Shakespeare, revised edition (Boston: D. C. Heath & Co., 1916).

Shakespeare, William, and Emma Smith, *King Henry V*, Shakespeare in Performance (Cambridge: Cambridge University Press, 2002).

Shakespeare, William, and Evelyn Smith, *Shakespeare's Comedy of As You Like It*, Teaching of English Series (London: Thomas Nelson & Sons, 1926).

Shakespeare's King Henry IV. Part I, Teaching of English Series, 33 (London: Thomas Nelson & Sons, 1925).

Shakespeare's King Henry V, Teaching of English Series, 114 (London: Thomas Nelson & Sons, 1927).

Shakespeare's Tragedy of Coriolanus, Teaching of English Series (London: Thomas Nelson & Sons, 1926).

Shakespeare's Tragedy of King Lear, Teaching of English Series, 96 (London: Thomas Nelson & Sons, 1926).

Shakespeare, William, and J. C. Smith, *As You Like It*, Heath's English Classics (Boston: D. C. Heath & Co., 1902).

Shakespeare, William, and C. C. Stopes, *Shakespeare's Sonnets*, King's Classics (London: De la More Press, 1904).

Shakespeare, William, and C. L. Thomson, *A Midsummer Night's Dream*, The Carmelite Shakespeare (London: Horace Marshall and Son, 1924).

Shakespeare, William, and Grace Trenery, *Much Ado About Nothing*, The Arden Shakespeare (London: Methuen & Co., 1924).

Shakespeare, William, and Charlotte Whipple Underwood, *Shakespeare's The Merchant of Venice*, Macmillan's Pocket Classics (New York: Macmillan, 1899).

Shakespeare, William, and Laura Jewry Valentine, *The Works of William Shakspeare*, Chandos Classics (London: Frederick Warne & Co., 1868).

The Works of William Shakspeare, 'Universal' Edition (London: Frederick Warne and Co., 1889).

The Works of William Shakspeare, 'Victorian' Edition (London: Frederick Warne and Co., 1896).

The Works of William Shakspeare. Life, Glossary, &c. (London: Frederick Warne & Co., 1875).

Shakespeare, William, and Alice Walker, *Troilus and Cressida*, New Cambridge Shakespeare (Cambridge: Cambridge University Press, 1969).

Shakespeare, William, Alice Walker, and J. Dover Wilson, *Othello*, New Cambridge Shakespeare (Cambridge: Cambridge University Press, 1957).

Shakespeare, William, and Agnes Russell Weekes, *As You Like It*, University Tutorial Series (London: W. B. Clive, University Tutorial Press, 1909).

Cymbeline, University Tutorial Series (London: W. B. Clive, University Tutorial Press, 1919).

The Tempest, University Tutorial Series (London: W. B. Clive, University Tutorial Press, 1909).

Shakespeare, William, and Richard Grant White, *Mr. William Shakespeare's Comedies, Histories, Tragedies, and Poems*, Riverside Shakespeare, 4 vols (Boston: Houghton Mifflin and Company, 1883), 1.

Shakespeare, William, Esther Wood, Goldwin Smith, and William H. Fleming, *The Personal Shakespeare*, 15 vols (New York: Doubleday, Page & Co., 1904).

Shakespeare, William, William Aldis Wright, William George Clark, and Evangeline M. O'Connor, *The Works of William Shakespeare: With Prefaces, Notes, Glossaries, a Life of Shakespeare, and a History of Early English Drama*, Elsinore Edition (New York: University Society, 1901).

Shakespeare, William, and Charlotte Mary Yonge, *The Second Part of Shakespeare's King Henry IV* (Westminster: National Society's Depository, 1884).

Shakespeare's King Henry V (Westminster: National Society's Depository, 1885).

Valentine, Laura Jewry, *Shakespearian Tales in Verse, Illustrated* (London: F. Warne & Co., 1881).

Secondary Criticism

Aaron, Jane, 'Lamb, Mary Anne (1764–1847), Children's Writer', in *Oxford Dictionary of National Biography* (Oxford: Oxford University Press, 2004), doi.org/10.1093/ref:odnb/15918.

Abbott, Don Paul, '"A New Genus": Mary Wollstonecraft and the Feminization of Elocution', *Rhetorica: A Journal of the History of Rhetoric*, 36.3 (2018), 269–95.

Alexander, Catherine, 'Shakespeare and War: A Reflection on Instances of Dramatic Production, Appropriation, and Celebration', *Exchanges: The Warwick Research Journal*, 1.2 (2014), 279–96.

Alexander, Peter, *Shakespeare's Henry VI and Richard III*, Shakespeare Problems, 3 (Cambridge: Cambridge University Press, 1929).

Altick, Richard D., *The English Common Reader: A Social History of the Mass Reading Public, 1800–1900*, 2nd ed. (Columbus: Ohio State University Press, 1998).

'From Aldine to Everyman: Cheap Reprint Series of the English Classics 1830–1906', *Studies in Bibliography*, 11 (1958), 3–24.

'An Entertainment for Elizabeth I at Elvetham, 1591', *The British Library*, www.bl.uk/collection-items/an-entertainment-for-elizabeth-i-at-elvetham-1591.

Bajetta, Carlo, 'The Authority of Editing: Thoughts on the Function(s) of Modern Textual Criticism', *Textus*, 19 (2006), 305–22.

Barber, Virginia, 'The Women's Revolt in the MLA', *Change: The Magazine of Higher Learning*, 4.3 (1972), 24–27.

Barchas, Janine, 'Why K. M. Metcalfe (Mrs Chapman) Is "Really the Originator in the Editing of Jane Austen"', *The Review of English Studies*, 68.285 (2017), 583–611.

Barnard, John, and D. F. McKenzie, eds., *The Cambridge History of the Book in Britain, vol. IV: 1557–1695* (Cambridge: Cambridge University Press, 2002).

Bate, Jonathan, and Sonia Massai, 'Adaptation as Edition', in *The Margins of the Text* ed. D. C. Greetham (Ann Arbor: University of Michigan Press, 1997), pp. 129–53.

Battiscombe, Georgina, *Charlotte Mary Yonge: The Story of an Uneventful Life; With an Introduction by E. M. Delafield* (London: Constable and Company, 1943).

Bayer, Mark, 'Henry Norman Hudson and the Origins of American Shakespeare Studies', *Shakespeare Quarterly*, 68.3 (2017), 271–95.

Bell, Alan, and Katherine Duncan-Jones, 'Lee, Sir Sidney (1859–1926), Second Editor of the *Dictionary of National Biography* and Literary Scholar', *Oxford Dictionary of National Biography* (Oxford: Oxford University Press, 2009), doi.org/10.1093/ref:odnb/34470.

Benzie, William, *Dr. F. J. Furnivall: Victorian Scholar Adventurer* (Norman, OK: Pilgrim Books, 1983).

Berg, Daria, *Women and the Literary World in Early Modern China, 1580–1700* (London: Routledge, 2013).

Bernstein, Susan David, *Roomscape: Women Writers in the British Museum from George Eliot to Virginia Woolf* (Edinburgh: Edinburgh University Press, 2013).

Bingham, Adrian, '"An Era of Domesticity"? Histories of Women and Gender in Interwar Britain', *Cultural and Social History*, 1.2 (2004), 225–33.

'Biographies of Yale's First Women Ph.D.'s | Women Faculty Forum', http://wff .yale.edu/biographies-yales-first-women-phds.

Birch, Dinah, 'Education', in *The Cambridge History of Victorian Literature*, ed. Kate Flint (Cambridge: Cambridge University Press, 2012), pp. 329–49.

Our Victorian Education (Oxford: Blackwell, 2008).

Blunden, Edmund, and Sayoni Basu, 'Nichols, Robert Malise Bowyer (1893–1944), Poet and Playwright', in *Oxford Dictionary of National Biography* (Oxford: Oxford University Press, 2016), doi.org/10.1093/ref:odnb/35223.

Booth, Alison, 'Fighting for Lives in the *ODNB*, or Taking Prosopography Personally', *Journal of Victorian Culture*, 10.2 (2005), 267–79.

Bottoms, Janet, '"Doing Shakespeare": How Shakespeare Became a School "Subject"', *Shakespeare Survey*, 66 (2013).

'"To Read Aright": Representations of Shakespeare for Children', *Children's Literature*, 32 (2004), 1–14.

Bourne, Claire M. L., '"Typographical Distinction": Alice Walker's Edward Capell's Shakespeare', in the *Women and Book History* seminar (Shakespeare Association of America, Los Angeles, 2018).

Bowers, Fredson, 'Practical Texts and Definitive Editions', in *Essays in Bibliography, Text, and Editing* (Charlottesville, VA: Published for the Bibliographical Society of the University of Virginia by the University Press of Virginia, 1975), pp. 412–39.

Braber, Ben, 'Within Our Gates: A New Perspective on Germans in Glasgow during the First World War', *Journal of Scottish Historical Studies*, 29.2 (2009), 87–105.

Brown, Cynthia Farr, 'Gildersleeve, Virginia Crocheron (1877–1965), College Administrator and International Affairs Expert', *American National Biography* (Oxford: Oxford University Press, 2000), doi.org/10.1093/anb/9780198606697.article.0900297.

Brown, Paul, 'Stealing Soldiers' Hearts: Appropriating *Henry V* and Marching Shakespeare's Boys off to the Great War', *Vides*, 3 (2015), 11.

Bruckner, Lynne Dickson, 'Ben Jonson's Branded Thumb and the Imprint of Textual Paternity', in *Printing and Parenting in Early Modern England*, ed. Douglas A. Brooks (Aldershot: Ashgate, 2005), pp. 109–30.

Burden, Emily, 'Pre-Victorian Prudery: *The Family Shakespeare* and the Birth of Bowdlerism' (master's thesis, University of Birmingham, 2007).

Burgess, Dorothy, *Dream and Deed: The Story of Katharine Lee Bates* (Norman: University of Oklahoma Press, 1952).

Burton, Dolores, *Shakespeare's Grammatical Style: A Computer-Assisted Analysis of Richard II and Anthony and Cleopatra*, Dan Danciger Publication Series (Austin: University of Texas Press, 1973).

Burton, Dolores M., 'Automated Concordances and Word Indexes: The Early Sixties and the Early Centers', *Computers and the Humanities*, 15.2 (1981), 83–100.

Butler, Martin, 'The Making of the Oxford "Ben Jonson"', *The Review of English Studies*, 62.257 (2011), 738–57.

Buurma, Rachel Sagner, and Laura Heffernan, 'Search and Replace: Josephine Miles and the Origins of Distant Reading', *Modernism/Modernity Print Plus*, 3.1 (2018), https://modernismmodernity.org/forums/posts/search-and-replace.

Caesar, Adrian, 'Brooke, Rupert Chawner (1887–1915), Poet', in *Oxford Dictionary of National Biography* (Oxford: Oxford University Press, 2017), doi.org/10.1093/ref:odnb/32093.

Carson, Christie, and Peter Kirwan, *Shakespeare and the Digital World: Redefining Scholarship and Practice* (Cambridge: Cambridge University Press, 2014).

Clare, Hilary, 'Evelyn Smith, Part 1', *Folly*, November 1995, pp. 1–5.

'Evelyn Smith, Part 2', *Folly*, March 1996, pp. 6–11.

Clear, Caitriona, 'Cumann Na MBan', in *The Oxford Companion to Irish History* (Oxford: Oxford University Press, 2002).

Cloud, Random, 'FIAT FLUX', in *Crisis in Editing: Texts of the English Renaissance*, ed. Randall McLeod (New York: AMS Press, 1994).

Cochran, Robert, *Louise Pound: Scholar, Athlete, Feminist Pioneer* (Lincoln: University of Nebraska Press, 2009).

'Pound, Louise (1872–1958), Folklorist', *American National Biography* (Oxford: Oxford University Press, 2000), doi.org/10.1093/anb/9780198606697.article.0900606.

Cohler, Deborah, 'Sapphism and Sedition: Producing Female Homosexuality in Great War Britain', *Journal of the History of Sexuality*, 16.1 (2007), 68–94.

Coker, Cait, and Kate Ozment, 'Our Mission', *Women in Book History Bibliography*, www.womensbookhistory.org/our-mission.

Cole, Sarah, 'Siegfried Sassoon', in *The Cambridge Companion to the Poetry of the First World War*, ed. Santanu Das (Cambridge: Cambridge University Press, 2013), pp. 94–104.

'Collecting Everyman's Library: 1906–1982', everymanslibrarycollecting.com.

Colley, Linda, *Shakespeare and the Limits of National Culture* (Egham: Royal Holloway, University of London, 1999).

Collins, Tracy J. R., 'Athletic Fashion, *Punch*, and the Creation of the New Woman', *Victorian Periodicals Review*, 43.3 (2010), 309–35.

Court, Franklin E., *Institutionalizing English Literature: The Culture and Politics of Literary Study, 1750–1900* (Stanford, CA: Stanford University Press, 1992).

Craig, Maggie, *When the Clyde Ran Red: A Social History of Red Clydeside* (Edinburgh: Birlinn, 2018).

Cullhed, Sigrid Schottenius, *Proba the Prophet: The Christian Virgilian Cento of Faltonia Betitia Proba*, Mnemosyne Supplements (Leiden: Brill, 2015).

Cummings, Brian, 'Shakespeare's First Folio and the Fetish of the Book', *Cahiers Élisabéthains*, 93.1 (2017), 50–69.

Cunningham, Patricia A., *Reforming Women's Fashion, 1850–1920: Politics, Health, and Art* (Kent, Ohio: Kent State University Press, 2003).

Currey, R. N., and Sayoni Basu, 'Gibson, Wilfrid Wilson (1878–1962), Poet', in *Oxford Dictionary of National Biography* (Oxford: Oxford University Press, 2009), doi.org/10.1093/ref:odnb/33392.

Cuthbertson, Guy, 'Dymock Poets (Act. 1913–1915)', in *Oxford Dictionary of National Biography* (Oxford University Press, 2009), doi.org/10.1093/ref:odnb/100255.

Dabbs, Thomas, 'Shakespeare and the Department of English', in *English as a Discipline, or Is There a Plot in This Play?*, ed. James C. Raymond (Tuscaloosa: University of Alabama Press, 1996), pp. 82–98.

Das, Santanu, 'Reframing First World War Poetry: An Introduction', in *The Cambridge Companion to the Poetry of the First World War*, ed. Santanu Das, Cambridge Companions to Literature (Cambridge: Cambridge University Press, 2013).

David, Deirdre, *Rule Britannia: Women, Empire, and Victorian Writing* (Ithaca, NY: Cornell University Press, 1995).

De Grazia, Margreta, *Shakespeare Verbatim* (Oxford: Oxford University Press, 1991).

Deazley, Ronan, *On the Origin of the Right to Copy: Charting the Movement of Copyright Law in Eighteenth Century Britain (1695–1775)* (London: Hart Publishing, 2004).

Decker, Christopher, 'Shakespeare Editions', in *Shakespeare in the Nineteenth Century*, ed. Gail Marshall (Cambridge: Cambridge University Press, 2012), pp. 16–38.

Delap, Lucy, 'The Superwoman: Theories of Gender and Genius in Edwardian Britain', *The Historical Journal*, 47.1 (2004), 101–26.

Delery, Clayton J., 'The Subject Presumed to Know: Implied Authority and Editorial Apparatus', *Text: Transactions of the Society for Textual Scholarship*, 5 (1991), 63–80.

Depledge, Emma, *Shakespeare's Rise to Cultural Prominence: Politics, Print and Alteration, 1642–1700* (Cambridge: Cambridge University Press, 2018).

Desmet, Christy, '*Shakespeariana* and Shakespeare Societies in North America, 1883–1893', *Borrowers and Lenders: The Journal of Shakespeare and Appropriation*, 2.2 (2006).

Dobson, Michael, 'Bowdler and Britannia: Shakespeare and the National Libido', ed. Stanley Wells, *Shakespeare Survey*, 46 (1993), 137–44.

The Making of the National Poet: Shakespeare, Adaptation and Authorship, 1660–1769 (Oxford: Oxford University Press, 1994).

Donaldson, E. Talbot, *Speaking of Chaucer* (London: Athlone Press, 1977).

Dor, Juliette, 'Caroline Spurgeon (1869–1942) and the Institutionalisation of English Studies as a Scholarly Discipline', *Philologie Im Netz*, Supplement 4 (2009), 55–66.

Doran, Madeleine, *Henry VI, Parts II and III: Their Relation to the Contention and the True Tragedy* (Iowa City: The University, 1928).

Duffy, Maureen, *A Thousand Capricious Chances: A History of the Methuen List, 1889–1989* (London: Methuen, 1989).

Dyhouse, Carol, 'The British Federation of University Women and the Status of Women in Universities, 1907–1939', *Women's History Review*, 4.4 (1995), 465–85.

    No Distinction of Sex? Women in British Universities, 1870–1939, Women's History (London: UCL Press, 1995).

Edwards, Philip, *Threshold of a Nation: A Study in English and Irish Drama* (Cambridge: Cambridge University Press, 1979).

Edwards, Ruth Dudley, *Victor Gollancz: A Biography* (London: Faber & Faber, 2012).

Egan, Gabriel, '"A Complicated and Unpleasant Investigation": The Arden Shakespeare 1899–1924' (presented at Open the Book, Open the Mind: The 2007 meeting of the Society for History of Authorship, Reading, and Publishing (SHARP), University of Minnesota, Minneapolis, 2007).

    The Struggle for Shakespeare's Text: Twentieth-Century Editorial Theory and Practice (Cambridge: Cambridge University Press, 2010).

Eggert, Paul, *The Work and the Reader in Literary Studies: Scholarly Editing and Book History* (Cambridge: Cambridge University Press, 2019).

English, Richard, *Irish Freedom: The History of Nationalism in Ireland* (London: Pan, 2007).

Erhart, Walter, 'The Gender of Philology – A Genealogy of *Germanistik*', in *Gendered Academia: Wissenschaft und Geschlechterdifferenz, 1890–1945*, ed. Miriam Kauko, Sylvia Mieszkowski, and Alexandra Tischel (Gottingen: Wallstein Verlag, 2005), pp. 41–64.

'Esther Cloudman Dunn Papers, 1864–1977 Finding Aid', *Five College Archives & Manuscript Collections*, https://asteria.fivecolleges.edu/findaids/smitharc hives/manosca325_bioghist.html.

Estill, Laura, 'Introduction: Special Issue, Digital Shakespeare Texts', *Renaissance & Reformation/Renaissance et Reforme*, 42.3 (2019), 167–70.

Falle, George, 'Sir Walter Scott as Editor of Dryden and Swift', *University of Toronto Quarterly*, 36.2 (1967), 161–80.

Fenwick, Gillian, 'Lee, Elizabeth (1857/8–1920), Biographer and Translator', in *Oxford Dictionary of National Biography* (Oxford: Oxford University Press, 2004), doi.org/10.1093/ref:odnb/41160.

Finnerty, Páraic, *Emily Dickinson's Shakespeare* (Amherst: University of Massachusetts Press, 2006).

Fleissner, Jennifer L., 'Dictation Anxiety: The Stenographer's Stake in *Dracula*', in *Literary Secretaries/Secretarial Culture*, ed. Leah Price and Pamela Thurschwell (Aldershot: Ashgate, 2005), pp. 63–90.

Fleming, Juliet, 'The Renaissance Collage: Signcutting and Signsewing', *Journal of Medieval and Early Modern Studies*, 45.3 (2015), 443–56.

Flint, Kate, *The Woman Reader 1837–1914* (Oxford: Oxford University Press, 1995).

Franklin, Colin, *Shakespeare Domesticated: The Eighteenth-Century Editions* (Aldershot: Scholar Press, 1991).

Gabler, Hans Walter, *Text Genetics in Literary Modernism and Other Essays* (Cambridge: Open Book Publishers, 2018), doi.org/10.11647/OBP.0120.

Galey, Alan, *The Shakespearean Archive* (Cambridge: Cambridge University Press, 2014).

Galey, Alan, and Rebecca Niles, 'Moving Parts: Digital Modeling and the Infrastructures of Shakespeare Editing', *Shakespeare Quarterly*, 68.1 (2017), 21–55.

Gaskell, Philip, *From Writer to Reader: Studies in Editorial Method* (Oxford: Clarendon Press, 1978).

Geduld, Harry M., *Prince of Publishers: A Study of the Work and Career of Jacob Tonson* (Bloomington: Indiana University Press, 1969).

Gibson, Rex, 'Editing Shakespeare for School Students', in *Problems of Editing*, ed. Christa Jansohn (Berlin: Walter de Gruyter, 1999), pp. 180–99.

——— '"O, What Learning Is!" Pedagogy and the Afterlife of *Romeo and Juliet*', *Shakespeare Survey*, 49 (1996), 141–52.

Gilbert, Sandra M., and Susan Gubar, *The Madwoman in the Attic: The Woman Writer and the Nineteenth-Century Literary Imagination* (New Haven, CT: Yale University Press, 1980).

Gilliver, Peter, *The Making of the Oxford English Dictionary* (Oxford: Oxford University Press, 2016).

——— 'Women and the Oxford English Dictionary', *Oxford Words Blog*, 2016, https://blog.oxforddictionaries.com/2016/03/08/women-and-the-oed.

'The Glasgow School of Art Home Front Memorial', *Glasgow School of Art: Archives & Collections*, https://gsaarchives.net/collections/index.php/nmc-1721.

Glazener, Nancy, *Literature in the Making: A History of US Literary Culture in the Long Nineteenth Century* (Oxford: Oxford University Press, 2015).

Goodblatt, Chanita, '"The University Is a Paradise, Rivers of Knowledge Are There": Evelyn Mary Spearing Simpson', in *Women Editing/Editing Women: Early Modern Women Writers and the New Textualism*, ed. Ann Hollinshead Hurley and Chanita Goodblatt (Newcastle: Cambridge Scholars, 2009), pp. 257–84.

Goodwin, Gordon, and David Huddleston, 'William Lee', in *Oxford Dictionary of National Biography* (Oxford: Oxford University Press, 2004), doi.org/10.1093/ref:odnb/16317.

Gossett, Suzanne, 'Emendations, Reconstructions, and the Uses of the Past', *Text*, 17 (2005), 35–54.

——— '"To Foster Is Not Always to Preserve": Feminist Inflections in Editing *Pericles*', in *In Arden: Editing Shakespeare: Essays in Honour of Richard Proudfoot*, ed. Ann Thompson and Gordon McMullan (London: Arden Shakespeare, 2003), pp. 65–80.

——— 'Why Should a Woman Edit a Man?', in *Women Editing/Editing Women: Early Modern Women Writers and the New Textualism*, ed. Ann Hollinshead Hurley and Chanita Goodblatt (Newcastle: Cambridge Scholars, 2009), pp. 25–34.

Graff, Gerald, 'Is There a Conversation in This Curriculum? Or, Coherence without Disciplinarity', in *English as a Discipline, or Is There a Plot in This Play?*, ed. James C. Raymond (Tuscaloosa: University of Alabama Press, 1996), pp. 11–28.

Grant, Stephen H., *Collecting Shakespeare: The Story of Henry and Emily Folger* (Baltimore, MD: Johns Hopkins University Press, 2014).

Gray, Erik, *Milton and the Victorians* (Ithaca, NY: Cornell University Press, 2015).

Green, A. C., 'The Difference between McKerrow and Greg', *Textual Cultures*, 4.2 (2009), 31–53.

Green, Stephanie, *The Public Lives of Charlotte and Marie Stopes*, Dramatic Lives (London: Pickering & Chatto, 2013).

'The Serious Mrs. Stopes: Gender, Writing and Scholarship in Late-Victorian Britain', *Nineteenth-Century Gender Studies*, 5.3, 2009, www.ncgsjournal .com/issue53/green.htm.

Greenblatt, Stephen, *Shakespearean Negotiations: The Circulation of Social Energy in Renaissance England* (Berkeley: University of California Press, 1988).

Greene, David, 'Robert Atkinson and Irish Studies', *Hermathena*, 102, 1966, 6–15.

Greetham, D. C., 'A History of Textual Scholarship', in *The Cambridge Companion to Textual Scholarship*, ed. Neil Fraistat and Julia Flanders (Cambridge: Cambridge University Press, 2013), pp. 16–41.

The Pleasures of Contamination: Evidence, Text, and Voice in Textual Studies (Bloomington: Indiana University Press, 2010).

Griffiths, Fiona J., *The Garden of Delights: Reform and Renaissance for Women in the Twelfth Century*, The Middle Ages Series (Philadelphia: University of Pennsylvania Press, 2007).

Grigely, Joseph, *Textualterity* (Ann Arbor: University of Michigan Press, 1995).

'Guide to the Chaucer Research Project Records 1886–1965', www.lib.uchicago .edu/e/scrc/findingaids/view.php?eadid=ICU.SPCL.CHAUCER&q= chaucer,.

'Guide to the Edith Rickert Papers 1858–1960', *University of Chicago, Special Collections Research Center*, www.lib.uchicago.edu/e/scrc/findingaids/view .php?eadid=ICU.SPCL.RICKERTE.

Gustafson, Sandra M., 'Eloquent Shakespeare', in *Shakespearean Educations: Power, Citizenship, and Performance*, ed. Coppélia Kahn, Heather S. Nathans, and Mimi Godfrey (Newark: University of Delaware Press, 2011), pp. 71–93.

'GWI History – Graduate Women International (GWI)', *Graduate Women International (GWI)*, www.graduatewomen.org/who-we-are/our-story/gwi-history.

Gwynn, E. J., and Arthur Sherbo, 'Dowden, Edward (1843–1913), Literary Scholar and Poet', in *Oxford Dictionary of National Biography* (Oxford: Oxford University Press, 2013), doi.org/10.1093/ref:odnb/32882.

Hair, Paul Edward Hedley, *Arts, Letters, Society: A Miscellany Commemorating the Centenary of the Faculty of Arts at the University of Liverpool* (Liverpool: Liverpool University Press, 1996).

Hall, Lesley, '"Sentimental Follies" or "Instruments of Tremendous Uplift"? Reconsidering Women's Same-Sex Relationships in Interwar Britain', *Women's History Review*, 25.1 (2016), 124–42.

Hall, Lesley A., 'Stopes, Charlotte Brown Carmichael (1840–1929), Feminist and Literary Scholar', in *Oxford Dictionary of National Biography* (Oxford: Oxford University Press, 2005), doi.org/10.1093/ref:odnb/53016.

Hall, Ruth, *Marie Stopes: A Biography* (London: Virago, 1978).

Hamilton, Ian, *Keepers of the Flame: Literary Estates and the Rise of Biography* (London: Hutchinson, 1992).

Hammond, Mary, *Reading, Publishing and the Formation of Literary Taste in England, 1880–1914* (Aldershot: Ashgate, 2006).

Hanley, Terence E., 'G. G. Pendarves (1885–1938)', http://tellersofweirdtales.blogspot.com/2016/05/gg-pendarves-1885-1938.html.

Harding, James E., *The Love of David and Jonathan: Ideology, Text, Reception*, BibleWorld (Abingdon, Oxon: Routledge, 2014).

Harvey, Kate, '"A Classic for the Elders": Marketing Charles and Mary Lamb in the Nineteenth Century', *Actes Des Congrès de La Société Française Shakespeare*, 34 (2016).

'Shakespeare's History Plays and Nationhood in Children's Literature and Education', in *Children's Literature on the Move: Nations, Translations, Migrations*, ed. Nora Maguire and Beth Rodgers (Dublin: Four Courts Press, 2013).

Hateley, Erica, *Shakespeare in Children's Literature: Gender and Cultural Capital* (New York: Routledge, 2009).

Haveley, Cicely Palser, 'Mary Cowden Clarke's Labours of Love', in *Women, Scholarship and Criticism: Gender and Knowledge c. 1790–1900*, ed. Joan Bellamy, Anne Laurence, and Gill Perry (Manchester: Manchester University Press, 2000), pp. 110–24.

Heathorn, Stephen, *For Home, Country, and Race: Gender, Class, and Englishness in the Elementary School, 1880–1914* (Toronto: University of Toronto Press, 2000).

'"Let Us Remember That We, Too, Are English": Constructions of Citizenship and National Identity in English Elementary School Reading Books, 1880–1914', *Victorian Studies*, 38.3 (1995), 395–427.

Heffernan, Megan, 'Turning Sonnets into Poems: Textual Affect and John Benson's Metaphysical Shakespeare', *Shakespeare Quarterly*, 64.1 (2013), 71–98.

Hennessey, Oliver, *Yeats, Shakespeare, and Irish Cultural Nationalism* (Lanham, MD: Fairleigh Dickinson University Press, 2014).

Hernandez-Delgado, Julio L., 'The Helen Gray Cone Collection, 1859–1934, Finding Aid', https://library.hunter.cuny.edu/sites/default/files/documents/archives/finding_aids/Helen_Gray_Cone_1859_1934.pdf.

Hinojosa, Lynne W., *The Renaissance, English Cultural Nationalism, and Modernism, 1860–1920* (Basingstoke: Palgrave Macmillan, 2009).

'History', *Mount Holyoke College*, 2012, www.mtholyoke.edu/about/history.

'History | HMS Victory', www.hms-victory.com/history.

Holderness, Graham, Bryan Loughrey, and Andrew Murphy, '"What's the Matter?" Shakespeare and Textual Theory', *Textual Practice*, 9.1 (1995), 93–119.

Hollingsworth, Mark G., 'Nineteenth-Century Shakespeares: Nationalism and Moralism' (DPhil dissertation, University of Nottingham, 2007).

Honigmann, E. A. J., 'The New Bibliography and Its Critics', in *Textual Performances: The Modern Reproduction of Shakespeare's Drama*, ed. Lukas Erne and Margaret Jane Kidnie, (Cambridge: Cambridge University Press, 2004), pp. 77–93.

Hooks, Adam G., 'Afterword: The Folio as Fetish', in *The Cambridge Companion to Shakespeare's First Folio*, ed. Emma Smith (Cambridge: Cambridge University Press, 2016), pp. 185–96.

'Precedent Bartlett', in the Women and Book History Seminar (Shakespeare Association of America, Los Angeles, 2018).

Housman, A. E., 'The Application of Thought to Textual Criticism', in *The Classical Papers of A. E. Housman, 1915–1936*, 3 vols (Cambridge: Cambridge University Press, 1972), III, 1058–69.

Howard-Hill, T. H., 'Alice Walker', ed. William Baker and Kenneth Womack, in *Twentieth-Century British Book Collectors and Bibliographers*, The Dictionary of Literary Biography, 201 (Detroit, MI: Gale Research, 1999), pp. 297–305.

'Walker, Alice (1900–1982)', in *Oxford Dictionary of National Biography* (Oxford: Oxford University Press, 2004), doi.org/10.1093/ref:odnb/60296.

Howsam, Leslie, *Past into Print: The Publishing of History in Britain, 1850–1950* (London: British Library; Toronto: University of Toronto Press, 2009).

'What the Victorian Empire Learned: A Perspective on History, Reading and Print in Nineteenth-Century Textbooks', *Journal of Victorian Culture*, 20.20 (2019), 1–16.

Howsam, Leslie, Christopher Stray, Alice Jenkins, James A. Secord, and Anna Vaninskaya, 'What the Victorians Learned: Perspectives on Nineteenth-Century Schoolbooks', *Journal of Victorian Culture*, 12.2 (2007), 262–85.

Hudson, Derek, *Munby: A Man of Two Worlds. The Life and Diaries of Arthur J. Munby, 1828–1910* (London: John Murray, 1972).

Hughes, C. E., and Betty T. Bennett, 'Clarke, Mary Victoria Cowden (1809–1898), Literary Scholar and Writer', in *Oxford Dictionary of National Biography* (Oxford: Oxford University Press, 2004), doi.org/10.1093/ref:odnb/5521.

Ioppolo, Grace, '"Much They Ought Not to Have Attempted": Editors of Collected Editions of Shakespeare from the Eighteenth to the Twentieth Centuries', in *The Culture of Collected Editions*, ed. Andrew Nash (Basingstoke: Palgrave Macmillan, 2003), pp. 157–71.

Jackson, Russell, 'Victorian Editors of *As You Like It* and the Purposes of Editing', in *The Theory and Practice of Text-Editing*, ed. Ian Small and Marcus Walsh (Cambridge: Cambridge University Press, 1991), pp. 142–56.

Jenkinson, Jacqueline, 'Refugees Welcome Here: Caring for Belgian Refugees in Scotland during the First World War', *History Scotland*, May–June 2018, 35–42.

Johnson, Nan, 'Shakespeare in American Rhetorical Education, 1870–1920', in *Shakespearean Educations: Power, Citizenship, and Performance*, ed. Coppélia Kahn, Heather S. Nathans, and Mimi Godfrey (Newark: University of Delaware Press, 2011), pp. 112–30.

Jones, Jennifer, and Josephine Castle, 'Women in UK Universities, 1920–1980', *Studies in Higher Education*, 11.3 (1986), 289–97.

Jowett, John, 'Disintegration, 1924', *Shakespeare*, 10.2 (2014), 171–87.

'Editing Shakespeare's Plays in the Twentieth Century', *Shakespeare Survey*, 59 (2006), 1–19.

Kahan, Jeffrey, *The Quest for Shakespeare: The Peculiar History and Surprising Legacy of the New Shakspere Society* (Basingstoke: Palgrave Macmillan, 2017).

Kaye, Elaine, 'Maurice, Mary Atkinson (1797–1858)', in *Oxford Dictionary of National Biography* (Oxford: Oxford University Press, 2004), doi.org/10.1093/ref:odnb/51769.

Kemp, Sandra, Charlotte Mitchell, and David Trotter, 'Weekes, A. R. [Agnes Russell Weekes] and Weekes, R. K. [Rose Kirkpatrick Weekes]', in *Edwardian Fiction: An Oxford Companion* (Oxford: Oxford University Press, 1997).

Kermode, Frank, 'In the Forest of Arden', *The Independent* (London, 18 March 1995), www.independent.co.uk/arts-entertainment/books/in-the-forest-of-arden-1611731.html.

Kernan, Mary Ann, 'The Launch of the First Series of the Arden Shakespeare in 1899: An Exploration of Bourdieu's Concept of Consecration', *Logos*, 27.2 (2016), 32–47.

King, Edmund G. C., 'Editors', in *The Cambridge Companion to Shakespeare's First Folio*, ed. Emma Smith (Cambridge: Cambridge University Press, 2016), pp. 120–36.

Kingsley-Smith, Jane, *The Afterlife of Shakespeare's Sonnets* (Cambridge: Cambridge University Press, 2019).

Kitzes, Adam H., 'The Hazards of Expurgation: Adapting *Measure for Measure* to the Bowdler *Family Shakespeare*', *The Journal for Early Modern Cultural Studies*, 13.2 (2013), 43–68.

Knights, Ben, 'Reading as a Man: Women and the Rise of English Studies in England', in *Gendered Academia: Wissenschaft und Geschlechterdifferenz 1890–1945*, ed. Miriam Kauko, Sylvia Mieszkowski, and Alexandra Tischel (Gottingen: Wallstein Verlag, 2005).

Knowles, Richard, *Shakespeare Variorum Handbook: A Manual of Editorial Practice*, 2nd ed. (New York: Modern Language Association of America, 2003), www.mla.org/content/download/3330/81674/variorum_hndbk.pdf

Krebs, Paula M., *Gender, Race, and the Writing of Empire: Public Discourse and the Boer War* (Cambridge: Cambridge University Press, 2004).

Kumar, Krishan, *The Making of English National Identity*, Cambridge Cultural Social Studies (Cambridge: Cambridge University Press, 2003).

Lavagnino, John, *Shakespeare and the Digital World: Redefining Scholarship and Practice*, ed. Christie Carson and Peter Kirwan (Cambridge: Cambridge University Press, 2014).

Lawrie, Alexandra, *The Beginnings of University English: Extramural Study, 1885–1910* (Basingstoke: Palgrave Macmillan, 2014).

Lee, Lily Xiao Hong, and Sue Wiles, *Biographical Dictionary of Chinese Women: Tang through Ming, 618–1644* (New York: Routledge, 2014).

Lenker, Lagretta Tallent, 'Shaw: The Bellicose Pacifist', *SHAW: The Annual of Bernard Shaw Studies*, 28.1 (2008), 1–10.

Lerer, Seth, *Children's Literature: A Reader's History, from Aesop to Harry Potter* (Chicago: University of Chicago Press, 2008).

Levenson, Jill L., 'Framing Shakespeare: Introductions and Commentary in Critical Editions of the Plays', in *Shakespeare and Textual Studies*, ed. Margaret Jane Kidnie and Sonia Massai (Cambridge: Cambridge University Press, 2015), pp. 377–90.

Levine, Philippa, ed., *Gender and Empire* (Oxford: Oxford University Press, 2007).

Lewalski, Barbara K., *The Life of John Milton* (Oxford: Blackwell Publishing, 2003).

Liddington, Jill, *The Road to Greenham Common: Feminism and Anti-Militarism in Britain since 1820* (Syracuse, NY: Syracuse University Press, 1991).

Liddington, Jill, and Elizabeth Crawford, '"Women Do Not Count, Neither Shall They Be Counted": Suffrage, Citizenship and the Battle for the 1911 Census', *History Workshop Journal*, 71.1 (2011), 98–127.

Lim, Jessica Wen Hui, 'Barbauld's Lessons: The Conversational Primer in Late Eighteenth-Century British Children's Literature', *Journal for Eighteenth-Century Studies*, 43.1 (2020), 101–20.

London, Bette, 'Secretary to the Stars: Mediums and the Agency of Authorship', in *Literary Secretaries/Secretarial Culture*, ed. Leah Price and Pamela Thurschwell (Aldershot: Ashgate, 2005), pp. 91–110.

Lootens, Tricia, 'Shakespeare, King of What? Gender, Nineteenth-Century Patriotism, and the Case of *Poet-Lore*', *Borrowers and Lenders: The Journal of Shakespeare and Appropriation*, 8.1 (2013), 8.

MacKenzie, John M., *Propaganda and Empire: The Manipulation of British Public Opinion, 1880–1960* (Manchester: Manchester University Press, 1984).

Maguire, Laurie, and Emma Smith, 'On Editing', *Shakespeare*, 15.3 (2019), 293–309.

Maguire, Laurie E., 'Feminist Editing and the Body of the Text', in *A Feminist Companion to Shakespeare*, ed. Dympna Callaghan (Oxford: Oxford University Press, 2000), pp. 59–79.

'How Many Children Had Alice Walker?', in *Printing and Parenting in Early Modern England*, ed. Douglas A. Brooks (Aldershot: Ashgate, 2005), pp. 327–50.

Shakespearean Suspect Texts: The 'Bad' Quartos and Their Contexts (Cambridge: Cambridge University Press, 1996).

Maley, Willy, 'British Ill Done?: Recent Work on Shakespeare and British, English, Irish, Scottish and Welsh Identities', *Literature Compass*, 3.3 (2006), 487–512.

'Shakespeare, Easter 1916, and the Theatre of the Empire of Great Britain', *Studies in Ethnicity and Nationalism*, 16.2 (2016), 189–205.

'Malone Society Publication List', *The Malone Society*, 2017, http://malonesociety
    .com/wp-content/uploads/2012/02/Publication-List-July-2017.pdf.
Marcus, Leah S., 'A Man Who Needs No Introduction', in *Shakespeare and
    Textual Studies*, ed. Margaret Jane Kidnie and Sonia Massai (Cambridge:
    Cambridge University Press, 2015), pp. 285–99.
    How Shakespeare Became Colonial: Editorial Tradition and the British Empire
    (London: Routledge, 2017).
    Unediting the Renaissance: Shakespeare, Marlowe, Milton (London: Routledge,
    1996).
Marsden, Jean I., 'Shakespeare for Girls: Mary Lamb and *Tales from Shakespeare*',
    Children's Literature, 17.1 (2009), 47–63.
Marshall, Gail, and Ann Thompson, 'Mary Cowden Clarke', in *Jameson, Cowden
    Clarke, Kemble, Cushman*, ed. Gail Marshall, Great Shakespeareans (London:
    Bloomsbury Arden Shakespeare, 2011), VII, 58–91.
Massai, Sonia, 'Editing Shakespeare in Parts', *Shakespeare Quarterly*, 68.1 (2017),
    56–79.
    Shakespeare and the Rise of the Editor (Cambridge: Cambridge University Press,
    2007).
Maus, Katharine Eisaman, 'A Womb of His Own: Male Renaissance Poets in the
    Female Body', in *Printing and Parenting in Early Modern England*, ed.
    Douglas A. Brooks (Aldershot: Ashgate, 2005), pp. 89–108.
McGann, Jerome J., *The Textual Condition*, Princeton Studies in Culture/Power/
    History (Princeton, NJ: Princeton University Press, 1991).
McKenzie, D. F., *Bibliography and the Sociology of Texts* (Cambridge: Cambridge
    University Press, 1986).
McKerrow, Ronald Brunlees, *Prolegomena for the Oxford Shakespeare: A Study in
    Editorial Method* (Oxford: Clarendon Press, 1939).
McLuskie, Kathleen E., 'Remembering Charlotte Stopes', in *Women Making
    Shakespeare: Text, Performance and Reception*, ed. Gordon McMullan, Lena
    Cowen Orlin, and Virginia Mason Vaughan (London: Bloomsbury Arden
    Shakespeare, 2014), pp. 195–205.
McMullan, Gordon, 'Reflections on the Politics of Editing a Complete
    Works of Shakespeare', *Contemporary Theatre Review*, 25.1 (2015),
    76–79.
McMurtry, Jo, *English Language, English Literature: The Creation of an Academic
    Discipline* (Hamden, CT: Archon Books, 1985).
Midgley, Clare, 'Bringing the Empire Home: Women Activists in Imperial
    Britain, 1790s–1930s', in *At Home with the Empire: Metropolitan Culture
    and the Imperial World*, ed. Catherine Hall and Sonya O. Rose (Cambridge:
    Cambridge University Press, 2006), pp. 230–50.
Millgate, Michael, *Thomas Hardy: A Biography Revisited* (Oxford: Oxford
    University Press, 2006).
Mitchell, Charlotte, 'Charlote M. Yonge's Bank Account: A Rich New Source of
    Information on Her Work and Her Life', *Women's Writing*, 17.2 (2010),
    380–400.

Molidor, Jennifer, 'Dying for Ireland: Violence, Silence, and Sacrifice in Dorothy Macardle's *Earth-Bound: Nine Stories of Ireland* (1924)', *New Hibernia Review/Iris Éireannach Nua*, 12.4 (2008), 43–61.

Muir, Kenneth, 'The Order of Shakespeare's Sonnets', *College Literature*, 10.3 (1983), 244–50.

Murphy, Andrew, 'An Irish Catalysis: W. B. Yeats and the Uses of Shakespeare', ed. Peter Holland, *Shakespeare Survey*, 64 (2011), 208–19.

'The Birth of the Editor', in *Concise Companion to Shakespeare and the Text*, ed. Andrew Murphy (Chichester: Wiley-Blackwell, 2010), pp. 93–108.

Shakespeare for the People: Working-Class Readers, 1800–1900 (Cambridge: Cambridge University Press, 2008).

Shakespeare in Print: A History and Chronology of Shakespeare Publishing (Cambridge: Cambridge University Press, 2003).

'Shakespeare's Irish Lives: The Politics of Biography', *Shakespeare Survey*, 68 (2015), 267–81.

'Shakespeare's Rising: Ireland and the 1916 Tercentenary', in *Celebrating Shakespeare: Commemoration and Cultural Memory*, ed. Clara Calvo and Coppélia Kahn (Cambridge: Cambridge University Press, 2015), pp. 161–81.

Murphy, Kate, 'A Marriage Bar of Convenience? The BBC and Married Women's Work 1923–39', *Twentieth Century British History*, 25.4 (2014), 533–61.

Neilson, William Allan, 'Office of President William Allan Neilson Files, 1917–1939, Finding Aid', *Five College Archives & Manuscript Collections*, http://asteria.fivecolleges.edu/findaids/smitharchives/manosca13.html.

Neville, Sarah, 'Rethinking Scholarly Commentary in the Age of Google', *Textual Cultures*, 12.1 (2019), 1–26.

'New Data on the Sexual Dimorphism of the Hand Stencils in El Castillo Cave (Cantabria, Spain)', *Journal of Archaeological Science: Reports*, 14 (2017), 374–81.

Nicholl, Charles, *The Lodger: Shakespeare on Silver Street* (London: Penguin, 2008).

Norcia, Megan A., *X Marks the Spot: Women Writers Map the Empire for British Children, 1790–1895* (Athens: Ohio University Press, 2010).

O'Day, Rosemary, 'Women and Education in Nineteenth Century England', in *Women, Scholarship and Criticism: Gender and Knowledge c. 1790–1900*, ed. Joan Bellamy, Anne Laurence, and Gill Perry (Manchester: Manchester University Press, 2000), pp. 91–109.

Olwell, Victoria, 'The Body Types: Corporeal Documents and Body Politics circa 1900', in *Literary Secretaries/Secretarial Culture*, ed. Leah Price and Pamela Thurschwell (Aldershot: Ashgate, 2005), pp. 48–62.

'Our Story – Poet Lore', https://poetlore.com/about/ourstory.

Palmieri, Patricia Ann, *In Adamless Eden: The Community of Women Faculty at Wellesley* (New Haven, CT: Yale University Press, 1995).

Pask, Kevin, *The Emergence of the English Author: Scripting the Life of the Poet in Early Modern England* (Cambridge: Cambridge University Press, 1997).

Perrin, Noel, *Dr. Bowdler's Legacy: A History of Expurgated Books in England and America* (Boston: David R. Godine, 1992).

Petersen, Stephen, '"I Do Know Your Tongue": The Shakespeare Editions of William Rolfe and H. H. Furness as American Cultural Signifiers', *The Kentucky Review*, 13.1 (1996), 3–44.

Peterson, William S., 'Furnivall, Frederick James (1825–1910)', in *Oxford Dictionary of National Biography* (Oxford: Oxford University Press, 2004), doi.org/10.1093/ref:odnb/33298.

Ponder, Melinda M., *From Sea to Shining Sea: The Story of the Poet of 'America the Beautiful'* (Chicago: Windy City Publishers, 2017).

Potter, Lois, 'Editing Desdemona', in *In Arden: Editing Shakespeare: Essays in Honour of Richard Proudfoot*, ed. Ann Thompson and Gordon McMullan (London: Arden Shakespeare, 2003), pp. 81–94.

Price, Leah, *The Anthology and the Rise of the Novel: From Richardson to George Eliot* (Cambridge: Cambridge University Press, 2000).

'The Poetics of Pedantry from Thomas Bowdler to Susan Ferrier', *Women's Writing*, 7.1 (2000), 75–88.

'Publications', *The Early English Text Society*, http://users.ox.ac.uk/~eets/publications.html.

Rasmussen, Eric, 'Editorial Memory: The Origin and Evolution of Collation Notes', in *Shakespeare and Textual Studies*, ed. Margaret Jane Kidnie and Sonia Massai (Cambridge: Cambridge University Press, 2015), pp. 391–97.

Rawlinson, Mark, 'Later Poets of the First World War', in *The Cambridge Companion to the Poetry of the First World War*, ed. Santanu Das (Cambridge: Cambridge University Press, 2013), pp. 81–93.

Renck, Anneliese Pollock, *Female Authorship, Patronage, and Translation in Late Medieval France: From Christine de Pizan to Louise Labé* (Turnhout: Brepols, 2018).

Rendall, Jane, 'The Condition of Women, Women's Writing and the Empire in Nineteenth-Century Britain', in *At Home with the Empire: Metropolitan Culture and the Imperial World*, ed. Catherine Hall and Sonya O. Rose (Cambridge: Cambridge University Press, 2006), pp. 101–21.

Roberts, David, *The Ladies: Female Patronage of Restoration Drama, 1660–1700* (Oxford: Clarendon Press, 1989).

Roberts, Jeanne Addison, 'Women Edit Shakespeare', *Shakespeare Survey*, 59 (2006), 136–46.

'Rose Mary Crawshay Prize', *The British Academy*, www.thebritishacademy.ac.uk/rose-mary-crawshay-prize.

Rosenberg, Rosalind, 'The Legacy of Dean Gildersleeve', *Barnard College*, 2010, https://web.archive.org/web/20100624022420/http://beatl.barnard.columbia.edu/learn/documents/gildersleeve.htm.

'Virginia Gildersleeve: Opening the Gates', *Living Legacies: Great Moments and Leading Figures in the History of Columbia University*, www.columbia.edu/cu/alumni/Magazine/Summer2001/Gildersleeve.html.

Rossini, Gill, *Same Sex Love, 1700–1957: A History and Research Guide* (South Yorkshire: Pen & Sword History, 2017).

Rozmovits, Linda, *Shakespeare and the Politics of Culture in Late Victorian England* (Baltimore, MD: Johns Hopkins University Press, 1998).

Ruthven, K. K., 'Textuality and Textual Editing', *Meridian: The La Trobe University English Review*, 4.1 (1985), 85–87.

Saenger, Paul, 'Benito Arias Montano and the Evolving Notion of Locus in Sixteenth-Century Printed Books', *Word & Image*, 17.1–2 (2001), 119–37.

Salzman, Paul, *Editors Construct the Renaissance Canon, 1825–1915* (Basingstoke: Palgrave Macmillan, 2018).

Samuel, Raphael, *Island Stories: Unravelling Britain, vol. II: Theatres of Memory*, ed. Alison Light, Sally Alexander, and Gareth Stedman Jones (London: Verso, 1998).

Scaravelli, Enrico, *The Rise of Bardolatry in the Restoration: Paratexts of Shakespearean Adaptations and Other Texts 1660–1737* (Bern, Switzerland: Peter Lang CH, 2015).

Schabert, Ina, 'A Double-Voiced Discourse: Shakespeare Studies by Women in the Early 20th Century', in *Gendered Academia: Wissenschaft und Geschlechterdifferenz 1890–1945*, ed. Miriam Kauko, Sylvia Mieszkowski, and Alexandra Tischel (Gottingen: Wallstein Verlag, 2005).

Scheil, Katherine West, *She Hath Been Reading: Women and Shakespeare Clubs in America* (Ithaca, NY: Cornell University Press, 2012).

Schoch, Richard W., *Shakespeare's Victorian Stage: Performing History in the Theatre of Charles Kean* (Cambridge: Cambridge University Press, 1998).

Schoenbaum, S., *Shakespeare's Lives*, new edition (Oxford: Clarendon Press, 1991).

Schwarz, Judith, '"Yellow Clover": Katharine Lee Bates and Katharine Coman', *Frontiers: A Journal of Women Studies*, 4.1 (1979), 59.

Sedelow, Sally Yeates, 'The Computer in the Humanities and Fine Arts', *ACM Computing Surveys (CSUR)*, 2.2 (1970), 89–110.

Seymour, Terry I., 'Great Books by the Millions: J. M. Dent's Everyman's Library', in *The Culture of the Publisher's Series, vol. II: Nationalisms and the National Canon*, ed. John Spiers (Basingstoke, Hampshire: Palgrave Macmillan, 2011), pp. 166–72.

Shaw, A. G. L., 'Arthur, Sir George, First Baronet (1784–1854)', in *Oxford Dictionary of National Biography* (Oxford: Oxford University Press, 2004), doi.org/10.1093/ref:odnb/707.

Sicherman, Barbara, *Well-Read Lives: How Books Inspired a Generation of American Women* (Chapel Hill: University of North Carolina Press, 2010).

Sillars, Stuart, 'Reading Illustrated Editions: Methodology and the Limits of Interpretation', *Shakespeare Survey*, 62 (2009), 162–81.

Simmers, George, 'Despised and Rejected', *Great War Fiction*, 2009, https://greatwarfiction.wordpress.com/2009/12/05/despised-and-rejected.

Skinner, David, 'A Critical and Historical Analysis of Charles and Mary Lamb's *Tales from Shakespeare* and Thomas Bowdler's *The Family Shakespeare*' (doctoral dissertation, University of Sheffield, 2011).

Smith, Bonnie G., *The Gender of History: Men, Women, and Historical Practice* (Cambridge, MA: Harvard University Press, 1998).

Smith, Emma, *The Cambridge Introduction to Shakespeare* (Cambridge: Cambridge University Press, 2007).

  Shakespeare's First Folio: Four Centuries of an Iconic Book (Oxford: Oxford University Press, 2016).

Smith, G. G., and Sandra Miley Cooney, 'Masson, David Mather', in *Oxford Dictionary of National Biography* (Oxford: Oxford University Press, 2004), doi.org/10.1093/ref:odnb/34924.

Smith, Helen, *'Grossly Material Things': Women and Book Production in Early Modern England* (Oxford: Oxford University Press, 2012).

Smith, Nadia Clare, *Dorothy Macardle: A Life* (Dublin: Woodfield Press, 2007).

  'From Dundalk to Dublin: Dorothy Macardle's Narrative Journey on Radio Éireann', *The Irish Review*, 42 (2010), 27–42.

Solomon, Barbara Miller, *In the Company of Educated Women: A History of Women and Higher Education in America* (New Haven, CT: Yale University Press, 1985).

Spencer, Jane, *Literary Relations: Kinship and the Canon 1660–1830* (Oxford: Oxford University Press, 2005).

Spevack, Marvin, 'What Price Shakespeare?: James Orchard Halliwell-Phillipps and the Shilling Shakespeares of the 1860s', *The Papers of the Bibliographical Society of America*, 96.1 (2002), 23–47.

Stallybrass, Peter, 'Against Thinking', *PMLA*, 122.5 (2007), 1580–87.

Sununu, Andrea, '"I Long to Know Your Opinion of It": The Serendipity of a Malfunctioning Timing Belt, or The Guiney–Tutin Collaboration in the Recovery of Katherine Philips', *Women's Writing*, 24.3 (2017), 258–79.

Sutherland, John, *The Longman Companion to Victorian Fiction* (London: Routledge, 2014).

Sutherland, Kathryn, 'Writings on Education and Conduct: Arguments for Female Improvement', in *Women and Literature in Britain, 1700–1800*, ed. Vivien Jones (Cambridge: Cambridge University Press, 2000), pp. 25–45.

Taylor, Gary, 'General Introduction', in *The Oxford Shakespeare: A Textual Companion*, ed. Stanley Wells, Gary Taylor, John Jowett, and William Montgomery (Oxford: Oxford University Press, 1987).

  Reinventing Shakespeare: A Cultural History from the Restoration to the Present (London: Hogarth Press, 1990).

  'Textual and Sexual Criticism: A Crux in *The Comedy of Errors*', *Renaissance Drama*, 19 (1988), 195–225.

'Theodor Benfey | German Scholar', *Encyclopedia Britannica* (Encyclopedia Britannica, 2018), www.britannica.com/biography/Theodor-Benfey.

Thompson, Ann, 'A Club of Our Own: Women's Play Readings in the Nineteenth Century', *Borrowers and Lenders: The Journal of Shakespeare and Appropriation*, 2.2 (2006), 14.

'Feminist Theory and the Editing of Shakespeare: *The Taming of the Shrew* Revisited', in *Shakespeare, Feminism and Gender*, ed. Kate Chedgzoy, New Casebooks (Basingstoke: Palgrave, 2001), pp. 49–69.

'Teena Rochfort Smith, Frederick Furnivall, and the New Shakspere Society's Four-Text Edition of Hamlet', *Shakespeare Quarterly*, 49 (1998), 125–39.

Thompson, Ann, and Sasha Roberts, 'Mary Cowden Clarke: Marriage, Gender and the Victorian Woman Critic of Shakespeare', in *Victorian Shakespeare, vol. II: Literature and Culture*, ed. Gail Marshall and Adrian Poole (New York: Palgrave Macmillan, 2003), pp. 170–89.

Women Reading Shakespeare, 1600–1900: An Anthology (Manchester: Manchester University Press, 1997).

Thompson, John B., *Merchants of Culture: The Publishing Business in the Twenty-First Century*, 2nd ed. (Cambridge: Polity Press, 2015).

Trettien, Whitney, 'Media, Materiality, and Time in the History of Reading: The Case of the Little Gidding Harmonies', *PMLA*, 133.5 (2018), 1135–51.

Tribble, Evelyn B., '"Like a Looking-Glas in the Frame": From the Marginal Note to the Footnote', in *The Margins of the Text*, ed. D. C. Greetham (Ann Arbor: University of Michigan Press, 1997), pp. 229–44.

Tudeau-Clayton, Margaret, and Willy Maley, eds., *This England, That Shakespeare: New Angles on Englishness and the Bard* (Farnham: Ashgate, 2010).

Turner, James, *Philology: The Forgotten Origins of the Modern Humanities* (Princeton, NJ: Princeton University Press, 2015).

Tyler, Elizabeth Muir, *England in Europe: English Royal Women and Literary Patronage, c. 1000–c. 1150* (Toronto: University of Toronto Press, 2017).

Urkowitz, Steven, '"If I Mistake in Those Foundations Which I Build Upon": Peter Alexander's Textual Analysis of "Henry VI Parts 2 and 3"', *English Literary Renaissance*, 18.2 (1988), 230–56.

Vandiver, Elizabeth, 'Early Poets of the First World War', in *The Cambridge Companion to the Poetry of the First World War*, ed. Santanu Das (Cambridge: Cambridge University Press, 2013), pp. 69–80.

Vaughan, Alden T., and Virginia Mason Vaughan, *Shakespeare's Caliban: A Cultural History* (Cambridge: Cambridge University Press, 1991).

Velz, John W., 'Joseph Crosby and the Shakespeare Scholarship of the Nineteenth Century', *Shakespeare Quarterly*, 27.3 (1976), 316–28.

Wall, Wendy, *The Imprint of Gender: Authorship and Publication in the English Renaissance* (Ithaca, NY: Cornell University Press, 1993).

Walsh, Brendan, *The Pedagogy of Protest: The Educational Thought and Work of Patrick H. Pearse* (Oxford: Peter Lang, 2007).

Walsh, Marcus, *Shakespeare, Milton, and Eighteenth-Century Literary Editing: The Beginnings of Interpretative Scholarship* (Cambridge: Cambridge University Press, 1997).

Wayne, Valerie, 'The Gendered Text and Its Labour', in *The Oxford Handbook of Shakespeare and Embodiment: Gender, Sexuality, Race*, ed. Valerie Traub (Oxford: Oxford University Press, 2016), pp. 549–68.

'Remaking the Texts: Women Editors of Shakespeare, Past and Present', in *Women Making Shakespeare: Text, Performance and Reception*, ed. Gordon McMullan, Lena Cowen Orlin, and Virginia Mason Vaughan (London: Bloomsbury Arden Shakespeare, 2014), pp. 57–67.

'The Sexual Politics of Textual Transmission', in *Textual Formations and Reformations*, ed. Laurie E. Maguire and Thomas L. Berger (Newark: University of Delaware Press, 1998).

Weedon, Alexis, *Victorian Publishing: The Economics of Book Production for a Mass Market, 1836–1916* (Aldershot: Ashgate, 2003).

Wells, Stanley, 'Old and Modern Spelling', in *Re-editing Shakespeare for the Modern Reader*, Oxford Shakespeare Studies (Oxford: Clarendon Press, 1984), pp. 5–31.

Werstine, Paul, 'Housmania: Episodes in Twentieth-Century "Critical" Editing of Shakespeare', in *Textual Performances: The Modern Reproduction of Shakespeare's Drama*, ed. Lukas Erne and Margaret Jane Kidnie (Cambridge: Cambridge University Press, 2004), pp. 49–62.

'Narratives about Printed Shakespeare Texts: "Foul Papers" and "Bad" Quartos', *Shakespeare Quarterly*, 41.1 (1990), 65.

West, Anthony James, *The Shakespeare First Folio: The History of the Book, vol. II: A New Worldwide Census of First Folios* (Oxford: Oxford University Press, 2003).

Wolff, Tatiana, 'English', in *Bedford College, University of London: Memories of 150 Years*, ed. J. Mordaunt Crook (London: Royal Holloway and Bedford New College, 2001), pp. 95–108.

Wolfson, Susan J., 'Explaining to Her Sisters: Mary Lamb's *Tales from Shakespear*', in *Women's Re-visions of Shakespeare: On the Responses of Dickinson, Woolf, Rich, H.D., George Eliot and Others*, ed. Marianne Novy (Urbana: University of Illinois Press, 1990), pp. 16–40.

Woudhuysen, H. R., 'Some Women Editors of Shakespeare: A Preliminary Sketch', in *Women Making Shakespeare: Text, Performance and Reception*, ed. Gordon McMullan, Lena Cowen Orlin, and Virginia Mason Vaughan (London: Bloomsbury Arden Shakespeare, 2014), pp. 79–88.

Xiong, Victor Cunrui, *Historical Dictionary of Medieval China* (Lanham, MD: Rowman & Littlefield, 2009).

Yarn, Molly G., 'A Correction to the Identity of "Mrs Furnivall" in Harvard's Houghton Library Archives', *Notes and Queries*, 65.3 (2018), 401–2.

'"All the Youth of England Are on Fire (for Shakespeare)": A Review of Evelyn Smith's *Henry V*, *The Hare: A Journal of Untimely Reviews in Early Modern Theatre*, 5.2 (2021), https://thehareonline.com.

'Katharine Lee Bates and Women's Editions of Shakespeare for Students', in *Women's Labour and the History of the Book in Early Modern England*, ed. Valerie Wayne (London: Arden Shakespeare, an imprint of Bloomsbury Publishing, 2020), pp. 187–203.

'Rickert's Network of Women Editors', in *Collaborative Humanities Research and Pedagogy: The Networks of John Matthews Manly and Edith Rickert*, ed. Katherine Ellison and Susan Kim (Basingstoke: Palgrave Macmillan, forthcoming).

Yeandle, Peter, 'Lessons in Englishness and Empire, c. 1880–1914: Further Thoughts on the English/British Conundrum', in *History, Nationhood and the Question of Britain*, ed. Helen Brocklehurst and Robert Phillips (Basingstoke: Palgrave Macmillan, 2004), pp. 274–88.

Yeats, George, 'Shakespeare's Victorian Legacy: Text as Monument and Emendation as Desecration in the Mid-Nineteenth Century', *Victorian Literature and Culture*, 40.2 (2012), 469–486.

Young, Alan R., 'John Dicks's Illustrated Edition of "Shakspere for the Millions"', *The Papers of the Bibliographical Society of America*, 106.3 (2012), 285–310.

Steam-Driven Shakespeare, or Making Good Books Cheap: Five Victorian Illustrated Editions (New Castle, DE: Oak Knoll Press, 2017).

Zarnowiecki, Matthew, 'Responses to Responses to Shakespeare's Sonnets: More Sonnets', *Critical Survey*, 28.2 (2016), 10–26.

Ziegler, Georgianna, 'Alice Reads Shakespeare: Charles Dodgson and the Girl's Shakespeare Project', in *Reimagining Shakespeare for Children and Young Adults*, ed. Naomi Miller (New York: Routledge, 2013).

'Introducing Shakespeare: The Earliest Versions for Children', *Shakespeare*, 2.2 (2006), 132–51.

'Women and Shakespeare', in *Shakespeare in the Nineteenth Century*, ed. Gail Marshall (Cambridge: Cambridge University Press, 2012), pp. 205–28.

Index

The names of all women editors with entries in Appendix A (active 1800–1950) are in bold. As Appendix A functions as an annotated bibliography, the information contained therein has not been indexed; however, I encourage readers to investigate the appendix for more details, including biographies of those women not covered in the text and details of publishers and series not discussed at length.

In cases of collaboration or partnership, the index centres women's contributions to editorial projects, rather than rehearse familiar male attributions. Although pragmatic concessions have been made, on the whole, men's names lead readers to their female collaborators – rarely the other way around.

For EU product safety concerns, contact us at Calle de José Abascal, 56–1°,
28003 Madrid, Spain or eugpsr@cambridge.org.

www.ingramcontent.com/pod-product-compliance
Ingram Content Group UK Ltd.
Pitfield, Milton Keynes, MK11 3LW, UK
UKHW020401140625
459647UK00020B/2583